The Prophe
in the Qur'an, the B

A new detailed commentary on the Qur'anic Chapter of Joseph

Louay Fatoohi

Luna Plena Publishing

Birmingham

First published: August 2007
Production Reference: 1010807

Published by:
Luna Plena Publishing
Birmingham, UK.
www.lunaplenapub.com

ISBN 978-1-906342-00-5

Cover design by:
Mawlid Design
www.mawliddesign.com

First Published in Malaysia 2005 by the Islamic Book Trust

بِسْمِ ٱللَّهِ ٱلرَّحْمَـٰنِ ٱلرَّحِيمِ

In the Name of Allah the Merciful, the Compassionate

نَحْنُ نَقُصُّ عَلَيْكَ أَحْسَنَ ٱلْقَصَصِ بِمَآ أَوْحَيْنَآ إِلَيْكَ هَـٰذَا ٱلْقُرْءَانَ وَإِن كُنتَ مِن قَبْلِهِۦ لَمِنَ ٱلْغَـٰفِلِينَ

We narrate to you [O Muhammad!] the best of narratives, by revealing this Qur'an to you; and before it you were one of the unaware (12.3).

About the Author

Louay Fatoohi was born in Baghdad, Iraq, in 1961 to a Christian family. He converted to Islam when he was twenty years old. He obtained a BSc in Physics from the College of Science, University of Baghdad, in 1984. In 1992, he and his wife Shetha moved to the United Kingdom where they have settled. Dr Fatoohi obtained his PhD in Astronomy from the Physics Department, Durham University, in 1998. He works as the Editorial Director of Packt Publishing.

The author of several books and many articles in Arabic and English, Dr Fatoohi is particularly interested in Qur'anic exegesis (Tafsir), history in the Qur'an, and comparative religion. His latest book is *Jihad in the Qur'an: The Truth from the Source* (2nd Edition 2004). He is currently finishing a book on *The Mystery of the Historical Jesus.*

Contents

Preface

The full knowledge contained in the Qur'an will always be beyond what anyone can encompass. This is due to the depth and breadth of the knowledge imbedded in the divine text, on the one hand, and the limitedness of how much any person can fathom of that knowledge, on the other. It is virtually impossible for any interpretation of the Qur'an, regardless of the degree of knowledge of the exegete, to claim to be complete and inclusive of all meanings of a Qur'anic text, or to have the final say on its meanings. There will always be an opportunity to learn something new from and about this divine Book. This is one fact underlined by Prophet Muhammad's description of the Qur'an as a Book "whose lessons never end and whose miracles never vanish."[1] The depth of the knowledge contained in the Qur'an combined with the limited means of any exegete mean that the attempts to study and interpret the Qur'anic text must never cease.

Since the revelation of the Qur'an fourteen centuries ago, numerous scholars have assiduously studied it. These tremendous efforts resulted in countless studies and interpretations of the Qur'an that helped and will continue to help billions of people study this divine text. However, unlike the unerring text that was revealed by Allah, exegeses of the Qur'an reflect the understanding and views of their human authors, and human beings do err.

Many exegetical books of the Qur'an suffer from a serious methodological flaw. When interpreting the Qur'anic text, these books systematically rely on information whose accuracy and authenticity are unverifiable or questionable, or that is simply incorrect and inauthentic. Because of this fundamental shortcoming, which is discussed in Chapter 1, many interpretational attempts read into the Qur'anic text meanings that it does not really have.

In addition to abandoning this flawed method completely, exegetes also need to make as much use as possible of the well-known methodology of using the Qur'anic text to interpret itself. This double approach, which I have diligently followed in this book, protects the exegetical attempt against many potential errors and inaccuracies.

It is necessary for the person who studies any Qur'anic text to be acquainted with previous interpretational attempts. More important, the exegete needs to be able to look at the Qur'anic text and examine it independently of its common interpretations. This is essential to ensure that the exegete reads the Qur'anic text *directly*, rather than through a particular understanding of that text. Unfortunately, most exegetes show undue influence by particular interpretations. This prevents them from approaching the Qur'anic text with impartiality and open-mindedness.

Each of the 114 Qur'anic "suwar (chapters)" has its special characteristics, and so has the "sūra (chapter)" of Joseph. Through relating a unique story whose episodes were carefully and skillfully weaved by the subtle hand of Allah, this sūra offers great lessons that capture the heart with its beauty and humble the mind with its wisdom. Like all other Qur'anic suwar, which scholars have been studying since the revelation of the Qur'an, the sūra of Joseph has had its share of research and interpretational attempts by the exegetes of the Qur'an. Offering another analysis and interpretation of this sūra must, therefore, be justified by the interpretation being genuinely new and significantly different from or adding to the already existing interpretations. The interpretation in this book differs considerably from the classical interpretations of the sūra of Joseph. Its analysis of the Qur'anic verses leads to many conclusions that are different from views that are commonly accepted by exegetes.

I stated above that the success of an interpretational attempt of a Qur'anic text does not mean more than a success in unveiling *some* of its meanings. Naturally, any exegetical attempt is also subject to failure. I cannot claim that this interpretation is free of mistakes, or that I have succeeded in interpreting all the Qur'anic text that I studied. No doubt, this study has its own mistakes and shortcomings, as is the case with any modest, limited human attempt to study the sublime divine text.

The most that I can say in favor of this interpretation is that it has *avoided many of the flaws that are common* in interpretations of the Qur'an in general and of the sūra of Joseph in particular. I think that this attempt is, in general, *more accurate* than previous attempts to interpret this sūra.

While I explained in detail how each interpretation of a Qur'anic text was arrived at, I highlighted in many places my inability to choose between more than one possible interpretation. I have also carefully distinguished between interpretations that I see "possible," i.e. are apparently consistent with the text but lack supportive evidence, and those that I consider "probable," i.e. possible interpretations that are supported by evidence.

This exegetical journey may be described as an attempt to relive the story of Joseph with all of its explicit and implicitly details in the Qur'an. I have found it at times useful, or even necessary, to mention possible details that could be linked with the story of Joseph, although they are not supported by Qur'anic evidence. I hope I have worked hard enough to differentiate between such possible details and those that the Qur'anic text mentions explicitly or implicitly.

I have not restricted myself to giving my interpretation, but I have mentioned also the most important or common alternatives that have been suggested by others. Furthermore, I have not concentrated exclusively on arguments that support my interpretation, but also mentioned what might be seen as counter arguments and explained what made me discard them.

The material of this book occupies twelve chapters which are briefly reviewed here.

The *first Chapter* tackles two topics that are essential to cover before embarking on the attempt to interpret the sūra of Joseph in the following chapters. The first topic is the Qur'an's special style in relating history. The second concerns common problems that many interpretational attempts of the Qur'anic text suffer from. Examples of common flaws in the interpretations of the sūra of Joseph are given. The chapter also contains a brief outline of the story of Joseph.

The next nine chapters, from the second to the tenth, include an analysis and interpretation of the whole of the sūra of Joseph. The verses are studied sequentially. Each verse is first cited in full and then followed with my commentary. The verses under study have been highlighted with a special printing style.

The sūra of Joseph starts with three and ends with ten general verses that are not part of the story of Joseph. *Chapter two* has been dedicated to the study of the first three (1-3) verses, and *Chapter ten* to the last ten (102-111). The story of Joseph, which occupies ninety eight (4-101) verses, is studied in Chapters 3-9. Each one of these seven chapters focuses on a particular stage of the story.

Chapter three analyzes verses 4-14 which describe events that took place when Joseph was still living in his father's house. The *fourth Chapter* interprets verses 15-20 which recount how Joseph was taken to Egypt.

The period from the entry of Joseph into Egypt until he was put in jail, which is related in verses 21-35, is studied in *Chapter five*. Verses 36-53, which cover the time that Joseph spent in prison, are analyzed in *Chapter six*.

In *Chapter seven*, verses 54-68 are examined. These verses describe Joseph's release from prison and his subsequent appointment to a high office in Egypt. The chapter also studies the visit of Joseph's half brothers to him during the years of drought and his attempt to make them bring his brother to Egypt. Verses 69-79 are covered in *Chapter eight* which looks at Joseph's meeting with his brother and how he kept him in Egypt.

Chapter nine focuses on the last verses of the story of Joseph, 80-101. These verses describe how Jacob, Joseph's father, lost his sight because of his grief, how his sight was miraculously restored by Joseph's shirt, and finally how he came with the rest of his extended family to live with Joseph in Egypt. The last ten verses of the sūra of Joseph, 102-111, which contain general sermons, are studied in *Chapter ten*.

Chapters 2-10 study miraculous aspects of the Qur'an through analyzing its text. *Chapter eleven* takes a different approach to the study of the miraculousness of the Qur'an. It compares information from the story of Joseph with historical information about ancient Egypt. The chapter attempts to determine the time and place in Egypt in which Joseph lived. The research approach of this chapter is the same one used to study the story of prophet Moses and the early history of the Israelites in our book *History Testifies to the Infallibility of the Qur'an: Early History of the Children of Israel* (Malaysia: A. S. Noordeen, 1999).

A third approach to studying the miraculous nature of the Qur'an is represented by comparing the Qur'anic text with other religious texts. The most suitable text to compare the sūra of Joseph with is the Biblical story of this prophet. This is dealt with in *Chapter twelve*, which is the last chapter of the book.

The book has two appendices containing the transliteration conventions and the Qur'anic terms and names used in the book.

Although this book contains a great deal of linguistic analysis of Qur'anic text, reading it does not require familiarity with the Arabic language or the Qur'an. I have taken every effort to explain everything that needs explaining to the reader who is unfamiliar with the Qur'an and/or Arabic.

I have tried my best to make this book as complete and comprehensive as it should be while maintaining the readability and smooth flow of the text. Additional details and background information have, therefore, been put in endnotes.

Each cited verse has been followed by a combination of two numbers identifying its sūra and its position in that sūra. For instance, the combination 12.11 refers to the 11th verse of the 12th sūra.

In recognition of the fact that the deep Qur'anic text can be translated only with limited accuracy, I have included the original Arabic text in addition to my suggested translation. Those who understand Arabic can refer to the original instead of relying completely on the provided translation.

I have also added in square brackets any explanatory text needed to clarify the translation. Round brackets have been used to add alternative texts, such as the English meaning of a term that is cited in its Arabic origin.

A number of different printing styles are used in the book. A special font has been used for the English translation of the Qur'anic text. The same font, but in italics, is also used for the Roman transliterations of the Qur'an. Roman transliterations of non-Qur'anic Arabic text use the same font of the ordinary text, but in italics.

Writing this book has been a dream that I have had for a long time. I thank Allah who has made it come true. Ever since Allah guided me to the Qur'an I have found in the sūra of Joseph special beauty that took over my heart, and deep knowledge and insightful wisdom that captured my mind.

Among the people who helped me with this book, I would like to thank in particular my wife Dr Shetha Al-Dargazelli for her many invaluable comments on earlier drafts. I would also like to thank my brothers Duraid and Faiz for their important comments. Shetha, Duraid, and Faiz have also kindly made the Qur'anic text very close to the Uthmani script. I am also deeply indebted to my friends Tariq Chaudhry and Alessandro Ansa for their excellent reviews of the book.

Readers are welcome to send any feedback they may have to *fatoohi_louay@gmail.com.*

Allah is the source of every good, and all thanks are due to Him. I thank Allah Almighty for any success this book has had in its interpretation of the Qur'anic text whose full meanings are beyond the comprehension of any creature. I ask Him for forgiveness for every mistake that I have made. The Messenger of Allah, our Master Muhammad, said: "Deeds are judged by the intentions behind them, and every person earns according to what he has intended."[2] May Allah make this book the fruit of good intention.

Prayer and peace be upon the Prophet of the Qur'an our Master Muhammad and upon his lineage and companions.

1

History and Prophet Joseph in the Qur'an, and Qur'anic Exegesis

In this chapter, we will first study characteristics of the Qur'an's style in recounting history. We will then commence our study of the Qur'anic story of Joseph with an outline of its main events. In the last section of the chapter, we will tackle common problems in the interpretational attempts of the Qur'an.

1.1 Narration of History in the Qur'an

It is necessary to talk briefly about the characteristic style of the Qur'an in relating history before we start our study of the story of Joseph. This information is vital for understanding the Qur'anic stories. Before that, however, it is important to highlight a particular attribute which characterizes the Qur'anic text in general and which is manifested in different forms. This quality is the use of succinctness in the Book of Allah. One manifestation of this is that a Qur'anic text does not mention explicitly information that can be concluded from or found in another Qur'anic text. This is better explained with examples from the Qur'an, such as the following set of verses which start with Allah's command to Moses and Aaron:

فَأْتِيَاهُ فَقُولَآ إِنَّا رَسُولَا رَبِّكَ فَأَرْسِلْ مَعَنَا بَنِىٓ إِسْرَٰٓءِيلَ وَلَا تُعَذِّبْهُمْ قَدْ جِئْنَٰكَ بِـَٔايَةٍ مِّن رَّبِّكَ
وَٱلسَّلَٰمُ عَلَىٰ مَنِ ٱتَّبَعَ ٱلْهُدَىٰٓ ﴿٤٧﴾ إِنَّا قَدْ أُوحِىَ إِلَيْنَآ أَنَّ ٱلْعَذَابَ عَلَىٰ مَن كَذَّبَ وَتَوَلَّىٰ ﴿٤٨﴾
قَالَ فَمَن رَّبُّكُمَا يَٰمُوسَىٰ ﴿٤٩﴾ قَالَ رَبُّنَا ٱلَّذِىٓ أَعْطَىٰ كُلَّ شَىْءٍ خَلْقَهُۥ ثُمَّ هَدَىٰ ﴿٥٠﴾ قَالَ فَمَا
بَالُ ٱلْقُرُونِ ٱلْأُولَىٰ ﴿٥١﴾ قَالَ عِلْمُهَا عِندَ رَبِّى فِى كِتَٰبٍ لَّا يَضِلُّ رَبِّى وَلَا يَنسَى ﴿٥٢﴾.

(سورة طه).

So go you both to him [Pharaoh] and say: "We are two messengers from your Lord; therefore send the Children of Israel with us and do not torment them; we have brought to you a sign from your Lord, and peace be upon

> him who follows the right guidance (20.47). Verily it has been revealed to us that torture will come upon him who rejects [the Message] and turns away" (20.48). He said: "So who is your Lord, O Moses?" (20.49). He said: "Our Lord is He who created everything, then guided it [to its course]" (20.50). He said: "Then what about the former generations?" (20.51). He said: "The knowledge thereof is with my Lord, in a book; my Lord errs not, nor does He forget" (20.52).

The Qur'an tells us in verses 20.47 and 20.48 the essence of the message that Allah ordered Moses and Aaron to convey to Pharaoh. When it then informs us in verse 20.49 of the debate that Moses and Aaron had with Pharaoh, the Qur'an does not mention what the two prophets said to Pharaoh, because it is the same message mentioned in the previous two verses. The verse starts with Pharaoh's reply to the message. It is as if the Qur'an says implicitly after verses 20.48 "and Moses and Aaron went to Pharaoh and conveyed to him what Allah had ordered them to tell him."

Note also the Qur'an's use of the verb قَالَ "He said" without specifying the identity of the speaker in each case. The reason is that the context leaves no ambiguity that the speakers are Moses and Pharaoh and makes clear also who said what.

After this quick reference to the Qur'an's style of using succinct phrases and sentences in conveying the intended meanings, let us now examine the Qur'an's style in relating history.

The Qur'an contains many historical stories about good and evil individuals and nations that lived before the time of Prophet Muhammad. It highlights the didactic lessons in those stories. The Qur'an is not interested in pure history but rather in the educational dimensions of historical events. This divine Book, therefore, has a unique style in relating history that differentiates it from historical documents written by man. Studying the Qur'anic stories requires familiarity with the Qur'an's style in relating history.

Succinctness is one attribute that differentiates the Qur'an's way of recounting history from traditional story telling. This attribute is an extension of the Qur'an's general style of using succinct eloquence which I mentioned earlier. So often the Qur'an bypasses minor details that are given prominence in traditional recounting of history. For instance, it is common for the Qur'an not to mention the names of main characters and places in a story. Notable examples of prominent characters in Qur'anic stories whose names are not mentioned include Joseph's eleven brothers, the wife and two sons of Adam and, from the story in the sūra of al-Kahf (18), Moses' companion and the righteous person whom Moses met.

Furthermore, Allah might even refer to a prophet without mentioning his name, as in the following verses:

أَلَمْ تَرَ إِلَى ٱلْمَلَإِ مِنۢ بَنِىٓ إِسْرَٰٓءِيلَ مِنۢ بَعْدِ مُوسَىٰٓ إِذْ قَالُوا۟ لِنَبِىٍّ لَّهُمُ ٱبْعَثْ لَنَا مَلِكًا نُّقَٰتِلْ فِى سَبِيلِ
ٱللَّهِ قَالَ هَلْ عَسَيْتُمْ إِن كُتِبَ عَلَيْكُمُ ٱلْقِتَالُ أَلَّا تُقَٰتِلُوا۟ قَالُوا۟ وَمَا لَنَآ أَلَّا نُقَٰتِلَ فِى سَبِيلِ ٱللَّهِ وَقَدْ
أُخْرِجْنَا مِن دِيَٰرِنَا وَأَبْنَآئِنَا فَلَمَّا كُتِبَ عَلَيْهِمُ ٱلْقِتَالُ تَوَلَّوْا۟ إِلَّا قَلِيلًا مِّنْهُمْ وَٱللَّهُ عَلِيمٌۢ بِٱلظَّٰلِمِينَ
﴿٢٤٦﴾ وَقَالَ لَهُمْ نَبِيُّهُمْ إِنَّ ٱللَّهَ قَدْ بَعَثَ لَكُمْ طَالُوتَ مَلِكًا قَالُوٓا۟ أَنَّىٰ يَكُونُ لَهُ ٱلْمُلْكُ عَلَيْنَا
وَنَحْنُ أَحَقُّ بِٱلْمُلْكِ مِنْهُ وَلَمْ يُؤْتَ سَعَةً مِّنَ ٱلْمَالِ قَالَ إِنَّ ٱللَّهَ ٱصْطَفَىٰهُ عَلَيْكُمْ وَزَادَهُۥ بَسْطَةً فِى
ٱلْعِلْمِ وَٱلْجِسْمِ وَٱللَّهُ يُؤْتِى مُلْكَهُۥ مَن يَشَآءُ وَٱللَّهُ وَٰسِعٌ عَلِيمٌ ﴿٢٤٧﴾ وَقَالَ لَهُمْ نَبِيُّهُمْ إِنَّ ءَايَةَ
مُلْكِهِۦٓ أَن يَأْتِيَكُمُ ٱلتَّابُوتُ فِيهِ سَكِينَةٌ مِّن رَّبِّكُمْ وَبَقِيَّةٌ مِّمَّا تَرَكَ ءَالُ مُوسَىٰ وَءَالُ هَٰرُونَ تَحْمِلُهُ
ٱلْمَلَٰٓئِكَةُ إِنَّ فِى ذَٰلِكَ لَءَايَةً لَّكُمْ إِن كُنتُم مُّؤْمِنِينَ ﴿٢٤٨﴾. (سورة البقرة).

Have you not considered [O Muhammad!] how the chiefs of the Children of Israel who came after Moses said to a prophet of theirs: "Set up for us a king and we will fight in the way of Allah." He said: "May it be that you would not fight if fighting was ordained for you?" They said: "Why would we not fight in the way of Allah having been driven out of our homes, and for the sake of our children?" But when fighting was ordained for them, they turned away except a few of them; and Allah knows the wrongdoers (2.246). And their prophet said to them: "Surely Allah has raised Saul to be a king for you." They said: "How can he hold kingship over us when we have a greater right to kingship than he, and he has not been granted abundant wealth?" He said: "Surely Allah has chosen him in preference to you, and He has increased him abundantly in knowledge and physique; and Allah grants His kingdom to whom He pleases"; and Allah is Embracing, Knowing (2.247). And their prophet said to them: "Surely the sign of His kingship is that there shall come to you the Ark, in which there is tranquility from your Lord and a remnant of what the house of Moses and the house of Aaron have left, which will be carried by angels; surely there is a sign in this for you if you are believers" (2.248).

It is notable that although Allah refers to Saul with his name, He refers to the prophet in the three verses with his status, i.e. as a prophet, without revealing his name. Allah has His own divine reason for this.

There are also many instances of places and cities that Allah refers to in various places in the Qur'an without specifying them explicitly, such as the place to which prophet Adam descended (2.36, 7.24), the village to which prophet Jonah was sent (10.98), and the birth place of prophet Jesus (19.23).

Let us take another example. The Qur'an mentions in lengthy detail in several places the suffering of a prophet at the hand of his disbelieving people, and Allah's subsequent revenge on those people. Nevertheless, not many details are given about the revenge itself, as often only the type of punishment is mentioned and the perishing of the disbelievers is stressed. For instance, Allah reveals in several suwar various details about the story of prophet Hūd, but He does not mention many details of the event of punishing the disbelievers:

فَأَنجَيْنَـٰهُ وَٱلَّذِينَ مَعَهُۥ بِرَحْمَةٍ مِّنَّا وَقَطَعْنَا دَابِرَ ٱلَّذِينَ كَذَّبُوا۟ بِـَٔايَـٰتِنَا وَمَا كَانُوا۟ مُؤْمِنِينَ ﴿٧٢﴾. (سور الأعراف).

So We saved him and those with him by a mercy from Us, and We cut off the last of those who rejected Our signs and did not become believers (7.72).

وَلَمَّا جَآءَ أَمْرُنَا نَجَّيْنَا هُودًا وَٱلَّذِينَ ءَامَنُوا۟ مَعَهُۥ بِرَحْمَةٍ مِّنَّا وَنَجَّيْنَـٰهُم مِّنْ عَذَابٍ غَلِيظٍ ﴿٥٨﴾ وَتِلْكَ عَادٌ ۖ جَحَدُوا۟ بِـَٔايَـٰتِ رَبِّهِمْ وَعَصَوْا۟ رُسُلَهُۥ وَٱتَّبَعُوٓا۟ أَمْرَ كُلِّ جَبَّارٍ عَنِيدٍ ﴿٥٩﴾ وَأُتْبِعُوا۟ فِى هَـٰذِهِ ٱلدُّنْيَا لَعْنَةً وَيَوْمَ ٱلْقِيَـٰمَةِ ۗ أَلَآ إِنَّ عَادًا كَفَرُوا۟ رَبَّهُمْ ۗ أَلَا بُعْدًا لِّعَادٍ قَوْمِ هُودٍ ﴿٦٠﴾. (سورة هود).

And when Our decree came to pass, We saved Hūd and those who believed with him with a mercy from Us, and We saved them from a severe torment (11.58). And that was [the people of] 'Ād; they denied the signs of their Lord, disobeyed His messengers, and followed the bidding of every insolent oppressor (11.59). And they were pursued by a curse in this world and on the Day of Resurrection; Lo! Surely 'Ād disbelieved in their Lord; surely, away with 'Ād, the people of Hūd (11.60).

فَكَذَّبُوهُ فَأَهْلَكْنَـٰهُمْ ۗ إِنَّ فِى ذَٰلِكَ لَـَٔايَةً ۖ وَمَا كَانَ أَكْثَرُهُم مُّؤْمِنِينَ ﴿١٣٩﴾. (سورة الشُّعَرَاء).

So they rejected him; therefore We destroyed them. Surely there is a sign in this, but most of them would not believe (26.139).

The event of the punishment represents the end and climax of the struggle of Hūd against his people. Details of this event would have been given particular importance in traditional story telling. The Qur'an, in contrast, mentions only Allah's aid to His prophet and His destruction of the disbelievers.

Another characteristic of the Qur'an's style in recounting stories is that the details of any particular story are usually found in more than one place in the Book of Allah. One example of that is the story of Moses. Building a complete picture of any story in the Qur'an requires compiling all its details from the various suwar. The story of Joseph is mentioned in its entirety in the sūra that is named after that prophet; this is an exception, not the rule.

An event may be described in different, but consistent, ways in different suwar, to reflect what Allah wants to emphasize and highlight in the respective sūra. For example, a historical conversation may be cited in different suwar using a number of different wordings to convey the meaning of that dialog. We must not forget that often the original language of a dialog was not the Arabic of the Qur'an, if Arabic at all, such as the dialogs between various prophets and their peoples. The verses below, which come from different suwar, describe the first dialog between Allah and Moses. They use different wordings to describe the same events. These suwar also differ with respect to the type and amount of information they give about that debate:

إِذْ قَالَ مُوسَىٰ لِأَهْلِهِۦٓ إِنِّىٓ ءَانَسْتُ نَارًا سَـَٔاتِيكُم مِّنْهَا بِخَبَرٍ أَوْ ءَاتِيكُم بِشِهَابٍ قَبَسٍ لَّعَلَّكُمْ تَصْطَلُونَ ﴿٧﴾ فَلَمَّا جَآءَهَا نُودِىَ أَنۢ بُورِكَ مَن فِى ٱلنَّارِ وَمَنْ حَوْلَهَا وَسُبْحَـٰنَ ٱللَّهِ رَبِّ ٱلْعَـٰلَمِينَ ﴿٨﴾ يَـٰمُوسَىٰٓ إِنَّهُۥٓ أَنَا ٱللَّهُ ٱلْعَزِيزُ ٱلْحَكِيمُ ﴿٩﴾ وَأَلْقِ عَصَاكَ فَلَمَّا رَءَاهَا تَهْتَزُّ كَأَنَّهَا جَآنٌّ وَلَّىٰ مُدْبِرًا وَلَمْ يُعَقِّبْ يَـٰمُوسَىٰ لَا تَخَفْ إِنِّى لَا يَخَافُ لَدَىَّ ٱلْمُرْسَلُونَ ﴿١٠﴾ إِلَّا مَن ظَلَمَ ثُمَّ بَدَّلَ حُسْنًۢا بَعْدَ سُوٓءٍ فَإِنِّى غَفُورٌ رَّحِيمٌ ﴿١١﴾ وَأَدْخِلْ يَدَكَ فِى جَيْبِكَ تَخْرُجْ بَيْضَآءَ مِنْ غَيْرِ سُوٓءٍ فِى تِسْعِ ءَايَـٰتٍ إِلَىٰ فِرْعَوْنَ وَقَوْمِهِۦٓ إِنَّهُمْ كَانُوا۟ قَوْمًا فَـٰسِقِينَ ﴿١٢﴾. (سورة النمل).

When Moses said to his family: "Surely I have perceived a fire. I shall either bring you tidings thence, or bring you a burning firebrand so that you may warm yourselves" (27.7). So when he came to the fire he heard a call: "Blessed is Whoever is in the fire and whoever is around it, and glory be to Allah, the Lord of the people (27.8). O Moses! It is Me, Allah, the Invincible, the Wise" (27.9). "Throw down your staff." And when he saw it moving as if it was a snake, he turned away fleeing without retracing his steps; [and it was said to him]: "O Moses! Fear not, for messengers are not to fear in My presence (27.10). Neither he who, after doing wrong, does good instead of evil, for surely I am Forgiving, Merciful" (27.11). "Enter your hand into your bosom, it will come out white, showing no harm; [go with this] among nine signs to Pharaoh and his people; surely they are a rebellious people [against Me] (27.12).

فَلَمَّا قَضَىٰ مُوسَى ٱلْأَجَلَ وَسَارَ بِأَهْلِهِۦٓ ءَانَسَ مِن جَانِبِ ٱلطُّورِ نَارًا قَالَ لِأَهْلِهِ ٱمْكُثُوٓا۟ إِنِّىٓ ءَانَسْتُ نَارًا لَّعَلِّىٓ ءَاتِيكُم مِّنْهَا بِخَبَرٍ أَوْ جَذْوَةٍ مِّنَ ٱلنَّارِ لَعَلَّكُمْ تَصْطَلُونَ ﴿٢٩﴾ فَلَمَّآ أَتَىٰهَا نُودِىَ مِن شَـٰطِئِ ٱلْوَادِ ٱلْأَيْمَنِ فِى ٱلْبُقْعَةِ ٱلْمُبَـٰرَكَةِ مِنَ ٱلشَّجَرَةِ أَن يَـٰمُوسَىٰٓ إِنِّىٓ أَنَا ٱللَّهُ رَبُّ ٱلْعَـٰلَمِينَ ﴿٣٠﴾ وَأَنْ أَلْقِ عَصَاكَ فَلَمَّا رَءَاهَا تَهْتَزُّ كَأَنَّهَا جَآنٌّ وَلَّىٰ مُدْبِرًا وَلَمْ يُعَقِّبْ يَـٰمُوسَىٰٓ أَقْبِلْ وَلَا تَخَفْ إِنَّكَ مِنَ ٱلْـَٔامِنِينَ ﴿٣١﴾ ٱسْلُكْ يَدَكَ فِى جَيْبِكَ تَخْرُجْ بَيْضَآءَ مِنْ غَيْرِ سُوٓءٍ وَٱضْمُمْ إِلَيْكَ

جَنَاحَكَ مِنَ الرَّهْبِ فَذَٰنِكَ بُرْهَـٰنَانِ مِن رَّبِّكَ إِلَىٰ فِرْعَوْنَ وَمَلَإِيْهِ إِنَّهُمْ كَانُواْ قَوْمًا فَـٰسِقِينَ ﴿٣٢﴾
قَالَ رَبِّ إِنِّى قَتَلْتُ مِنْهُمْ نَفْسًا فَأَخَافُ أَن يَقْتُلُونِ ﴿٣٣﴾ وَأَخِى هَـٰرُونُ هُوَ أَفْصَحُ مِنِّى لِسَانًا
فَأَرْسِلْهُ مَعِىَ رِدْءًا يُصَدِّقُنِىٓ إِنِّىٓ أَخَافُ أَن يُكَذِّبُونِ ﴿٣٤﴾ قَالَ سَنَشُدُّ عَضُدَكَ بِأَخِيكَ وَنَجْعَلُ
لَكُمَا سُلْطَـٰنًا فَلَا يَصِلُونَ إِلَيْكُمَا بِـَٔايَـٰتِنَآ أَنتُمَا وَمَنِ ٱتَّبَعَكُمَا ٱلْغَـٰلِبُونَ ﴿٣٥﴾. (سورة القصص).

Then, when Moses had fulfilled the term and left in the night with his family, he perceived [at a distance] a fire at the side of the Mount and said to his family: "Tarry here; I have perceived a fire that I might bring to you tidings thence, or a firebrand that you may warm yourselves" (28.29). And when he came to the fire, he heard a call from the right coast of the valley in the spot that was blessed because of the tree: "O Moses! It is Me, Allah, the Lord of the people" (28.30). "Throw down your staff"; and when he saw it move as if it was a snake, he turned away fleeing without retracing his steps. [And it was said to him]: "O Moses! Draw nigh and do not fear for you are one of those who are secure (28.31). Enter your hand into your bosom and it will come out white, showing no harm; and guard your heart from fear, for these shall be two proofs from your Lord to Pharaoh and his chiefs; for they are a rebellious people [against Me]" (28.32). He said: "My Lord! I have killed one of them and I fear that they will kill me (28.33). My brother Aaron speaks better than me, therefore make him a messenger and a helper to confirm me; I fear that they will accuse me of telling lies" (28.34). He said: "We shall strengthen you with your brother, and We shall give to you both authority so they shall not be able to reach you [for harm] on account of our signs; you both and those who follow you will be the victorious" (28.35).

وَإِذْ نَادَىٰ رَبُّكَ مُوسَىٰٓ أَنِ ٱئْتِ ٱلْقَوْمَ ٱلظَّـٰلِمِينَ ﴿١٠﴾ قَوْمَ فِرْعَوْنَ أَلَا يَتَّقُونَ ﴿١١﴾. قَالَ
رَبِّ إِنِّىٓ أَخَافُ أَن يُكَذِّبُونِ ﴿١٢﴾ وَيَضِيقُ صَدْرِى وَلَا يَنطَلِقُ لِسَانِى فَأَرْسِلْ إِلَىٰ هَـٰرُونَ
﴿١٣﴾ وَلَهُمْ عَلَىَّ ذَنۢبٌ فَأَخَافُ أَن يَقْتُلُونِ ﴿١٤﴾ قَالَ كَلَّا فَٱذْهَبَا بِـَٔايَـٰتِنَآ إِنَّا مَعَكُم مُّسْتَمِعُونَ
﴿١٥﴾ فَأْتِيَا فِرْعَوْنَ فَقُولَآ إِنَّا رَسُولُ رَبِّ ٱلْعَـٰلَمِينَ ﴿١٦﴾ أَنْ أَرْسِلْ مَعَنَا بَنِىٓ إِسْرَٰٓءِيلَ
﴿١٧﴾. (سورة الشعراء).

And when your Lord [O Muhammad!] called Moses [saying]: "Go to the wrongdoing people (26.10). The people of Pharaoh. Will they not act dutifully [towards Me]?" (26.11). He said: "My Lord! I fear that they will accuse me of telling lies (26.12). And my breast will be straitened, and my tongue will not speak fluently, therefore make Aaron a messenger [to help me] (26.13). And they have a charge of crime against me, so I fear that they will kill me" (26.14). He said: "By no means [will they hurt you]. So go you both with Our signs; We shall be with you, hearing (26.15). So, both of you go to Pharaoh and say: 'We are messengers of the Lord of the people (26.16). Let the Children of Israel leave with us'" (26.17).

There is another prominent attribute that characterizes the Qur'an's non-traditional style in relating historical stories. Successive verses may mention disconnected events that did not happen immediately after each other. One form this style takes is citing a past event in the middle of more recent ones, in order to stress a certain point; so events may not be cited in their chronological order. In such cases, where the citing of each event represents a change in the narrative context, the accounts of various events are linked by إِذْ "*idh* (when)," rather than by ثُمَّ "*thumma* (then)" or فَـ "*fa* (therefore or so)" both of which indicate that the events are mentioned in their chronological order. The following examples show the special use of "*idh*":

وَٱتَّقُواْ يَوْمًا لَّا تَجْزِى نَفْسٌ عَن نَّفْسٍ شَيْـًٔا وَلَا يُقْبَلُ مِنْهَا عَدْلٌ وَلَا تَنفَعُهَا شَفَـٰعَةٌ وَلَا هُمْ
يُنصَرُونَ ﴿١٢٣﴾ وَإِذِ ٱبْتَلَىٰٓ إِبْرَٰهِـۧمَ رَبُّهُۥ بِكَلِمَـٰتٍ فَأَتَمَّهُنَّ قَالَ إِنِّى جَاعِلُكَ لِلنَّاسِ إِمَامًا قَالَ وَمِن
ذُرِّيَّتِى قَالَ لَا يَنَالُ عَهْدِى ٱلظَّـٰلِمِينَ ﴿١٢٤﴾ وَإِذْ جَعَلْنَا ٱلْبَيْتَ مَثَابَةً لِّلنَّاسِ وَأَمْنًا وَٱتَّخِذُواْ مِن
مَّقَامِ إِبْرَٰهِـۧمَ مُصَلًّى وَعَهِدْنَآ إِلَىٰٓ إِبْرَٰهِـۧمَ وَإِسْمَـٰعِيلَ أَن طَهِّرَا بَيْتِىَ لِلطَّآئِفِينَ وَٱلْعَـٰكِفِينَ وَٱلرُّكَّعِ
ٱلسُّجُودِ ﴿١٢٥﴾ وَإِذْ قَالَ إِبْرَٰهِـۧمُ رَبِّ ٱجْعَلْ هَـٰذَا بَلَدًا ءَامِنًا وَٱرْزُقْ أَهْلَهُۥ مِنَ ٱلثَّمَرَٰتِ مَنْ ءَامَنَ
مِنْهُم بِٱللَّهِ وَٱلْيَوْمِ ٱلْأَخِرِ قَالَ وَمَن كَفَرَ فَأُمَتِّعُهُۥ قَلِيلًا ثُمَّ أَضْطَرُّهُۥٓ إِلَىٰ عَذَابِ ٱلنَّارِ وَبِئْسَ ٱلْمَصِيرُ
﴿١٢٦﴾ وَإِذْ يَرْفَعُ إِبْرَٰهِـۧمُ ٱلْقَوَاعِدَ مِنَ ٱلْبَيْتِ وَإِسْمَـٰعِيلُ رَبَّنَا تَقَبَّلْ مِنَّآ إِنَّكَ أَنتَ ٱلسَّمِيعُ ٱلْعَلِيمُ
﴿١٢٧﴾. (سورة البقرة).

And guard yourselves [O you who believe!] against a day when no soul shall avail another in the least, neither shall any compensation be accepted from it, nor shall intercession benefit it, nor shall they be helped (2.123). And *idh* (when) Abraham's Lord tried him with certain words and fulfilled them; He said: "Surely I will make you a guide for people." He [Abraham] said: "Will you also [make guides] from my offspring?" He said: "My covenant does not cover the wrongdoers" (2.124). And *idh* (when) We made the House [the Ka'ba in Mecca] a resort for people and a sanctuary, [ordering them]: "Take the place where Abraham lives as a place of prayer." And We made a covenant with Abraham and Ishmael: "Purify My House for the circumambulators, those in retreat, and those who bow down and prostrate themselves [in worship]" (2.125). And *idh* (when) Abraham said: "My Lord, make this a safe town and provide its people with fruits, to those among them who believe in Allah and the Last Day." He said: "And whoever disbelieves, I shall grant him provisions for a short while, then I shall drive him to the torment of the Fire; and it is an evil destination" (2.126). And *idh* (when) Abraham and Ishmael were raising the foundations of the House [they used to say]: "Our Lord! Accept from us [our discharging of this duty]; surely You are the Hearing, the Knowing" (2.127).

The word "*idh*" in verse 2.124 starts a new context: the speech about Abraham. Verse 2.125 refers to an event that followed the building of the Ka'ba, and verse 2.126 mentions Abraham's prayer that happened at a later time. Verse 2.127 then returns to the earlier stage of building the Ka'ba by Abraham and his son Ishmael. These events did not take place immediately after each other; they are different events, hence Allah uses "*idh*" to refer to them.[3]

Despite its special style in recounting historical information, the Qur'an presents all historical accounts, like other information in the Qur'an, as factual information that describes real events exactly as they occurred. This means that the growing human knowledge of the history of events documented in the Qur'an can be used as sources for studying the Book of Allah.

1.2 The Story of Prophet Joseph in the Qur'an

The story of Joseph in the Qur'an is mentioned in its entirety in the one sūra that carries his name. The sūra of Joseph is the twelfth sūra of the one hundred and fourteen suwar in the Qur'an. It consists of one hundred and eleven verses.

The name of Joseph occurs only twice outside this sūra. First, with a number of other prophets in a verse that talks about his great grandfather Abraham, and second, when a believer in Egypt at the time of Moses reminded his people of Joseph who lived there about four centuries earlier:

وَوَهَبْنَا لَهُۥٓ إِسْحَـٰقَ وَيَعْقُوبَ ۚ كُلًّا هَدَيْنَا ۚ وَنُوحًا هَدَيْنَا مِن قَبْلُ ۖ وَمِن ذُرِّيَّتِهِۦ دَاوُۥدَ وَسُلَيْمَـٰنَ
وَأَيُّوبَ وَيُوسُفَ وَمُوسَىٰ وَهَـٰرُونَ ۚ وَكَذَٰلِكَ نَجْزِى ٱلْمُحْسِنِينَ ﴿٨٤﴾. (سورة الأنعام).

And We gave Isaac and Jacob to him [Abraham], each of whom We did guide; and Noah did We guide before; and his [Abraham's] descendants, David, Solomon, Job, Joseph, and Aaron; and thus do We reward the good-doers (6.84).

وَلَقَدْ جَآءَكُمْ يُوسُفُ مِن قَبْلُ بِٱلْبَيِّنَـٰتِ فَمَا زِلْتُمْ فِى شَكٍّ مِّمَّا جَآءَكُم بِهِۦ ۖ حَتَّىٰٓ إِذَا هَلَكَ قُلْتُمْ لَن
يَبْعَثَ ٱللَّهُ مِنۢ بَعْدِهِۦ رَسُولًا ۚ كَذَٰلِكَ يُضِلُّ ٱللَّهُ مَنْ هُوَ مُسْرِفٌ مُّرْتَابٌ ﴿٣٤﴾. (سورة غافر).

And surely Joseph came to you [O my people!] in times gone by with clear proofs, but you ever remained in doubt about what he brought to you. When he died, you said: "Allah will not send a messenger after him." Thus does Allah cause to err him who is extravagant, a doubter (40.34).

The sūra of Joseph was revealed in Mecca, i.e. before the immigration of the Prophet to the city of "al-Madīna."[4] Some scholars think that the first three verses and the seventh verse of this sūra were revealed in al-Madīna. There is nothing in those verses, however, that justifies this assumption.

The story starts with little Joseph recounting to his father a visionary dream in which he saw eleven stars and the sun and the moon prostrating to him. Jacob instructed his son not to relate the dream to his half brothers. They had fostered envy for Joseph because they thought that their father loved him more than them. The Qur'an then tells us about a plan that Joseph's brothers worked out to get rid of Joseph. After obtaining the permission of their father to take Joseph with them to where they graze their cattle, they threw him in a well.

Joseph's brothers thought that some travelers would find their young brother and take him far from the land of their father. Pretending to cry for losing Joseph, they returned to their father carrying their brother's shirt which they had smeared with some blood. They claimed that a wolf devoured Joseph when they left him unattended. As for little Joseph, travelers in a caravan found him, took him away, and sold him in Egypt. The person who bought Joseph is seen a few years later occupying the high position of the "'Azīz."

When Joseph grew into an extremely handsome young man, the wife of the 'Azīz tried to seduce him. Joseph rejected her advances. Women in the city then started to talk about the woman's fondness of Joseph. She invited them to her house, and in their presence threatened Joseph with imprisonment if he would not obey her. The chaste Joseph preferred being thrown unjustly in jail to committing fornication, so the 'Azīz's wife and her accomplices put him in prison.

At some point, Joseph was joined in prison by two men. Having seen in him signs of righteousness and paranormal abilities, the two prisoners asked Joseph to interpret a dream each of them had seen. Joseph successfully interpreted the dreams: one prisoner would be killed, and the second would be freed and returned to work as the cupbearer of the king. Joseph asked the latter, when he is back in the king's service, to relate to the king the injustice that he was made to suffer. Satan made the cupbearer forget about Joseph who, therefore, stayed in jail.

A few years later, the king saw a dream and asked his court for an interpretation, but they could not oblige. This time the cupbearer remembered Joseph, so he asked for permission to go and ask his former prison mate for the interpretation. Joseph told him that there was going to be seven years of plenteous crops, followed by seven years in which there would be little harvest, before a year of copious rain sets in.

Having heard Joseph's interpretation, the king asked for Joseph to be brought to him. Joseph, while still in prison, requested through the messenger that the king questions the women who conspired against him. The wife of the 'Azīz confessed to what she did to Joseph and acknowledged her sin.

After setting Joseph free, the king wanted to have him close to him and appoint him in a high position. Joseph asked the king to be put in charge of the storehouses of the land. His wish was granted.

During the years of famine that Joseph had predicted, his brothers came to Egypt asking for food. They were allowed into Joseph's office, and he recognized them. They, however, did not recognize their brother. He gave them provisions but told them not to come back asking for more without bringing their half brother.

When they returned to their father, they told him about Joseph's decision and asked him to send their half brother Benjamin[5] with them to get more provisions. Jacob, who agreed to send Joseph with them years earlier, first refused to send his other son. Then he agreed to do so if his sons would take an oath to return Benjamin unless something out of their control prevents them from doing so. They took the oath, so Benjamin went with his brothers to ask for provisions in Egypt. This time Joseph secretly revealed his real identity to Benjamin who was being mistreated by his older brothers.

With the collusion of Benjamin, Joseph worked out a plan to keep his brother with him in Egypt, but without revealing his real identity to his other ten brothers. He accused Benjamin of stealing the drinking cup of the king and, consequently, took him as a slave and refused to allow him to return with his brothers.

Joseph's brothers' first reaction to the developing event was to claim that their other half brother, i.e. Joseph, had also committed a robbery. Later, they tried to convince Joseph to allow Benjamin to go back with them and take one of them as a slave in stead. This offer, which Jacob's sons put forward because they had promised their father to bring back Benjamin with them, was turned down by Joseph. Jacob, who was still very sad for the disappearance of his son Joseph, though well aware through divine knowledge that he was still alive, lost his sight as a result of his continued sadness for losing Joseph.

Jacob sent his sons for the third time to Egypt, this time to look for both Joseph and Benjamin. When Joseph's brothers met him, he revealed his identity to them. Completely stunned by the revelation, they showed serious regret for what they had done and repented for their sinful acts.

Joseph then asked them to take his shirt and put it on his father's face in order to restore his sight. He also asked them to bring all of their families, along with his father and mother, to Egypt. When Joseph's shirt was put on Jacob's face, his sight was restored. Jacob's sons asked their father to pray to Allah to forgive them for what they had done.

In Egypt, Jacob, Joseph's mother, and his brothers prostrated in respect to Joseph who was occupying a high position. Joseph then drew his father's attention to the fact that this was the interpretation and realization of the dream that he saw when he was still a young boy. In the last verse of the story of Joseph, we see this noble prophet in a magnificent thanksgiving prayer to Allah for the favors that He conferred on him and his family.

After the story of Joseph, the sūra concludes with ten general verses.

1.3 Problems in the Exegesis of the Qur'an

Since the revelation of the Qur'an, Muslim scholars have shown great interest in studying and interpreting the Qur'an. These enormous efforts have resulted in a huge number of exegetical books. Some of these works focus on interpreting particular verses or suwar, whereas others attempt to interpret the Book of Allah in its entirety. Examples of the latter category of exegetical books, mostly referred to as "Tafsīr (exegesis) of so and so" after their respective authors, include the following which I will quote from in this book and which represent the main schools of exegesis:

1) *Al-Jāmi' li Aḥkām al-Qur'an (The Collection of the Rules of the Qur'an),* by Muhammad al-Qurṭubī (d. 1272 CE).

2) *Tafsīr of Ibn Kathīr,* by Ismā'īl Ibn Kathīr (1301-1372 CE).

3) *Ad-Dur al-Manthūr fī at-Tafsīr bi al-Ma'thūr (The Spread Jewels in Interpreting with the Reported Opinions),* by Jalāl ad-Dīn as-Suyūṭī (d. 1505 CE).

4) *Tafsīr of al-Jalālayn*[6], by Jalāl ad-Dīn as-Suyūṭī and Jalāl ad-Dīn al-Maḥallī.

5) *Tafsīr of al-'Ayyāshī,* by Muhammad al-'Ayyāshī.

6) *Tafsīr Nūr ath-Thaqalayn (The Tafsīr of the Light of the Two Species),* by 'Abd 'Alī bin Jum'a al-'Arūsī al-Ḥuwayzī. This work cites

extensively from al-'Ayyāshī.

7) *Tafsīr al-Qummī*, by 'Alī bin Ibrāhīm al-Qummī.

8) *Tafsīr aṭ-Ṭabaṭabā'ī*, by Muhammad aṭ-Ṭabaṭabā'ī (1892-1981).

9) *At-Tibyān fī Tafsīr al-Qur'an (Revealing the Interpretion of the Qur'an)*, by Muhammad aṭ-Ṭūsī (995-1067 CE).

10) *Jāmi' al-Bayān fī Tafsīr al-Qur'an (The Compilation of the Clarification in Interpreting the Qur'an)*, by Muhammad aṭ-Ṭabarī (840-922 CE).

Muslim exegetes agree on the authenticity of the text of the Qur'an. They do differ, nevertheless, in their interpretations of that text. There are instances where different interpretations of one Qur'anic text can be reconciled and should, thus, be all considered possible. There are many cases, however, where different interpretations contradict each other, so they cannot all be correct. Using research resources and methodologies that are available to him, an exegete often tries hard to reach what he thinks is the correct interpretation of the Qur'anic text. While the Qur'an is a divine text that is completely true, any interpretation of this blessed text is a human attempt that may succeed or fail.

Exegetes' mistakes differ in their nature and consequences. There are mistakes which can be described as "individual" or "isolated" because they affect a particular verse or set of verses. For instance, misunderstanding a particular word or clause in a verse leads to misinterpreting that verse or one set of verses. The worst mistakes, however, are those which can be called "methodological." These reflect flaws in the methodology used in the interpretation. The negative effects of these mistakes are not restricted to the interpretation of a particular verse or sūra, but extend to any Qur'anic text that they may be applied to. Let us study some of the worst methodological mistakes that many exegetes have inherited from each other and whose effects, therefore, can be seen in many exegetical books.

The first of these serious methodological mistakes is the failure to follow the principle of "the Qur'an interprets itself." The Qur'an is one entity whose different verses and suwar cannot be studied in complete isolation from each other. There are many examples that show that understanding a verse in one sūra requires relating it to another verse in a different sūra. Neglecting the interrelations between different parts of the Qur'anic text results in, at best, the inability to interpret the relevant verses, and, at worst, erroneous interpretations.

After citing the verse وَنَزَّلْنَا عَلَيْكَ ٱلْكِتَـٰبَ تِبْيَـٰنًا لِّكُلِّ شَىْءٍ "and We have revealed the Book to you [O Muhammad!] explaining clearly everything" (from 16.89) in the introduction to his voluminous exegetical work of the Qur'an, aṭ-Ṭabaṭabā'ī beautifully points out that the Qur'an cannot be "an explanation of everything but not of itself." Then he cites the following two verses that describe the Qur'an: هُدًى لِلنَّاسِ وَبَيِّنَاتٍ مِنَ الْهُدَىٰ وَالْفُرْقَانِ "a guidance to people and clear proofs of guidance and distinction [between right and wrong]" (from 2.185) and وَأَنزَلْنَا إِلَيْكُمْ نُورًا مُبِينًا "and We have sent down to you [O people!] a clear light" (from 4.174), and goes on to comment: "how can the Qur'an be guidance, proof, distinction [between right and wrong], and clear light to people with respect to all of their needs, if it does not satisfy their need to understand it, which is the greatest need?"

The principle of "the Qur'an interprets itself" does not exclude other sources of information and knowledge for studying the Qur'anic text. It, rather, means that there is so much that cannot be properly understood without consulting the Qur'an itself. For instance, when studying the meaning of a particular word in a verse, it is certainly useful to know what external linguistic sources have to say. What is indispensable, however, is studying the variations of that word in the Qur'an itself and the contexts in which they occur.

Exegetes neglect or underestimate the fact that "the Qur'an interprets itself"; this has made them rely completely on extra-Qur'anic sources to interpret the Qur'anic text. This has led exegetes to use information, from a variety of sources, much of which lacks any supportive evidence. We will see examples of this later when we examine some of the interpretations that have been suggested for verses of the sūra of Joseph. The problem is that exegetes often accept the authenticity of a narrative simply because it is attributed to particular historians or exegetes. They ignore the possibility that those older historians and exegetes could have erred by propagating an inauthentic narrative, or that the narrative was wrongly attributed to those scholars, something that is usually impossible to confirm or reject. It is rather puzzling, as well as disappointing, to find that many exegetes do not make a distinction between narratives that can be linked to a Qur'anic text, so there is reason to think they *may* be true, and those that seem impossible to relate to any Qur'anic text, hence remain hypothetical.

The problem is further exacerbated by the failure of many exegetes and historians to deal with reported narratives rationally and logically, and to carefully examine their accuracy and plausibility. Exegetical books are full of hundreds, in fact thousands, of narratives that defy common sense. Some of these contradict the Qur'an itself, as we will see later. Let us look at one example of those completely ridiculous, yet amazingly popular, narratives that have no foundations in the Book of Allah. This narrative has been cited by exegetes when interpreting verse 80 of the sūra of Joseph: "So, when they [Joseph's brothers] despaired of [convincing] him, they conferred privately. The eldest among them said: 'Do you not know that your father has taken from you a covenant in Allah's name, and how you gave away Joseph before? Therefore I will not depart from this land until my father permits me or Allah judges for me, and He is the best of judges'." Al-Qurṭubī attributes to the old exegete Ibn 'Abbās the following narrative, which occurs in very or slightly similar, longer or shorter, versions in many exegetical books, such as those of al-'Ayyāshī, al-Ḥuwayzī, aṭ-Ṭabarī, al-Qummī and as-Suyūṭī:

> When Judah [one of Joseph's brothers] would get angry and take the sword, not even a hundred thousand [fighters] would be able to repel him. The hairs of his chest would stand like large needles and penetrate his clothes. It was reported that Judah, who was the most volatile among his brothers, said to them: "Either you sort out the king [meaning Joseph who had detained his brother Benjamin with him] and I sort out the people of Egypt, or you sort out the people of Egypt and I sort out the king and those who are with him." His brothers said: "You sort out the king and those who are with him, and we will sort out the people of Egypt." So, he sent out one of his brothers to count the markets in Egypt, which they found to be nine. Each of them picked a market.
>
> Judah then entered Joseph's office and said: "O king! If you do not give our brother back to us I will make such a cry that would make every pregnant woman in your city suffer a miscarriage." That was a special attribute in them [Joseph's brothers] when they got angry. Joseph angered Judah by saying something to him. Judah, therefore, became angry; his anger increased, and his hair penetrated his clothes.
>
> This was the case with everyone of Jacob's sons. When one of them would get angry, he would get goose bumps, his body would grow, the hairs of his back would protrude through his clothes, and a drop of blood would fall from each hair. If he would hit the ground with his foot, the earth would quake and buildings would collapse. If he would make a cry, every pregnant woman, animal, and bird would give birth, even if the fetus was not fully-grown. His anger would not go unless he shed blood or was touched by the hand of one of the offspring of Jacob.
>
> When Joseph realized that the anger of his brother Judah had reached its climax, he asked in Coptic a young son of his to touch

> Judah between his shoulders without letting the latter see him. He did that, so Judah's anger disappeared and he threw away the sword. He turned right and left expecting to see one of his brothers but he could not see any of them. He left in a hurry to his brothers and asked them: "Was anyone of you with me [in the presence of Joseph]?" They replied: "No." He said: "Where has Simeon [one of their brothers] gone?" They answered: "To the mountain."
>
> Judah left and met his brother who was carrying a massive rock. Judah asked Simeon: "What do you want to do with this?" Simeon replied: "I will go to the market that was assigned to me and smash with this rock the head of everyone there." Judah said: "Return this rock or throw it in the sea, and do not say anything to anyone. I swear by the One who took Abraham as His close friend that a hand of someone from Jacob's offspring has touched me."
>
> Then, they entered Joseph's office. The latter, who was the strongest among them, said: "O you Hebrews! Do you think that there is no one who is stronger than you?" He turned to a massive rock of the rocks of the mill and kicked it with his foot, pushing it through the wall. Then he caught Judah with one hand and wrestled him to the ground.

The details of this popular story speak for its unreliability and inauthenticity.

Perhaps, among the worst forms of the misguided methodology of using unreliable narratives in interpreting the Qur'an is the use of information from the Bible. This tendency, in turn, is a result of the equally important mistake of equating the Old Testament with the Torah and the New Testament with the Injīl. Allah's descriptions in the Qur'an of the Torah which He revealed to Moses and the Injīl which He inspired to Jesus clearly show that these divine Books are substantially different from the Old and New Testaments. The latter were written and edited by people to serve particular purposes. The huge amount of inaccurate and erroneous information in the Old and New Testaments makes it incumbent to treat any unverifiable Biblical information with a great deal of caution and suspicion. No piece of Biblical information should be presumed to be accurate unless there is supportive extra-Biblical evidence. It is perhaps even justified to think that such information is more likely to be incorrect. The Qur'an is the only book whose full contents is absolutely true. This fact is confirmed by the accuracy, consistency, and truthfulness of this unique Book.

Let's cite an example on the exegetes' almost unconditional, and certainly unjustified, trust in Biblical narratives. Most of the exegesis books that I have consulted — namely those of as-Suyūṭī, al-Jalālayn, Ibn Kathīr, al-Qurṭubī, aṭ-Ṭūsī, al-Ḥuwayzī, al-Qummī, and aṭ-Ṭabarī — state in their commentary on verse 18 that Joseph's brother smeared his shirt with the blood of a goat. This identification of the animal used is simply copied from the Bible (Genesis, 37:31). The Qur'an does not contain any evidence to support this claim, so adding it to an interpretation of the Qur'anic text is unjustified and misleading.

The inattentiveness of some exegetes has made them use Biblical narratives in interpreting the Qur'anic text even when that Biblical information contradicts the Qur'an! For instance, many exegetes — such as al-Qurṭubī, Ibn Kathīr, aṭ-Ṭūsī, and aṭ-Ṭabarī (in their commentary on verse 12.100); al-Jalālayn (in their interpretation of verse 12.15); and as-Suyūṭī (when commenting on verse 12.42) — have cited the opinion of some that Joseph was seventeen when his brothers threw him in the well. In fact, this figure, which is copied from the Bible (Genesis, 37:2), clearly contradicts the Qur'an. Verses 12.12-13 imply, and verse 12.19 explicitly states, that Joseph was a "young boy" when he was cast down the well!

Unfortunately, many exegetical books look more like attempts to reconcile the Qur'anic narrative with Biblical information than efforts to interpret the Qur'anic text.

If all of this was not sad enough, many exegetical books contain a large number of unfounded stories that undermine the status of prophets. It seems that these exegetes have copied those stories without thinking about their significance and implications. Strangely enough, in other parts of their books, the propagators of such stories fiercely defend the "infallibility" of prophets as if they are not the same people who cited those disrespectful stories! Let us look at some of such stories which involve prophets Jacob and Joseph.

One story claims that Allah tested Jacob with the loss of his son for years because when one day he slaughtered a big lamb, he refused to feed a poor, hungry man. In other words, losing Joseph was a punishment for Jacob. This claim is mentioned by al-'Ayyāshī and al-Ḥuwayzī at the beginning of their respective commentaries on the sūra of Joseph, and is repeated by al-Ḥuwayzī in his interpretation of verses 12.24 and 12.86.

Some exegetical books claim that Joseph ended in prison as a result of his desire to commit fornication with the wife of the 'Azīz. The Qur'anic version of this event is that he chose to enter prison in preference to committing fornication with that woman!

A particular misinterpretation of the following verse has become common in some commentaries on the Qur'an, such as those of al-'Ayyāshī, al-Ḥuwayzī, aṭ-Ṭabarī, al-Qummī, and al-Qurṭubī who attributes the interpretation to Ibn 'Abbās: "And he said to that of the two whom he knew would be saved: 'Mention me in the presence of your lord'. But Satan made him forget to make a mention to his lord, so he [Joseph] remained in the prison several years" (12.42). According to this interpretation, Joseph complained to someone other than Allah, i.e. his prison mate, about his difficult circumstances, so Allah punished him by making him stay in prison for several years! In support of this misinterpretation, al-Ḥuwayzī cites the following two sayings which are falsely attributed to Prophet Muhammad: "I am surprised how my brother Joseph sought help from a creature instead of the Creator" and "had it not been for what he [Joseph] said [his request for help from the prisoner], he would not have stayed that long in prison." In his commentary, aṭ-Ṭabarī also mentions these two sayings in a number of different wordings. Ibn Kathīr mentions the second saying, but he considers it to be very weak in authenticity.

Some exegetes, such as al-Qurṭubī and al-Ḥuwayzī, cite another false saying attributed to the Prophet which criticizes Joseph's request to the king to put him in charge of the storehouses of the land — a request which in fact reflects Joseph's special knowledge of future events as we will see later. That saying states: "May Allah show mercy to my brother Joseph. Had he not said [to the king] 'put me in charge of the storehouses of the land' (from 12.55), he [the king] would have put him in charge immediately, but [because he said that] He [Allah] postponed it for a year."

Another accusation leveled at Jacob is that he complained about his sorrow over losing Joseph to someone other than Allah so Allah sent the angel Gabriel to criticize him. This is mentioned by al-'Ayyāshī, al-Ḥuwayzī and aṭ-Ṭabarī in their commentaries on verse 12.86. Al-'Ayyāshī's interpretations of verses 12.87 and 12.95 carry also the accusation to Jacob that he wrote to the 'Azīz of Egypt complaining about the calamities that have struck him, so Allah reprimanded him for this guilt! The sūra of Joseph is full of references to Jacob's extraordinary patience and refusal to complain to anyone other than Allah, but that has not prevented exegetes from mentioning the fabricated story about this prophet's alleged complaints.

Al-Qurṭubī mentions another fanciful story in his commentary on verse 12.84. This one claims that Jacob's lengthy loss of contact with Joseph and his loss of sight were divine punishments for him. The given explanation for the alleged punishments is that Jacob was one day praying when he turned to have a look at the sleeping little Joseph! Another example comes from al-Ḥuwayzī's commentary on verse 12.99.

This exegete claims that Joseph did not dismount his horse when he went out to receive his father when he came to Egypt, so Allah decided not to make anyone of his offspring a prophet!

Such defamatory stories have no foundations in the Qur'an, and they are in essence similar to the numerous Biblical stories that accuse prophets of committing all kinds of evil acts and misbehavior. For instance, the authors of the Bible have made up a story which accuses prophet[7] David of committing adultery with the wife of one of the leaders of his army, whose name was Uriah, while the latter was taking part in a war. The Bible claims that David then sent Uriah to the front to be killed, so he was able to take Uriah's wife for good! Amazingly, the Biblical authors knew all too well that this kind of behavior is a major sin as they claim that the Lord became angry with David for what he did.[8] That did not prevent them from attributing that evil to David and spicing up the story with lots of details!

When comparing the Qur'an and the Bible, one cannot fail to notice that the latter does not include the concept of "veneration of the prophets" which is stressed in various verses and suwar in the Qur'an. Most of the stories in historical and exegetical Islamic literature that attribute sinful acts of prophets belong to the same class of Biblical stories that reflect total ignorance of the meanings and implications of Allah's election of someone to be a prophet. I believe that such stories which have Biblical features must be classified with the inauthentic sayings and narratives that are labeled by scholars as إسرائيليّات "*isrā'īliyyāt* (Israelitic)" in reference to their suspected Jewish sources. The Book of Allah does not contain a shred of evidence that confirms such stories. To the contrary, the Qur'an's description of the status of prophets and details of their stories invalidate all such false accusations.

Having seen the huge difference between the Qur'an and the Bible, some Israelite clerics and others tried to bridge the unbridgeable gap between the beautiful and authentic Qur'anic concepts and the corrupt concepts of the Bible. They thought that by simply tampering with Islamic literature they can distort Islamic concepts and bring them nearer to Biblical ones. Allah, however, had decided to protect the Qur'an, ensure the integrity of its text, and make it immune to any attempt to change or tamper with it. Those text manipulators were, therefore, forced to find other Islamic literature to interfere with. Even the sayings of Prophet Muhammad did not escape this manipulation. Scholars who have studied the sayings of the Prophet have long identified a number of such false sayings as "Israelitic."

The worst mistake in the commentaries of the sūra of Joseph that I have studied occurs in al-Ḥuwayzī's work. In the beginning of his commentary on the sūra of Joseph, this exegete attributes to Imām 'Alī bin Abī Ṭālib, the cousin of Prophet Muhammad and his closest follower, the following awful false saying: "Do not teach your women the sūra of Joseph and do not read it to them, for it contains seductions. Teach them the sūra of an-Nūr for it contains lessons." Al-Ḥuwayzī attributes another equally terrible saying to Imām Muhammad al-Bāqir, the great spiritual scholar: "It is disliked for women to learn the sūra of Joseph"! Such sayings clearly and explicitly contradict Allah's descriptions of His Book. Allah has made reading and studying the Qur'an — that is all parts of it without exception — a duty on every Muslim. Naturally, there are numerous authentic Prophetic sayings that urge the Muslim to learn and teach the Qur'an, such as: "The best among you is he who learns and teaches the Qur'an."[9]

The Book of Allah is one entity which cannot and must not be divided as al-Ḥuwayzī does. Regarding the flagrant comments on the sūra of Joseph that this exegete attributes to two great Muslim scholars, it suffices to remember that it is this particular sūra in which Allah has chosen to include His magnificent description of the Qur'anic stories: "We narrate to you [O Muhammad!] the best of narratives, by revealing this Qur'an to you; and before it you were one of the unaware" (12.3). In fact, there are many Prophetic sayings that praise this blessed sūra, such as "teach your people the sūra of Joseph. Allah will make the death experience of any Muslim who reads it or teaches it to his family and servants easy, and He will give him the ability not to envy a Muslim."

A number of interpretations of the sūra of Joseph, such as the commentaries of al-'Ayyāshī and al-Ḥuwayzī on verse 12.42, and as-Suyūṭī, aṭ-Ṭabarī, Ibn Kathīr, and al-Qurṭubī on verse 12.50, attribute the following saying, though in a variety of wordings, to Prophet Muhammad: "I am surprised at the patience and nobility of Joseph, may Allah forgive him, when he was asked about the lean and fat cows. If I was in his position, I would not have answered their query without laying a condition that they release me first. I am also surprised at the patience and nobility of Joseph, may Allah forgive him, when the messenger [of the king] came to him. Had I been in his position, I would have rushed to the door to leave, but he wanted to get the vindication first." I do not believe that the master of patience and nobility Prophet Muhammad could have said that. Aṭ-Ṭabaṭabā'ī has also rejected the authenticity of this saying. It is interesting to note that this saying contradicts completely false sayings ascribed to Prophet Muhammad cited earlier which criticize Joseph for his supposed impatience!

After this brief introduction to the special style and contents of the Qur'an, the story of Joseph, and some of the common methodological problems in Qur'anic exegesis, we are now ready to start our most enjoyable spiritual journey to study the sūra of Joseph.

2

The Beginning of the Sūra of Joseph

We will start in this chapter our study of the sūra of Joseph. This chapter will only focus on the first three verses, which are general and not part of the story of Joseph. The story commences in verse 4, and we will start studying it in the next chapter.

> الٓر تِلْكَ ءَايَـٰتُ ٱلْكِتَـٰبِ ٱلْمُبِينِ ﴿١﴾
>
> *Alif, lām, rā'.* Those are the verses of the manifest Book (1).

Starting with the letters الٓر "*alif, lām, rā',*" the sūra of Joseph is one of *twenty nine suwar* that start with حروف مُقَطَّعة "separate letters." These letters occur only at the very beginning of Qur'anic suwar. Three of those twenty nine suwar start with one letter, nine suwar start with two letters, thirteen suwar start with three letters, two suwar start with four letters and another two with five letters.[10]

There are *fourteen different combinations of separate letters*, which consist of thirty eight letters in total. In the twenty nine times in which they occur in the Qur'an, these combinations of letters contain seventy eight letters. The *fourteen different combinations* contain *fourteen different letters*, which represent half of the twenty eight letters of the Arabic alphabet. These letters are: ا "*alif,*" ح "*ḥā',*" هـ "*hā',*" ط "*ṭā',*" ي "*yā',*" ك "*kāf,*" ل "*lām,*" م "*mīm,*" ن "*nūn,*" س "*sīn,*" ع "*'ayn,*" ص "*ṣād,*" ق "*qāf,*" and ر "*rā'.*"

The separate letters have remained one of the enigmas that have confounded exegetes of the Qur'an. In fact, aṭ-Ṭabaṭabā'ī says at the beginning of his interpretation of sūra 26 that aṭ-Ṭabrasī[11] mentions eleven different interpretations that have been suggested for those letters. One interpretation suggests that these letters are "separated names of Allah which if people know how to combine together they would know the greatest name of Allah."[12]

Another interpretation suggests that "these are oaths that Allah has sworn with, as if He has sworn with these letters that the Qur'an is His word. These letters are venerable because they are the building blocks of His revealed Books, His Beautiful Names, and sublime attributes, and they are the origins of the languages of the various nations." A third opinion sees the separate letters as "references to the signs of Allah, His tests, how long nations last, and how long those people live." Another view suggests that these letters "are meant to point out how long this nation [the Islamic nation] would last, calculated by means of numerology." These are only samples of the interpretations that have been put forward.

Aṭ-Ṭabaṭabā'ī has an opinion that is worth noting:

> If you consider the suwar which share the same starting separate letters — such as those that include "*mīm*," "*rā'*," "*ṭā*" and "*sīn*," or "*ḥā*" and "*mīm*" — you will find that the suwar that share the same letters have similarities in content and context, something they do not share with other suwar. This is confirmed by the fact that those suwar start with similar phrases. For instance, the suwar that have the separate letters "*ḥā*" and "*mīm*" start with تَنزِيلُ ٱلْكِتَـٰبِ مِنَ ٱللَّهِ "[This is] the revelation of the Book from Allah" (e.g. 40; 45; 46) or something similar. The suwar with the letter "*rā*" starts with تِلْكَ ءَايَـٰتُ ٱلْكِتَـٰبِ ٱلْمُبِينِ "Those are the verses of the Book" (e.g. 10; 12; 15) or something close. The same applies to the beginnings of the suwar that start with "*ṭā*" and "*sīn*." The suwar that have "*mīm*" in their separate letters start by rejecting any doubt over the authenticity of the Book or the like.
>
> It could be surmised, therefore, that there is a special link between the separate letters and the contents of the suwar that start with them. This is supported by the fact that sūra 7 which starts with "*alif, lām, mīm, ṣād*" almost combines the contents of the suwar that start with the letters "*alif, lām, mīm*" and the sūra of "Ṣād" which starts with the letter "*ṣād*." Similarly, sūra 13 which starts with "*alif, lām, mīm, rā*" appears to combine the contents of the suwar that start with the letters "*alif, lām, mīm*" and those that start with the letter "*rā'*."
>
> This indicates that those letters are hidden symbols between Allah and His Messenger, which we can know nothing about other than they have special links with the contents of those suwar. Perhaps, if one would compare the contents of the suwar that start with the same separate letters, more about this matter would become apparent.

Scholars have noticed that the number 19 makes some amazing appearances in the Qur'an. It has also been shown that the separate letters have intriguing relations with this number. I can add the observation that some combinations of separate letters are followed by clauses that consist of nineteen letters. In verse 12.1, for instance, the clause تِلْكَ ءَايَـٰتُ ٱلْكِتَـٰبِ ٱلْمُبِينِ "those are the verses of the manifest Book" consists of nineteen letters. Although such observations highlight miraculous aspects in the linguistic structure of the Qur'an, they do not shed much light on the *meanings* of those separate letters.

Some may question describing those letters as "separate," given that some of those combinations of letters are treated as words, as is the case with طه "*Ṭā'hā*" and يس "*Yā'sīn*" which are commonly believed to be names of Prophet Muhammad. In reply to that, let me note the difference between these two combinations of separate letters and the two names of the Messenger which occur in the Qur'an, "Muḥammad" and "Aḥmad." These two names share one root: حَمْد "*ḥamd* (praise)"; "Muḥammad" means "most praised" and "Aḥmad" "most praising." On the contrary, when viewed as words, neither "*Ṭā'hā*" nor "*Yā'sīn*" can be derived from an Arabic root. All that can be said is that the word "*Ṭā'hā*" is a combination of the letters "*ṭā*" and "*hā*;" and "*Yā'sīn*" is a combination of "*yā*" and "*sīn*."

Ibn Kathīr states that the clause "those are the verses of the manifest Book" means "these are verses of the Book, which is the manifest Qur'an, i.e. the clear Book that reveals, explains, and clarifies the vague issues." Al-Qurṭubī points out that some exegetes think that this clause means "it is those the verses that you were promised in the Torah."

The problem with the interpretation of Ibn Kathīr is that it neglects the fact that the verse contains the demonstrative pronoun تِلْكَ "*tilka* (those)," which is used to refer to *distant* things; he treats the verse as if it contains the demonstrative pronoun هذه "*hādhihi* (these)," which refers to *close* things. Al-Qurṭubī, on the other hand, does consider the fact that the verse contains "those" rather than "these." He suggests that Allah refers to "the verses of the manifest Book" with "those" because those verses were mentioned in the Torah. He does not, however, identify the mentioned verses.

The fact is that the demonstrative pronoun "*tilka*," which can mean "those" or "that" depending on the context, has a special use in the Qur'an that differentiates it from other words, including the demonstrative pronoun "*hādhihi* (this/these)." The former is used to refer to things that are distant in time or place. For instance, Allah recounts stories of prophets Abraham, his sons, and grandsons before addressing the

Children of Israel as follows:

﴿تِلْكَ أُمَّةٌ قَدْ خَلَتْ لَهَا مَا كَسَبَتْ وَلَكُم مَّا كَسَبْتُمْ وَلَا تُسْـَٔلُونَ عَمَّا كَانُوا۟ يَعْمَلُونَ ﴿١٣٤﴾. (سورة البقرة).

That is a nation that has passed away. They shall have what they earned and you shall have what you earn. You will not be called upon to answer for what they did (2.134).

In another example, after referring to wrongful nations that He had destroyed, Allah goes on to say:

تِلْكَ ٱلْقُرَىٰ نَقُصُّ عَلَيْكَ مِنْ أَنۢبَآئِهَا وَلَقَدْ جَآءَتْهُمْ رُسُلُهُم بِٱلْبَيِّنَـٰتِ فَمَا كَانُوا۟ لِيُؤْمِنُوا۟ بِمَا كَذَّبُوا۟ مِن قَبْلُ كَذَٰلِكَ يَطْبَعُ ٱللَّهُ عَلَىٰ قُلُوبِ ٱلْكَـٰفِرِينَ ﴿١٠١﴾. (سورة الأعراف).

Those towns we recount to you [O Muhammad!] the stories of; their messengers came to them with clear proofs, but they would not believe what they had already denied. Thus does Allah set a seal on the hearts of the disbelievers (7.101).

The following verse refers to ٱلـدَّارُ ٱلْأَخِـرَةُ "[the] Last Abode" which Allah mentions many times in the His Book:

تِلْكَ ٱلدَّارُ ٱلْـَٔاخِرَةُ نَجْعَلُهَا لِلَّذِينَ لَا يُرِيدُونَ عُلُوًّا فِى ٱلْأَرْضِ وَلَا فَسَادًا وَٱلْعَـٰقِبَةُ لِلْمُتَّقِينَ ﴿٨٣﴾. (سورة القصص).

That Last Abode We shall give to those who do not seek loftiness nor to cause corruption on earth. And the [good] end is for the dutiful ones (28.83).

Finally, let me cite the following verse which mentions the belief of Jews and Christians that *only they* can enter paradise, then uses the word "*tilka* (those)" to refer to such beliefs:

وَقَالُوا۟ لَن يَدْخُلَ ٱلْجَنَّةَ إِلَّا مَن كَانَ هُودًا أَوْ نَصَـٰرَىٰ تِلْكَ أَمَانِيُّهُمْ قُلْ هَاتُوا۟ بُرْهَـٰنَكُمْ إِن كُنتُمْ صَـٰدِقِينَ ﴿١١١﴾. (سورة البقرة).

And they [the People of the Book] say: "No one shall enter paradise except he who is a Jew or a Christian". Those are [nothing more than] their desires. Say [O Muhammad!]: "Produce your proof if you are truthful" (2.111).

The demonstrative pronoun "*tilka*" occurs in the Qur'an mainly in contexts similar to these above. "*Tilka*" occurs in three verses at the beginning of the clause تِلْـكَ ءَايَـٰتُ ٱللَّهِ "those are the verses of Allah" which resembles the clause تِلْـكَ ءَايَـٰتُ ٱلْكِتَـٰبِ ٱلْمُبِينِ "those are the verses of the manifest Book" in the sūra of Joseph which we are analyzing here. Studying those three verses, therefore, is particularly relevant to this discussion. These are the said three verses, each with the two verses preceding it:

وَلَمَّا بَرَزُوا۟ لِجَالُوتَ وَجُنُودِهِۦ قَالُوا۟ رَبَّنَآ أَفْرِغْ عَلَيْنَا صَبْرًا وَثَبِّتْ أَقْدَامَنَا وَٱنصُرْنَا عَلَى ٱلْقَوْمِ ٱلْكَـٰفِرِينَ ﴿٢٥٠﴾ فَهَزَمُوهُم بِإِذْنِ ٱللَّهِ وَقَتَلَ دَاوُۥدُ جَالُوتَ وَءَاتَـٰهُ ٱللَّهُ ٱلْمُلْكَ وَٱلْحِكْمَةَ وَعَلَّمَهُۥ مِمَّا يَشَآءُ وَلَوْلَا دَفْعُ ٱللَّهِ ٱلنَّاسَ بَعْضَهُم بِبَعْضٍ لَّفَسَدَتِ ٱلْأَرْضُ وَلَـٰكِنَّ ٱللَّهَ ذُو فَضْلٍ عَلَى ٱلْعَـٰلَمِينَ ﴿٢٥١﴾. تِلْكَ ءَايَـٰتُ ٱللَّهِ نَتْلُوهَا عَلَيْكَ بِٱلْحَقِّ وَإِنَّكَ لَمِنَ ٱلْمُرْسَلِينَ ﴿٢٥٢﴾.
(سورة البقرة).

And when they [Saul and his soldiers] came out against Goliath and his soldiers, they said: "Our Lord! Bestow on us patience, make our steps firm, and assist us against the disbelieving people" (2.250). So they defeated them by Allah's permission. And David killed Goliath, and Allah gave him [David] kingship and wisdom, and taught him whatever He willed. And had Allah not repelled people with each other, the earth would have certainly been in a state of disorder; but Allah is full of favor to the people (2.251). Those are the verses of Allah that We recite to you [O Muhammad!] with truth; and surely you are one of the messengers (2.252).

يَوْمَ تَبْيَضُّ وُجُوهٌ وَتَسْوَدُّ وُجُوهٌ فَأَمَّا ٱلَّذِينَ ٱسْوَدَّتْ وُجُوهُهُمْ أَكَفَرْتُم بَعْدَ إِيمَـٰنِكُمْ فَذُوقُوا۟ ٱلْعَذَابَ بِمَا كُنتُمْ تَكْفُرُونَ ﴿١٠٦﴾ وَأَمَّا ٱلَّذِينَ ٱبْيَضَّتْ وُجُوهُهُمْ فَفِى رَحْمَةِ ٱللَّهِ هُمْ فِيهَا خَـٰلِدُونَ ﴿١٠٧﴾ تِلْكَ ءَايَـٰتُ ٱللَّهِ نَتْلُوهَا عَلَيْكَ بِٱلْحَقِّ وَمَا ٱللَّهُ يُرِيدُ ظُلْمًا لِّلْعَـٰلَمِينَ ﴿١٠٨﴾. (سورة آل عمران).

On the Day when some faces shall turn white and some faces shall turn black; as to those whose faces turned black [it will be said]: "Did you disbelieve after believing? Taste therefore the torment for your disbelief" (3.106). And as to those whose faces turned white, they shall be in Allah's mercy; they will be in it forever (3.107). Those are the verses of Allah which We recite to you [O Muhammad!] with truth; and Allah does not desire any injustice to the people (3.108).

وَفِى خَلْقِكُمْ وَمَا يَبُثُّ مِن دَآبَّةٍ ءَايَـٰتٌ لِّقَوْمٍ يُوقِنُونَ ﴿٤﴾ وَٱخْتِلَـٰفِ ٱلَّيْلِ وَٱلنَّهَارِ وَمَآ أَنزَلَ ٱللَّهُ مِنَ ٱلسَّمَآءِ مِن رِّزْقٍ فَأَحْيَا بِهِ ٱلْأَرْضَ بَعْدَ مَوْتِهَا وَتَصْرِيفِ ٱلرِّيَـٰحِ ءَايَـٰتٌ لِّقَوْمٍ يَعْقِلُونَ ﴿٥﴾ تِلْكَ ءَايَـٰتُ ٱللَّهِ نَتْلُوهَا عَلَيْكَ بِٱلْحَقِّ فَبِأَىِّ حَدِيثٍۭ بَعْدَ ٱللَّهِ وَءَايَـٰتِهِۦ يُؤْمِنُونَ ﴿٦﴾
(سورة الجاثية).

And in the creation of yourselves [O people!] and the beasts that He scatters there are signs for a people of certainty [about faith] (45.4). And in the alteration of the night and day, in what Allah sends down of sustenance from the sky thereby reviving the earth after its death, and in the changing of the winds there are signs for a people who understand (45.5). Those are the verses of Allah which We recite to you [O Muhammad!] with truth; then in what speech other than Allah's and His signs would they believe? (45.6).

It is obvious in all these verses that ءَايَـٰتُ ٱللَّهِ "the verses of Allah" which are referred to with the demonstrative pronoun "*tilka*" are the verses that are mentioned before the clause تِلْكَ ءَايَـٰتُ ٱللَّهِ "those are the verses of Allah." One clear piece of evidence on this is that in each of the three occurrences of the clause "those are the verses of Allah" there is a relation between what follows that clause and the verses that precede it, as explained below.

In the case of the verses of sūra 2, after relating the story of David, Allah followed the clause "those are the verses of Allah" with وَإِنَّكَ لَمِنَ ٱلْمُرْسَلِينَ "and surely you are one of the messengers." This stresses that Prophet Muhammad could not have known that story had he not been a Messenger, i.e. in receipt of divine revelation.[13]

In verse 3.108, it is clear that following the sentence تِلْكَ ءَايَـٰتُ ٱللَّهِ نَتْلُوهَا عَلَيْكَ بِٱلْحَقِّ "those are the verses of Allah which We recite to you with truth" with وَمَا ٱللَّهُ يُرِيدُ ظُلْمًا لِّلْعَـٰلَمِينَ "and Allah does not desire any injustice to the people" is intended to stress that what is mentioned earlier in verses 106 and 107, that is the entrance of one party into hell and another into paradise, does not reflect injustice, but rather divine justice.

Finally, the sentence فَبِأَىِّ حَدِيثٍۭ بَعْدَ ٱللَّهِ وَءَايَـٰتِهِۦ يُؤْمِنُونَ "then in what speech other than Allah's and His signs would they believe?" in verse 45.6 emphasizes the strength of the argument about the creation of Allah in verses 45.4-5.

This discussion clearly shows that the clause "those are the verses of Allah" refers to verses that are mentioned immediately before the clause itself. In the first verse of the sūra of Joseph, however, it is notable that the demonstrative pronoun "those" is preceded *only* by the separate letters: "*alif, lām, rā'*. Those are the verses of the manifest Book." This makes me conclude that the separate letters "*alif, lām, rā*" must themselves be "the verses of the manifest Book" which are referred to with "those."

Some may question the conclusion above to suggest that "the verses of the manifest Book" which Allah refers to with "those" are not the separate letters "*alif, lām, rā*" but all of the Qur'anic verses that were revealed *before* the sūra of Joseph. According to this view, verse 12.1 simply stresses the divine origin of the Qur'anic verses that Allah had previously revealed. There are two very important points that undermine this alternative interpretation.

First, the word "those" is used in *all* such verses, including the examples that I cited, to refer to specific verses which are mentioned *explicitly* and *immediately* before the verse or the clause in which "those" occurs. The assumption that the clause "the verses of the manifest Book" in the first verse of the sūra of Joseph refers *in general* to all Qur'anic verses that had already been revealed rather than to specific verses means that the word "those" is used in a way that is different from its use in the other similar verses. My interpretation that "the verses of the manifest Book" is a reference to "*alif, lām, rā*" agrees with the use of "those" in those other verses.

Second, "the verses of the manifest Book" and very similar clauses occur seven times in the Book of Allah in addition to its appearance at the beginning of the sūra of Joseph. In all those verses, the clause occurs *after the separate letter at the beginning of the respective sūra*:

الٓر تِلْكَ ءَايَـٰتُ ٱلْكِتَـٰبِ ٱلْحَكِيمِ ﴿١﴾. (سورة يونس).

Alif, lām, rā'. Those are the verses of the wise Book (10.1).

الٓمٓر تِلْكَ ءَايَـٰتُ ٱلْكِتَـٰبِ وَٱلَّذِىٓ أُنزِلَ إِلَيْكَ مِن رَّبِّكَ ٱلْحَقُّ وَلَـٰكِنَّ أَكْثَرَ ٱلنَّاسِ لَا يُؤْمِنُونَ ﴿١﴾. (سورة الرّعْدِ).

Alif, lām, mīm, rā'. Those are the verses of the Book. And that which has been sent down to you [O Muhammad!] from your Lord is the truth, but most people do not believe (13.1).

الٓر تِلْكَ ءَايَـٰتُ ٱلْكِتَـٰبِ وَقُرْءَانٍ مُّبِينٍ ﴿١﴾. (سورة الحِجْرِ).

Alif, lām, rā'. Those are the verses of the Book and a manifest Qur'an (15.1).

طسٓمٓ ﴿١﴾ تِلْكَ ءَايَـٰتُ ٱلْكِتَـٰبِ ٱلْمُبِينِ ﴿٢﴾. (سورة الشُّعَراءِ).

Ṭā', sīn, mīm (26.1). Those are the verses of the manifest Book (26.2).

طسٓ تِلْكَ ءَايَـٰتُ ٱلْقُرْءَانِ وَكِتَابٍ مُّبِينٍ ﴿١﴾. (سورة النَّمْلِ).

Ṭā', sīn. Those are the verses of the Qur'an and a manifest Book (27.1).

طسٓمٓ ﴿١﴾ تِلْكَ ءَايَـٰتُ ٱلْكِتَـٰبِ ٱلْمُبِينِ ﴿٢﴾. (سورة القَصَصِ).

Ṭā', sīn, mīm (28.1). Those are the verses of the manifest Book (28.2).

الٓمٓ ﴿١﴾ تِلْكَ ءَايَـٰتُ ٱلْكِتَـٰبِ ٱلْحَكِيمِ ﴿٢﴾. (سورة لُقمان).

Alif, lām, mīm (31.1). Those are the verses of the wise Book (31.2).

This consistent style must be indicative of a clear relation between the clause تِلْكَ ءَايَـٰتُ ٱلْكِتَـٰبِ "those are the verses of the Book,"[14] which occurs once in the form تِلْكَ ءَايَـٰتُ ٱلْقُرْءَانِ "those are the verses of the Qur'an," and the separate letters. In other words, "the verses of the Book" or "the verses of the Qur'an" which the verses above refer to are the separate letters that precede those two clauses.

There is another significant observation that relates to the contexts in which the clause "those are the verses of Allah" appears. This clause has a similar structure to the clause "those are the verses of the Book." The two clauses also have close meanings as "the verses of the Book" are one type of "the verses of Allah." In none of its three appearances, however, does the clause "those are the verses of Allah" occur in contexts similar to that of "those are the verses of the Book," i.e. after separate letters. This is another confirmation that there is a link between the clause "the verses of the Book" and the separate letters.

We have seen that Allah refers to the separate letters in seven verses, including verse 1 of the sūra of Joseph, using the clause "the verses of the Book" and in an eighth verse using the clause "the verses of the Qur'an"; so, is there any difference in meaning between these two clauses, or are they simply two wordings that have the same meaning? Exegetes in general do not make a distinction in meaning between the two clauses, assuming that the Qur'an is the Book and the Book is the Qur'an. For instance, in his comment on the clause "those are the verses of the manifest Book," al-Qurṭubī suggests that: "Allah means by 'the manifest Book' the manifest Qur'an, i.e. which is manifest in what it permits and what it forbids; in its legal limits, rulings, guidance, and blessing." Ibn Kathīr is of the same understanding, stating in his interpretation of the same verse: "these are verses of the Book, which is the manifest Qur'an, i.e. the clear Book that reveals, explains, and clarifies the vague issues."

There is, however, a difference between the terms "Book" and "Qur'an" in the Qur'an. An adequate explanation of this is rather lengthy, touches on complicated topics, and requires a dedicated study. In brief, "the Qur'an" is the name of the *Arabic Book* that Allah revealed to Prophet Muhammad, whereas "the Book" is a broader term which includes all the Books that Allah has revealed, as we will see in the next verse. Since "the Qur'an" is one of the forms in which "the Book" has been revealed, the latter term is used at times to refer to "the Qur'an."

> إِنَّآ أَنزَلْنَـٰهُ قُرْءَٰنًا عَرَبِيًّا لَّعَلَّكُمْ تَعْقِلُونَ ﴿٢﴾
>
> We have sent it down as an Arabic Qur'an that you may understand (2).

"The Book" represents divine knowledge whose language cannot be understood except by an elite of Allah's creation. Allah has therefore revealed "the Book" to people in the form of Books that are written in human languages which they can understand. Every divine Book that Allah revealed to a prophet represents an *embodiment or manifestation* of "the Book" in a particular human language, and is sent to people who speak that language. Those people would then have the responsibility of spreading what they learn from the revealed Book to other peoples who do not speak that language. The Qur'an, for instance, represents a revelation of "the Book" *in Arabic*, so that it can be understood and taught by those who speak that language.

In addition to the verse above, there are a number of verses in various Qur'anic suwar which emphasize that the Qur'an is a *clarification and expounding* of "the Book" *in Arabic*:

وَكَذَٰلِكَ أَنزَلْنَٰهُ حُكْمًا عَرَبِيًّا وَلَئِنِ ٱتَّبَعْتَ أَهْوَآءَهُم بَعْدَ مَا جَآءَكَ مِنَ ٱلْعِلْمِ مَا لَكَ مِنَ ٱللَّهِ مِن وَلِيٍّ وَلَا وَاقٍ ﴿٣٧﴾. (سورة الرّعدِ).

And thus We have sent it down as Wisdom in Arabic; and if you [O Muhammad!] follow their [the disbelievers'] low desires after the knowledge that has come to you, you shall not have a friend or a protector against Allah (13.37).

وَكَذَٰلِكَ أَنزَلْنَٰهُ قُرْءَانًا عَرَبِيًّا وَصَرَّفْنَا فِيهِ مِنَ ٱلْوَعِيدِ لَعَلَّهُمْ يَتَّقُونَ أَوْ يُحْدِثُ لَهُمْ ذِكْرًا ﴿١١٣﴾. (سورة طَهَ).

And thus We have sent it down as an Arabic Qur'an, and have detailed in it threats that they [people] may act dutifully or that it may cause them to remember (20.113).

حمٓ ﴿١﴾ وَٱلْكِتَٰبِ ٱلْمُبِينِ ﴿٢﴾ إِنَّا جَعَلْنَٰهُ قُرْءَٰنًا عَرَبِيًّا لَّعَلَّكُمْ تَعْقِلُونَ ﴿٣﴾. (سورة الزّخْرُفِ).

Ḥa', mīm (43.1). And the manifest Book (43.2). We have made it an Arabic Qur'an that you may understand (43.3).

حمٓ ﴿١﴾ تَنزِيلٌ مِّنَ ٱلرَّحْمَٰنِ ٱلرَّحِيمِ ﴿٢﴾ كِتَٰبٌ فُصِّلَتْ ءَايَٰتُهُ قُرْءَٰنًا عَرَبِيًّا لِّقَوْمٍ يَعْلَمُونَ ﴿٣﴾. (سورة فُصِّلَت).

Ḥa', mīm (41.1). [It is] a revelation from ar-Raḥmān [Allah], the Merciful (41.2). A Book whose verses have been *fuṣṣilat* (detailed) as an Arabic Qur'an for a people of knowledge (41.3).

Note, for example, the clause "a Book whose verses have been *fuṣṣilat* (detailed) in Arabic," where the passive voice فُصِّلَتْ "*fuṣṣilat*" means "detailed," "explained," "expounded" ...etc.

Interestingly, "the Book" is not mentioned explicitly in verses 13.37,

20.113, and 43.3. It is, nevertheless, the referent of the attached pronoun هاء "*hā'* (it)" in the words أَنزَلْنَٰهُ "*anzalnāhu* (sent it down)" in verses 13.37 and 20.113, فِيهِ "*fīhi* (in it)" in verse 20.113, and جَعَلْنَٰهُ "*ja'alnāhu* (made it)" in verse 43.3. It is also the referent of the implicit pronoun in يُحْدِثُ "it may cause" in verse 20.113. This conclusion becomes totally obvious when comparing those verses with verse 41.3 which mentions the word "Book" explicitly.

These verses leave no doubt whatsoever that the Arabic nature of the Qur'an is an inherent attribute of this Book. The Arabic Text that Allah has called "the Qur'an" is a clarification and expounding of "the Book" which people cannot understand. Translating the Qur'anic text, therefore, is bound to produce a text that does not represent the Qur'an. Any translation of the Qur'an is merely an interpretation of it. As an interpretation of the meanings of the Qur'an is not itself a Qur'an, a translation of the Qur'an does not represent the Qur'an. Only Allah knows all the meanings and knowledge that are contained in the Arabic Qur'an, so any translation or interpretation of a Qur'anic text is, by definition, limited, even if correct.

Note Allah's emphasis that He revealed the Qur'an in Arabic that people may "understand" (12.2; 43.3) and "act dutifully" (20.113). This points out that Allah revealed "the Book" in the form of an Arabic Text to give people the opportunity to understand the truth and become knowledgeable and dutiful. Had Allah revealed "the Book" in its original form, people would not have understood anything of it and would not have acquired dutifulness and knowledge, so He revealed it as an "Arabic Qur'an."[15] In fact, the original form of the Book might well be incommunicable, not only incomprehensible, to people.

نَحْنُ نَقُصُّ عَلَيْكَ أَحْسَنَ ٱلْقَصَصِ بِمَآ أَوْحَيْنَآ إِلَيْكَ هَٰذَا ٱلْقُرْءَانَ وَإِن كُنتَ مِن قَبْلِهِۦ لَمِنَ ٱلْغَٰفِلِينَ ﴿٣﴾
We narrate to you [O Muhammad!] the best of narratives, by revealing this Qur'an to you; and before it you were one of the unaware (3).

Allah stresses in His speech to the Prophet that the narratives that He revealed to him in the Qur'an are the best stories. In addition to being totally truthful and void of any false information, these narratives are more than mere accurate accounts of events. They are didactic stories that have lessons that guide those who follow them to Allah. Are there, then, any stories better than those that Allah relates to draw their reader closer to Him?

Al-Qurṭubī says in his exegesis that "scholars have disagreed as to why this sūra, from among all the suwar, has been called أَحْسَنَ ٱلْقَصَصِ 'the best of narratives’,” and he cites the opinions of a number of scholars. Al-Qurṭubī’s statement, however, reflects a fundamental misunderstanding of the phrase “the best of narratives.” The latter *does not refer exclusively to the story of Joseph* but rather to *all stories that are mentioned in the Qur’an.* The story of Joseph is among “the best of narratives” because it is one of the Qur’anic stories. The description “best of narratives” applies to all of the stories in the Qur’an in the same way the description الْقَصَصُ الْحَقُّ “truthful narratives” in the following verse applies to all Qur’anic stories, including Joseph’s, and is not restricted to the story of Jesus which occurs immediately before the verse:

إِنَّ هَـٰذَا لَهُوَ ٱلْقَصَصُ ٱلْحَقُّ وَمَا مِنْ إِلَـٰهٍ إِلَّا ٱللَّهُ وَإِنَّ ٱللَّهَ لَهُوَ ٱلْعَزِيزُ ٱلْحَكِيمُ ﴿٦٢﴾. (سورة آل عِمْرَان).

> Surely these are the truthful narratives; and there is no god save Allah, and Allah is the Invincible, the Wise (3.62).

Allah’s words “We narrate to you [O Muhammad!] the best of narratives, by revealing this Qur’an to you” are similar to what He says about أَحْسَنَ ٱلْحَدِيثِ “the best of speech” in this verse:

ٱللَّهُ نَزَّلَ أَحْسَنَ ٱلْحَدِيثِ كِتَـٰبًا مُّتَشَـٰبِهًا مَّثَانِىَ تَقْشَعِرُّ مِنْهُ جُلُودُ ٱلَّذِينَ يَخْشَوْنَ رَبَّهُمْ ثُمَّ تَلِينُ جُلُودُهُمْ وَقُلُوبُهُمْ إِلَىٰ ذِكْرِ ٱللَّهِ ذَٰلِكَ هُدَى ٱللَّهِ يَهْدِى بِهِۦ مَن يَشَآءُ وَمَن يُضْلِلِ ٱللَّهُ فَمَا لَهُۥ مِنْ هَادٍ ﴿٢٣﴾. (سورة الزّمر).

> Allah has sent down the best of speech, a consistent Book that is in pairs. The skins of those who fear their Lord shudder because of it, then their skins and hearts soften to the remembrance of Allah. That is Allah’s guidance, with which He guides whom He wills. As for him whom Allah sends astray, there is no guide (39.23).

The statement “Allah has sent down the best of speech” does not mean that sūra 39 only or its 23rd verse in particular is “the best of speech.” This is a description of the Book, in parts and as a whole, so “the best of speech” includes the verse above, but is not exclusive to it.

The story of Joseph differs from other relatively long stories in the Qur’an in being mentioned in its entirety in one sūra. The sūra of Joseph, in turn, is distinguished from other Qur’anic suwar in that most of its verses relate to one story. This seems to be the reason that describing the Qur’anic stories *in general* as “the best of narratives” occurs in this sūra *in particular.*

The last part of verse 3 of the sūra of Joseph reminds the Prophet that he did not know any of those stories before the inspiration of the Qur’an came to him. A similar reminder occurs in other verses that talk about historical events that Allah describes as أَنۢبَآءِ ٱلْغَيْبِ "*anbā' al-ghayb* (tidings of the unseen)."[16] The information about those historical events is described in that manner because those events happened far in the past. The aim of this reminder is to stress that the Messenger and his people could not have known those details had Allah not revealed them in the Qur'an:

تِلْكَ مِنْ أَنۢبَآءِ ٱلْغَيْبِ نُوحِيهَآ إِلَيْكَ مَا كُنتَ تَعْلَمُهَآ أَنتَ وَلَا قَوْمُكَ مِن قَبْلِ هَـٰذَا فَٱصْبِرْ إِنَّ ٱلْعَـٰقِبَةَ لِلْمُتَّقِينَ ﴿٤٩﴾. (سورة هود).

Those are some tidings of the unseen which We reveal to you [O Muhammad!]; you did not know them nor did your people before this [the Qur'an]; so be patient; the [prosperous] end is for the dutiful ones (11.49).

For instance, in the following verse, Allah refers to the lottery that prophet Zachariah took part in to take custody of Mary:

ذَٰلِكَ مِنْ أَنۢبَآءِ ٱلْغَيْبِ نُوحِيهِ إِلَيْكَ وَمَا كُنتَ لَدَيْهِمْ إِذْ يُلْقُونَ أَقْلَـٰمَهُمْ أَيُّهُمْ يَكْفُلُ مَرْيَمَ وَمَا كُنتَ لَدَيْهِمْ إِذْ يَخْتَصِمُونَ ﴿٤٤﴾. (سورة آل عِمْرَان).

These are some tidings of the unseen which We reveal to you [O Muhammad!]; and you were not with them when they cast their pens [to decide] which one of them should be charged with the care of Mary, and you were not with them when they disputed [the matter] (3.44).

The following verse from the sūra of Joseph refers to the plot of Joseph's brothers to get rid of him, which the Prophet learned about through the Qur'an:

ذَٰلِكَ مِنْ أَنۢبَآءِ ٱلْغَيْبِ نُوحِيهِ إِلَيْكَ وَمَا كُنتَ لَدَيْهِمْ إِذْ أَجْمَعُوٓا۟ أَمْرَهُمْ وَهُمْ يَمْكُرُونَ ﴿١٠٢﴾. (سورة يوسف).

These are some tidings of the unseen which We reveal to you [O Muhammad!], and you were not with them when they concerted their plans together when they were scheming (12.102).

Finally, this is what Allah says about His revelation to prophet Moses:

وَلَقَدْ ءَاتَيْنَا مُوسَى ٱلْكِتَـٰبَ مِنۢ بَعْدِ مَآ أَهْلَكْنَا ٱلْقُرُونَ ٱلْأُولَىٰ بَصَآئِرَ لِلنَّاسِ وَهُدًى وَرَحْمَةً لَّعَلَّهُمْ يَتَذَكَّرُونَ ﴿٤٣﴾ وَمَا كُنتَ بِجَانِبِ ٱلْغَرْبِىِّ إِذْ قَضَيْنَآ إِلَىٰ مُوسَى ٱلْأَمْرَ وَمَا كُنتَ مِنَ ٱلشَّـٰهِدِينَ ﴿٤٤﴾ وَلَـٰكِنَّآ أَنشَأْنَا قُرُونًا فَتَطَاوَلَ عَلَيْهِمُ ٱلْعُمُرُ وَمَا كُنتَ ثَاوِيًا فِىٓ أَهْلِ مَدْيَنَ تَتْلُوا۟ عَلَيْهِمْ ءَايَـٰتِنَا وَلَـٰكِنَّا كُنَّا مُرْسِلِينَ ﴿٤٥﴾ وَمَا كُنتَ بِجَانِبِ ٱلطُّورِ إِذْ نَادَيْنَا وَلَـٰكِن رَّحْمَةً مِّن رَّبِّكَ لِتُنذِرَ قَوْمًا مَّآ أَتَىٰهُم مِّن نَّذِيرٍ مِّن قَبْلِكَ لَعَلَّهُمْ يَتَذَكَّرُونَ ﴿٤٦﴾. (سورة القَصَص).

And We gave Moses the Book, after We destroyed the generations of old, as clear testimonies for people, a guidance, and a mercy, that they may remember (28.43). And you [O Muhammad!] were not on the western side [of the Mount] when We handed to Moses the matter, and you were not one of the witnesses (28.44). But We brought forth generations, and their lives dragged on for them; and you were not dwelling with the people of Midian, reciting to them Our verses, but We have sent [you as] a Messenger (28.45). And you were not on the side of the Mount when We called [Moses], but this [knowledge that We have revealed to you] is a mercy from your Lord for you to warn a people to whom no warner before you came, that they may give heed (28.46).

Note how Allah reminds the Prophet in these verses of sūra 28 that he was not on the western side of the Mount to know about the Tablets of the Torah, which He wrote for Moses there, nor was he living among the people of Midian to know of what happened to Moses after fleeing the wrath of Pharaoh in Egypt. Allah explains to the Prophet his acquisition of this knowledge saying "but We have sent [you as] a Messenger," meaning that Prophet Muhammad came to know about these events because Allah made him one of His messengers. That knowledge is proof that Muhammad is indeed a Messenger of Allah. Finally, Allah reminds His Messenger that he was not on the side of the Mount when Allah called on Moses, but that He has given him this knowledge as a mercy from Him so that he would warn people who had not had a warner before him "that they may give heed" to the warning.

3

Prophet Joseph in the House of His Father Prophet Jacob

We will now start our study of the story of Joseph by focusing in this chapter on the period when Joseph was still a child living with his father Jacob, before his brothers abandoned him in a far, foreign land.

> إِذْ قَالَ يُوسُفُ لِأَبِيهِ يَٰٓأَبَتِ إِنِّي رَأَيْتُ أَحَدَ عَشَرَ كَوْكَبًا وَٱلشَّمْسَ وَٱلْقَمَرَ رَأَيْتُهُمْ لِي سَٰجِدِينَ ﴿٤﴾
>
> When Joseph said to his father: "O my father! I saw eleven stars,[17] the sun, and the moon; I saw them prostrating to me" (4).

I have pointed out in §1.1 that the Qur'an uses the word "*idh*," which means "when," when starting a new context or citing past events. In this verse, the word "*idh*" starts the narration of the story of Joseph, with Joseph telling his father about a vision he saw.

The verb رأى "*ra'ā*" generally means "saw." It is used, however, in a number of Qur'anic verses in association with *visions*, including ones seen by ordinary people, such as the visions of Joseph's two prison mates and the king, which we will study later.

The verse does not state explicitly that Joseph saw that vision in his sleep, but there is consensus among exegetes that it was a *sleep vision* rather than a *waking vision*. The king referred to his vision with the verb أَرَىٰ "*arā* (see)" in verse 12.43, and his court called it a "dream" in their reply to him in verse 12.44. There is only one other verse that uses the verb رأى "*ra'ā*" to refer explicitly to a *visionary dream* that was seen by prophet Abraham.[18]

I will refer to Joseph's vision with the term "dream," though the implication is that it was a *visionary dream*, i.e. one that had prognostic qualities.

One thing that draws attention in verse 12.4 is Joseph's use of the verb رَأَيْتُ "[I] saw" twice. He first said "I saw eleven stars, the sun, and the moon," and then followed up saying "I saw them prostrating to me." Exegetes have suggested a number of explanations for this, but I do not find any of them convincing.[19]

It is possible that repeating "saw" refers to Joseph's astonishment at seeing eleven stars, the sun, and the moon's prostration to him. The interpretation that seems to me more likely, nevertheless, is that the repetition reflects Joseph's hesitation, which itself is the result of his politeness and humbleness, as he described to his father the greatly significant scene of the prostration of "eleven stars, the sun, and the moon." Joseph wanted to tell his father that he saw "eleven stars, the sun, and the moon" prostrating to him, but when he was about to mention the prostration he stopped in hesitation and shyness, and then continued as he had to tell his father about what he saw.

Some might think that Joseph's hesitation and shyness do not mean that he knew the exact meaning of the prostration of the "eleven stars, the sun, and the moon" to him, but that he realized that this dream meant that he would attain a high status. It is more likely that Joseph knew that the eleven stars represented his brothers, and the sun and moon denoted his parents. This explains his embarrassment when he spoke to his father about his vision; he knew that it meant that his father would prostrate to him. Note that this interpretation can include the interpretation above that Joseph was astonished at what he saw. In other words, Joseph's embarrassment as he related the vision to his father was accompanied by astonishment at its significance.

Some exegetes think that the sun refers to Joseph's mother and the moon to his father. It seems that this view is derived from the fact that the gender of the Arabic word for "sun" is feminine and that for "moon" masculine. This, however, does not rule out using the sun to refer to Jacob and the moon to Joseph's mother, as the reference here is merely symbolic. The exegetes' opinion ignores the possibility that the genders of the words "sun" and "moon" in the language that Jacob and his family spoke were different from their equivalents in the Arabic of the Qur'an.

I agree with the exegetes who think that the sun stands for Jacob and the moon for Joseph's mother. I am inclined to this view because the sun is the source of the moon's light and the largest of the two luminaries, something that corresponds to the status of Jacob relative to his wife. Jacob was the spiritual sun of guidance of the time.

There is also a special, subtle meaning in the appearance of Jacob in his son's vision as a sun. Jacob was going to lose his sight some years after Joseph saw his vision. His appearance in the vision as a source of light refers to the fact that he was going to regain his sight by the time he would prostrate to Joseph, as we will see later on.

It is common practice in speech and writing to mention the sun and moon before the stars. Additionally, since the sun and the moon stood for Jacob and his wife, and the eleven stars represented Joseph's brothers, one would expect Joseph to mention the two luminaries before the stars when recounting his dream. Joseph, however, mentions them in the reverse order. The explanation of this is that Joseph's brothers were going to meet and prostrate to him in Egypt before his parents meet and prostrate to him. Joseph's account of his dream reflects stunning accuracy in reporting subtle details that are already extremely difficult to spot.

It should be noted that the prostration is a mark of "greeting," not "worshipping." I will get back to this point in Chapter 9 when I talk about verse 12.100 which mentions the fulfillment of the vision.

قَالَ يَـٰبُنَىَّ لَا تَقْصُصْ رُءْيَاكَ عَلَىٰٓ إِخْوَتِكَ فَيَكِيدُوا۟ لَكَ كَيْدًا ۖ إِنَّ ٱلشَّيْطَـٰنَ لِلْإِنسَـٰنِ عَدُوٌّ مُّبِينٌ ﴿٥﴾

He said: "O my son! Do not relate your vision to your brothers, otherwise they would scheme against you a scheme; Satan is a manifest enemy to man (5).

The first thing that Jacob said to his son is not to disclose his vision to his brothers lest they plan some evil against him under the influence of Satan, the manifest enemy of man. The Arabic word كَيْدًا "*kaydan*," which I have translated as "scheme," means a plot that is often accompanied with some secrecy. The plot may have the negative connotation of aiming to cause harm, as is the case here.

Some exegetes, such as al-Jalālayn and aṭ-Ṭabaṭabā'ī, conclude from Jacob's command to Joseph that his other sons would have realized that the dream meant that they, their father, and their step-mother would prostrate to Joseph. Some may also argue that Jacob's order to his son not to *disclose* the dream to his brothers and not only not to *interpret* it to them means that they were capable of interpreting it.

It is a distinct possibility that Joseph's brothers would have known that the eleven stars signified them, if they were eleven brothers at the time, i.e. their youngest brother Benjamin was already born. Even if they would fail to recognize that, they would have certainly noticed the clear revelation of the vision that Joseph was destined to attain a high status. This would have further fueled their envy toward Joseph, whom they were already mistreating. This would have been a sufficient reason for Jacob to advise Joseph not to disclose his vision to his brothers.

It is possible that some of the meanings of the vision would have become clear to Joseph's brothers. What is certain, however, is that Joseph's brothers would not have recognized the more subtle meanings of their brother's vision. Interpreting visions requires very special knowledge. There is no indication that Allah had granted this kind of knowledge to Joseph's brothers. The misbehavior of the latter at the time shows that they were far from deserving such a great favor.

Aṭ-Ṭabaṭabā'ī notes that Jacob instructed Joseph not to disclose the vision to his brothers before he interpreted the vision to his son in the next verse. He attributes this to Jacob's immense love for Joseph and his awareness of the envy of Joseph's brothers and their anger at their brother.

Aṭ-Ṭabaṭabā'ī makes another remark on the fascinating Qur'anic text that is worth mentioning. When warning Joseph, Jacob did not only *suspect* that revealing the dream *may* make his other sons devise a plot. He was rather *certain* that this would happen: فَيَكِيدُواْ لَكَ كَيْدًا "otherwise they would scheme against you a scheme." He then followed that with the explanation that "Satan is a manifest enemy to man." Aṭ-Ṭabaṭabā'ī adds in his comment on this verse that the whispering of *Satan* was another source for the enmity of Joseph's brothers' toward him, in addition to the envy that *their lower selves* had for their brother. In this way, he attributes the enmity of Joseph's brothers to two sources, internal and external.

وَكَذَٰلِكَ يَجْتَبِيكَ رَبُّكَ وَيُعَلِّمُكَ مِن تَأْوِيلِ ٱلْأَحَادِيثِ وَيُتِمُّ نِعْمَتَهُۥ عَلَيْكَ وَعَلَىٰٓ ءَالِ يَعْقُوبَ كَمَآ أَتَمَّهَا عَلَىٰٓ أَبَوَيْكَ مِن قَبْلُ إِبْرَٰهِيمَ وَإِسْحَٰقَ إِنَّ رَبَّكَ عَلِيمٌ حَكِيمٌ ﴿٦﴾

And thus your Lord will choose you, teach you a share of *ta'wīl al-aḥādīth* (the interpretation of talks), and perfect His favor on you and on the lineage of Jacob, as He perfected it before on your fathers[20] Abraham and Isaac; your Lord is Knowledgeable, Wise" (6).

This verse is a continuation of Jacob's speech to Joseph. The word وَكَذَٰلِكَ "And thus" refers to Joseph's vision, as if Jacob said to his son "and as the vision shows......."

Jacob's saying "And thus your Lord will choose[21] you" means "and thus, as the dream shows, Allah has chosen you." The choosing here seems to mean Allah's election of Joseph for prophethood.

Jacob goes on describing Allah's favors to Joseph: "teach you a share of *ta'wīl al-aḥādīth* (the interpretation of talks), and perfect His favor on you," and concludes by mentioning the favors that Allah will confer on the lineage of Jacob: "and on the lineage of Jacob, as He perfected it before on your fathers Abraham and Isaac." Let's now study the nature of the divine favors that Jacob mentions, starting with تَأْوِيلِ ٱلْأَحَادِيثِ "*ta'wīl al-aḥādīth*" which I have translated as "the interpretation of talks." This phrase occurs three times in the Qur'an, all in the sūra of Joseph: in verse 6, where Jacob is the speaker; in verse 21, which is a direct speech from Allah; and in verse 101, where the speaker is Joseph.

The word تَأْوِيل "*ta'wīl*" means "interpreting/interpretation" or "explaining/explanation." This word occurs also in the sūra of Joseph in other than the phrase "*ta'wīl al-aḥādīth*," where it also means "interpretation." Some exegetes have different opinions about the meaning of "*ta'wīl*."[22]

Regarding the term "*aḥādīth*,"[23] there is consensus among exegetes that it means "dreams" and that, accordingly, "*ta'wīl al-aḥādīth*" means the "interpretation of dreams." No doubt, this view was influenced by the mention in the sūra of Joseph of Joseph's successful interpretation of a number of dreams. What exegetes seem to have overlooked, however, is that there is a special Qur'anic phrase for the interpretation of dreams: تَأْوِيلِ ٱلْأَحْلَـٰمِ "*ta'wīl al-aḥlām*"; the word "*aḥlām*" means "dreams." This term is used by the court of the king who was in power when Joseph was in prison: قَالُوٓا۟ أَضْغَـٰثُ أَحْلَـٰمٍ وَمَا نَحْنُ بِتَأْوِيلِ ٱلْأَحْلَـٰمِ بِعَـٰلِمِينَ "They said: '[These are] medleys of dreams, and we are not knowledgeable in the *ta'wīl al-aḥlām* (interpretation of dreams)'" (12.44). This was in reply to the king's request to his court for an interpretation for his dream. In his request, the king referred to the interpretation of dreams with **تعبير الرؤى** "interpretation of dreams" when he said يَـٰٓأَيُّهَا ٱلْمَلَأُ أَفْتُونِى فِى رُءْيَـٰىَ إِن كُنتُمْ لِلرُّءْيَا تَعْبُرُونَ "O chiefs! Give me your opinions about my dream, if you can interpret dreams."[24] This throws doubts on the common interpretation that equates "*ta'wīl al-aḥādīth*" with "*ta'wīl al-aḥlām*."

In fact, the word "*aḥādīth*" in the Qur'an has a different meaning from "dreams," as shown in the other two verses in which this term occurs:

ثُمَّ أَرْسَلْنَا رُسُلَنَا تَتْرَا كُلَّ مَاجَآءَ أُمَّةً رَّسُولُهَا كَذَّبُوهُ فَأَتْبَعْنَا بَعْضَهُم بَعْضًا وَجَعَلْنَـٰهُمْ أَحَادِيثَ فَبُعْدًا لِّقَوْمٍ لَّا يُؤْمِنُونَ ﴿٤٤﴾. (سورة المؤمنون).

Then We sent Our messengers in succession. Whenever a messenger came to his nation, they called him a liar, so We made some of them [the nations] follow others [in punishment] and We made them *aḥādīth*, so away with people who do not believe (23.44).

فَقَالُوا۟ رَبَّنَا بَـٰعِدْ بَيْنَ أَسْفَارِنَا وَظَلَمُوٓا۟ أَنفُسَهُمْ فَجَعَلْنَـٰهُمْ أَحَادِيثَ وَمَزَّقْنَـٰهُمْ كُلَّ مُمَزَّقٍ إِنَّ فِى ذَٰلِكَ لَـَٔايَـٰتٍ لِّكُلِّ صَبَّارٍ شَكُورٍ ﴿١٩﴾. (سورة سَبَإٍ).

So they [the people of Sheba] said: "Our Lord! Make the stages between our journeys longer"; and they wronged themselves, so We made them *aḥādīth* and scattered them with utter scattering; surely there are signs in this for every patient, grateful person (34.19).

The word "*aḥādīth*" is the plural of "*ḥadīth*." The latter occurs in a number of verses, including the following:

ٱللَّهُ لَآ إِلَـٰهَ إِلَّا هُوَ لَيَجْمَعَنَّكُمْ إِلَىٰ يَوْمِ ٱلْقِيَـٰمَةِ لَا رَيْبَ فِيهِ وَمَنْ أَصْدَقُ مِنَ ٱللَّهِ حَدِيثًا ﴿٨٧﴾. (سورة النِّسَاء).

Allah, there is no god but He. He will surely gather you [O people!] together on the Day of Resurrection whereof there is no doubt; and who is more true *ḥadīthan* (in "*ḥadīth*") than Allah? (4.87).

أَوَلَمْ يَنظُرُواْ فِى مَلَكُوتِ ٱلسَّمَـٰوَٰتِ وَٱلْأَرْضِ وَمَا خَلَقَ ٱللَّهُ مِن شَىْءٍ وَأَنْ عَسَىٰٓ أَن يَكُونَ قَدِ ٱقْتَرَبَ أَجَلُهُمْ فَبِأَىِّ حَدِيثٍ بَعْدَهُۥ يُؤْمِنُونَ ﴿١٨٥﴾. (سورة الأعْراف).

Do they not consider the kingdom of the heavens and the earth and whatever things Allah has created, and that their term may have become nigh? In what *ḥadīth* beyond this would they then believe? (7.185).

وَهَلْ أَتَىٰكَ حَدِيثُ مُوسَىٰٓ ﴿٩﴾. (سورة طه).

And has the *ḥadīth* of Moses reached you [O Muhammad!]? (20.9).

هَلْ أَتَىٰكَ حَدِيثُ ضَيْفِ إِبْرَٰهِيمَ ٱلْمُكْرَمِينَ ﴿٢٤﴾. (سورة الذاريَات).

Has the *ḥadīth* of the guests of Abraham reached you [O Muhammad!]? (51.24).

It is obvious from the verses that contain the word "*aḥādīth*" or "*ḥādīth*" that this word means "speech that contains news or a story." Note that modern Arabic has the noun حَدَثْ "*ḥadath*" which means "event" and the verb حَدَثَ "*ḥadatha*" which means "took place," both of which are clearly related to the word حَديث "*ḥadīth*" whose verb is حَدَّثَ "*ḥaddatha* (spoke to)".

Therefore, the phrase "*ta'wīl al-aḥādīth*" refers to the ability to "know the حَدَثْ '*ḥadath* (event)' that lies behind a particular حَديث '*ḥadīth* (speech or talk).'" The *ta'wīl* of a *ḥadīth* means tracing it back to its *awwal* or "origin"; the origin of a *ḥadīth* is obviously the *ḥadath* (event) that it originated from.

A *ḥadīth* can be a dream, but *aḥādīth* are not confined to dreams. This is why the Qur'an differentiates between "*ta'wīl al-aḥādīth*" and "*ta'wīl al-aḥlām*." One piece of evidence that the former includes the latter is that the paranormal abilities that Joseph had exceeded the interpretation of dreams. We will see later as we follow the story of Joseph that he was able to know various events before they took place, such as predicting the kind of food that he and his prison mates would get.

Naturally, since "*ta'wīl al-aḥādīth*" represents the ability to know the origin of events, it must also imply the ability to distinguish between true and false *aḥādīth*. *Ta'wīl* of a true *ḥadīth* means determining the original event(s) that it refers to, whereas the *ta'wīl* of an untrue *ḥadīth* means knowing the reason for forging it.

In its three occurrences, the phrase "*ta'wīl al-aḥādīth*" is preceded by the preposition مِن "*min*," which literally means "of/from" and which I have translated as "a share of." Comparing this phrase with other terms that refer to branches of divine knowledge, such as the words كِتَاب "*kitāb* (Book)" and حِكْمَة "*ḥikma* (Wisdom)," shows that these two terms are not usually preceded by "*min*" (e.g. 2.129), except in a smaller number of verses (e.g. 2.131). I conclude from the presence of the word "*min*" in *all* three occurrences of "*ta'wīl al-aḥādīth*" that this word is meant to indicate the limitedness of the given knowledge. In other words, the use of "*min*" refers to the fact that "*ta'wīl al-aḥādīth*" is a huge branch of knowledge and that Allah granted Joseph "a share of" it.[25]

Jacob's interpretation of Joseph's dream, and particularly his conclusion that Allah would teach his son "*ta'wīl al-aḥādīth*" or "the interpretation of talks," indicates that Jacob himself had the ability of "interpreting talks"! This conclusion is also supported by Jacob's words "and perfect His favor on you and on the lineage of Jacob" which reflect his realization that the eleven stars stood for Joseph's brothers, and the sun and moon denoted himself and Joseph's mother. Indeed, the realization of Joseph's dream brought great favors to all of Jacob's family, as we will see later on. In fact, Joseph might well have recounted his dream to his father because Jacob was known to have the ability to "interpret talks," including "dreams."

It is clear that Jacob interpreted the dream to Joseph in general terms, not in detail. This could be due to the limitedness of Jacob's ability to interpret talks or simply because he did not want to disclose all that he knew from the dream to his young son.

We come now to Jacob's following words on whose interpretation exegetes have disagreed: "and perfect His favor on you and on the lineage of Jacob, as He perfected it before on your fathers Abraham and Isaac." Some believe that this verse refers to the conferment of prophethood on Joseph, and other kinds of favors on his sons. Other exegetes think that it indicates that all of Jacob's sons were going to become prophets. A third group of exegetes suggest that the verse refers to the conferment of favors other than prophethood on Joseph and his sons.

The view of many exegetes that Joseph's ten older brothers were not prophets stems from their belief that "infallible" prophets cannot misbehave in the way Joseph's brothers did in their mistreatment of Joseph and Benjamin. This position, nevertheless, is based on one, but certainly not the only, possible understanding of the concept of the infallibility of prophets. For instance, some exegetes, including those who believe that the Asbāṭ were Jacob's sons, think that committing minor sins before receiving prophethood does not contradict the concept of the infallibility of prophets. It is possible that Jacob's sons became prophets at a later stage and that they changed completely by Allah's will. In this case, granting prophethood to all of Jacob's sons would be the greatest form of the favors that the verse above mentions. I will examine below the important and controversial issue of the prophethood of Joseph's brothers in detail.

The exegetes' disagreement about the possible prophethood of Joseph's brothers reflects their disagreement on whether they are the prophets whom the Qur'an calls الأَسْبَاط "*al-Asbāṭ* (the Asbāṭ)" in five verses. I will study first four of those verses, and address later the fifth verse which uses the term "*Asbāṭ*" in a special way:

﴿قُولُوٓاْ ءَامَنَّا بِٱللَّهِ وَمَآ أُنزِلَ إِلَيْنَا وَمَآ أُنزِلَ إِلَىٰٓ إِبْرَٰهِـۧمَ وَإِسْمَـٰعِيلَ وَإِسْحَـٰقَ وَيَعْقُوبَ وَٱلْأَسْبَاطِ وَمَآ أُوتِىَ مُوسَىٰ وَعِيسَىٰ وَمَآ أُوتِىَ ٱلنَّبِيُّونَ مِن رَّبِّهِمْ لَا نُفَرِّقُ بَيْنَ أَحَدٍ مِّنْهُمْ وَنَحْنُ لَهُۥ مُسْلِمُونَ ﴿١٣٦﴾. (سورة البَقَرة).

Say [O People of the Book!]: "We believe in Allah; and in that which has been sent down to us; and in that which was sent down to Abraham, Ishmael, Isaac, Jacob, and the *Asbāṭ*; and in that which was given to Moses and Jesus; and in that which was given to the prophets from their Lord. We do not make any distinction between any of them, and to Him we are Muslims (we submit)" (2.136).

﴿أَمْ تَقُولُونَ إِنَّ إِبْرَٰهِـۧمَ وَإِسْمَـٰعِيلَ وَإِسْحَـٰقَ وَيَعْقُوبَ وَٱلْأَسْبَاطَ كَانُواْ هُودًا أَوْ نَصَـٰرَىٰ قُلْ ءَأَنتُمْ أَعْلَمُ أَمِ ٱللَّهُ وَمَنْ أَظْلَمُ مِمَّن كَتَمَ شَهَـٰدَةً عِندَهُۥ مِنَ ٱللَّهِ وَمَا ٱللَّهُ بِغَـٰفِلٍ عَمَّا تَعْمَلُونَ ﴿١٤٠﴾. (سورة البَقَرة).

Or do you [O People of the Book!] say that Abraham, Ishmael, Isaac, Jacob, and the *Asbāṭ* were Jewish or Christian? Say [O Muhammad!]: "Do you know best, or Allah does?" And who is more of a wrongdoer than he who conceals a testimony that he has from Allah? And Allah is not unaware of what you do (2.140).

﴿قُلْ ءَامَنَّا بِٱللَّهِ وَمَآ أُنزِلَ عَلَيْنَا وَمَآ أُنزِلَ عَلَىٰٓ إِبْرَٰهِيمَ وَإِسْمَـٰعِيلَ وَإِسْحَـٰقَ وَيَعْقُوبَ وَٱلْأَسْبَاطِ وَمَآ أُوتِىَ مُوسَىٰ وَعِيسَىٰ وَٱلنَّبِيُّونَ مِن رَّبِّهِمْ لَا نُفَرِّقُ بَيْنَ أَحَدٍ مِّنْهُمْ وَنَحْنُ لَهُۥ مُسْلِمُونَ

﴿٨٤﴾. (سورة آل عِمْرَان).

Say [O Muhammad!]: "We believe in that which has been sent down to us; and in that which was sent down to Abraham, Ishmael, Isaac, Jacob, and the *Asbāṭ*; and in that which was given to Moses, Jesus, and the prophets from their Lord. We do not make any distinction between any of them, and to Him we are Muslims (we submit)" (3.84).

إِنَّآ أَوْحَيْنَآ إِلَيْكَ كَمَآ أَوْحَيْنَا إِلَىٰ نُوحٍ وَٱلنَّبِيِّـۧنَ مِنۢ بَعْدِهِۦ وَأَوْحَيْنَآ إِلَىٰٓ إِبْرَٰهِيمَ وَإِسْمَـٰعِيلَ وَإِسْحَـٰقَ وَيَعْقُوبَ وَٱلْأَسْبَاطِ وَعِيسَىٰ وَأَيُّوبَ وَيُونُسَ وَهَـٰرُونَ وَسُلَيْمَـٰنَ وَءَاتَيْنَا دَاوُۥدَ زَبُورًا ﴿١٦٣﴾. (سورة النِّسَاء).

We have revealed to you [O Muhammad!] as we revealed to Noah and the prophets after him; and [as] We revealed to Abraham, Ishmael, Isaac, Jacob, the *Asbāṭ*, Jesus, Job, Jonah, Aaron, and Solomon. And We gave David a Book (4.163).

These verses leave no doubt that the Asbāṭ were prophets. As to the identity of those Asbāṭ, exegetes are split into two groups. One group believes that the Asbāṭ were Jacob's twelve sons, whereas the majority believe that they were not his sons but descendants. The word Asbāṭ, whose singular is سِبْط "*sibṭ*," means in general "descendants." Some exegetes claim that each one of the Asbāṭ was a descendant of one of the sons of Jacob. Another opinion that is mentioned by some scholars is that the word "Asbāṭ" means the "tribes of the Israelites," as Arabs are divided into different "clans" and non-Arabs into different "peoples." This opinion suggests that the word "Asbāṭ" was used to refer to the tribes of the Israelites before the revelation of the Qur'an. It is clear that this opinion has developed as a result of rejecting the view that the Asbāṭ were the sons of Jacob, rather than led to that view.

There is nothing in the verses above that contradicts the view that the Asbāṭ were Jacob's *sons* rather than his *descendants*; it is possible that they were called "the Asbāṭ" in reference to one of their grandfathers. But does the Qur'an contain anything that indicates that the Asbāṭ were indeed Jacob's twelve sons rather than some of his descendants? The arguments below make it clear that the answer is in the affirmative.

The best starting point of the investigation to determine the identity of the Asbāṭ is studying the places in which this term appears. In all of the verses above, the term "Asbāṭ" appears in one phrase which mentions the name of the *father* of the prophets, Abraham; then his *sons* prophets Ishmael and Isaac; then prophet Jacob *son* of prophet Isaac; then the prophets known as "the Asbāṭ": إِبْرَٰهِيمَ وَإِسْمَـٰعِيلَ وَإِسْحَـٰقَ وَيَعْقُوبَ وَٱلْأَسْبَاطِ

"Abraham, Ishmael, Isaac, Jacob, and the Asbāṭ." In other words, the verse refers to a *father, then his son, then his other son, then the son of the latter, and then grandsons.* Allah does not say explicitly whose grandsons those prophets were, but the fact that the verse mentions *successive* generations of prophets who descend from the same lineage leaves no doubt that the prophets who are mentioned at the end of the phrase are grandsons of the fathers who are mentioned earlier. The Asbāṭ are Jacob's sons.

The word "Asbāṭ" is preceded by the definite article "the" instead of being followed by a pronoun or word that attributes them explicitly to their fathers, such as "the Asbāṭ of so and so." This must mean that the context in which this word occurs clarifies its meaning, i.e. the grandfather(s) in question must be mentioned in the same context. Since "Asbāṭ" occurs after the *fathers* "Abraham, Ishmael, Isaac, Jacob," it is clear that the aforementioned fathers are the fathers of those grandsons.

Every human being is a grandson, and therefore every group of people are *grandsons* of innumerable grandfathers. Why, then, does Allah call those prophets in particular "the Asbāṭ," i.e. "the grandsons"? Why did He not say, for instance, "Abraham, Ishmael, Isaac, Jacob, and his sons" or "Abraham, Ishmael, Isaac, Jacob, Joseph, and his brothers" instead of "Abraham, Ishmael, Isaac, Jacob, and the Asbāṭ"? Those prophets were *special grandsons,* so Allah described them as "the Asbāṭ," i.e. "the grandsons," to emphasize their distinction.

In fact, exegetes agree that the term "the Asbāṭ" indicates that those referred to were prophets and at the same time grandsons of prophets, something that makes them special grandsons. This view, nevertheless, does not necessarily mean that the Asbāṭ were Jacob's sons or exclude the possibility that this name included other prophets from later generations who descended from Jacob. The problem with this view, however, is that it cannot explain using that term exclusively for a *particular group* of prophets who descended from Jacob. The verses cited earlier name a number of prophets who were from the lineage of Jacob but were not included in the term "the Asbāṭ."

On the contrary, the view that "the Asbāṭ" were only Joseph and his brothers perfectly explains calling this particular group of prophets "the Asbāṭ." Each one of this *unique group of grandsons* differs from any other prophet in that he was son of a prophet, who was himself son of a prophet, who was himself a brother of a prophet and son of a prophet. The Asbāṭ differed from other prophets from the lineage of Jacob in that they were *direct grandsons* of Abraham, Ishmael, Isaac, and Jacob. In other words, the phrase "Abraham, Ishmael, Isaac, Jacob, and the Asbāṭ" names *successive generations* of prophets.

It is significant that "the Asbāṭ" does not occur in any context other than the phrase "Abraham, Ishmael, Isaac, Jacob, and the Asbāṭ." It neither occurs separated with any word from the name of Jacob, which is preceded by the name of his father Isaac, which is in turn preceded by the name of his brother Ishmael, in turn preceded by the name of his father Abraham. It should also be noted that although He separated in verses 2.136 and 4.84 between names of prophets with the word وَمَآ "and in that which," Allah did not separate between the names of "Abraham, Ishmael, Isaac, Jacob, and the Asbāṭ." He separated the names of these prophets immediately after "the Asbāṭ" from the names of other prophets with "and in that which." This also suggests that the Asbāṭ represent the immediate generation after Jacob, i.e. his sons. Moses, Jesus and the other prophets who are mentioned in those two verses were also descendants of Abraham, but they were not direct descendants of "Abraham, Ishmael, Isaac, Jacob, and the Asbāṭ," hence their names are separated from the names of their grandfathers.

Note also the absence of Joseph's name from the prophets' names that are mentioned in the verses that contain the phrase "Abraham, Ishmael, Isaac, Jacob, and the Asbāṭ" despite the fact that Allah has dedicated for Joseph's story one of the longer suwar in the Qur'an. Does this not suggest that Joseph is not mentioned explicitly in those verses because he is one of the Asbāṭ mentioned in those verses? Indeed, when Allah mentions in another verse the names of several prophets — including Abraham, Ishmael, Isaac, and Jacob — but not "the Asbāṭ," the name of Joseph does get mentioned explicitly:

وَتِلْكَ حُجَّتُنَآ ءَاتَيْنَـٰهَآ إِبْرَٰهِيمَ عَلَىٰ قَوْمِهِۦ نَرْفَعُ دَرَجَـٰتٍ مَّن نَّشَآءُ إِنَّ رَبَّكَ حَكِيمٌ عَلِيمٌ ﴿٨٣﴾ وَوَهَبْنَا لَهُۥٓ إِسْحَـٰقَ وَيَعْقُوبَ كُلًّا هَدَيْنَا وَنُوحًا هَدَيْنَا مِن قَبْلُ وَمِن ذُرِّيَّتِهِۦ دَاوُۥدَ وَسُلَيْمَـٰنَ وَأَيُّوبَ وَيُوسُفَ وَمُوسَىٰ وَهَـٰرُونَ وَكَذَٰلِكَ نَجْزِى ٱلْمُحْسِنِينَ ﴿٨٤﴾ وَزَكَرِيَّا وَيَحْيَىٰ وَعِيسَىٰ وَإِلْيَاسَ كُلٌّ مِّنَ ٱلصَّـٰلِحِينَ ﴿٨٥﴾ وَإِسْمَـٰعِيلَ وَٱلْيَسَعَ وَيُونُسَ وَلُوطًا وَكُلًّا فَضَّلْنَا عَلَى ٱلْعَـٰلَمِينَ ﴿٨٦﴾. (سورة الأنعام).

And that was Our argument which we gave to Abraham against his people; We raise in degrees whom We please; surely your Lord [O Muhammad!] is Wise, Knowing (6.83). And We gave Isaac and Jacob to him, each of whom We did guide; and Noah did We guide before; and his [Abraham's] descendants, David, Solomon, Job, Joseph, and Aaron; and thus do We reward the good-doers (6.84). And Zachariah, John, Jesus, and Ilyās; each one of them was of the righteous (6.85). And Ishmael, al-Yasa', Jonah, and Lot; and to every one We gave favor above the people (6.86).

Let us look again at verse 4.163 and the verse that follows it:

إِنَّآ أَوْحَيْنَآ إِلَيْكَ كَمَآ أَوْحَيْنَآ إِلَىٰ نُوحٍ وَٱلنَّبِيِّـۧنَ مِنۢ بَعْدِهِۦ وَأَوْحَيْنَآ إِلَىٰٓ إِبْرَٰهِيمَ وَإِسْمَـٰعِيلَ
وَإِسْحَـٰقَ وَيَعْقُوبَ وَٱلْأَسْبَاطِ وَعِيسَىٰ وَأَيُّوبَ وَيُونُسَ وَهَـٰرُونَ وَسُلَيْمَـٰنَ وَءَاتَيْنَا دَاوُۥدَ زَبُورًا
﴿١٦٣﴾ وَرُسُلًا قَدْ قَصَصْنَـٰهُمْ عَلَيْكَ مِن قَبْلُ وَرُسُلًا لَّمْ نَقْصُصْهُمْ عَلَيْكَ وَكَلَّمَ ٱللَّهُ مُوسَىٰ
تَكْلِيمًا ﴿١٦٤﴾. (سورة النِّسَاء).

We have revealed to you [O Muhammad!] as we revealed to Noah and the prophets after him; and [as] We revealed to Abraham, Ishmael, Isaac, Jacob, the Asbāṭ, Jesus, Job, Jonah, Aaron, and Solomon. And We gave David a Book (4.163). And [other] messengers We have already recounted their stories to you [O Muhammad!], and messengers We have not; and Allah spoke to Moses with speech (4.164).

Note the reference to the messengers whose stories Allah related to Prophet Muhammad and others whose stories He did not. Note also that the stories of all prophets who are named in the verse above have been mentioned in the Qur'an. Does this not confirm that the Asbāṭ are themselves prophets whose stories have been mentioned in the Qur'an? If so, who are those prophets whose story has been mentioned in the Qur'an and who are particularly suited to be referred to *collectively* with the term "the Asbāṭ"? If Joseph was one of those prophets, who would the others be other than his brothers? This observation rules out the possibility that the Asbāṭ include in addition to Joseph and his brothers some sons of theirs, for the Qur'an has not related to us stories about immediate grandsons of Jacob.

The following verse shows us the Asbāṭ sitting next to their dying *father* and referring to their *fathers* إِبْرَٰهِيمَ وَإِسْمَـٰعِيلَ وَإِسْحَـٰقَ "Abraham, Ishmael, and Isaac." Their *immediate relationship* to these prophets is the reason they are named "the Asbāṭ":

أَمْ كُنتُمْ شُهَدَآءَ إِذْ حَضَرَ يَعْقُوبَ ٱلْمَوْتُ إِذْ قَالَ لِبَنِيهِ مَا تَعْبُدُونَ مِنۢ بَعْدِى قَالُوا۟ نَعْبُدُ إِلَـٰهَكَ
وَإِلَـٰهَ ءَابَآئِكَ إِبْرَٰهِـۧمَ وَإِسْمَـٰعِيلَ وَإِسْحَـٰقَ إِلَـٰهًا وَٰحِدًا وَنَحْنُ لَهُۥ مُسْلِمُونَ ﴿١٣٣﴾. (سورة
البَقَرة).

Or were you [O People of the Book!] witnesses when death visited Jacob, when he said to his sons: "What will you worship after me?" They said: "We will worship your God; the God of your fathers Abraham, Ishmael, and Isaac, [who is] one God, and to Him we submit [as Muslims]"

(2.133).

Note that the verse uses the word لِبَنِيه "to his sons" instead of "the Asbāṭ." This agrees with my observation that using the term "Asbāṭ" requires a special context that gives the term its meaning, such as being preceded by the names of the fathers, as is the case in the four verses above.

Exegetes who refuse to accept that Joseph's brothers became prophets have also overlooked or misunderstood several Qur'anic references that show that Joseph's brothers changed later in their lives to become righteous men. I will address those references when I study the verses in which they occur, but I would like to comment here on verse 2.133 above in particular. Note that the verse uses the word لِبَنِيه "to his sons" instead of "Joseph and his brothers"; the latter phrase used in verse 7 of the sūra of Joseph which we will study shortly: لَقَدْ كَانَ فِي يُوسُفَ وَإِخْوَتِهِ آيَاتٌ لِلسَّائِلِينَ "Surely in [the story of] Joseph and his brothers there are signs for the inquirers." The reason for this difference is that verse 12.7 talks about Joseph and his brothers at the beginning of their story, when Satan made them carry enmity for Joseph and Benjamin. By the latter stage of Jacob's life of verse 2.133, Allah had conferred favors on Joseph's brothers, making them righteous men and brothers for Allah's sake and not for blood alone. This is why they are referred to *collectively*.

There is another point that confirms the observation above and the view that the term "his sons" was not only used for the linguistic function of attributing the sons to their father Jacob. The verse treats all of Jacob's sons as one. It attributes to them one answer to their father's question, and indicates that they took, in front of him, one pledge not to worship other than Allah, the One — the God of their fathers Abraham, Ishmael, Isaac, and Jacob — and to surrender to Him.

The fact that Jacob's sons mentioned their righteous grandfathers, the fathers of Jacob, in their reply to their father indicates that they had also become prophets. Their reference to those great grandfathers represents an oath to be worthy of the title of "the Asbāṭ" which they carried as a result of their blood relationship to those great prophets who were also their fathers.

Additionally, note that the dream of Joseph, which was going to materialize *after the entry of Jacob and his family to Egypt*, did not distinguish between Joseph's ten half brothers and Benjamin who, like Joseph, had suffered at the hands of his ten half brothers. Each one of Joseph's eleven brothers appeared as a star in his dream. The entry of Jacob and his family to Egypt occurred after genuine repentance of his ten sons:

قَالُوٓاْ أَءِنَّكَ لَأَنتَ يُوسُفُ قَالَ أَنَا۠ يُوسُفُ وَهَـٰذَآ أَخِى قَدْ مَنَّ ٱللَّهُ عَلَيْنَآ إِنَّهُۥ مَن يَتَّقِ وَيَصْبِرْ فَإِنَّ ٱللَّهَ لَا يُضِيعُ أَجْرَ ٱلْمُحْسِنِينَ ﴿٩٠﴾ قَالُواْ تَٱللَّهِ لَقَدْ ءَاثَرَكَ ٱللَّهُ عَلَيْنَا وَإِن كُنَّا لَخَـٰطِـِٔينَ ﴿٩١﴾ قَالَ لَا تَثْرِيبَ عَلَيْكُمُ ٱلْيَوْمَ يَغْفِرُ ٱللَّهُ لَكُمْ وَهُوَ أَرْحَمُ ٱلرَّٰحِمِينَ ﴿٩٢﴾. (سورة يوسف).

They [Joseph's brothers] said: "Are you indeed Joseph?" He said: "I am Joseph, and this is my brother; Allah has indeed conferred on us favors; surely, as for he who acts dutifully and patiently, Allah does not waste the reward of the good-doers" (12.90). They said: "By Allah! Allah has indeed preferred you over us, and we have been sinners" (12.91). He said: "You shall not be rebuked today. [May] Allah forgive you, and He is the most Merciful of the merciful ones" (12.92).

قَالُواْ يَـٰٓأَبَانَا ٱسْتَغْفِرْ لَنَا ذُنُوبَنَآ إِنَّا كُنَّا خَـٰطِـِٔينَ ﴿٩٧﴾ قَالَ سَوْفَ أَسْتَغْفِرُ لَكُمْ رَبِّىٓ إِنَّهُۥ هُوَ ٱلْغَفُورُ ٱلرَّحِيمُ ﴿٩٨﴾. (سورة يوسف).

They said: "O our father! Ask forgiveness for our sins. We have certainly been sinners" (12.97). He said: "I shall ask for forgiveness for you from my Lord; certainly He is the Forgiving, the Merciful" (12.98).

This explains the symbolization of each of the ten brothers as a star, like Benjamin, in Joseph's dream. No matter how sinful a person is, he becomes a new person once Allah has forgiven him. Aṭ-Ṭabaṭabā'ī has beautifully noted that "seeing the family of Jacob in the form of the sun, the moon, and eleven stars, all of which are high heavenly globes with brilliant lights and huge orbits, indicates that they would attain a high status." The elevation of the status of Joseph's brothers after Allah forgave them was like rising from the ground high up into heaven.

It is clear from the discussion above that the Qur'an leaves no doubt whatsoever that "the Asbāṭ" were Joseph and his brothers on whom Allah conferred the favor of prophethood. The latter is the greatest of the favors that Jacob referred to in his interpretation of Joseph's dream: وَيُتِمُّ نِعْمَتَهُۥ عَلَيْكَ وَعَلَىٰٓ ءَالِ يَعْقُوبَ "and [He will] perfect His favor on you and on the lineage of Jacob." The belief of most exegetes that the Asbāṭ cannot be Joseph's brothers is the result of a particular understanding, or more accurately "misunderstanding," of the concept of the infallibility of prophets.

I have postponed discussing the fifth verse that mentions the term "the Asbāṭ" which, as I have already pointed out, uses this term in a special meaning:

وَقَطَّعْنَـٰهُمُ ٱثْنَتَىْ عَشْرَةَ أَسْبَاطًا أُمَمًا وَأَوْحَيْنَآ إِلَىٰ مُوسَىٰٓ إِذِ ٱسْتَسْقَىٰهُ قَوْمُهُۥٓ أَنِ ٱضْرِب بِّعَصَاكَ

ٱلْحَجَرَ فَٱنۢبَجَسَتْ مِنْهُ ٱثْنَتَا عَشْرَةَ عَيْنًا قَدْ عَلِمَ كُلُّ أُنَاسٍ مَّشْرَبَهُمْ وَظَلَّلْنَا عَلَيْهِمُ ٱلْغَمَـٰمَ وَأَنزَلْنَا عَلَيْهِمُ ٱلْمَنَّ وَٱلسَّلْوَىٰ كُلُوا۟ مِن طَيِّبَـٰتِ مَا رَزَقْنَـٰكُمْ وَمَا ظَلَمُونَا وَلَـٰكِن كَانُوٓا۟ أَنفُسَهُمْ يَظْلِمُونَ ﴿١٦٠﴾. (سورة الأعراف).

> And We divided them *asbāṭān*, twelve nations. And We revealed to Moses when his people asked him for water: "Strike the rock with your staff," so twelve springs gushed forth out of it; each people knew their drinking place; and We made the clouds overshadow them and We sent to them manna and quails [saying]: "Eat of the good things We have given you." And they did not wrong Us, but they did wrong themselves (7.160).

Exegetes in general believe that the term "*asbāṭān*" here means "groups." It seems that this refers to Allah's division of the Israelites into twelve nations, each representing the descendants of one of the twelve Asbāṭ. It is not clear whether this division is related or not to the events mentioned in the verse.

After this detour to study the identity of the Asbāṭ, let us get back to the sūra of Joseph and Jacob's interpretation of his son's dream.

Jacob's use of the phrase "the lineage of Jacob" instead of "your brothers" when talking to Joseph in verse 6 indicates that he was referring to all of his family, including himself and his wife. Jacob recognized the identity of the characters in Joseph's visionary dream and knew that it refers to good that will come to all of them.

Note that Jacob mentioned separately Allah's favor on Joseph, "and [He will] perfect His favor on you," and Allah's favor on the rest of his family, "and on the lineage of Jacob," and that he mentioned Allah's favor on Joseph first. This agrees chronologically with what was going to happen and the causal relation between the different events. Joseph received his share of Allah's favor, which the visionary dream revealed, including the favor of prophethood, *before* his brothers and their families received their share. The verses indicate that Joseph was a prophet at least since his early youth, whereas his brothers had still not become prophets even many years later when they came to Egypt seeking provisions. Additionally, Allah's favor to Joseph of elevating him to a high position of power in Egypt was the *cause* of the favor to Jacob's family, as Joseph supplied them with provisions and brought them to Egypt where they lived a comfortable life. As we will see later on, some of the favors that Joseph's dream referred to are mentioned by Joseph in his thanksgiving prayer at the end of the Qur'anic story:

وَقَدْ أَحْسَنَ بِىٓ إِذْ أَخْرَجَنِى مِنَ ٱلسِّجْنِ وَجَآءَ بِكُم مِّنَ ٱلْبَدْوِ مِنۢ بَعْدِ أَن نَّزَغَ ٱلشَّيْطَـٰنُ بَيْنِى

وَبَيْنَ إِخْوَتِيٓ إِنَّ رَبِّى لَطِيفٌ لِّمَا يَشَآءُ إِنَّهُۥ هُوَ ٱلْعَلِيمُ ٱلْحَكِيمُ ﴿١٠٠﴾ رَبِّ قَدْ ءَاتَيْتَنِى مِنَ ٱلْمُلْكِ وَعَلَّمْتَنِى مِن تَأْوِيلِ ٱلْأَحَادِيثِ ﴿١٠١﴾. (سورة يوسف).

> And He has indeed been kind to me, as He released me from the prison and brought you from the nomad desert after Satan had sown seeds of dissent between me and my brothers (from 12.100). My Lord! You have given me a share of kingship and taught me a share of *ta'wīl al-aḥādīth* (from 12.101).

Aṭ-Ṭabaṭabā'ī makes a beautiful remark on Jacob's use of the word رَبُّكَ "your Lord" instead of "Allah" in his speech to Joseph: "And thus your Lord will choose you, teach you a share of *ta'wīl al-aḥādīth* (the interpretation of talks), and perfect His favor on you and on the lineage of Jacob, as He perfected it before on your fathers Abraham and Isaac; your Lord is Knowledgeable, Wise." He points out that this is intended to emphasize that Joseph was the main cause of the coming of those favors.

Jacob's words at the end of the verse that "your Lord is Knowledgeable, Wise" are a reference to the fact that there is divine knowledge and wisdom behind Allah's election of Joseph and Jacob's lineages, and Abraham and Isaac before them, to be the recipients of His favors. This verse is reminiscent of Allah's saying elsewhere in the Qur'an:

وَإِذَا جَآءَتْهُمْ ءَايَةٌ قَالُوا۟ لَن نُّؤْمِنَ حَتَّىٰ نُؤْتَىٰ مِثْلَ مَآ أُوتِىَ رُسُلُ ٱللَّهِ ٱللَّهُ أَعْلَمُ حَيْثُ يَجْعَلُ رِسَالَتَهُۥ سَيُصِيبُ ٱلَّذِينَ أَجْرَمُوا۟ صَغَارٌ عِندَ ٱللَّهِ وَعَذَابٌ شَدِيدٌۢ بِمَا كَانُوا۟ يَمْكُرُونَ ﴿١٢٤﴾. (سورة الأنعام).

> And when a verse comes to them [the disbelievers], they say: "We will not believe till we are given the like of what Allah's messengers were given." Allah knows best to whom He gives His Message. Humiliation before Allah and severe torment will befall the guilty ones because of what they scheme (6.124).

Allah stresses here that He knows best the secrets behind choosing particular people to convey His Message.

لَّقَدْ كَانَ فِى يُوسُفَ وَإِخْوَتِهِۦٓ ءَايَٰتٌ لِّلسَّآئِلِينَ ﴿٧﴾

Surely in [the story of] Joseph and his brothers there are signs for the inquirers (7).

The particle ل "*lām* (l)" in the word لَقَد "*laqad*," which is translated as "surely," is used for an oath. So, Allah here stresses that "in [the story of] Joseph and his brothers there are signs for the inquirers."

The story of Joseph and his brothers is one of the Qur'anic stories which Prophet Muhammad had no knowledge of before the revelation of the Qur'an — something that Allah highlighted when He said: "We narrate to you [O Muhammad!] the best of narratives, by revealing this Qur'an to you; and before it you were one of the unaware." The word آيَاتٌ in the verse above, which also means "verses," means "signs" or "proofs" here.

Most exegetes believe that the word لِلسَّائِلِينَ "for the inquirers" indicates that some people tried to test the Prophet by asking him about the story of Joseph. The Arabs of Mecca, where this verse was revealed, did not know about the Israelite prophets and their stories. This is why some exegetes think that those enquirers where actually commissioned by the Jews of al-Madīna. According to this interpretation of "the inquirers," Allah revealed the sūra of Joseph in response to that challenge and as proof that Muhammad was indeed His Messenger. Those who mentioned this interpretation include aṭ-Ṭūsī, who copied it from az-Zajjāj, and al-Qurṭubī. According to this interpretation, the word "signs" means "signs and proofs of the prophethood of Muhammad."

The "inquirers," nevertheless, could refer to those who seek the truth, as there are countless magnificent lessons and sermons in this story to guide seekers of the true religion. If this is the meaning of "inquirers," then the word "signs" would mean "proofs of the divine origin of the Qur'an" for the enquirer about the verity of the Qur'an, and would mean "lessons" and "sermons" for the believer in the Qur'an who is seeking knowledge and learning.

إِذْ قَالُواْ لَيُوسُفُ وَأَخُوهُ أَحَبُّ إِلَىٰٓ أَبِينَا مِنَّا وَنَحْنُ عُصْبَةٌ إِنَّ أَبَانَا لَفِى ضَلَٰلٍ مُّبِينٍ ﴿٨﴾

When they said: "Verily Joseph[26] and his brother are dearer to our father than us, though we are a band; surely, our father is in manifest error (8).

Unlike verses 4-6, verse 7 does not include any details about the story of Joseph; it only comments on that story. Because verse 7 is parenthetic, and therefore intercepts the narration of the story of Joseph, returning to the story in verse 8 represents the start of a new context. This is why verse 8 starts with "*idh* (when)," as explained in §1.1.

The change in context might actually be greater than it looks. The dialogue described in the verse above might have taken place long, that is years, after Joseph saw his visionary dream. The separation of verse 12.7 between Joseph's narration of his dream to his father and Jacob's interpretation of that dream, on the one hand, and the rest of the story of Joseph, on the other, is probably a reference to the relatively long time between the occurrence of the dream and subsequent events of the story which start in this verse.

This verse contains the first explicit clarification of Jacob's advice and warning to Joseph in verse 5 of his brothers' envy toward him: "otherwise they would scheme against you a scheme; Satan is a manifest enemy to man." It shows that Joseph's ten brothers were upset that Jacob loved Joseph and Benjamin more than them. They also thought that their father was wrong in doing so: "surely, our father is in manifest error," because he ignored the fact that they were a عُصْبَةٌ "*'uṣba* (band)." This term indicates that they acted as a group, helped each other and were powerful, so they thought they were better than their *two young and weak* brothers.

Exegetes believe that Joseph's brothers were in charge of providing for the family, taking on tasks such as herding the cattle. This interpretation is supported by the denouncement of Joseph's brothers of what they saw as their father's error in loving their two young and weak brothers more than them. Obviously, Joseph and Benjamin were unable to do the kind of vital jobs that their older brothers could do. No doubt, prophet Jacob looked after and provided guidance to all of his sons, but he showed special care for Joseph and Benjamin.

The use of the word وَأَخُوهُ "*wa akhūhu* (and his brother)" by Joseph's brothers highlights the fact that Joseph and Benjamin were from a different mother.

It is clear that Joseph and Benjamin were younger than their half brothers. Though unclear in the Qur'an, it is likely that Joseph was the older of the two brothers.

The fact that Joseph's brothers mentioned Joseph before Benjamin indicates that Jacob's love for Joseph was greater than his love for Benjamin. It could also be the result of Joseph being older than Benjamin. Given that the conversation of Joseph's brothers probably occurred a few years after Joseph saw his dream, the possibility that Joseph was older than Benjamin implies the other possibility that the latter had not been born when Joseph saw his dream. There does not seem to be a way to prove or disprove the latter possibility, but if it was true then it is another indication that Joseph's dream could not have been interpreted without knowledge of "*ta'wīl al-aḥādīth*," because the number of Joseph's brothers at the time was ten, whereas the number of stars seen by Joseph was eleven. In this case, the birth of Jacob's eleventh son was another future event that was foretold by the dream.

ٱقْتُلُوا۟ يُوسُفَ أَوِ ٱطْرَحُوهُ أَرْضًا يَخْلُ لَكُمْ وَجْهُ أَبِيكُمْ وَتَكُونُوا۟ مِنۢ بَعْدِهِۦ قَوْمًا صَـٰلِحِينَ ﴿٩﴾

Kill Joseph or cast him to some land, so that your father pays attention exclusively to you, and after him you will be a righteous people" (9).

This verse is a continuation of the deliberations of Joseph's ten half brothers. It is obvious that they concluded that the solution to their problem was simply to separate Joseph from his father. They are shown in the verse above discussing two possible ways of carrying this out: killing Joseph, or taking him to a land where he would not be able to contact his father again. Some exegetes have suggested that the aim of the second suggestion was also killing Joseph, as it meant casting Joseph to an uninhibited land to die. I do not agree with this view. I think that the aim of the suggestion was to keep Joseph away from his father.

Aṭ-Ṭabaṭabā'ī has cleverly noted in his comment on this verse that the goal of the attempt of Joseph's ten brothers to get rid of him, to have their "father pays attention exclusively" to them, means that they actually revered and loved their father. He stresses that had that not been the case, Jacob's sons would have thought of getting rid of their father or intimidating him. They simply wanted to be the exclusive recipients of the love of their father whom they loved and respected. In fact, there is nothing in the sūra of Joseph suggesting that Jacob's sons disobeyed their father or deceived him in any matter other than Joseph's.

Aṭ-Ṭabaṭabā'ī points out also that the complaint of Joseph's brothers about Jacob's love for Joseph and Benjamin, and their plot to make Joseph disappear, meant that Jacob's love was not the ordinary kind of love that a father has for his younger children. Had that love been of this kind, it would not have bothered Joseph's brothers a lot; they would have simply had to wait until Joseph and Benjamin got older to see Jacob's special love for his two sons disappear. Aṭ-Ṭabaṭabā'ī's remark is undoubtedly true, but I also see in the sūra of Joseph explicit and implicit references that Jacob's love for Joseph was special and differed even from his love for Benjamin. Let us discuss this in some detail.

Many years after getting rid of Joseph, Jacob's sons were still mistreating Benjamin. We will see later that Jacob would not entrust his sons with Benjamin:

فَلَمَّا رَجَعُوٓا۟ إِلَىٰٓ أَبِيهِمْ قَالُوا۟ يَـٰٓأَبَانَا مُنِعَ مِنَّا ٱلْكَيْلُ فَأَرْسِلْ مَعَنَآ أَخَانَا نَكْتَلْ وَإِنَّا لَهُۥ لَحَـٰفِظُونَ ﴿٦٣﴾ قَالَ هَلْ ءَامَنُكُمْ عَلَيْهِ إِلَّا كَمَآ أَمِنتُكُمْ عَلَىٰٓ أَخِيهِ مِن قَبْلُ فَٱللَّهُ خَيْرٌ حَـٰفِظًا وَهُوَ أَرْحَمُ ٱلرَّٰحِمِينَ ﴿٦٤﴾. (سورة يوسف).

So when they returned to their father, they said: "O our father! The measure has been withheld from us, so send with us our brother so that we may get the measure; and surely we shall be protective of him" (12.63). He said: "Should I entrust you with him, would I be doing other than what I did before when I entrusted you with his brother? So, Allah is the best protector, and He is the most Merciful of the merciful ones" (12.64).

This verse also shows that Jacob's sons used to mistreat Benjamin:

وَلَمَّا دَخَلُوا۟ عَلَىٰ يُوسُفَ ءَاوَىٰٓ إِلَيْهِ أَخَاهُ قَالَ إِنِّىٓ أَنَا۠ أَخُوكَ فَلَا تَبْتَئِسْ بِمَا كَانُوا۟ يَعْمَلُونَ ﴿٦٩﴾. (سورة يوسف).

And when they entered Joseph's place, he admitted his brother to his private place and said: "I am your brother, so do not be grieved at what they have been doing" (12.69).

The persistence of Jacob's sons on mistreating Benjamin means that Jacob continued to treat Benjamin in a different way to his treatment of his other sons even after he had grown up. This, in turn, means that Jacob did not treat Benjamin in a special way because he was young, but because he recognized in his son some qualities that merited that treatment. Indeed, there is not in the sūra of Joseph anything suggesting that Benjamin misbehaved as his ten brothers did. His good manners might explain the continuation of his father's special care for him. Jacob's love for Joseph, however, was different even from his love for Benjamin.

It is clear from Jacob's interpretation of Joseph's dream that he was in possession of divine knowledge that allowed him to know so much about Joseph, his nearness to Allah, the good that Allah had ordained for him, and his distinction from his brothers. Jacob's care for Joseph was exceptional. Jacob knew, for example, from Joseph's dream, that all of Joseph's eleven brothers, including Benjamin, would prostrate to him. This stressed Joseph's distinction from his brothers.

One indication that Jacob's love for Joseph was unique is his reaction years later when he lost contact with his oldest son and Benjamin, who stayed in Egypt, as we will see later on. Jacob prayed: "may Allah bring them all together to me; surely He is the Knowing, the Wise" (from 12.83), using the word "all" to refer to Joseph, Benjamin, and his oldest son. Yet we see him in the next verse express his sadness for Joseph in particular: "And he turned away from them, and said: 'Alas, my grief for Joseph!'. And his eyes became white because of the grief, for he kept within him lots of grief" (12.84).

The Qur'an shows unambiguously the superior status of Joseph with respect to his brothers. For instance, the sūra of Joseph focuses on

Joseph in particular rather than any of his brothers, including Benjamin. Any mention of any of his eleven brothers occurs in the context of narrating Joseph's story. Additionally, Joseph is the only prophet among the Asbāṭ who is mentioned in person outside the sūra of Joseph, namely in the following two verses:

وَوَهَبْنَا لَهُۥٓ إِسْحَـٰقَ وَيَعْقُوبَ ۚ كُلًّا هَدَيْنَا ۚ وَنُوحًا هَدَيْنَا مِن قَبْلُ ۖ وَمِن ذُرِّيَّتِهِۦ دَاوُۥدَ وَسُلَيْمَـٰنَ وَأَيُّوبَ وَيُوسُفَ وَمُوسَىٰ وَهَـٰرُونَ ۚ وَكَذَٰلِكَ نَجْزِى ٱلْمُحْسِنِينَ ﴿٨٤﴾. (سورة الأنعام).

And We gave Isaac and Jacob to him [Abraham], each of whom We did guide; and Noah did We guide before; and his [Abraham's] descendants, David, Solomon, Job, Joseph, and Aaron; and thus do We reward the good-doers (6.84).

وَلَقَدْ جَآءَكُمْ يُوسُفُ مِن قَبْلُ بِٱلْبَيِّنَـٰتِ فَمَا زِلْتُمْ فِى شَكٍّ مِّمَّا جَآءَكُم بِهِۦ ۖ حَتَّىٰٓ إِذَا هَلَكَ قُلْتُمْ لَن يَبْعَثَ ٱللَّهُ مِنۢ بَعْدِهِۦ رَسُولًا ۚ كَذَٰلِكَ يُضِلُّ ٱللَّهُ مَنْ هُوَ مُسْرِفٌ مُّرْتَابٌ ﴿٣٤﴾. (سورة غافر).

And surely Joseph came to you [O my people!] in times gone by with clear proofs, but you ever remained in doubt about what he brought to you. When he died, you said: "Allah will not send a messenger after him." Thus does Allah cause to err him who is extravagant, a doubter (40.34).

Although Joseph's brothers complain in 12.8 that Jacob loves Joseph and Benjamin more than them, we see them in the next verse thinking that removing Joseph *only* is sufficient to make their father pay attention exclusively to them. Why did they not think of removing Benjamin also? The answer is that it is Jacob's care for Joseph in particular which was troubling them, because it exceeded by far Jacob's care for Benjamin. Joseph's brothers perceived Joseph as the barrier between them and their father; they concluded that removing him would bring them close to their father.

But why did Joseph's brothers want their father pay attention exclusively to them? The answer to this question can be found in the last part of the verse above where they say "and after him you will be a righteous people." The phrase "after him" means "after Joseph," i.e. "after the disappearance of Joseph." Joseph's brothers fully believed that prophet Jacob was the source of special blessings, and that his love and care for someone was the source of much good, success, and blessings for that person. They, therefore, linked taking Joseph away from their father, in which case Jacob's attention would be exclusively focused on them, to becoming "righteous people."[27]

Despite Joseph's attempts not to reveal to his brothers the blessings that Allah conferred on him, the effects of those blessings would have shown on him. Joseph's brothers thought that his nearness to his father made him receive those blessings from Jacob and at the same time prevented them from getting those blessings. They concluded that taking Joseph away from his father would make them receive blessings that were until then exclusively for Joseph. They failed to recognize that Jacob's special care for Joseph stemmed from his knowledge of Joseph's special spiritual status, which they could not recognize, and that they would not get the same treatment as Joseph from their father even if Joseph was not around. The blessings that Allah had ordained for Joseph were not going to go to someone else even if that person lived as near to Jacob as Joseph did. This is something that Joseph's brothers were destined to realize after taking Joseph away from their father. Jacob drew Joseph near to him physically because he was already close to him spiritually, not the other way round.

> قَالَ قَآئِلٌ مِّنْهُمْ لَا تَقْتُلُوا۟ يُوسُفَ وَأَلْقُوهُ فِى غَيَٰبَتِ ٱلْجُبِّ يَلْتَقِطْهُ بَعْضُ ٱلسَّيَّارَةِ إِن كُنتُمْ فَٰعِلِينَ ﴿١٠﴾
>
> One of them said: "Do not kill Joseph, but cast him down into the bottom[28] of the well where some caravanners will pick him up, if you would do something [to him]" (10).

Exegetes have disagreed on the identity of Jacob's son who suggested throwing Joseph down a well instead of killing him. Names that were mentioned include Judah, Simeon, Levi, and Reuben, and some thought it was "the eldest son."[29]

The fact is that the exegetes' guesses of the name of that brother, all of which use Biblical names of Joseph's brothers, have no foundation in the Qur'an. This reflects the common tendency among exegetes, discussed in §1.3, of not focusing on the Qur'anic text only, but relying on various narratives, such as those of the Old Testament.

The suggestion in verse 12.10 is a response to the ones in 12.9. In the latter verse, two suggestions were put forward: killing Joseph, or casting him to a land faraway from where their father lived: "Kill Joseph or cast him to some land." The speaker in verse 12.10 replies to the first suggestion in verse 12.9 by saying "do not kill Joseph," then moves on to present a plan to carry out the second suggestion of banishing Joseph to some land: "but cast him down into the bottom of the well where some caravanners will pick him up." Al-Jalālayn say in their interpretation of 12.15 that Joseph's brothers wanted to kill him by throwing him into "the bottom of the well," but this is a clear misunderstanding.

The suggestion of casting Joseph in a well indicates that the person who suggested it was talking about one particular well. It is clear, for instance, that, having already objected to killing Joseph, he was talking about a well that was not as much filled with water as would cause Joseph to drown: "Do not kill Joseph." His words "where some caravanners will pick him up" indicate that the well was on a travel route that is used so often that Joseph was bound to be rescued by travelers before dying of hunger or cold. It is clear that the well was not on a travel route that crosses the area where Jacob was living.

Al-Qurṭubī has pointed out that leaving Joseph on a travel route would spare his brothers the trouble of taking him to a land that is far enough from his parent's home, as the travelers would do that for them. It should be noted, however, that Joseph's brothers would not have succeeded in convincing their father to take Joseph on a long journey away from home. In fact, Jacob permitted his sons to take Joseph with them for a few hours only, as we will see later on.

So, Joseph's brothers wanted to get rid of him by making some travelers take him away to a far land. But why did one of them suggest casting Joseph in a well so that travelers would pick him, instead of giving or selling him to travelers? The answer is that Joseph would have resisted such a plot, spoken in front of the potential buyers, and exposed his brothers' evil act. This would have caused the plot of Joseph's brothers to fail, and perhaps even landed them in trouble. Throwing Joseph in the well would spare them this kind of trouble, and at the same time achieve their goal. The scene of a young child in the bottom of a well was certain to force whoever finds him to take him out, if not to rescue him from death then to enslave him, as indeed happened.

The speaker ends his speech with the clause "if you would do something [to him]," urging his brothers to follow his suggestion if they plan to do anything.

قَالُوا۟ يَـٰٓأَبَانَا مَا لَكَ لَا تَأْمَ۫نَّا عَلَىٰ يُوسُفَ وَإِنَّا لَهُۥ لَنَـٰصِحُونَ ﴿١١﴾
They said: "O our father! Why do you not entrust us with Joseph? Surely we seek good for him (11).

The conversation between Joseph's brothers ended with the suggestion of one of them that they should cast Joseph in "the bottom of the well," which implies that the plan was unanimously approved. Indeed, we find them afterward, in the verse above, trying to convince their father to allow them to take Joseph, obviously to carry out their plan.

Jacob's sons' question to their father "why do you not entrust us with Joseph?" shows that they were well aware that he did not believe that Joseph would be safe with them, so he was not going to allow them to take him. They sought to convince their father with kind words, hence the start of their speech with the loving phrase "O our father!," as noted by aṭ-Ṭabaṭabā'ī.

Trying to lay a sense of guilt on their father for not entrusting them with Joseph, they went on to say: "Why do you not entrust us with Joseph?" hoping to persuade him to allow them to take Joseph away. They followed their gentle criticism with a confirmation that they sought only good for Joseph: "Surely we seek good for him."

﴿أَرْسِلْهُ مَعَنَا غَدًا يَرْتَعْ وَيَلْعَبْ وَإِنَّا لَهُ لَحَٰفِظُونَ ﴿١٢﴾﴾

Send him with us *ghadan* (in the early morning) to enjoy himself and play, and surely we shall be protective of him" (12).

Here we see Joseph's brothers getting to the goal of their speech to their father, disclosing what they wanted him to do: to allow them to take Joseph with them. After confirming to their father in the previous verse that they were worthy of his trust to take care of Joseph and that they would be only a source of good for their brother, "surely we seek good for him," Joseph's brothers set out to assure Jacob that they were able to protect Joseph against any possible source of external harm: "surely we shall be protective of him."

It is interesting to note the pretext that Joseph's brothers used to convince their father to send Joseph with them. They claimed that they wanted to take Joseph with them to "enjoy himself and play." The verb يَرْتَعْ "*yarta'*," translated here as "enjoy himself," means relax and move freely in the grazing place. It seems that they meant taking Joseph to where they used to graze their cattle. It is clear from this pretext that Joseph was very young — a conclusion that is consistent with Joseph's brothers' appeal to their father in the previous verse to "entrust" them with Joseph, and their declaration that they would "protect" him.

It is common to interpret the word غَدًا "*ghadan*," which I have translated as "in the early morning," as "the following day." There is more than one reason to reject the suggestion that Joseph's brothers specified in their request to their father "the following day" as the date to take their brother with them. First, the aim of Joseph's brothers was to abandon him in a land faraway. They could do this on any day that Joseph was permitted to go with them, for it is certain that they would go out to graze the cattle daily.

Second, Joseph's brothers were all too aware that they had a difficult task in trying to persuade their father to let them take Joseph and that they would have to talk to him many times before getting his permission.

It is not possible, therefore, that when they spoke to their father about that matter, they asked him to send Joseph with them on the "*the following day.*"

Third, Joseph's brothers' pretext was that they wanted to take Joseph to "enjoy himself and play." Specifying a particular day, let alone "the following day," would have made their father very suspicious of their intention, particularly as they used to go to graze the cattle daily.

If we add to all of this the fact that Joseph's brothers were very keen not to raise their father's doubts and to win his confidence to agree to their request, it looks certain that they did not specify "the following day" as the date to take their brother with them. The word "*ghadan*" must mean something else other than "the following day."

As seen in my translation of this verse, I believe that "*ghadan*" refers to the early time of the day, i.e. the first hours of the morning. The word in question shares the same linguistic root with the word غَـدَاة "*ghadāt*," whose plural is غُـدُو "*ghuduw*." These are two verses in which these two words occur:

وَٱصْبِرْ نَفْسَكَ مَعَ ٱلَّذِينَ يَدْعُونَ رَبَّهُم بِٱلْغَدَوٰةِ وَٱلْعَشِيِّ يُرِيدُونَ وَجْهَهُۥ وَلَا تَعْدُ عَيْنَاكَ عَنْهُمْ تُرِيدُ زِينَةَ ٱلْحَيَوٰةِ ٱلدُّنْيَا وَلَا تُطِعْ مَنْ أَغْفَلْنَا قَلْبَهُۥ عَن ذِكْرِنَا وَٱتَّبَعَ هَوَىٰهُ وَكَانَ أَمْرُهُۥ فُرُطًا ﴿٢٨﴾. (سورة الكهف).

And withhold yourself [O Muhammad!] in patience with those who call on their Lord in the *ghadāt* (morning) and evening, seeking Him; and let not your eyes pass beyond them, desiring the riches of this world's life. And do not follow the person whose heart We have made unmindful to Our remembrance, who follows his low desires, and whose case has gone beyond all bounds (18.28).

وَٱذْكُر رَّبَّكَ فِى نَفْسِكَ تَضَرُّعًا وَخِيفَةً وَدُونَ ٱلْجَهْرِ مِنَ ٱلْقَوْلِ بِٱلْغُدُوِّ وَٱلْءَاصَالِ وَلَا تَكُن مِّنَ ٱلْغَـٰفِلِينَ ﴿٢٠٥﴾. (سورة الأعراف).

And remember your Lord [O Muhammad!] within yourself humbly, in fear, and in a low voice in the *ghuduw* (mornings) and late afternoons, and do not be one of the heedless (7.205).

The reason that Joseph's brothers asked their father to send their little brother with them "in the early morning" is probably because that event took place in summer when the weather starts to turn very hot as the sun rises in the sky. In order to make Jacob agree to allow Joseph to go with them, Joseph's brothers suggested that they would take Joseph with them to play and enjoy himself in the early hours of the morning, implying that one of them would return him home before it got too hot. Joseph's brothers, thus, used the word "*ghadan*" to convince their father *to let them take Joseph with them, not to specify the exact day they wanted to take their brother on.*

I will discuss again why "*ghadan*" must mean "in the early morning" when I study in the next chapter the occurrence of the word عِشَآءً "*'ishā'an*" in verse 12.16.

قَالَ إِنِّى لَيَحْزُنُنِىٓ أَن تَذْهَبُوا۟ بِهِۦ وَأَخَافُ أَن يَأْكُلَهُ ٱلذِّئْبُ وَأَنتُمْ عَنْهُ غَٰفِلُونَ ﴿١٣﴾
He said: "It saddens me that you should take him away, and I fear that a wolf might devour him while you are not attending to him" (13).

Jacob's first response to his sons' request was to tell them that sending Joseph with them would sadden him. Many exegetes think that this means that Jacob's love for Joseph was so strong that he did not want anyone to take him away and that Joseph's departure would sadden him. This interpretation, nevertheless, sounds weak as it portrays Jacob as a father who was too attached to his son that he could not let him ago away even for a few hours.

More important, this interpretation is not really supported by the verse. Note that Jacob did not say that "separation from Joseph" would sadden him, which would have justified that interpretation, but instead he said that "taking Joseph away by his brothers" would make him sad. Jacob was well aware of the ill feelings that Joseph's brothers fostered toward their brothers, so he was concerned about leaving Joseph with his brothers away from his watchful eyes lest they mistreat him.

Jacob did not reveal to his sons why Joseph's going with them would cause him sadness, though they all knew. He was hopeful that the hostile feelings of his sons toward Joseph would change, so perhaps he thought that voicing his suspicions would only deepen those feelings. Jacob preferred, thus, to follow that with a reference to his fear for Joseph being devoured by a wolf while his brothers are inattentive of him.

Note the kindness of Jacob's reply. He did not only refrain from explicitly accusing his sons of being a source of danger to Joseph, but he went further by implying that he thought they would certainly defend their brothers should he face any danger, and that they would leave him exposed to danger only *inadvertently, not deliberately.* This verse reflects the efforts that Jacob exerted to change his sons' feelings toward Joseph.

It is worth noting that Jacob's concern that Joseph could be devoured by a wolf whilst in his brothers' care is another indication that Joseph was a young child at the time. Jacob's concern suggests that he was aware of wolves frequenting the cattle's grazing place.

قَالُواْ لَئِنْ أَكَلَهُ ٱلذِّئْبُ وَنَحْنُ عُصْبَةٌ إِنَّآ إِذًا لَّخَٰسِرُونَ ﴿١٤﴾
They said: "If a wolf would devour him despite the fact that we are a band, we are then certainly a failing group" (14).

Responding to their father's apprehension, Jacob's sons stressed that if a wolf could devour Joseph despite their presence, that would mean that they were a powerless and useless group. They meant that since they were not a powerless group, a wolf would not be able to devour Joseph, thus urging their father to let Joseph go with them.

Joseph's brothers defended themselves against what could be implied in their father's saying "and I fear that a wolf might devour him while you are not attending to him," but they did not comment on his first statement: "It saddens me that you should take him away." Their refrainment confirms my observation above that Jacob's words do not indicate explicitly that his sadness was because of Joseph going with his brothers. Jacob was keen on helping his sons get rid of their ill feelings toward Joseph.

4

Prophet Joseph on His Way to Egypt

This chapter examines the story of Joseph beginning from when his brothers take and abandon him away from his father's house to his entry into Egypt.

> فَلَمَّا ذَهَبُوا بِهِ وَأَجْمَعُوا أَن يَجْعَلُوهُ فِي غَيَابَتِ الْجُبِّ وَأَوْحَيْنَا إِلَيْهِ لَتُنَبِّئَنَّهُم بِأَمْرِهِمْ هَـٰذَا وَهُمْ لَا يَشْعُرُونَ ﴿١٥﴾
>
> So when they took him away and agreed that they should throw him to the bottom of the well, and We revealed to him: "You will certainly inform them of this affair of theirs while they are unaware" (15).

Although stressing that Joseph's brothers took him, the verse does not state explicitly whether that happened with or without Jacob's permission. Significantly, this verse occurs after a verse in which Jacob's sons had the last words in their conversation with their father as they tried to convince him: "They said: 'If a wolf would devour him despite the fact that we are a band, we are then certainly a failing group'." This implies that Joseph's brothers took him with their father's permission. Indeed, we will see later in the story Jacob remind his sons, when they asked him to send Benjamin with them to Egypt, that he "entrusted" them with Joseph but they betrayed that trust: "He said: 'Should I entrust you with him, would I be doing other than what I did before when I entrusted you with his brother? So, Allah is the best protector, and He is the most Merciful of the merciful ones'" (12.64). This proves that Jacob's sons took Joseph with the permission of their father. Note that the verb آمَنَ على "entrust someone with" is the same verb that occurred in Joseph's brothers' request, "O our father! Why do you not entrust us with Joseph? Surely we seek good for him," implying that at the end Jacob agreed to the request.

I have already shown that Jacob was aware that Joseph's brothers harbored evil for their brother; why, then, did he agree that they take him? The answer to this question has two sides that may be described as "apparent" and "subtle." I will start with the former. We have seen in our study of Jacob's reply, "It saddens me that you should take him away, and I fear that a wolf might devour him while you are not attending to him," that he was so keen on changing the attitude of his sons toward Joseph that he did not want to say explicitly that he saw them as a source of potential danger to Joseph. He preferred to attribute any harm that may occur to Joseph to an external source, mentioning a wolf. It seems that Jacob reckoned that if Joseph's brothers would take him with them that might improve the way they felt about Joseph, so he agreed to their request.

We should not forget that the verse "send him with us *ghadan* (in the early morning) to enjoy himself and play, and surely we shall be protective of him" does not refer to a discussion that occurred on *one day* between Jacob and his sons and ended up with him agreeing to their request to take Joseph with them the next day. This is what many may think because of mistaking the word غَدًا "*ghadan*" to mean "the following day," when in fact it means "in the early morning" of any day. This verse refers to the pretext that Joseph's brothers used to persuade their father to send Joseph with them, a pretext that they would have used in their discussion with him over many days until he agreed in good faith to their request.

Jacob's keenness on changing his sons' feelings toward Joseph may not be sufficient to explain the great risk that he took by allowing them to take Joseph away. This takes us from the "apparent" to the "subtle" explanation of Jacob's acceptance of his sons' request: Allah made Jacob agree to his sons' request so that the story of Joseph would unravel as He decreed.

The verb وَأَجْمَعُوٓا "and [they] agreed" indicates that *all* of Joseph's brothers agreed to throw him to the bottom of the well. This is in line with my already mentioned conclusion that the fact that the conversation about how to get rid of Joseph ended with the verse "one of them said: 'Do not kill Joseph, but cast him down into the bottom of the well where some caravanners will pick him up, if you would do something [to him]'" (12.10) means that they all agreed to that plan. Note that the verb يَجْعَلُوهُ "[they] should put him" shows that by putting Joseph in the well, Joseph's brothers did not intend to kill him, but wanted some passers-by to rescue him and take him to a land far from where his father lived.

After Jacob's sons lowered Joseph to the bottom of the well, Allah revealed to him: "You will certainly inform them of this affair of theirs while they are unaware." He told Joseph that one day he will mention this plot to his brothers, and that this would come as a complete surprise to them. Indeed, this is what happened many years later in Egypt. Verses 12.89-90 describe how Joseph reminded his brothers of their evil scheme against him while they were totally unaware that the dignitary they had been visiting was in fact their brother Joseph whom they cast to the bottom of the well years earlier: "He said: 'Do you know how you treated Joseph and his brother when you were ignorant?' (12.89). They said: 'Are you indeed Joseph?'. He said: 'I am Joseph and this is my brother; Allah has indeed conferred on us favors; surely, as for he who acts dutifully and patiently, Allah does not waste the reward of the good-doers' (12.90)."

Allah's revelation brought much kindness, care, and mercy to the child Joseph who was in grave distress. Joseph would have badly missed his father when he realized what his brothers were going to do to him. Allah's consolation, however, was greater than any consolation that Joseph could have received from any human being, including his father.[30]

﴿وَجَآءُوٓ أَبَاهُمْ عِشَآءً يَبْكُونَ ١٦﴾

And they came to their father *'ishā'an* (at night), weeping (16).

Joseph's brothers returned home pretending to cry for their brother. The mention of the verse that the time of the return was عِشَآءً "*ishā'an* (at night)" confirms my interpretation of the word "*ghadan*" in verse 12.12 as meaning "in the early morning." Allah tells us that after taking their brother with them in the early morning, Joseph's brothers came back at night without him.

Al-Qurṭubī believes that Joseph's brothers chose to return at night because they thought that this would help them make up the story about what happened, as their faces would not be visibile in the darkness of the night. But even if that was true, they must have given their father another reason for getting back late. Let us remember that verse 12.12 indicates that Joseph was with his brothers in the early hours of the morning of a summer day, which means that they got back 10-12 hours after they should have brought Joseph back to his father. They were supposed to return him before the sun reached a high point in the sky and it became too hot.

Joseph's brothers were keen on pretending that they cared about Joseph and were sad to lose him, so they would have been expected to tell their father about Joseph's death immediately after they knew about it. What, then, was their excuse for returning late? We will see in the next two verses Joseph's brothers untruthfully claim that a wolf has devoured Joseph, and that they could find only his blood-stained shirt. This leads me to conclude that Joseph's brothers must have claimed that they could not come back before night because they kept on looking for Joseph's body until the night set in.

Probably, Joseph's brothers thought that getting back at night would provide cover for their lie. If they had told their father about what had happened to Joseph in the morning he would have certainly asked them to take him to where they left Joseph or found his shirt. By returning during the night, they guaranteed that Jacob would not be able to go before the next morning to wherever Joseph was supposed to have been devoured by the wolf and they found his shirt. If Jacob went there in the morning and did not find anything supporting his sons' claims, that would not represent a problem for them. They could claim that beasts or the elements had removed any trace of their brother. In fact, we will see in verse 12.18 that Jacob knew that it was useless to try to search for Joseph, so his only reaction to the news of losing his son was to leave the matter in the hands of Allah.

The well that Joseph's brothers chose was far enough from their home to prevent Joseph from returning home should the person who found him try to identify his family and return him home. This could have been one reason that *forced* them not to come back before night.

قَالُوا۟ يَٰٓأَبَانَآ إِنَّا ذَهَبْنَا نَسْتَبِقُ وَتَرَكْنَا يُوسُفَ عِندَ مَتَٰعِنَا فَأَكَلَهُ ٱلذِّئْبُ وَمَآ أَنتَ بِمُؤْمِنٍ لَّنَا وَلَوْ كُنَّا صَٰدِقِينَ ﴿١٧﴾

They said: "O our father! We went to race with one another and left Joseph with our belongings, so a wolf devoured him; and you will not believe us though we are truthful" (17).

Joseph's brothers started their speech to their father with the loving phrase "O our father!" to create a friendly atmosphere that might help to make him believe the painful details they were going to tell him.

The use of Joseph's brothers of the clause ذَهَبْنَا نَسْتَبِقُ "we went to race with one another"[31] instead of the verb استبقنا "we raced with one another" means that their race included going to a relatively far distance from the starting point. The fake story about the race was used by Joseph's brothers to justify leaving Joseph alone with their belongings, as it is obvious that young Joseph could not take part in this activity.

Joseph's brothers deliberately combined their claim of being busy racing with the claim about Joseph being devoured by a wolf. The latter is a danger that Jacob himself suggested: "and I fear that a wolf might devour him while you are not attending to him." They thought that their story was thus more likely to be believed by their father as he himself had acknowledged this possibility.

It is clear from their plan that Joseph's brothers wanted to convince their father that Joseph was actually dead, not merely missing. They thought that only Joseph's death would make Jacob ultimately forget his son.

By saying to their father "you will not believe us though we are truthful," Jacob's sons suggested that they had to convey to him what happened even though they were aware of his suspicions about their intention. They stressed that their story was true by reminding their father that his failure to believe them was due to the suspicions that he already had, not because their story was fake. They tried to make their father develop doubts about the suspicions that were inevitably going to appear in his mind about their story, and thus making him believe it.

وَجَآءُو عَلَىٰ قَمِيصِهِۦ بِدَمٍ كَذِبٍ قَالَ بَلْ سَوَّلَتْ لَكُمْ أَنفُسُكُمْ أَمْرًا فَصَبْرٌ جَمِيلٌ وَٱللَّهُ ٱلْمُسْتَعَانُ عَلَىٰ مَا تَصِفُونَ ﴿١٨﴾

And they came with false blood on his shirt. He said: "[No,] rather your souls have suggested to you [doing] something [evil]; so, [my course is] perfect patience. And it is Allah whose help is sought against what you describe" (18).

Joseph's brothers brought his shirt to their father after smearing it with blood, which was not actually Joseph's, as proof that their brother was devoured by a wolf. The plan that Joseph's brothers followed to deceive Jacob reflects their failure to appreciate the depth of the knowledge of this prophet. Allah conferred on Jacob "*ta'wīl al-aḥādīth* (the interpretation of talks)," making him able to read through simple things and signs present and future events, as we saw in his interpretation of his son's dream. Jacob, therefore, was not going to believe his sons' story about the death of Joseph. He knew through Joseph's dream, and whatever other sources of knowledge that Allah made available to him, certain facts about the future of Joseph and the rest of the family. Indeed, we will see later how Jacob tells critics of his undiminished hope of seeing Joseph again, years after his disappearance: "and I know from Allah what you do not know" (from 12.86).

I should cite a particular event that reveals the extent of Jacob's sons' underestimation of the knowledge and paranormal abilities that Allah conferred on their father. Many years after the sudden disappearance of Joseph, Jacob was one day able to smell the scent of his son through a shirt that Joseph sent to him, when the shirt was still at a far distance from Jacob's living place: "And when the camel caravan had departed, their father said: 'I perceive the scent of Joseph; may you not disbelieve me!'" (12.94). The recipient of such divine favor was undoubtedly able to know that the blood on the shirt, which he could touch and carefully examine, was not Joseph's.

Indeed, Jacob's first reaction to his sons' claims was: "[No,] rather your souls have suggested to you [doing] something [evil]." This is a direct accusation from Jacob to his sons that they have worked out a scheme for Joseph and that their account of what happened had no relation to truth.

Jacob's words "so, [my course is] perfect patience" refer to his reaction to what happened. The صَبْرٌ جَمِيلٌ "*ṣabrun jamīlun*," which I translate as "perfect patience," is "the patience that is not associated with any complaint," as explained by the Prophet.[32]

Note that Jacob's reply "so, [my course is] perfect patience" refers to his patience not only with Joseph's calamity, but also with the state of his sons. Jacob did not react negatively to what his sons did. He did not throw them out of the house, for example. He followed those words with the sentence "and it is Allah whose help is sought against what you describe." Here, Jacob refers to his sons' lies about what happened and asks Allah for help in exposing those lies and revealing the truth.

Before moving to the next verse, we need to stop a little to ponder on Jacob's reaction in this extremely difficult situation. There is no doubt that losing the son that he had special love for caused great sadness to Jacob, especially as he did not know the condition of his son then, and what was going to happen to him. Jacob's knowledge that Allah had ordained great good for Joseph in the future was a source of consolation for him, but that would not have prevented him from feeling sad for his son whom he could not see anymore, know his condition, or help.

Jacob's sadness must have been amplified by the fact that Joseph's brothers were responsible for his disappearance, and that the good faith that he put in them had contributed directly to the sad unfolding of events. Despite all that, faith and wisdom never departed Jacob when he was disputing his sons' story and later asking for patience and help from Allah during that crisis. How beautiful, then, is the reaction of this knowledgeable prophet to his grave calamity, and how great is his perfect patience! This divine test has made Jacob draw nearer to Allah.

No doubt, Jacob would have remembered in this grave calamity his great grandfather, prophet Abraham, whom Allah also tested with his son. One day, Allah ordered Abraham in a dream to slaughter his son Ishmael. When Abraham and Ishmael were about to carry out Allah's command, Allah intervened. He ordered Abraham not to sacrifice his son, and gave him a huge animal to sacrifice instead:

فَلَمَّا بَلَغَ مَعَهُ ٱلسَّعْىَ قَالَ يَـٰبُنَىَّ إِنِّىٓ أَرَىٰ فِى ٱلْمَنَامِ أَنِّىٓ أَذْبَحُكَ فَٱنظُرْ مَاذَا تَرَىٰ قَالَ يَـٰٓأَبَتِ

ٱفْعَلْ مَا تُؤْمَرُ سَتَجِدُنِىٓ إِن شَآءَ ٱللَّهُ مِنَ ٱلصَّـٰبِرِينَ ﴿١٠٢﴾ فَلَمَّآ أَسْلَمَا وَتَلَّهُۥ لِلْجَبِينِ
﴿١٠٣﴾ وَنَـٰدَيْنَـٰهُ أَن يَـٰٓإِبْرَٰهِيمُ ﴿١٠٤﴾ قَدْ صَدَّقْتَ ٱلرُّءْيَآ إِنَّا كَذَٰلِكَ نَجْزِى ٱلْمُحْسِنِينَ
﴿١٠٥﴾ إِنَّ هَـٰذَا لَهُوَ ٱلْبَلَـٰٓؤُا۟ ٱلْمُبِينُ ﴿١٠٦﴾ وَفَدَيْنَـٰهُ بِذِبْحٍ عَظِيمٍ ﴿١٠٧﴾. (سورة
الصّافاتِ).

And when he [Abraham's son, Ishmael] was old enough to work with him [his father Abraham], he [Abraham] said: "O son! I see in a dream that I am sacrificing you, so let me know what you think." He [Ishmael] said: "O father! Do what you are commanded to do; Allah-willing, you will find me one of those with patience" (37.102). So when they submitted [to Allah's command], and he [Abraham] laid him [Ishmael] on his forehead (37.103). And We called to him saying: "O Abraham! (37.104). You have fulfilled the vision." Indeed, this is how we reward the good-doers (37.105). Surely this was a manifest trial (37.106). And we ransomed him [Ishmael] with a tremendous sacrifice (37.107).

Great stances such as these reveal some of the unique nature of Allah's prophets and the close servants whom He has chosen for Himself and distinguished from other people.

> وَجَآءَتْ سَيَّارَةٌ فَأَرْسَلُوا۟ وَارِدَهُمْ فَأَدْلَىٰ دَلْوَهُۥ ۖ قَالَ يَـٰبُشْرَىٰ هَـٰذَا غُلَـٰمٌ ۚ وَأَسَرُّوهُ بِضَـٰعَةً ۚ وَٱللَّهُ عَلِيمٌۢ بِمَا
> يَعْمَلُونَ ﴿١٩﴾
>
> And there came a caravan[33]. They [the caravanners] sent someone to draw some water, and he let down his bucket; he said: "O good news! Here is a young boy"; and they concealed him as an article of merchandise, and Allah was aware of what they were doing (19).

In the verse above, the Qur'an takes us back to the place where Jacob's sons left their brother hoping that some travelers would help him out of the well and take him to a far land: "One of them said: 'Do not kill Joseph, but cast him down into the bottom of the well where some caravanners will pick him up, if you would do something [to him]'" (12.10). Verse 12.19 tells us that this was exactly what happened. A caravan of travelers arrived to the area and sent someone to get them water from the well in which Joseph was thrown. When that traveler sent the bucket down the well, he was surprised to see Joseph, something that he considered to be "good news." His words "here is a young boy" show that Joseph was a little child then, as we have seen implied by the Qur'an earlier on.

While it is unclear how long Joseph stayed in the well, he was probably found shortly after he was cast there. As I explained in my interpretation of verse 12.10, Joseph's brothers would have chosen a well that is on a travel route to ensure that their brother gets rescued and does not die at the bottom of the well.

The verb أسرّ "*asarra*" means "to make something a secret" or "to treat it as a secret," hence I have translated the clause وَأَسَرُّوهُ بِضَـٰعَةً as "and they concealed him as an article of merchandise," i.e. the travelers hid Joseph with their goods. Exegetes have disagreed about the identity of the plural pronoun implied in the verb وَأَسَرُّوهُ "and they concealed him." Some agree with the old exegete Mujāhid that it refers to the caravanners. The others accept Ibn 'Abbās' view that it refers to Joseph's brothers.

The latter group of exegetes, who represent the majority, think that Joseph's brothers threatened to kill him if he revealed the truth, and forced him to pretend that he was their slave in order to sell him to the caravan. The Qur'anic verse, however, contains absolutely nothing to support this view. In fact, this interpretation reflects the exegetes' influence by the Biblical narrative which claims that Joseph's brothers sold him to caravanners.

I think that this interpretation is completely wrong. I am inclined toward the apparent meaning of the verse that the implied plural pronoun in وَأَسَرُّوهُ "and they concealed him" refers to travelers in the caravan. It is clear that the conjunction وَ "and" links this verb to the plural verb أَرْسَلُوا "[they] sent" which precedes it in the same verse and which definitely refers to the caravanners, not to Joseph's brothers. Additionally, the clause "and they concealed him as an article of merchandise" makes it clear that the reference is to the travelers not to Joseph's brothers.[34]

Allah's words "and Allah was aware of what they were doing" are a reminder that He was present and watching when the travelers took Joseph away from his father's land, that He was aware of everything they were doing, and that they were not able to do anything that He would not allow to happen. This reminder brings to mind what Allah said in a previous verse when Joseph's brothers put him in the well: "and We revealed to him: 'You will certainly inform them of this affair of theirs while they are unaware'." In verse 12.19 Allah gives a reminder that He was present, witnessing everything that was taking place, and that none of those events would have taken place had He not wanted them to happen for subtle goals that subsequent events would unveil.

وَشَرَوْهُ بِثَمَنٍ بَخْسٍ دَرَٰهِمَ مَعْدُودَةٍ وَكَانُوا۟ فِيهِ مِنَ ٱلزَّٰهِدِينَ ﴿٢٠﴾

And they sold him for a low price, a few silver coins, and they were disinterested in keeping him (20).

Note that the words شَرَوْهُ "they sold him," كَانُوا۟ "they were," and ٱلزَّٰهِدِينَ "disinterested in keeping" refer to the same plural pronoun implied in the verbs أَرْسَلُوا۟ "[they] sent," أَسَرُّوهُ "they concealed him," and يَعْمَلُونَ "they were doing" in the previous verse. Since the selling of Joseph occurred in Egypt, as we will see when we study the next verse, it is obvious that the sellers must have been the travelers not Joseph's brothers. This confirms my comments on the previous verse that it was caravanners not Joseph's brothers who concealed Joseph with their goods.

There are three opinions about the meaning of the adjective بَخْسٍ "*bakhsin*," which I have translated as "low." The first two indicate that "*bakhsin*" means "unjust" and "forbidden," respectively. The third and most common view suggests that this word means "undervalued." In the latter case, describing the price as "undervalued" may indicate that it was below the average price of a slave at the time. It is more likely, however, that the meaning is that any fee that the travelers would receive for Joseph would be "low," because anyone who would sell Joseph would inevitably be a loser, for giving away this noble servant of Allah for money. Support for this interpretation of the meaning of "*bakhsin*" could be seen in the phrase "a few silver coins," which emphasizes the cheapness of the price for which Joseph was sold, and the clause "and they were disinterested in keeping him," which stresses the sellers' ignorance of Joseph's status.

Allah then states that this low price was "a few silver coins." The term دَرَٰهِمَ "coins" refers to whatever currency was in use at the time. Some exegetes have pointed out that the adjective مَعْدُودَةٍ "*ma'dūdatin*," which means literally "countable," means "few." They suggest that coins were weighed when they were many but counted when there was only a few of them as they would be easy to count. It seems that the caravanners sold Joseph for a few coins because he had not cost them any money. They had not bought him as a slave, so any money they would take would have been a net profit.

Allah ends this verse by emphasizing that the caravanners' treatment of Joseph, selling him for money, reflects their disinterest in him: "and they were disinterested in keeping him." This underlines their ignorance of Joseph's real status and their failure to treat him as he deserves. This emphasis on the caravanners' ignorance of Joseph's status is an indirect reference to Joseph's great status in the sight of Allah.

There is a great lesson in Allah's test of Joseph, who is noble in His sight, with that temporary state of humiliation in this transient world.

5

Prophet Joseph in Egypt

In this chapter, we will study what happened to Joseph from his arrival to Egypt until his unjust imprisonment.

وَقَالَ ٱلَّذِي ٱشْتَرَىٰهُ مِن مِّصْرَ لِامْرَأَتِهِۦٓ أَكْرِمِي مَثْوَىٰهُ عَسَىٰٓ أَن يَنفَعَنَآ أَوْ نَتَّخِذَهُۥ وَلَدًا وَكَذَٰلِكَ مَكَّنَّا لِيُوسُفَ فِي ٱلْأَرْضِ وَلِنُعَلِّمَهُۥ مِن تَأْوِيلِ ٱلْأَحَادِيثِ وَٱللَّهُ غَالِبٌ عَلَىٰٓ أَمْرِهِۦ وَلَٰكِنَّ أَكْثَرَ ٱلنَّاسِ لَا يَعْلَمُونَ ﴿٢١﴾

And the man who bought him from Egypt said to his wife: "Give him an honorable abode; he may prove useful to us, or we may adopt him as a son." And thus did We establish Joseph in the land, and so We could teach him a share of *ta'wīl al-aḥādīth* (the interpretation of talks); and Allah has full control over His affair, but most people do not know (21).

This verse starts with announcing the arrival of the little child Joseph to Egypt, where he was bought by an unidentified man. The latter took him home, handed him to his wife, and asked her to look after him: "give him an honorable abode."

The word مثوى "*mathwā*," from which مثواه "*mathwāhu*" in the verse above is derived, means "place of living." That man asked his wife to prepare a nice place for Joseph to live in. It is clear from the man's instruction to his wife that he felt Joseph was special, so he did not want him to be treated like a normal slave. Indeed, he followed his request to his wife with an explanation for this special treatment: "he may prove useful to us, or we may adopt him as a son." Every working slave is useful for his master; by saying "he may prove useful to us," the man must have meant that Joseph might be more useful then normal slaves.

This conclusion is confirmed by the rest of the speech of the master to his wife: "or we may adopt him as a son." Joseph must have looked a very distinguished child to the person who bought him that the latter thought of the possibility of adopting him. Many exegetes have concluded from this that the man had no offspring and that he was barren. They also suggested that he was sexually impotent. There is actually nothing in the verse that explicitly confirms any of those suggestions. It is possible that

Joseph's exceptional good manners, beauty, and intelligence made the man think of adopting him.

After telling us that Joseph settled in the home of that man in Egypt, Allah describes that event saying: "and thus did We establish Joseph in the land." The verb مَكَّنَّا "*makkannā*," translated here as "did We establish," shares the same root with the word مكان "*makān* (place)." It is as if Allah has said: "and thus We did provide for Joseph a place in the land."[35]

Note that the word وَكَذَٰلِكَ "and thus" in the sentence وَكَذَٰلِكَ مَكَّنَّا لِيُوسُفَ فِي الْأَرْضِ وَلِنُعَلِّمَهُ مِن تَأْوِيلِ الْأَحَادِيثِ "and thus did We establish Joseph in the land, and so We could teach him a share of *ta'wīl al-aḥādīth* (the interpretation of talks)" stresses indirectly that "establishing Joseph in the land" and "teaching him a share of the interpretation of talks" were Allah's response to the scheming of those who sought evil for him. The phrase فِي الْأَرْضِ "in the land" refers to what Joseph's brothers said in the past: اقْتُلُوا يُوسُفَ أَوِ اطْرَحُوهُ أَرْضًا "kill Joseph or cast him to some land," as if Allah is responding to their plot by saying that "while they wanted to cast Joseph to *some land*, We have *established him in the land*."

The conjunction و "and" at the beginning of "and so We could teach him a share of *ta'wīl al-aḥādīth* (the interpretation of talks)" stresses that teaching "the interpretation of talks" to Joseph is another favor that Allah conferred on him in addition to establishing him in the land. The particle ل "*lām* (so)" in وَلِنُعَلِّمَهُ "and so We could teach him" underlines the connection between establishing Joseph in the land and teaching him "the interpretation of talks." Allah was going to make that place and its special circumstances a school and means for granting Joseph such knowledge.

Some exegetes, such as aṭ-Ṭabarī, have pointed out that the pronoun هـ "*ha*' (his)" in the word أَمْرِهِ "his affair" refers to Joseph who is mentioned at the beginning of the verse. The meaning of وَاللَّهُ غَالِبٌ عَلَىٰ أَمْرِهِ, in which أَمْرِهِ occurs, would therefore be "and Allah is in control of Joseph's affair." I think, however, that the pronoun in أَمْرِهِ refers to Allah, not Joseph, who is mentioned at the beginning of the clause وَاللَّهُ غَالِبٌ عَلَىٰ أَمْرِهِ "and Allah has full control over His affair," hence أَمْرِهِ is translated as "His affair."

This clause is actually similar to the Qur'anic clause إِنَّ اللَّهَ بَالِغُ أَمْرِهِ "surely Allah will attain His affair" (from 65.3); this clause occurs in a different sūra and is unrelated to the story of Joseph. The clause "and Allah has full control over His affair" is a general statement that means that Allah is capable of achieving what He wants, a fact that is emphasized in many verses.[36] However, Allah's affair that is mentioned in this particular place in the sūra of Joseph is what Allah planned for Joseph: establish him in the land and teach him the interpretation of talks. Allah reminds us here that what

Joseph's brothers wanted for Joseph was different from what He wanted, and that it is His will that prevails. Clearly, Allah showed much kindness and care for Joseph and took direct control of his affair.

The clause "and Allah has full control over His affair" continues the talk about what Allah has given Joseph, but it is of course a general fact that is always true. It is a common Qur'anic style to follow the description of a special case with more general lessons that can be derived from it. We will encounter more uses of this style in the sūra of Joseph.

The clause "but most people do not know" refers to people's ignorance of the fact that "Allah has full control over His affair." This is not restricted to the ignorance of those who do not know about or believe in Allah, such as the polytheists. It also includes the ignorance of those who know that Allah is the Creator who is capable of everything, but whose knowledge has not materialized into faith. To this latter kind of ignorance belongs the ignorance, mentioned by aṭ-Ṭabaṭabā'ī, of those who mistake the apparent causes of events for their real causes. They are unaware of the fact that it is Allah who gives a cause its effectiveness, and that He can disable any cause whenever He wants.

﴿وَلَمَّا بَلَغَ أَشُدَّهُۥٓ ءَاتَيْنَـٰهُ حُكْمًا وَعِلْمًا وَكَذَٰلِكَ نَجْزِى ٱلْمُحْسِنِينَ ﴿٢٢﴾﴾

And when he attained his full strength, We gave him Wisdom and Knowledge; and thus do We reward the good-doers (22).

Exegetes have expressed different views about the age that is meant by the clause وَلَمَّا بَلَغَ أَشُدَّهُۥٓ "and when he attained his full strength." Their estimates have ranged between the age of puberty and sixty. Studying the references to the "attainment of full strength" in the Qur'an leads me to conclude that it is the age of reaching mental and physical maturity. Contrary to what some exegetes say, attaining full strength does not represent any particular age. It changes from one person to another, though the average is 16-18 years.[37]

Allah informs us that after Joseph's attainment of full strength, He gave him "Wisdom and Knowledge." The word حُكْمًا "*ḥukman*," which I have translated as "Wisdom," is derived from the Arabic verb for "judge." "Wisdom" is the ability to pass sound "judgments," i.e. the ability to distinguish between right and wrong. "Knowledge," on the other hand, has various forms and kinds. No doubt, the knowledge referred to in this verse includes "the interpretation of talks," so this verse refers to Allah's fulfillment of His promise in the previous verse: "and so We could teach him a share of *ta'wīl al-aḥādīth* (the interpretation of talks)." Fulfilling this promise is itself a confirmation of Allah's saying in that verse: "and Allah has full control over His affair."

Allah's words "and thus do We reward the good-doers" in praising Joseph as one of the "good-doers" show that Joseph adhered to the religion of his father despite losing contact with him since his early childhood. It is possible to understand the word وَكَذَٰلِكَ "and thus" in two slightly different ways. It could be seen as a reference to Allah's conferment of "Wisdom and Knowledge" on Joseph. In this case, the meaning of the clause would be that Allah rewards every good-doer with "Wisdom and Knowledge," although the kind and degrees of these would differ from one person to another. It is also possible to understand "and thus" as referring to the act of rewarding good-doers in general, in which case the clause would mean that Allah rewards the good-doers with good, without specifying the nature of that reward.

Finally, it should be noted that this verse which refers to Joseph's attainment of his full strength occurs immediately after the verse that recounts the purchasing of Joseph in Egypt. This reminds us of the Qur'anic unconventional style of relating stories. It may bypass the events of a number of years to move directly to talk about a later stage.

وَرَٰوَدَتْهُ ٱلَّتِى هُوَ فِى بَيْتِهَا عَن نَّفْسِهِۦ وَغَلَّقَتِ ٱلْأَبْوَٰبَ وَقَالَتْ هَيْتَ لَكَ قَالَ مَعَاذَ ٱللَّهِ إِنَّهُۥ رَبِّىٓ أَحْسَنَ مَثْوَاىَ
إِنَّهُۥ لَا يُفْلِحُ ٱلظَّٰلِمُونَ ﴿٢٣﴾

And she in whose house he was living tried to seduce him. She locked the doors and said: "Come forward." He said: "I seek refuge in Allah! Surely my Lord has made good my abode; surely the wrongdoers do not prosper" (23).

Some exegetes think that the verb رَٰوَدَتْ "*rāwadat*," translated here as "[she] tried to seduce," means "asked gently." In fact, that verb is derived from أراد "*arāda* (wanted)" and does not necessarily imply a sense of gentleness. Indeed, we will see that what that woman did was anything but asking kindly. Thus, the meaning of the verse is that the woman "wanted" Joseph to surrender to her.

The words "and she in whose house he was living" specify the identity of the woman in question. She was the lady in whose house Joseph had ended up, and so she is the one whose husband spoke to about Joseph in verse 12.21. One may think that it is possible that Joseph's abode could have changed during that time. For instance, the man who bought Joseph in Egypt could have sold him later on, and thus Joseph ended up in the house of the woman who wanted to seduce him. What seems to rule out this possibility, however, is that Allah tells us "and thus did We establish Joseph in the land" after mentioning that the person "who bought him from

Egypt" asked his wife to offer Joseph a nice abode. These words refer to the settling down of Joseph in a specific place, which is the house of the man "who bought him from Egypt."

Exegetes have differed in their opinion about the origin of the word هَيْتَ "*hayta*," which I have translated as "come forward." There is no disagreement, however, on the fact that it was used by the woman to urge and encourage Joseph to comply with what she wanted.

Aṭ-Ṭabaṭabā'ī has cleverly noticed that Allah's description of the woman as "she in whose house he was living" implies a special emphasis on the difficult nature of the test that Joseph was put to. As everything was happening in the house of the woman herself, disobeying her was exceptionally difficult. The difficulty is further underlined by the fact that the woman locked the doors.[38]

Joseph's first reaction to the woman's advances was to say: "I seek refuge in Allah." Aṭ-Ṭabaṭabā'ī makes the beautiful observation that Joseph did not reject the woman's request because he feared her husband or because of any usual worldly fears that might develop inside a person in such circumstances. Joseph's reply shows that the real source of his chastity was Allah from whom he asked for help in that period of trial.

Joseph followed those words by saying "surely my Lord has made good my abode." Exegetes have interpreted these words in two different ways, depending on how they understood the word رَب "*rabb* (Lord)" in رَبِّيَ "*rabbī* (my Lord)." This word may be understood as referring to Allah or the lord of the house in which Joseph was living. If it referred to the man who said to his wife "give him an honorable abode; he may prove useful to us, or we may adopt him as a son," then Joseph's words would have expressed his abhorrence at the suggestion of betraying the person who provided him with a nice living place in a foreign land. According to the other view, "*rabbī*" is a reference to Allah, who Joseph mentioned in that difficult test when he said "I seek refuge in Allah." In this case, Joseph's words "I seek refuge in Allah! Surely my Lord has made good my abode" would mean asking Allah for help in that difficult situation, and remembering the favor that Allah had conferred on him when He made a living place available for him.

At first, the verse may seem equally accommodating of both interpretations, and that it is not possible to prefer one assumption to the other. The view that Joseph was referring to the lord of the house not to Allah, however, suggests that Joseph refused to commit fornication with the woman because of his appreciation of the fact that her husband had given him a nice place to live in! The alternative understanding of "*rabbī*" as a reference to Allah means that Joseph rejected the woman's advances because he thought her invitation amounts to abusing Allah's favor of establishing him in the land. This is a wise answer worthy of coming from Joseph. This interpretation of "*rabbī*" agrees also with the way Joseph began his reply to the woman. He mentioned Allah and asked Him for protection against what she was asking him to do. We will see in the next verse that the word رَبِّى "*rabbī*" in the clause "had he not seen the manifest proof of his Lord" also means "my Lord," i.e. "Allah."

There is another fact that undoubtedly proves my conclusion above. There are eleven references, in various wordings, to "Joseph's Lord" in the sūra of Joseph in verses 6, 23, 24, 33, 34, 35, 37, 50, 100, and 101. Significantly, in *all* of these, the referent is Allah.[39]

وَلَقَدْ هَمَّتْ بِهِۦ وَهَمَّ بِهَا لَوْلَآ أَن رَّءَا بُرْهَـٰنَ رَبِّهِۦ كَذَٰلِكَ لِنَصْرِفَ عَنْهُ ٱلسُّوٓءَ وَٱلْفَحْشَآءَ إِنَّهُۥ مِنْ عِبَادِنَا ٱلْمُخْلَصِينَ ﴿٢٤﴾

And surely she set out to do something to him and he set out to do something to her had he not seen the manifest proof of his Lord; thus [it was] so that We turned evil and lewdness away from him; [for] he is one of Our chosen servants (24).

The particle ل "*lām*" in وَلَقَد "and surely" is used for an oath, as if the verse starts with "and by Allah, surely ....." The object of the oath could be the clause هَمَّتْ بِهِ "she set out to do something to him," هَمَّتْ بِهِ وَهَمَّ بِهَا "she set out to do something to him and he set out to do something to her," or the longer clause هَمَّتْ بِهِ وَهَمَّ بِهَا لَوْلَا أَنْ رَّءَا بُرْهَـٰنَ رَبِّهِ "she set out to do something to him and he set out to do something to her had he not seen the manifest proof of his Lord."

Mentioning the woman's action, "she set out to do something to him," before Joseph's, "and he set out to do something to her," confirms that she was and remained the person who maintained the momentum of events.

I have translated the verb هَمَّ بِـ "*hamma bi*" as "set out to do something to [someone]." The reasons for this, admittedly, vague translation will become clearer later on.

The clause هَمَّتْ بِهِ "*hammat bihi* (she set out to do something to him)" clearly refers to actions taken by the woman to make Joseph consent to committing fornication. Exegetes agree on this. In contrast, the clause وَهَمَّ بِهَا "*wa hamma bihā* (and he set out to do something to her)" has seen exegetes split into two groups over its meaning.

The first group think that Joseph did want at some point to do what the woman wanted him to do, although, of course, he did not do it in the end. Old exegetes who are cited in various books as adopters of this view include Ibn 'Abbās, Mujāhid, Qutāda, 'Ukruma, al-Ḥasan, Sa'īd bin

Jubayr, Abū Naṣr al-Qushayrī, Ibn al-Anbārī, al-Naḥḥās, al-Māwardī, and others. There are other reports that distance some of these exegetes from that view. Interpretational details that have no support whatsoever in the Qur'an have been attributed to some of those exegetes. For instance, there is the claim that Joseph had taken off his clothes when he saw the proof of his Lord! In fact, the Qur'anic text indicates in verse 12.25 that Joseph was wearing his shirt when he wanted to leave the room.[40]

The second group of exegetes believe that although the view above of the first group does not accuse Joseph of committing fornication, it does attribute to him evil that cannot be committed by prophets. This second group, therefore, suggest alterative interpretations. Al-Ghazālī, for instance, has suggested that Joseph desired the woman in his sleep, not while awake. The majority of these exegetes, however, have claimed that the verb هَمَّ بِ "*hamma bi* (set out to do something to someone)" has two different meanings when used for the actions of the woman and Joseph's. They think that what Joseph "set out" to do to the woman was different from what she "set out" to do to him. For instance, in his voluminous commentary, aṭ-Ṭabaṭabā'ī dedicated for verse 12.24 more space than any other verse of the sūra of Joseph to stress that "and he set out to do something to her" does not mean that Joseph did any of the things that the almost identical clause "she set out to do something to him" means the woman did. Aṭ-Ṭabaṭabā'ī and others cite an interpretation that is, falsely, ascribed to one Imām stating that the woman set out to do something to Joseph, but he set out not to do anything to her. The flawed nature of this interpretation becomes clear when observing that the Qur'anic clause is "and he set out to do something to her," not "and he set out to do something."

The most common opinion among this group of exegetes is that Joseph set out to strike the woman or push her away from him. Another view is that Joseph's action was to wish that she was his wife, and a third claims that Joseph meditated over killing her. There are others who have suggested that "and he set out to do something to her" means that Joseph only thought of obeying her but never did.

One interpretation suggested by exegetes is that the negation in the clause "had he not seen the manifest proof of his Lord" applies to the clause "and he set out to do something to her." Grammatically, this means that the latter clause acts as the answer to the Arabic word لَوْلَا "*lawlā* (had [he] not)," although it occurs before it. According to this interpretation, the clause above actually means "had he not seen the manifest proof of his Lord, he would have set out to do something to her." This would mean that Joseph did not set out to do something to the woman because he saw the manifest proof of his Lord.

Most exegetes, however, are not inclined to this interpretation on linguistic grounds. They argue that the answer of "*lawlā*" cannot precede but has to follow it. Therefore, they do not accept that "and he set out to do something to her" is the answer of "had he not seen the manifest proof of his Lord," hence the latter does not negate the former. It is true that in the overwhelming number of verses in which "*lawlā*" occurs, its answer follows it. Nevertheless, some exegetes have equally rightly pointed to verses, though only a few in number, in which "*lawlā*" seems to follow rather than precede its answer.

There is, however, an extremely important fact that has gone unnoticed. In all of the four verses in which the answer of "*lawlā*" precedes it, the answer has a negative meaning, whereas the clause "and he set out to do something to her" is affirmative. These are the said four verses:

وَنَزَعْنَا مَا فِى صُدُورِهِم مِّنْ غِلٍّ تَجْرِى مِن تَحْتِهِمُ ٱلْأَنْهَـٰرُ وَقَالُوا۟ ٱلْحَمْدُ لِلَّهِ ٱلَّذِى هَدَىٰنَا لِهَـٰذَا
وَمَا كُنَّا لِنَهْتَدِىَ لَوْلَآ أَنْ هَدَىٰنَا ٱللَّهُ لَقَدْ جَآءَتْ رُسُلُ رَبِّنَا بِٱلْحَقِّ وَنُودُوٓا۟ أَن تِلْكُمُ ٱلْجَنَّةُ أُورِثْتُمُوهَا
بِمَا كُنتُمْ تَعْمَلُونَ ﴿٤٣﴾. (سورة الأعْرافِ).

And We will remove whatever ill-feeling is in their [the people of paradise] hearts. Rivers shall flow beneath them, and they shall say: "Praise be to Allah who guided us to this, and we would not have found the way, *lawlā* (had) Allah (not) guided us; surely, the messengers of our Lord brought the truth." And they shall be cried to that "this is paradise which you have been made to inherit for what you did" (7.43).

قُلْ مَا يَعْبَؤُا۟ بِكُمْ رَبِّى لَوْلَا دُعَآؤُكُمْ فَقَدْ كَذَّبْتُمْ فَسَوْفَ يَكُونُ لِزَامًۢا ﴿٧٧﴾. (سورة
الفُرقَـانِ).

Say [O Muhammad!]: "My Lord would not care for you, *lawlā* (had) it (not been for) calling you; but as you have rejected [the truth], it [the punishment] shall be inevitable" (25.77).

إِن كَادَ لَيُضِلُّنَا عَنْ ءَالِهَتِنَا لَوْلَآ أَن صَبَرْنَا عَلَيْهَا وَسَوْفَ يَعْلَمُونَ حِينَ يَرَوْنَ ٱلْعَذَابَ مَنْ
أَضَلُّ سَبِيلًا ﴿٤٢﴾. (سورة الفُرقَـانِ).

[The disbelievers say]: "He [Muhammad] almost led us astray from our gods, *lawlā* (had) we (not) adhered to them patiently!" And they will know, when they see the punishment, who is most astray off the [straight] path (25.42).

وَأَصْبَحَ فُؤَادُ أُمِّ مُوسَىٰ فَـٰرِغًا إِن كَادَتْ لَتُبْدِى بِهِۦ لَوْلَآ أَن رَّبَطْنَا عَلَىٰ قَلْبِهَا لِتَكُونَ مِنَ

ٱلْمُؤْمِنِينَ ﴿١٠﴾. (سورة القَصَص).

And the heart of Moses' mother became void [because of anxiety]. She almost disclosed it [Moses' story], *lawlā* (had) We (not) strengthened her heart so that she be one of the believers (28.10).

Let us examine the answers of "*lawlā*" in these verses. The first two answers, "we would not have found the way" and "my Lord would not care for you," contain the negative adverb "not." The last two answers, "he [Muhammad] almost led us astray from our gods" and "she almost disclosed it [Moses' story]," contain إن كَادَ "almost," which also has a negative undertone. On the contrary, the clause "and he set out to do something to her" is affirmative. I, therefore, disagree with the view that "and he set out to do something to her" is an advanced answer of "*lawlā*" in the clause "*lawlā* (had) he (not) seen the manifest proof of his Lord," and with the wrong conclusion that Joseph did not set out to do something to the woman.

Understanding verse 12.24 properly requires recognizing that the verb "*hamma*," translated as "set out," indicates *the intention to do something, and starting it, but it does not indicate the completion or incompletion of that action.* In the Qur'an, this verb is associated with actions that were not completed, as shown in the following verses:

أَلَا تُقَـٰتِلُونَ قَوْمًا نَّكَثُوٓا۟ أَيْمَـٰنَهُمْ وَهَـمُّوا۟ بِإِخْرَاجِ ٱلرَّسُولِ وَهُم بَدَءُوكُمْ أَوَّلَ مَـرَّةٍ ﴿١٣﴾.
(سورة التوْبَـةِ).

What! Will you not fight a [disbelieving] people who broke their oaths and *hammū* (set out) to drive the Messenger out [of the city] (from 9.13).

وَلَقَدْ قَالُوا۟ كَلِمَةَ ٱلْكُفْرِ وَكَفَرُوا۟ بَعْدَ إِسْلَـٰمِهِمْ وَهَـمُّوا۟ بِمَا لَمْ يَنَالُوا۟ ﴿٧٤﴾. (سورة التوْبَـةِ).

And surely they [the hypocrites] did speak the word of disbelief, and they disbelieved after embracing Islam, and they *hammū* (set out) to do that which they failed to achieve (from 9.74).

إِذْ هَمَّت طَّآئِفَتَانِ مِنكُمْ أَن تَفْشَلَا وَٱللَّهُ وَلِيُّهُمَـا وَعَلَى ٱللَّهِ فَلْيَتَوَكَّلِ ٱلْـمُؤْمِنُونَ ﴿١٢٢﴾.
(سورة آلِ عِمْرَان).

When two parties from among you [O you who believe!] *hammat* (set out) to show cowardice, and Allah was the guardian of both of them. It is in Allah that the believers should put their trust (3.122).

وَلَوْلَا فَضْلُ ٱللَّهِ عَلَيْكَ وَرَحْمَتُهُۥ لَـهَمَّت طَّآئِفَةٌ مِّنْهُمْ أَن يُضِلُّوكَ وَمَا يُضِلُّونَ إِلَّآ أَنفُسَهُمْ وَمَا يَضُرُّونَكَ مِن شَىْءٍ وَأَنـزَلَ ٱللَّهُ عَلَيْكَ ٱلْكِتَـٰبَ وَٱلْحِكْمَةَ وَعَلَّمَكَ مَا لَـمْ تَكُن تَعْلَمُ وَكَانَ فَضْلُ ٱللَّهِ عَلَيْكَ عَظِيمًا ﴿١١٣﴾. (سورة النِّسَاءِ).

> And were it not for Allah's favor upon you [O Muhammad!] and His mercy, a party of them [the disbelievers] would surely have *hammat* (set out) to lead you astray, and they lead no one astray but themselves, and they shall not harm you in the least. And Allah has sent down to you the Book and Wisdom, and He has taught you what you did not know; and Allah's favor on you has been great (4.113).

كَذَّبَتْ قَبْلَهُمْ قَوْمُ نُوحٍ وَٱلْأَحْزَابُ مِنۢ بَعْدِهِمْ وَهَمَّتْ كُلُّ أُمَّةٍۭ بِرَسُولِهِمْ لِيَأْخُذُوهُ وَجَـٰدَلُوا۟ بِٱلْبَـٰطِلِ لِيُدْحِضُوا۟ بِهِ ٱلْحَقَّ فَأَخَذْتُهُمْ فَكَيْفَ كَانَ عِقَابِ ﴿٥﴾. (سورة غافر).

> Before these [the people of Prophet Muhammad], the people of Noah and the parties after them denied [the signs of Allah], and every nation *hammat* (set out) to seize their messenger; and they argued using falsehood to refute the truth, so I seized them; how [terrible] then was My retribution! (40.5).

يَـٰٓأَيُّهَا ٱلَّذِينَ ءَامَنُوا۟ ٱذْكُرُوا۟ نِعْمَتَ ٱللَّهِ عَلَيْكُمْ إِذْ هَمَّ قَوْمٌ أَن يَبْسُطُوٓا۟ إِلَيْكُمْ أَيْدِيَهُمْ فَكَفَّ أَيْدِيَهُمْ عَنكُمْ وَٱتَّقُوا۟ ٱللَّهَ وَعَلَى ٱللَّهِ فَلْيَتَوَكَّلِ ٱلْمُؤْمِنُونَ ﴿١١﴾. (سورة المائدة).

> O you who believe! Remember Allah's favor on you when a people *hamma* (set out) to stretch forth their hands against you, but He withheld their hands from you; and act dutifully toward Allah; and in Allah let the believers put their trust (5.11).

All these verses use variations of the verb "*hamma* (set out)" that mean to intend to carry out an action and to start it, but not to finish it. It is equally important to notice that the incompletion of the action does not reflect a change in the person's intention, or his decision not to pursue what he set out to do, but rather represents his failure to complete the action because of the occurrence or intervention of an event that is out of his control. This is in complete agreement with the description of the verse of what happened between the wife of the 'Azīz and Joseph. The woman did not have her wish fulfilled because Allah did not allow it to happen, as stressed in the clause "had he not seen the manifest proof of his Lord."

Many exegetes have tried to *prove* that Joseph did not commit fornication by speculating on the details of the event that is described by the clause "she set out to do something to him and he set out to do something to her." This attempt is actually misleading. The real proof that nothing serious happened between Joseph and the woman is Allah's words "had he not seen the manifest evidence of his Lord; thus [it was] so that We turned evil and lewdness away from him; [for] he is one of Our chosen servants." In these words, Allah three times stresses Joseph's purity and vindicates him of any lewdness. First, He showed Joseph the proof: "had he not seen the manifest evidence of his Lord"; second, He turned evil and lewdness away from Joseph: "so that We turned evil and lewdness away from him"; third, He made Joseph one of His chosen servants: "he is one of Our chosen servants."

The details of the events that are referred to by "she set out to do something to him and he set out to do something to her" are unknown. This is why I have deliberately used a vague translation for the verb "*hamma bi* (to set out to do something to someone)." It can be stated with complete confidence, however, that Joseph did not commit the disobedience that the woman tried to force him to do, as clearly indicated by the latter part of the verse which vindicates Joseph.

I would like to point out the precision and beauty of the Qur'anic clause "thus [it was] so that We turned evil and lewdness away from him." By talking about *removing evil and lewdness away from Joseph*, as opposed to *taking Joseph away from them*, the verse emphasizes that it was not Joseph who sought evil and lewdness, but that he was tested with those bad things without him asking for or seeking them.

Unsurprisingly, exegetes have differed about the nature of the proof that is mentioned in "had he not seen the manifest proof of his Lord." It has been claimed that Joseph saw his father Jacob, an angel, or the husband of the woman. There have been other suggestions that have no obvious support in the Qur'an. The arrival of the proof from Allah was in response to Joseph's prayer in verse 12.23 at the start of his test when he asked for his Lord's help against the invitation of the woman by saying: "I seek refuge in Allah." However, the Qur'anic text does not reveal the nature of that proof which drove "evil and lewdness" away from Joseph.

Allah ends the verse with the sentence "he is one of Our chosen servants," explaining His special care for Joseph. Some exegetes read the passive participle مُخْلَصِينَ "*mukhlaṣīn* (chosen [ones])" as the active participle مُخْلِصِينَ "*mukhliṣīn*," which means "sincere [ones]." The Qur'an uses the active participle "*mukhliṣīn*" to refer to those who practice sincerity, but it uses the passive participle "*mukhlaṣīn*" when talking about those chosen by Allah, i.e. when Allah is the subject and those people are the object. Since the station of Joseph in verse 12.24 is that of being chosen, as Allah intervened to protect him from evil and lewdness, the word that the verse ends with must be "*mukhlaṣīn*," not "*mukhliṣīn*."[41]

The "lewdness" that Allah turned away from Joseph is clear, but what is the mentioned "evil"? One possibility is that this word refers to evil that would have happened to Joseph had he obeyed the woman, because her husband was about to arrive to the house, as we will see in the next verse, and would have taken revenge on Joseph. It is also possible that the evil refers to other forms of harm which would have occurred later to Joseph as a consequence of obeying the woman.

> وَٱسْتَبَقَا ٱلْبَابَ وَقَدَّتْ قَمِيصَهُۥ مِن دُبُرٍ وَأَلْفَيَا سَيِّدَهَا لَدَا ٱلْبَابِ قَالَتْ مَا جَزَآءُ مَنْ أَرَادَ بِأَهْلِكَ سُوٓءًا إِلَّآ أَن
> يُسْجَنَ أَوْ عَذَابٌ أَلِيمٌ ﴿٢٥﴾
>
> And they raced with one another to the door, and she tore his shirt from behind; and they met her lord at the door. She said: "What is the punishment of he who intends evil for your wife other than imprisonment or a painful torment?" (25).

It seems that Joseph recognized that there was no point in staying in the room and trying to convince the woman to stop her advances. He decided that leaving that place was his only option.

Unlike the previous events that took place between the woman and Joseph, it was Joseph who took the initiative this time as he ran to the door, with her running after him. Joseph and the woman raced to reach one destination, but they had two different objectives. Joseph's aim was to leave the house and retain his chastity and purity, whereas the woman's was to try to prevent him from leaving and force him to commit fornication. Note how the clause "raced with one another" reveals Joseph's and the woman's keenness on their two completely different goals.

Verse 12.23 talks about the woman locking *doors*, "she locked the doors," whereas verse 12.25 refers to *one door* at which they found her lord: "and they met her lord at the door." It is clear that the term "doors" includes many of the house doors; it certainly includes the door of the room in which Joseph and the woman were, and the external door of the house. Now, if we presume that the reference in this verse is to the door of the room, as is commonly suggested by exegetes, this means that the lord of the house had opened the external door and, for some reason, came to the door of the room in which Joseph and the woman were. The fact that the husband managed to reach the door of the internal room means that locking the doors would have locked people in rather than out; this is most improbable.

The interpretation that I find more likely is that the verse actually refers to the external door of the house. Joseph would have left the room so he could leave the house, otherwise the woman would have kept on following him wherever he went. When Joseph reached the external door and tried to open it, the woman was left with no option but to tear his shirt to prevent him from leaving, as he would not have left the house half naked.

According to this view, the woman tore Joseph's shirt *deliberately*. It happened when he was trying to open the external door to leave the house while she was standing behind him. I think this interpretation is more likely than the classical interpretation which depicts Joseph moving away from the woman toward the door of the room, while she is trying to pull him back from his shirt, and then tearing it *inadvertently*. The Qur'anic text "and she tore his shirt from behind" contains nothing to indicate that the woman tore Joseph's shirt unintentionally. This understanding, in fact, is the result of the common misinterpretation of what happened. Actually, the text suggests that the woman's action was deliberate.

It was clear to the woman's husband who was standing at the door that something suspicious was taking place between his wife and Joseph. The way Joseph looked with his torn shirt and the woman's expression must have made the husband understand what she was after. Therefore, she rushed to accuse Joseph of trying to rape her, and urged her husband to imprison or torture Joseph: "She said: 'What is the punishment of he who intends evil for your wife other than imprisonment or a painful torment?'." This clearly indicates that the woman did not really love Joseph, otherwise she would not have asked for him to be put in prison or tortured.

قَالَ هِيَ رَٰوَدَتْنِي عَن نَّفْسِي وَشَهِدَ شَاهِدٌ مِّنْ أَهْلِهَآ إِن كَانَ قَمِيصُهُۥ قُدَّ مِن قُبُلٍ فَصَدَقَتْ وَهُوَ مِنَ ٱلْكَٰذِبِينَ

﴿٢٦﴾

He said: "She tried to seduce me." And a witness from her own folk bore witness [saying]: "If his shirt was torn from the front, then she has spoken the truth and he is one of the liars (26).

It seems that Joseph's politeness and embarrassment at the situation prevented him from talking first to complain to the husband, despite the fact that he was the wronged person. This is the exact opposite of the behavior of the woman who rushed to make up an untrue story and accuse Joseph of assaulting her. Joseph rebuffed the accusation by saying the truth: it was she who tried to seduce him.

The text appears to suggest that it was the husband who sought to have a third person to investigate the contradictory accounts given by his wife and Joseph. The husband's decision not to accept what his wife said without investigating it first probably means that the situation that he witnessed, what he knew about Joseph, and perhaps what he knew about his wife also, made him doubt the accuracy of his wife's account.

There are a number of different accounts about the identity and age of the witness or testifier,[42] including a saying attributed to the Prophet stating that the witness was a small child who spoke in the cradle. This saying is clearly inauthentic, otherwise Allah would have mentioned in the Qur'an that He aided Joseph with the miracle of making a child speak in the cradle, as He mentioned the miracle of the speech of Jesus in the cradle. Additionally, the very occurrence of such a miracle would have been a stronger proof than the argument used by the testifier.

Note that Allah described the witness as being "from her own folk"; He did not use a description such as "child in the cradle." This means that the witness had been chosen deliberately to be one of the woman's relatives, and that he could not have been a child who miraculously and suddenly spoke in the cradle.

There are many possible reasons for the husband choosing a witness from his wife's relatives. Perhaps, he wanted to limit the spreading of the news among strangers, or ensure that the witness was not going to side unfairly with Joseph for one reason or another. It is possible that the husband already had suspicions that his wife was telling lies, so he wanted to have the opinion of someone who was not influenced by his own prejudice, i.e. someone who would give his wife, not Joseph, the benefit of the doubt. It is equally possible that the woman herself had a say in choosing the witness, and that she wanted a relative of hers. Choosing the witness might also have been the result of more than one of the reasons above.

We come now to the first half of the conclusion of that witness: "If his shirt was torn from the front, then she has spoken the truth and he is one of the liars." Such tearing would have meant that the woman was defending herself against Joseph's advances, and tore his shirt from the front while doing so.

﴿وَإِن كَانَ قَمِيصُهُۥ قُدَّ مِن دُبُرٍ فَكَذَبَتْ وَهُوَ مِنَ ٱلصَّـٰدِقِينَ ﴿٢٧﴾﴾

And if his shirt was torn from behind, then she has told a lie and he is one of the truthful" (27).

This is the second half of the testifier's view. The underlying logic is that if the shirt was torn from behind then Joseph must have had his back turned to the woman, which means that he was trying to get away from her, rather than assault her.

There are a number of points that are worth noting. First, the woman did not deny tearing the shirt, but her explanation for doing that contradicted Joseph's account. The task of the testifier, therefore, was not to decide who tore the shirt, but to find out the reason for that, i.e.

whether she was trying to defend herself or seduce Joseph. Second, the witness did not know which side of the shirt was torn, hence his mention of the two possibilities. This point is dealt with in more detail in the commentary on the next verse. Third, the witness first mentioned the possibility that exonerates the woman. Being one of her relatives, he was probably trying to be courteous.

> فَلَمَّا رَءَا قَمِيصَهُ قُدَّ مِن دُبُرٍ قَالَ إِنَّهُ مِن كَيْدِكُنَّ إِنَّ كَيْدَكُنَّ عَظِيمٌ ﴿٢٨﴾
>
> So when he saw his shirt torn from behind, he said: "Certainly, it is a women's scheme; surely, your scheme [O women!] is mighty (28).

Some think that these were the words of the witness, whereas others believe they were the husband's. I think that they must have been uttered by the witness. Some exegetes have pointed out that the clause "So when he saw his shirt" does not necessarily refer to seeing the shirt but simply knowing its state, i.e. as if the verse says "and since he knew that the shirt...." I find this interpretation to be weak. It is actually the result of attributing those words to the husband, not proof that he said them. The text is clearly talking about seeing visually. This, in turn, necessitates that the observer in question is the witness, not the husband. The observer is described as someone who had not seen the torn shirt before, whereas the husband had certainly seen it when he met Joseph and his wife at the door.

This conclusion agrees with my observation that the witness' coverage of the two possibilities of the shirt being torn from the front and the back means that he did not know which side was torn. It is also logical to think that, having asked the witness to give his opinion, the husband would have asked him also to look at the shirt to form a more complete view, hence the words above must belong to the witness. It is likely that the husband did not refrain deliberately from telling the witness which side of the shirt was torn; it would not have occurred to him that this could have any role in determining the guilty party. After hearing that the witness' conclusion would be decided by the side from which the shirt was torn, he brought the shirt to the witness to see it and deliver his final verdict.

When the witness saw that the shirt was torn from the back, he turned to the woman and said: "Certainly, it is a women's scheme; surely, your scheme [O women!] is mighty." As I explained in my interpretation of Jacob's warning to Joseph of his brothers' "*kayd*" in verse 12.5 in Chapter 3, this word, which I have translated as "scheme," means guile and plotting that could involve lies, as in this case. It was clear to the witness that everything that Joseph said was true, whereas everything that the woman said was merely a scheme built of lies and untrue accusations.

Note the witness' reference to women in general. It seems that this generalization derives from the common belief that women in general have a great deal of guile. Perhaps, the witness used the plural form in order to sound less direct in his criticism of the woman. We will see how Joseph will later become a victim to a group of women led by his master's wife.

يُوسُفُ أَعْرِضْ عَنْ هَٰذَا وَٱسْتَغْفِرِى لِذَنۢبِكِ إِنَّكِ كُنتِ مِنَ ٱلْخَاطِـِٔينَ ﴿٢٩﴾
O Joseph! Turn away from this; and you [O woman!], ask forgiveness for your sin; you were one of the sinners" (29).

Although these words are attributed by many exegetes to the husband, being a continuation of the previous verse means that they are the words of the witness. We will see more support for this conclusion below. The continuation of the witness' speech and the absence of any intervention by the husband mean that the latter agreed to the conclusion regarding what really took place between his wife and Joseph.

The witness asks Joseph here to ignore what happened: "O Joseph! Turn away from this." Many interpret this as an order to Joseph to keep what happened as a secret and not disclose it to anyone.

The words "and you [O woman!], ask forgiveness for your sin; you were one of the wrongdoers" are seen by some exegetes who ascribe them to the woman's husband as an order to her to ask forgiveness from the lord that she worshipped. My view that these are the words of the witness not the husband, however, means that it is likely that they actually urged the woman to ask forgiveness from her husband.

The witness' words to Joseph instructed him how he should handle what happened. There is no indication that they carried any religious connotations. Additionally, Joseph's religion was different from the religion of those people, so the witness was not in a position to give Joseph any religious advice. It is logical to similarly conclude that the words of the witness to the woman represented his advice about what she should do to overcome what happened, and that they did not involve any religious advice. The fact that the witness did not follow up "ask forgiveness" with an identification of whose forgiveness is to be sought implies that he referred to the husband.[43]

The rational and emotionless tone of the speech indicates that the speaker was not personally affected by those events. He was able to look at the whole issue in an objective, factual way that was not influenced by any personal involvement. The speaker cannot be the woman's husband, as I have indicated above.

Exegetes have attributed the husband's decision to keep his wife, despite accepting the witness' conclusion, either to his strong love for her, or his lack of any moral sensitivity. In fact, there are a number of possible interpretations for the husband's strange reaction. If the husband's strong love was the reason for keeping his wife, his knowledge that there was no affair between his wife and Joseph could have been one factor in his decision. That the husband lacked moral sensitivity is, however, not unlikely. We will see later in the Qur'an references to moral degeneration in that society, at least among the upper class.

One other possible explanation why the husband kept his wife could be that she had the upper hand and authority in the house, perhaps because she belonged to an influential family that the husband did not want to lose ties with. This could also be the reason that the husband asked for a witness from his wife's relatives. This possibility also explains why the husband kept Joseph in the house even after he knew of his wife's interest in him. It is clear that the woman wanted to keep Joseph, because she was still interested in him. The husband's decision to keep his wife could be due to more than one or all of the reasons above.

وَقَالَ نِسْوَةٌ فِي ٱلْمَدِينَةِ ٱمْرَأَتُ ٱلْعَزِيزِ تُرَٰوِدُ فَتَىٰهَا عَن نَّفْسِهِۦ قَدْ شَغَفَهَا حُبًّا إِنَّا لَنَرَىٰهَا فِي ضَلَٰلٍ مُّبِينٍ ﴿٣٠﴾

And women in the city said: "The wife of the 'Azīz is trying to seduce her servant; her love for him has possessed her; we surely think that she is in manifest error" (30).

This is the first occurrence of the term "'Azīz" in the sūra of Joseph. Although there is no explicit reference that the 'Azīz's wife is the same woman described in verse 12.23 as "she in whose house he was living," the context makes this fact clear. The 'Azīz had high status and considerable power and influence. The term "'Azīz" means "powerful one," "respected one"...etc. But the 'Azīz was not the king himself, as will be clear when analyzing other verses. Many exegetes have failed to notice this and used the titles "'Azīz" and "king" interchangeably.

This verse informs us that news of the attempts of the 'Azīz's wife to seduce Joseph was leaked to women in the city. One odd suggestion put forward by some exegetes, such as al-'Ayyāshī and al-Ḥuwayzī, is that it was Joseph who disclosed what happened. This contradicts Joseph's modesty and good manners. There is more than one possibility as to how that news leaked outside the house of the 'Azīz. The wife of the 'Azīz could have confided the affair to someone; the witness could have spoken about it to someone who in turn told others; someone else at the house of the 'Azīz who knew about the matter could have spread the news; or even the 'Azīz himself could have leaked the news inadvertently, though this is the less likely possibility.

It is important to note the women's use of تُرَٰوِدُ "*turāwidu* (is trying to seduce)" instead of the past tense verb راودت "*rāwadat* (tried to seduce)." It is clear that they were aware that the wife of the 'Azīz was still trying to seduce Joseph; she did not stop her attempts after the event of tearing the shirt.

The word فتى "*fatā*" means "young man." If it is attributed to someone, as in فَتَىٰهَا "*fatāhā* (her *fatā*)" in verse 12.30, then "*fatā*" means "servant." Exegetes think that "*fatāhā*" means "her slave" and indicates that Joseph was a slave in the house of the 'Azīz. This view might be supported by the fact that the 'Azīz "bought" Joseph. It is also possible, however, for the word "*fatā*" to mean the "servant" who is not necessarily a "slave."

The women's words "we surely think that she is in manifest error" reflect their belief that the 'Azīz's wife was wrong in trying to seduce Joseph. Their criticism of her behavior was not religiously driven, nor was it related to the fact that this married woman was seeking an extramarital affair. As I have already mentioned, that society had very low moral standards. What was wrong in those women's view is that the wife of the high ranking 'Azīz should be interested in one of her servants or slaves.

فَلَمَّا سَمِعَتْ بِمَكْرِهِنَّ أَرْسَلَتْ إِلَيْهِنَّ وَأَعْتَدَتْ لَهُنَّ مُتَّكَـًٔا وَءَاتَتْ كُلَّ وَٰحِدَةٍ مِّنْهُنَّ سِكِّينًا وَقَالَتِ ٱخْرُجْ
عَلَيْهِنَّ فَلَمَّا رَأَيْنَهُۥٓ أَكْبَرْنَهُۥ وَقَطَّعْنَ أَيْدِيَهُنَّ وَقُلْنَ حَٰشَ لِلَّهِ مَا هَٰذَا بَشَرًا إِنْ هَٰذَآ إِلَّا مَلَكٌ كَرِيمٌ ﴿٣١﴾

So when she heard of their guile, she sent for them, prepared for them a banquet, gave each of them a knife, and said [to Joseph]: "Come out to them." So when they saw him, they were impressed by him, cut their hands, and said: "Exalted is Allah! This is not a human being; he is none other than a noble angel" (31).

It is likely that the women mentioned in verse 12.30 belonged to the elite of society and knew the 'Azīz's wife personally. This explains how she heard about their gossip, her invitation to them, and their close relationships.

According to aṭ-Ṭabaṭabā'ī, the women's action is described in the verse as مَكْر "*makr* (guile)" because it aimed at causing a scandal for the 'Azīz's wife. He mentioned another explanation, which had previously been mentioned by aṭ-Ṭabarī, that the women used their gossip to cunningly make the 'Azīz's wife show them Joseph. Al-Qurṭubī mentions a third opinion, that the 'Azīz's wife had confided that matter to the women but they disclosed the secret, hence their action is described as "guile." The verse appears to suggest that aṭ-Ṭabaṭabā'ī's first view is the most likely.

In response to the gossip of those women, the 'Azīz's wife invited them to her house: "she sent for them." She prepared for her guests food, and a cunning plan also. Exegetes have disagreed on the meaning of the word مُتَّكَأ "*muttaka*" which I have translated as "banquet."[44]

Aṭ-Ṭabaṭabā'ī has noted that the order of the 'Azīz's wife to Joseph to join the women is worded as "come out to them," not "enter upon them." He thinks that Joseph must have been in a room located inside the place of the banquet where the women were sitting. Although aṭ-Ṭabaṭabā'ī's observation is accurate, his explanation does not sound convincing. In fact, there are a number of possible alternative interpretations. For instance, there is the unlikely explanation that the room in which the 'Azīz's wife received the women was "outside" the house, say in the garden, hence her order to Joseph to "come out to them." The Qur'an does indeed use the verb يخرج على "*yakhruj 'alā*" or يخرج إلى "*yakhruj ilā*," which means "to come out to," for the coming out of someone inside to someone outside; and it uses the verb يدخل على "*yadkhul 'alā* (to enter upon)" to refer to someone entering on someone who is inside. The use of the clause "come out to them" in verse 12.31, however, could be due to the fact that although the women were inside the house, they had come from outside. The entry of Joseph to the room of the women amounted to coming out of the house to them.

Nevertheless, I think the following deeper explanation is more likely. It is clear from the women's astonishment at Joseph's beauty that they had not seen him before. In fact, their words "the wife of the 'Azīz is trying to seduce her servant; her love for him has possessed her; we surely think that she is in manifest error" do not indicate that they were aware of Joseph's exceptional beauty. Let us remember that Joseph was brought to the house of that woman when he was still a young child, so it is possible that the 'Azīz's wife made sure that no one knew of his extraordinary beauty. Perhaps, she prevented him from showing himself to people. It is unlikely that Joseph himself would have avoided being seen by strangers for one reason or another, and the likelihood is that the 'Azīz's wife was behind him not appearing to people. This probably happened because she knew that if other women became aware of his exceptional beauty they would try to seduce him. The women mentioned in this verse tried indeed to do that after seeing Joseph. If this likely possibility is considered, the deeper meaning of the order of the 'Azīz's wife to Joseph, "come out to them," would be that he should come out not from his room, but also from his hideout so that they can see his beauty.

The women thought that the knife that each was given was for cutting the food, but the 'Azīz's wife had something completely different in mind. She ordered Joseph to come to the place of the women who were deeply impressed when they saw his beauty. The women could not take their eyes off Joseph, so each cut her hand with the knife with which she was supposed to cut the food.

This event raises the question as to how the 'Azīz's wife predicted what was going to happen to the women if they saw Joseph while using the knives! The 'Azīz's wife must herself have had that experience a number of times. She had cut her hand with the knife or got completely distracted from what she was doing when Joseph was around, as her attention would completely focus on him. Note that the verse stresses that the 'Azīz's wife gave *each woman* a knife: "gave each of them a knife." Perhaps, this emphasis indicates that giving each guest for a meal a knife was not the custom, and that the 'Azīz's wife did that deliberately to have all women cut their hands. It is also likely that the 'Azīz's wife ordered Joseph to stay in the women's room for sometime while she was urging the women to have food to make them cut their hands.[45]

What happened to those women, and other events in the story of Joseph in general, suggest that Joseph's special effect was not the result of his extreme beauty only. It is clear that this noble prophet had such spiritual presence that would have influence on all people in his vicinity. Different people, however, were affected differently, depending on their nature.

One reaction that the women showed to seeing Joseph is saying "Exalted is Allah! This is not a human being; he is none other than a noble angel." The phrase حَـٰشَ لِلَّهِ "*ḥāshā liLlāh*," which I have translated as "Exalted is Allah," is often used to deny and denounce something that is deemed to be wrong or unacceptable; this is how it is used in this verse, as if the women denied that Joseph could have been a mere human being. This does not mean that the women really thought that Joseph was more than a human being; their words simply emphasized that his beauty exceeded any human beauty they had ever seen.

Now, does the occurrence of the word "Allah" in "*ḥashā liLlāh*" mean that the women believed in Allah? One possibility is that this phrase is used metaphorically. Such phrases are often used because of their general meanings, which are not related to the presence of the name of Allah.

It is also possible that this is a reference to Allah. That society believed in a number of gods, as made clear in Joseph's speech to his prison mates in verse 12.40, which we will study later on: "You do not worship beside Him other than names which you and your fathers have coined, for which Allah has sent down no proof." It is possible, of course, that the society in which those women lived believed also in a head of gods. This head of gods was a distorted image of Allah whom they would have been called to worship by past prophets. Obviously, the Qur'an used the familiar name "Allah" rather than the ancient, unfamiliar name that the people of the 'Azīz would have used. The Arabs of the Arabian Peninsula before Islam also worshipped "Allah," but they had developed a distorted image of Him that is fundamentally different from the One God whom they learned about through prophets such as Abraham. The Qur'an came to restore the real image of Allah.

Clearly, likening Joseph to an angel was meant to emphasize Joseph's exceptional beauty. As I have already mentioned, Joseph's effect on the woman was also the result of his spirituality, but they were not in a position to realize that.

The use of the word "angel" raises the question whether those Egyptians believed in angels and whether they had a particular view about them. The answer seems to be yes, although this does not mean that the image of angel in that society was close to the Qur'anic image.

قَالَتْ فَذَٰلِكُنَّ ٱلَّذِى لُمْتُنَّنِى فِيهِ وَلَقَدْ رَٰوَدتُّهُۥ عَن نَّفْسِهِۦ فَٱسْتَعْصَمَ وَلَئِن لَّمْ يَفْعَلْ مَآ ءَامُرُهُۥ لَيُسْجَنَنَّ وَلَيَكُونًا مِّنَ ٱلصَّـٰغِرِينَ ﴿٣٢﴾

She said: "So, this is he whom you blamed me for, and certainly I have tried to seduce him, but he has sought protection [from Allah against my seduction]; and if he does not do what I bid him, he shall certainly[46] be imprisoned and he shall certainly be of those who are brought low" (32).

After the success of her plan to have the women cut their hands as a result of seeing Joseph, the 'Azīz's wife responded to their gossip. She said to them: "so, this is he whom you blamed me for," i.e. "this is the beautiful Joseph whom you blamed me for trying to seduce." She meant that had they been in her position, they would have tried the same, as evidenced by the impact that seeing Joseph had on them. This reflects the moral disintegration that had spread in that society, as it seems that having lovers was common practice among women.

Having proved to the women that each one of them would have tried to do the same with Joseph had he been her slave or servant, the 'Azīz's wife confessed to trying to seduce him and that he sought Allah's protection against her seduction. She also threatened to put him in jail and have him treated with humiliation if he insisted on rejecting her advances. It is clear from her threat that she was a woman with power, obviously for being the wife of the 'Azīz, but possibly also because she belonged to an influential family.

The threat of the 'Azīz's wife reminds us of her request to her husband, when he caught her trying to seduce Joseph, to put him in jail or torture him: "She said: 'What is the punishment of he who intends evil for your wife other than imprisonment or a painful torment?'." Her new threat to treat Joseph with cruelty and injustice if he would not obey her confirms that her interest in him was not real love.

Since the threat of the 'Azīz's wife was intended to force Joseph to accept her advances, it must have happened in his presence. This conclusion is confirmed in verse 12.50, which reveals that Joseph knew that the women who cut their hands were aware of the reason for putting him in jail.

قَالَ رَبِّ ٱلسِّجْنُ أَحَبُّ إِلَيَّ مِمَّا يَدْعُونَنِيٓ إِلَيْهِ وَإِلَّا تَصْرِفْ عَنِّي كَيْدَهُنَّ أَصْبُ إِلَيْهِنَّ وَأَكُن مِّنَ ٱلْجَٰهِلِينَ ﴿٣٣﴾

He said: "My Lord! The prison is dearer to me than that which they invite me to; and if You do not turn their scheming away from me, I shall incline toward them and become one of the ignorant" (33).

In his prayer to Allah, Joseph uses the plural feminine words يَدْعُونَنِيٓ "*yad'ūnanī* (they invite me)" and كَيْدَهُنَّ "*kaydahunnā* (their scheming)." He is, obviously, talking about the women in addition to the 'Azīz's wife. One possible explanation is that "they invite me" indicates that the women urged Joseph to obey the 'Azīz's wife, and that "their scheming" is another description of that pressure. The more likely interpretation, however, is that after seeing Joseph, those women themselves wanted to have affairs with him. They could have told him about that when they were in the house of the 'Azīz's wife or through some mediators. What makes this interpretation a lot more likely than the former is Joseph's words "I shall incline toward them." This particular interpretation highlights the already mentioned fact that the society was in a low moral state to the extent that it was common for married women, or at least those from the upper class, to have lovers.

Since the women's "scheming" must have occurred after the meeting described in the previous two verses, Joseph's prayer in this verse would also have happened sometime after that meeting.

Joseph's prayer in response to the threat of the 'Azīz's wife shows the purity and chastity of this chosen prophet. He prayed to Allah to turn the women away from him and let him enter prison, preferring to suffer the hardship of the prison to disobey his Lord.

There is tremendous politeness and courtesy in the prayer of this noble prophet. He was too embarrassed to ask his Lord to repel the women and at the same time protect him from the prison. He restricted himself to one request, as if he prayed to Allah: "turn this seduction away from me, and I will be content to enter the prison."

Joseph's prayer "and if You do not turn their scheming away from me, I shall incline toward them" reflects his reliance on Allah. It is an acknowledgement that his successful resistance to the seductive calls of the women was a gift from Allah.

In saying "and become one of the ignorant," Joseph describes fornication as a behavior of the ignorant people who do not know the right and wrong.

﴿فَٱسْتَجَابَ لَهُۥ رَبُّهُۥ فَصَرَفَ عَنْهُ كَيْدَهُنَّ إِنَّهُۥ هُوَ ٱلسَّمِيعُ ٱلْعَلِيمُ ﴿٣٤﴾

So, his Lord responded to him and turned away from him their scheming; He is the Hearing, the Knowing (34).

Allah responded to Joseph's request to turn the scheming of the women away from him. The verse does not appear to give details about how that happened, but it does say clearly that Allah protected Joseph from the disobedience that those women invited Joseph to commit.

Allah's mention of His Beautiful Names[47] "the Hearing" and "the Knowing" refers to His hearing of and responding to Joseph's prayer, and His knowledge of all that happened and will happen.

﴿ثُمَّ بَدَا لَهُم مِّنۢ بَعْدِ مَا رَأَوُا۟ ٱلْءَايَـٰتِ لَيَسْجُنُنَّهُۥ حَتَّىٰ حِينٍ ﴿٣٥﴾

Then it occurred to them after they had seen the signs that they should certainly imprison him for a while (35).

This verse informs us of the decision to put Joseph in prison. Aṭ-Ṭabarī cites the view that the plural pronoun in لَهُم "*lahum* (to them)" refers in fact to one person, and that the verse uses the plural form because it does not identify that person. I do not agree with this interpretation, particularly as the verb يَسْجُنُنَّ "they should certainly imprison" also occurs in the plural. I think that there were a *group* of people, not only one person, responsible for the imprisonment of Joseph. This conclusion agrees with the king's questioning, which we will see in Chapter 6, of the *group of women* about what happened to Joseph.

It is important to note the use of the masculine لَهُم "*lahum* (to them)," which refers to a group of more than two males or a mix of males and females, rather than the feminine لَهُنَّ "*lahunna* (to them)," which refers to a group of more than two females. This means that the women were not alone responsible for the imprisonment of Joseph. Clearly, they would have used someone with authority and power to put Joseph in jail.

It is not unlikely that this person was the 'Azīz. Aṭ-Ṭabaṭabā'ī thinks that the plural masculine pronoun refers to the 'Azīz's wife, the 'Azīz, and assistants of his. It is likely, however, that the other women also had a hand in what happened, at least in terms of incitement, as they were at the heart of the events. We will see later how Joseph asked the king to question those women about their scheming.

If those plans were put by the 'Azīz's wife, and perhaps the other women also, in order to seduce Joseph, then why would the 'Azīz himself join in the plot? It is possible, of course, that he was merely obeying his dominant wife. The imprisonment of Joseph was also useful to the 'Azīz because it took Joseph away from his wife. Additionally, it is not unlikely that the 'Azīz and the others imprisoned Joseph after falsely accusing him of trying to seduce his wife, and perhaps other women also, in order to distort the spreading rumors in the city about the attempts of those women to seduce Joseph.

Exegetes agree that "the signs" are proofs of Joseph's chastity and his rejection of lewdness. The 'Azīz, the witness, and the women saw one proof after another of Joseph's purity. Note the emphasis in the verse that seeing the signs was the cause for imprisoning Joseph. When the 'Azīz's wife, and perhaps the other women, became certain that Joseph was determined to keep his chastity and obedience to his Lord, they could not find any way of forcing him to obey them other than putting him in jail "for a while."

The said period in prison is that which would be taken for Joseph's determination to collapse and for him to surrender to the women's desires. The time that the 'Azīz was waiting for, however, was different. Perhaps, it was the time that would be taken for people to forget about his wife's interest in Joseph, or the time that his wife herself would take to lose her interest in Joseph. It is not possible to determine which meaning of "for a while" is more likely, because it is very difficult to specify with confidence the stance of the 'Azīz regarding his wife and Joseph in general.

The oath in "*layasjununnahu* (they should certainly imprison him)" refers to the determination of Joseph's persecutors to put him in jail. Imprisonment was a price that Joseph paid for adhering to Allah's commands and refusing to obey the women's call to disobey the Lord. By having Joseph jailed, the 'Azīz's wife carried out the threat she made in the presence of the women: "and if he does not do what I bid him, he shall certainly be imprisoned and he shall certainly be of those who are brought low." Joseph, however, preferred this end to disobeying Allah: "He said: 'My Lord! The prison is dearer to me than that which they invite me to'."

6

Prophet Joseph in Prison

After seeing in the previous chapter how Joseph was unjustly put in jail, we will follow in this chapter what happened to him in prison until Allah conferred on him the favor of freedom.

> وَدَخَلَ مَعَهُ ٱلسِّجْنَ فَتَيَانِ قَالَ أَحَدُهُمَآ إِنِّيٓ أَرَىٰنِيٓ أَعْصِرُ خَمْرًا وَقَالَ ٱلْأَخَرُ إِنِّيٓ أَرَىٰنِيٓ أَحْمِلُ فَوْقَ رَأْسِي
> خُبْزًا تَأْكُلُ ٱلطَّيْرُ مِنْهُ نَبِّئْنَا بِتَأْوِيلِهِۦٓ إِنَّا نَرَىٰكَ مِنَ ٱلْمُحْسِنِينَ ﴿٣٦﴾
>
> And two servants entered the prison with him. One of them said: "I see myself pressing wine," and the other said: "I see myself carrying bread on my head, whereof birds are eating. Inform us of its interpretation; surely we see you to be one of the good-doers" (36).

The previous verse ended with a reference to a vow by Joseph's persecutors to put him in jail. This and the following verses show that they did that.

The Qur'an starts the story of Joseph in jail by mentioning the imprisonment of two male servants[48] in the same jail. Note that the word مَعَهُ "*ma'ahu* (with him)" describes "place," not "time." This word does not mean that the two servants entered the prison at the "same time" with Joseph, but it means that they entered the "same prison" in which Joseph was put. The verse implies that the two servants entered the prison after Joseph; it does not say how long afterward.

In the next scene of Joseph in prison, the Qur'an shows us Joseph being asked by the two men to interpret their two dreams.[49] I stressed in §1.1 that historical events that are successively mentioned in the Qur'an did not necessarily occur immediately, or even shortly, after each other. It is wrong to rush to the conclusion that the two men saw their visions immediately after entering the prison. This wrong conclusion is drawn, for example, by al-'Ayyāshī who thinks that the two men saw their dreams on the night of entering the jail, and that they asked Joseph about their interpretations the following morning.

The two men's justification for asking Joseph to interpret the dreams for them is that he looked to them as "one of the good-doers." The men's realization that Joseph was a good-doer, and their consequent expectation that he can interpret their dreams accurately, must have occurred after they stayed with him long enough. This period of time could not have been a mere few hours. So, even if the men saw their dreams immediately after entering the prison, which is not something that the text suggests, their request to Joseph to interpret those dreams for them must have occurred some time after that, namely after realizing that he was "one of the good-doers."

Note also that the verse tells us that the two men asked Joseph at the same time to interpret their dreams for them, but it does not say whether they saw their two dreams on the same day.

The Qur'an uses the term مُحْسِن "*muḥsin*," which I have translated as "good-doer," to describe the person who has good attributes that Allah wants people to have, such as faith, truthfulness, trustworthiness, sincerity, mercifulness, generosity, forgiveness, and patience. These are qualities that people in general value and like, even if they do not possess them. Most of these qualities cannot be concealed. By their very nature, many of these qualities can be seen in the person's behavior.

Joseph was truly a "good-doer," as attested by verse 12.22: "And when he attained his full strength, We gave him Wisdom and Knowledge; and thus do We reward the good-doers." During their stay in prison, the two men would have seen clear signs of good action on Joseph's part, hence their words to him: "we see you to be one of the good-doers." The qualities above do not suggest that the good-doer is someone who can interpret dreams, so why did the men think that Joseph could interpret theirs?

One belief that was and still widespread among many people, across different religions and cultures, is that there is a cause-and-effect relation between having good qualities and acquiring paranormal or spiritual abilities. This could have been the reason that the two men asked Joseph to interpret their dreams for them. They thought that he had the ability to interpret dreams because he was a good-doer.

There is a more likely explanation for the men's request to Joseph to interpret their dreams. During their stay with Joseph in jail, they witnessed signs of his ability to interpret dreams, perform other paranormal feats, or both. Indeed, in the next verse, we will see Joseph himself mention paranormal abilities that Allah has conferred on him. According to this explanation, the two men's description of Joseph as a good-doer reflects their belief that his good qualities were the source of his paranormal abilities. Note that the men did not describe Joseph as مِنْ

المؤمنين "one of the believers," مِنَ المتقين "one of the dutiful ones," or with a description that attributes his paranormal abilities to his religion, as they were not believers in that religion.

Al-Ḥuwayzī cites the view of some exegetes that "one of the good-doers" means "someone who knows the interpretation of dreams." This view actually lacks any support in the Qur'an. In fact, it contradicts the fact that the words "*muḥsin* (good-doer)" and "*muḥsinīn* (good-doers)" always occur in the Qur'an in the sense that I mentioned above.

Note the use of the word بِتَأْوِيلِهِ "*bita'wīlihi* (of its interpretation)," which contains a singular pronoun, instead of بتأويلهما "*bita'wīlihimā* (of their interpretation)," which contains a dual pronoun, despite the fact that the reference is to the two dreams. The explanation of this is that the linguistic reference to the two dreams is not direct, as the singular pronoun in "*bita'wīlihi* (of its interpretation)" refers to the "subject" of the speech. In other words, it is as if the speaker had said "inform us of the interpretation of what we have said to you," which are the two dreams. It is a reference to the "speech" that contained the details of their dreams.

قَالَ لَا يَأْتِيكُمَا طَعَامٌ تُرْزَقَانِهِ إِلَّا نَبَّأْتُكُمَا بِتَأْوِيلِهِ قَبْلَ أَن يَأْتِيَكُمَا ذَٰلِكُمَا مِمَّا عَلَّمَنِي رَبِّي إِنِّي تَرَكْتُ مِلَّةَ قَوْمٍ لَّا يُؤْمِنُونَ بِاللَّهِ وَهُم بِالْآخِرَةِ هُمْ كَافِرُونَ ﴿٣٧﴾

He said: "No food comes [in due course] as sustenance for you but I will inform you of its kind before it comes to you; that is of what my Lord has taught me; I have forsaken the faith of a people who do not believe in Allah, and who are disbelievers in the hereafter (37).

I believe that the pronoun in the word بِتَأْوِيلِهِ "*bita'wīlihi*" refers to the food, hence my translation of that word to "of its kind." A different interpretation, nevertheless, has also been suggested by exegetes.[50]

In his study of the sūra of Joseph, Ṭahmāz has suggested that the food mentioned is not the prison food, which the prisoners would become familiar with. It is the food that is brought to them by their visitors. The kind and time of this food cannot be expected.[51]

Note that Joseph's ability to know the kind of food that would be given to the prisoners before it arrives differs from his ability to interpret dreams. Both are abilities to know future events, but the former is about gaining that knowledge through interpreting particular signs rather than dreams. This confirms the point that I raised in my comment on verse 12.6 in Chapter 3 that "*ta'wīl al-aḥādīth*," or "the interpretation of talks," that Allah conferred on Joseph *included* but was *not restricted* to "*ta'wīl al-aḥlām*," or "the interpretation of dreams." Allah best knows how many and what forms of "*ta'wīl al-aḥādīth*" He conferred on Joseph.

Since "*ta'wīl al-aḥādīth*" is about knowing past, present, and future events through interpreting various signs and information, it is clear that there are infinite forms of this kind of knowledge. Why, then, did Joseph mention in particular his ability to *predict the kind of food* that would be given in the prison? The answer lies in the identity of those he was speaking to. Joseph who had tremendous wisdom and knowledge was speaking to a drink bearer and to someone whose dream suggests that he was a baker. He was talking to two simple people whose professions were about serving food and drink; there would have been no nearer example to their appreciation than one about food.

Like every prophet of Allah, Joseph was commanded to call people, that is all people, anytime and anywhere to Islam, the religion of surrender to Allah.[52] He did not interpret the dreams to the two men immediately, but started first by calling them to his true religion. He started off his sermon by drawing their attention to a fact that they were unaware of: every kind of knowledge that he had, was given to him by his Lord.

It is not apparent from the verses whether the two men were already aware that Joseph was able, in addition to interpret dreams, to know the kind of food before it was brought to the prison cell. Clearly, Joseph purposefully started off his sermon by mentioning that "no food comes [in due course] as sustenance for you but I will inform you of its kind before it comes to you," in order to tell the two men that this and all other kinds of knowledge that he had were favors conferred on him by his Lord: "that is of what my Lord has taught me." He then told them that this knowledgeable Lord is "Allah": "I have forsaken the faith of a people who do not believe in Allah."

Joseph did not only want to tell his two prison mates that all those kinds of knowledge were from his Lord, Allah, but he intended to use this fact to convey to them the Message that Allah had commanded him to communicate to people. The ability to predict the kind of food, which he purposefully mentioned to the two men, and his ability to interpret dreams, which they wanted him to help them with, are two abilities about predicting future events. The fact that these two abilities were given to him by Allah must mean that Allah knows the future and the unseen. Yet Allah has revealed the tidings of the Day of Resurrection that will happen at some point in the future, so that Day must be a real future event. This is the thinking that underlines Joseph's words: "and who are disbelievers in the hereafter." In other words, Joseph told his two enquirers indirectly that since they have acknowledged that he had true knowledge that they had no access to, they must also accept that Allah is the true and only God, because He is the Lord who gave him that knowledge. Additionally, since they believed that Joseph knew of future events, through knowledge from Allah, it is logical for them to believe in the Day of Judgment which will occur in the future and which Joseph also knew about through Allah.

The people whose faith Joseph forsook were clearly the people of the 'Azīz. Joseph's words, of course, do not imply that he was one day a follower of the faith of those people and that he forsook it later. They mean that when he had to choose between entering jail and following the example of those people, he chose the former. By choosing prison, Joseph adhered to his religion and its high values, and refused to replace it with the polytheistic faith and moral degeneration of the people of the 'Azīz whose religion did not believe in Allah or the hereafter.

It is clear that Joseph had told his two fellow prisoners about what happened to him in the house of the 'Azīz. It is natural for prison mates to ask each other about the circumstances of their imprisonment, but Joseph had a special reason to tell his prison mates about his story. Joseph was a caller to Allah's way and one of His representatives on earth, so it was natural for people who listened to him to associate what he did and said with the Lord that he invited them worship. Joseph must have been extremely keen to clarify to his cell mates that he did not end up in prison because he was an evil man. He explained to them that he was imprisoned because he was a righteous person who did not want to be involved in vice.

It should be emphasized that Joseph's description of the 'Azīz's people as those who "do not believe in Allah" does not necessarily mean that they did not worship a god whom they considered as the head of gods. Such belief, however, does not represent "belief in Allah" according to the Qur'an. The Qur'anic definition of belief in Allah is to believe in Allah as He described Himself, including being *the One and only God*. Therefore, the Qur'an calls the association of another god with Allah as an act of "disbelief," not "belief" in Him. For instance, the polytheistic population of the Arabian Peninsula at the time of the revelation of the Qur'an worshipped Allah. However, because they worshipped other gods beside Him, Allah describes them in the Qur'an as disbelievers, as in the following verse:

وَمَا لَكُمْ لَا تُؤْمِنُونَ بِٱللَّهِ وَٱلرَّسُولُ يَدْعُوكُمْ لِتُؤْمِنُوا۟ بِرَبِّكُمْ وَقَدْ أَخَذَ مِيثَـٰقَكُمْ إِن كُنتُم مُّؤْمِنِينَ
﴿٨﴾. (سورة المجادلة).

And what reason have you that you should not believe in Allah, and the Messenger calls on you to believe in your Lord, and indeed He has made a covenant with you, if you are believers? (57.8).

A similar argument applies to the Qur'anic concept of the belief in the hereafter. For instance, merely believing in another life after death is not equivalent to believing in the hereafter. The latter means to believe in the Day of Resurrection as it really is, i.e. as described by Allah in the Qur'an. I will revisit this point in more detail in my comment on verse 12.39.

وَٱتَّبَعْتُ مِلَّةَ ءَابَآءِىٓ إِبْرَٰهِيمَ وَإِسْحَٰقَ وَيَعْقُوبَ مَا كَانَ لَنَآ أَن نُّشْرِكَ بِٱللَّهِ مِن شَىْءٍ ذَٰلِكَ مِن فَضْلِ ٱللَّهِ عَلَيْنَا وَعَلَى ٱلنَّاسِ وَلَٰكِنَّ أَكْثَرَ ٱلنَّاسِ لَا يَشْكُرُونَ ﴿٣٨﴾

And I have followed the religion of my fathers Abraham, Isaac, and Jacob; It never was for us to associate anything with Allah. This is of the favor of Allah upon us and upon people, but most people do not give thanks (38).

After telling the prisoners that he has forsaken the faith of the people who "do not believe in Allah, and who are disbelievers in the hereafter," Joseph revealed to his listeners that his faith is that of his "fathers Abraham, Isaac, and Jacob." He then went on to describe the monotheistic nature of the religion of his fathers: "It never was for us to associate anything with Allah."

Note how Joseph talks about his father Jacob and himself using the past tense as, he does with his other two forefathers Abraham and Isaac who had passed away: "It never was for us to associate anything with Allah." This emphasizes that his and his father's belief in the oneness of Allah, and their avoidance of polytheism, were as pre-determined and unchangeable as the belief of his grandfathers Abraham and Isaac, who had passed away.

Note Joseph's emphasis in this and the next verse on the oneness of Allah, and that it is the true religion whereas polytheism is a false religion. The oneness of Allah is the foundation of true religion, hence the person's embracement of Islam starts with reciting this Qur'anic declaration of the oneness of Allah: لَآ إِلَٰهَ إِلَّا ٱللَّهُ "*lā ilāha illā Allahu* (there is no god save Allah)" (from 47.19), followed by this verse which declares that Muhammad is a Messenger sent by Allah to convey the message of oneness of Allah: مُّحَمَّدٌ رَّسُولُ ٱللَّهِ "*Muḥammadun rasūlu Allah* (Muhammad is the Messenger of Allah)" (from 48.29). The Qur'an tells us that associating other gods with Allah is the one unforgivable sin:

إِنَّ ٱللَّهَ لَا يَغْفِرُ أَن يُشْرَكَ بِهِۦ وَيَغْفِرُ مَا دُونَ ذَٰلِكَ لِمَن يَشَآءُ وَمَن يُشْرِكْ بِٱللَّهِ فَقَدِ ٱفْتَرَىٰٓ إِثْمًا عَظِيمًا ﴿٤٨﴾. (سورة النساء).

Surely Allah does not forgive that anything should be associated with Him, but forgives what is less than that to whomsoever He pleases; and whoever associates anything with Allah, he has indeed committed a grave sin (4.48).

Joseph continues to stress that his and his forefathers' adherence to the oneness of Allah is a divine favor not only to themselves, but to all people. By making Abraham, Isaac, Jacob, and Joseph prophets, Allah created from among people messengers who taught them about the oneness of Allah, the belief in the hereafter, and all aspects of His true religion. It is in order to cite here the following saying of Prophet Muhammad: "The best that I and the prophets before me have said is '*lā ilāha illā Allah* (there is no god save Allah)'."

Joseph, then, adds: "but most people do not give thanks," emphasizing the fact that most people deny Allah's favor to them, and reject the Message of the prophets. The gravest form of the people's denial of Allah's favor is to associate others with Him. Joseph's sermon to his fellow inmates was itself an act of thanking Allah for His favor on him and his forefathers. It was an act of thankfulness like those that Allah had commanded prophet David and his family, as well as everyone else of course, to offer:

ٱعْمَلُوٓا۟ ءَالَ دَاوُۥدَ شُكْرًا وَقَلِيلٌ مِّنْ عِبَادِىَ ٱلشَّكُورُ ﴿١٣﴾. (سورة فاطر).

Give thanks, O family of David! And very few of My servants are grateful (from 34.13).

يَـٰصَـٰحِبَىِ ٱلسِّجْنِ ءَأَرْبَابٌ مُّتَفَرِّقُونَ خَيْرٌ أَمِ ٱللَّهُ ٱلْوَٰحِدُ ٱلْقَهَّارُ ﴿٣٩﴾

O my two fellow prisoners! Are divided lords better or Allah the One, the Conqueror? (39).

After talking to his prison mates about his true religion and comparing it with the false religion of the people who put him in jail, he called them with "O my two fellow prisoners!" to draw their attention to the comparison he was going to make between "divided lords" and "Allah the One, the Conqueror." Joseph used the indefinite form "divided lords" instead of the definite form "the divided lords" to make his statement universal, so applicable to all gods other than Allah, including those that the prisoners and their people worshipped. Saying "divided lords" instead of "lords" only stresses the fact that every group of "lords" are bound to be "divided."

Contrary to his use of the indefinite form in the first part of the comparison, Joseph used in the second part the phrase "Allah the One, the Conqueror," instead of the indefinite phrase "one, conquering god." Had he said "one, conquering god," the comparison would have been between "divided gods" and "*one god*," that is any god, yet the comparison had to be with "*the One God*." Therefore, Joseph mentioned the name of that one God, "Allah," and followed it with two of His Beautiful Names: "the One, the Conqueror."

He mentioned "the One" to emphasize the fact that Allah is the only God; there is no other god. Describing Allah as "the Conqueror" stresses that He is always the conqueror who cannot be defeated, so the belief in the existence of other gods beside Him is self-contradictory. Since Allah is the conqueror of everything else, there is no sense at all in the suggestion that there are other gods with Him. The fact that these alleged gods are under the control of Allah, the Conqueror, just like everything in the universe, negates any claimed distinction they are supposed to have over other creatures, and any divine qualities they are claimed to possess.[53]

The true religion is the religion of the oneness of God. This is not mere belief in *one god*, but the belief in *the One God*. A person may worship someone or something of whatever nature and considers him/it to be the only god. This is not a form of belief in the oneness of God, but another form of polytheism. To believe in the oneness of God is to believe that *Allah is the One God*. Note that the verse that represents the declaration of oneness in Islam mentions Allah specifically: "*lā ilāha illā Allah* (there is no god save Allah)"; it is not merely a declaration of belief in an unspecific one god, such as "there is no god but one."

Additionally, the belief that Allah is the One God does not mean merely the belief that the name of that One God is "Allah" yet imagine Him in whatever form. The belief in the oneness of Allah means the belief in the attributes with which He described Himself in the Qur'an, as in the following verses, for example:

هُوَ ٱللَّهُ ٱلَّذِى لَآ إِلَـٰهَ إِلَّا هُوَ عَـٰلِمُ ٱلْغَيْبِ وَٱلشَّهَـٰدَةِ هُوَ ٱلرَّحْمَـٰنُ ٱلرَّحِيمُ ﴿٢٢﴾ هُوَ ٱللَّهُ ٱلَّذِى لَآ إِلَـٰهَ إِلَّا هُوَ ٱلْمَلِكُ ٱلْقُدُّوسُ ٱلسَّلَـٰمُ ٱلْمُؤْمِنُ ٱلْمُهَيْمِنُ ٱلْعَزِيزُ ٱلْجَبَّارُ ٱلْمُتَكَبِّرُ سُبْحَـٰنَ ٱللَّهِ عَمَّا يُشْرِكُونَ ﴿٢٣﴾ هُوَ ٱللَّهُ ٱلْخَـٰلِقُ ٱلْبَارِئُ ٱلْمُصَوِّرُ لَهُ ٱلْأَسْمَآءُ ٱلْحُسْنَىٰ يُسَبِّحُ لَهُۥ مَا فِى ٱلسَّمَـٰوَٰتِ وَٱلْأَرْضِ وَهُوَ ٱلْعَزِيزُ ٱلْحَكِيمُ ﴿٢٤﴾. (سورة الحشر).

He is Allah other than whom there is no god, the Knower of the unseen and the visible. He is the Merciful, the Gracious (59.22). He is Allah other than whom there is no god. He is the King, the Holy, the Giver of Peace, the Granter of Security, the Guardian over all, the Invincible, the Supreme, the High; High is He above what they associate [with Him] (59.23). He is Allah, the Creator, the Maker, the Fashioner; His are the Beautiful Names;

Whatever is in the heavens and the earth glorifies Him. And He is the Invincible, the Wise (59.24).

لَّا تُدْرِكُهُ ٱلْأَبْصَـٰرُ وَهُوَ يُدْرِكُ ٱلْأَبْصَـٰرَ وَهُوَ ٱللَّطِيفُ ٱلْخَبِيرُ ﴿١٠٣﴾. (سورة الأنعام).

Eyes cannot reach Him, and He can reach every eye, and He is the Subtle, the Aware (6.103).

هُوَ ٱلَّذِى خَلَقَ ٱلسَّمَـٰوَاتِ وَٱلْأَرْضَ فِى سِتَّةِ أَيَّامٍ ثُمَّ ٱسْتَوَىٰ عَلَى ٱلْعَرْشِ يَعْلَمُ مَا يَلِجُ فِى ٱلْأَرْضِ وَمَا يَخْرُجُ مِنْهَا وَمَا يَنزِلُ مِنَ ٱلسَّمَآءِ وَمَا يَعْرُجُ فِيهَا وَهُوَ مَعَكُمْ أَيْنَ مَا كُنتُمْ وَٱللَّهُ بِمَا تَعْمَلُونَ بَصِيرٌ ﴿٤﴾ لَّهُ مُلْكُ ٱلسَّمَـٰوَاتِ وَٱلْأَرْضِ وَإِلَى ٱللَّهِ تُرْجَعُ ٱلْأُمُورُ ﴿٥﴾ يُولِجُ ٱلَّيْلَ فِى ٱلنَّهَارِ وَيُولِجُ ٱلنَّهَارَ فِى ٱلَّيْلِ وَهُوَ عَلِيمٌۢ بِذَاتِ ٱلصُّدُورِ ﴿٦﴾. (سورة الحديد).

It is He who created the heavens and the earth in six Days, then He mounted the throne. He knows that which goes deep down into the earth, and that which comes forth out of it; and that which comes down from the heaven, and that which goes up into it, and He is with you wherever you are; and Allah sees what you do (57.4). His is the kingdom of the heavens and the earth; and to Allah [all] affairs are referred back (57.5). He causes the night to pass into the day, and causes the day to pass into the night; and He is aware of what is in the hearts (57.6).

Naturally, a person cannot be in a state of belief in the oneness of Allah and polytheism at the same time, because these two states are, by definition, mutually exclusive. What many people do not know about these two contradictory states is that every person is bound to be in one of them at any one time. If the person is not a believer in the oneness of Allah, then he is bound to be a polytheist; and if he is not a polytheist, then he must be a believer in the oneness of Allah. It is impossible for a person to be a believer in the oneness of Allah and a polytheist at the same time. It is also impossible for a person not to be in one of those two states.

Note that atheism is not essentially different from polytheism. Atheism considers material "causes," such as natural laws, to be the real and ultimate force behind events. It suggests that these causes are self-sustained and do not need a god to continue to exist. Polytheism claims that there are other gods besides Allah; atheism, on the other hand, denies the existence of Allah, but ascribes to matter divine qualities, making it an equal alternative to Allah.

Thus, Joseph's words in verse 12.39 are not a denial of the existence of divided lords only, but of any lord other than Allah, as well as an emphasis that Allah is the god who is "the One, the Conqueror."

> مَا تَعْبُدُونَ مِن دُونِهِۦٓ إِلَّآ أَسْمَآءً سَمَّيْتُمُوهَآ أَنتُمْ وَءَابَآؤُكُم مَّآ أَنزَلَ ٱللَّهُ بِهَا مِن سُلْطَـٰنٍ ۚ إِنِ ٱلْحُكْمُ إِلَّا لِلَّهِ ۚ أَمَرَ أَلَّا تَعْبُدُوٓا۟ إِلَّآ إِيَّاهُ ۚ ذَٰلِكَ ٱلدِّينُ ٱلْقَيِّمُ وَلَـٰكِنَّ أَكْثَرَ ٱلنَّاسِ لَا يَعْلَمُونَ ﴿٤٠﴾
>
> You do not worship beside Him other than names which you and your fathers have coined, for which Allah has sent down no proof; The judgment rests only with Allah; He has commanded that you shall not worship other than Him; this is the right religion, but most people do not know (40).

The plural pronoun أَنتُمْ "*antum* (you)" in the phrase "you and your fathers" refers to the two prisoners as well as their people, whereas the word ءَابَآؤُكُم "*ābā'ukum* (your fathers)" refers to the past generations of their grandfathers. All were polytheists who worshipped gods other than Allah. Joseph started by refuting those pseudo gods, stressing that they were no more than names that did not correspond to real divine entities. He explained how this myth developed. The people who worshipped those gods had themselves coined the names of these alleged gods, i.e. they invented them. These pseudo gods were then worshipped by the following generations. Joseph went on to say that Allah, the true God and only source of truth, has not revealed any "proof" that those names belonged to real gods.

It was as if Joseph told his prison mates that the tidings about any god cannot come to people from themselves, as human beings have no way of knowing about the existence of any god. Any such knowledge must come from a god. This god must be Allah.

Joseph then said "the judgment rests only with Allah," before going on to explain that Allah has ruled that no other god should be worshipped because He is the only God.

Joseph describes Allah's command to "not worship other than Him" as "the right religion." He concludes by pointing out that most people are ignorant of the fact that the belief that Allah is the only God is the right religion: "but most people do not know." Note the similarity between the end of this verse and the end of verse 12.38: "but most people do not give thanks."

> يَـٰصَـٰحِبَىِ ٱلسِّجْنِ أَمَّآ أَحَدُكُمَا فَيَسْقِى رَبَّهُۥ خَمْرًا ۖ وَأَمَّا ٱلْـَٔاخَرُ فَيُصْلَبُ فَتَأْكُلُ ٱلطَّيْرُ مِن رَّأْسِهِۦ ۚ قُضِىَ ٱلْأَمْرُ ٱلَّذِى فِيهِ تَسْتَفْتِيَانِ ﴿٤١﴾
>
> O my two fellow prisoners! As for one of you, he shall give his lord wine to drink; and as for the other, he shall be crucified, so that birds shall eat from his head; the matter which you have inquired about is done" (41).

Joseph here uses the phrase "O my two fellow prisoners!" to focus their attention as he is about to change the subject of the speech to move to the interpretation of their dreams. He explained that one of them would end up giving his lord wine to drink, i.e. he would be released from jail and spared any expected punishment, and that the other would be crucified so that birds will feed from his head.

Ibn Kathīr thinks that Joseph did not specify the identity of each person in order not to upset the prisoner who was destined to be crucified. This explanation ignores the fact that not identifying the crucified prisoner would probably have made *both* prisoners greatly sad and concerned, the exact opposite to what Ibn Kathīr thought would happen. The unquestionable proof that Ibn Kathīr's explanation is wrong is the clarity of which interpretation belonged to what dream. It was absolutely clear that the person who was going to serve wine to his lord was the prisoner who saw himself "pressing wine," and the prisoner whose end would be on the cross and have birds eat from his head was the one who saw himself "carrying bread on his head, whereof birds are eating."

The use of the words أَحَدُكُمَا "*aḥadukumā* (one of you)" and ٱلْآخَرُ "*al-ākharu* (the other)" to refer to the two prisoners is in line with the Qur'an's style of using succinct, but clear, phrases and clauses. The clarity of which interpretation belonged to what dream made it possible to use these two words to refer to the two prisoners unambiguously without having to identify them in more detail.

Many exegetes claim that after Joseph had interpreted the two dreams, the person who was going to be crucified said to Joseph that he had lied about the dream, and that he did not actually see it. They say that this is why Joseph said "the matter which you have inquired about is done," meaning that the matter will happen as he interpreted it. Joseph's words, however, were not actually in reply to a comment by one of the prisoners, but an emphasis that his interpretation of the two dreams was true, and that it was inevitable that events will unfold as he described them. He stressed that because he had attributed his knowledge of "the interpretation of talks" to Allah when he said: "that is of what my Lord has taught me." Joseph wanted to remind his prison mates that since "the interpretation of talks" that he had was from Allah, hence represented true and genuine knowledge, his interpretations of the two dreams were bound to turn out to be true.

We will see in the next verses that the "lord" whom the pardoned prisoner would serve was the king. Probably, the work of that person as a cupbearer for the king after his release from prison means that he was simply reinstated in the job that he was doing before being put in jail. It is unlikely for a person that has just been freed from prison to start work immediately as a cupbearer for the king. In fact, the story suggests that both prisoners were in the service of the king when they were put in jail. This is further supported by the fact that this particular prison had a prisoner of another high ranking officer, the 'Azīz, so it was a special jail.

Since the dream of the released prisoner contained a reference to his vocation as a cupbearer, it is probable that the dream of the second prisoner means that he worked in the king's kitchen or was in charge of the preparation of his food. It seems that something that relates to the service of the two men led to them being charged and put in jail. The crucifixion of one of them means that the charge was serious and proven. It seems that the other prisoner was exonerated. The details about the cause of the imprisonment of the two men given by exegetes lack any support from the Qur'an.

It is notable that the interpretation of the dreams occupies one verse whereas the leading sermon with which Joseph started his speech occupies four verses, 12.37-40. This is a clear example on Joseph's use of the knowledge of "the interpretation of talks" that Allah conferred on him in the service of his Lord, inviting people to the right path.

وَقَالَ لِلَّذِى ظَنَّ أَنَّهُۥ نَاجٍ مِّنْهُمَا ٱذْكُرْنِى عِندَ رَبِّكَ فَأَنسَىٰهُ ٱلشَّيْطَـٰنُ ذِكْرَ رَبِّهِۦ فَلَبِثَ فِى ٱلسِّجْنِ بِضْعَ سِنِينَ ﴿٤٢﴾

And he said to that of the two whom he knew[54] would be saved: "Mention me in the presence of your lord." But Satan made him forget to make a mention to his lord, so he [Joseph] remained in the prison several years (42).

After interpreting the dreams to his two fellow prisoners, Joseph asked the prisoner who was destined to live, i.e. the one who was going to serve wine to his lord, to mention him to his lord: "mention me in the presence of your lord." Some think that this request means that Joseph wanted the prisoner to mention to his lord his good qualities and paranormal abilities that he may intervene and release him. I have already mentioned in my interpretation of verse 12.37, however, that Joseph would certainly have spoken to his prison mates about the injustice that led to his imprisonment, so his request must surely mean that he wanted the story of his victimization to be conveyed to the lord of that prisoner. As we will see in the next verses, that lord was the king himself. He would, therefore, be the ideal person to lift the injustice that befell Joseph, as the king had of course higher authority than Joseph's imprisoners, including the 'Azīz. We should note here also that Joseph's request meant that he knew that the king was the lord of that prisoner.

Allah then tells us that as the released prisoner forgot about Joseph, the latter was left for years totally forgotten in his jail: "so he remained in the prison several years." This verse seems to specify the total time that Joseph spent in jail, which means that the entry of the two men to the prison and their subsequent departure, one to his lord's palace and the other to the place of crucifixion, occurred shortly after Joseph was put in prison.

Exegetes have given a number of different opinions about the length of time Joseph stayed in prison, with estimates ranging between one year to fourteen years, and even longer. The word بِضْع "*biḍ'a*" cannot mean one or two, and it is unlikely to mean more than ten. Having translated this word to "several," an estimate of six years would not be far from the truth.

I touched only briefly in §1.3 on a common major misunderstanding of this verse, so I shall now address this issue in more detail. This misunderstanding has been advocated, among others, by al-'Ayyāshī, al-Ḥuwayzī, al-Qummī, al-Qurṭubī, and aṭ-Ṭūsī. It claims that the attached pronoun ـه "*hā'* (him/his)" in each of the words فَأَنسَاهُ "*fa-ansāhu* (but [Satan] made him forget)" and رَبِّهِ "*rabbihi* (his lord)" does not refer to the prisoner, but to Joseph himself. Thus, the "lord" in question would be Allah, not the lord of the prisoner, i.e. the king. It entails from this erroneous assumption that the meaning of the verse is that Satan made Joseph forget his Lord, so Allah left him in the prison for several years in punishment!

In order to justify this interpretation, exegetes have come up with an equally bad claim. They say that Satan made Joseph forget his Lord because Joseph did not ask for help from Allah but from a servant of Allah, as he asked the prisoner to mention him to his lord. Exegetes cite also all kinds of involved stories, whose sources remain a mystery, about an alleged rebuke of Allah to Joseph for seeking help from a prisoner instead of Him. It is not uncommon in such situations for exegetes to seek supportive evidence from sayings that are falsely attributed to Prophet Muhammad to confirm those stories, such as the following inauthentic sayings: "I am surprised how my brother Joseph sought help from a creature instead of the Creator," and "had it not been for what he [Joseph] said [his request for help from the prisoner], he would not have stayed that long in prison."

Those who reiterate such narratives overlook their complete contradiction with the image that the Qur'an draws of Joseph. They seem to have failed to recognize that their claims that Joseph forget Allah — asking the prisoner to mediate for him with his lord, instead of seeking the help of Allah — and was consequently punished by Allah who lengthened his stay in jail, amount to accusing Joseph of falling in the trap of polytheism. This false charge is thoroughly refuted by the Qur'anic text which describes Joseph as one of Allah's "chosen servants." It shows the piety and strength of faith of this noble prophet since his childhood, and his preference of suffering over disobeying Allah.

Strangely enough, many of the exegetes who propagate in parts of their exegetical writings those untrue and unfair stories about Joseph, desperately defend in others their special view of the concept of infallibility that they attribute to prophets and righteous people! The Qur'anic text refutes each and every assumption in those narratives that degrade Joseph's status and behavior, as we will see below.

One wrong assumption that those misleading narratives are based on is that Joseph's words to the prisoner "mention me in the presence of your lord" mean that he asked a servant *instead of* asking the Lord Himself. The truth, however, is that Islam does not consider seeking to achieve something through its natural means as dispensing with Allah. To dispense with Allah means to forget that Allah is the Lord of all means. In fact, it is impossible for a human being to live without seeking to achieve things through their usual means. For instance, a person makes a living by doing some work; does going to the work place, or attempting to convince a customer to buy goods, count as dispensing with Allah, because it does not represent seeking to make a living from Allah *directly*? Of course not.

Islam has made things easier for man, because Allah wants to ease things for people, not make them difficult: يُرِيدُ ٱللَّهُ بِكُمُ ٱلْيُسْرَ وَلَا يُرِيدُ بِكُمُ ٱلْعُسْرَ - "Allah desires ease for you, and He does not desire hardship for you" (from 2.185). Allah has permitted, for example, people to seek the help of each other. He has not described this as polytheism. For instance, the Muslim can borrow money when he is in need. Seeking financial help from someone is not an act of polytheism. Allah has even legislated for the relation between the lender and the borrower.

By saying to his fellow prisoner "mention me in the presence of your lord," Joseph sought help that he knew would not come without Allah's permission. This request is completely permissible. The propagators of those stories about Joseph have forgotten that he was a servant who used to worship and remember Allah day and night, so he was as far as can be from forgetting that everything is ultimately in the hands of Allah.

As already mentioned, those misleading stories rely on the claim that the pronoun in "*fa-ansāhu* (but [Satan] made him forget)" in the clause "but Satan made him forget to make a mention to his lord" refers to Joseph, and that "*rabbihi* (his lord)" refers to the Lord of Joseph, i.e. Allah. The truth is that this clause describes what happened to Joseph's request, "mention me in the presence of your lord," which precedes it. The speaker in the latter is Joseph, whereas the person spoken to is the prisoner. So, the pronouns in both "*fa-ansāhu* (but [Satan] made him forget)" and "*rabbihi* (his lord)" refer to the prisoner.

Note that Joseph's request mentions the "lord" of that prisoner, and that the clause describing the outcome of that request also contains the word "lord." Therefore, the second occurrence of this word must also mean the "lord of the prisoner," i.e. the king, not "Allah."

The Qur'anic text gives another clear proof that the person who forgot was the prisoner, and that what he forgot was to mention Joseph to his lord. It says in verse 12.45 about that prisoner: "and he of the two [prisoners] who had found deliverance and remembered after a period of time," which means he "remembered after a period of time" of "forgetfulness." Satan had made the prisoner forget Joseph's request in order to keep the latter in prison so that his belief might be weakened and his determination might be broken, so he would do what his imprisoners wanted him to do.

This is one of two instances where it is explicitly mentioned that Satan tried to influence Joseph indirectly by manipulating people around him. We will see in verse 12.100 how Joseph describes the division between him and his brothers as the result of "sewing of seeds of dissent" by Satan.

As for the claim that imprisonment was a punishment for Joseph, we have seen one proof after another that Joseph himself chose imprisonment coupled with obedience to Allah over disobedience to his Lord when he said: "My Lord! The prison is dearer to me than that which they invite me to" (from 12.33). Had he wanted, Joseph could have regained his freedom by choosing to obey his imprisoners instead of Allah.

وَقَالَ ٱلْمَلِكُ إِنِّىٓ أَرَىٰ سَبْعَ بَقَرَٰتٍ سِمَانٍ يَأْكُلُهُنَّ سَبْعٌ عِجَافٌ وَسَبْعَ سُنۢبُلَٰتٍ خُضْرٍ وَأُخَرَ يَابِسَٰتٍ يَٰٓأَيُّهَا
ٱلْمَلَأُ أَفْتُونِى فِى رُءْيَٰىَ إِن كُنتُمْ لِلرُّءْيَا تَعْبُرُونَ ﴿٤٣﴾

And the king said: "I see in a dream seven fat cows being devoured by seven lean ones; and seven green ears of grain and [seven] others dry; O chiefs! Give me your opinions about my dream, if you can interpret[55] dreams" (43).

After staying in prison for several years, signs of ease for Joseph started to appear as the king sought an interpretation for a dream he saw. This king was the "lord" of the prisoner whom Joseph had asked to mention him in front of, and whom Satan made him forget to do so. The king recounted his dream to his court, and asked them for their opinion about its meaning.

It is clear from the prisoners' request to Joseph to interpret their dreams, and the king's command to have his dream interpreted, that interpreting dreams was common among those people.[56]

Aṭ-Ṭabaṭabā'ī has pointed out that this verse does not say explicitly that the king saw one vision, so it is possible that the dream that involved the ears of grain was different from the one that involved the cows. There is no evidence to support this opinion. Interestingly, the Biblical narrative indicates that the king saw two different dreams.

قَالُوٓا۟ أَضْغَٰثُ أَحْلَٰمٍ ۖ وَمَا نَحْنُ بِتَأْوِيلِ ٱلْأَحْلَٰمِ بِعَٰلِمِينَ ﴿٤٤﴾

They said: "[These are] medleys of dreams, and we are not knowledgeable in the interpretation of dreams" (44).

In response to the king's request for the interpretation of his dream, the courtiers said that they thought his dream was "medleys of dreams," and that they did not know how to interpret dreams.

The word أَضْغَٰثُ "*aḍghāth* (medleys)" is the plural of the word ضِغْث "*ḍighth*." The latter occurs in Allah's instruction to prophet Job: وَخُذْ بِيَدِكَ ضِغْثًا فَٱضْرِب بِّهِۦ وَلَا تَحْنَثْ "and take in your hand a *ḍighth* (medley), and beat with it, and do not break your oath" (38.44). The word "*ḍighth*" means a handful of something, so it implies the sense of "medley," hence my translation of the plural "*aḍghāth*" to "medleys."

Some exegetes have suggested that the word "*aḍghāth*" implies that the dreams were untrue or meaningless. This suggestion is actually incorrect. The second half of the courtiers' reply, "and we are not knowledgeable in the interpretation of dreams," contradicts the claim that they suggested that the king's dream was meaningless. If that was really what they meant by the phrase "medleys of dreams," then there would have been no reason to say to the king that they did not know how to interpret dreams.

In fact, contrary to what many exegetes suggest, the courtiers' reply indicates that they did believe that the king's dream had a meaning. What they meant by the phrase "medleys of dreams" is that the dream looked for them like a *mixture* of scenes that are difficult to analyze, hence interpreting it required someone with special abilities to interpret dreams. This interpretation is confirmed by the suggestion of the king's cupbearer in the next verse to ask Joseph about the interpretation of the dream.

The word "*aḍghāth*" occurs also in one of the charges that the disbelievers leveled at Prophet Muhammad:

بَلْ قَالُوٓاْ أَضْغَٰثُ أَحْلَٰمٍۭ بَلِ ٱفْتَرَىٰهُ بَلْ هُوَ شَاعِرٌ فَلْيَأْتِنَا بِـَٔايَةٍ كَمَآ أُرْسِلَ ٱلْأَوَّلُونَ ﴿٥﴾ (سورة الأنبياء).

They [the disbelievers] rather said: '[the Qur'an is] *aḍghāth* (medleys) of dreams; rather, he [Prophet Muhammad] has forged it; rather, he is a poet [so he authored the Qur'an], so let him come up with a sign like the messengers of old (21.5).

Note that here also the word "*aḍghāth*" does not mean "meaningless things." What the disbelievers meant by that claim is that the verses of the Qur'an were not revealed by Allah as the Prophet said, but that they were medleys of dreams that he saw in his sleep. The reason for them using the word "*aḍghāth*" is that the Qur'an was not revealed at one time but intermittently over twenty two years. The disbelievers suggested that those verses were merely mixtures of dreams that the Prophet used to see in his sleep each now and then. They did not mean that the verses were meaningless because they were "medleys of dreams," but that since they were "medleys of dreams," then they were not "revealed by Allah" as claimed by the Prophet.

In addition to describing the Qur'an as "medleys of dreams," the disbelievers also called it "forgery" and "poetry," both of which refute its divine source, but do not imply that it was "meaningless."

وَقَالَ ٱلَّذِى نَجَا مِنْهُمَا وَٱدَّكَرَ بَعْدَ أُمَّةٍ أَنَا۠ أُنَبِّئُكُم بِتَأْوِيلِهِۦ فَأَرْسِلُونِ ﴿٤٥﴾

And he of the two [prisoners] who had found deliverance and remembered after a period of time said: "I can let you know its interpretation, so send me" (45).

The clause "he of the two [prisoners] who had found deliverance" refers obviously to the prisoner who was released, and whose dream was interpreted by Joseph as follows: "as for one of you, he shall give his lord wine to drink."

The matter that the cupbearer had forgotten and "remembered after a period of time" was Joseph's request to him: "mention me in the presence of your lord." Satan had made the cupbearer forget about Joseph: "But Satan made him forget to make a mention to his lord."[57]

Naturally, the king's cupbearer was present in the court when the king spoke about his dream. When he saw that none of the courtiers was able to interpret the king's dream he said: "I can let you know its interpretation, so send me," meaning "give me permission to go to someone I know who can interpret the dream, so you will know its meaning." Note how the cupbearer's words reflect his total confidence in Joseph's ability to interpret the dream.

> يُوسُفُ أَيُّهَا ٱلصِّدِّيقُ أَفْتِنَا فِي سَبْعِ بَقَرَٰتٍ سِمَانٍ يَأْكُلُهُنَّ سَبْعٌ عِجَافٌ وَسَبْعِ سُنۢبُلَٰتٍ خُضْرٍ وَأُخَرَ يَابِسَٰتٍ لَّعَلِّيٓ أَرْجِعُ إِلَى ٱلنَّاسِ لَعَلَّهُمْ يَعْلَمُونَ ﴿٤٦﴾
>
> Joseph, O truthful one! Expound for us [the meaning of a dream of] seven fat cows being devoured by seven lean ones; and seven green ears of grain and [seven] others dry, that I may go back to the people [with the interpretation] so they may know (46).

This verse shows the cupbearer talking to Joseph, which implies that the king agreed to his suggestion and sent for Joseph's interpretation.

The cupbearer and the other prisoner described Joseph as "one of the good-doers" when they were with him in the prison; this time, the cupbearer call's Joseph صِدِّيق "*ṣiddīq*," which is the superlative of صادق "*ṣādiq* (truthful one)." The cupbearer addressed Joseph with this word this time because he had witnessed Joseph's truthful and accurate interpretation of his and the other prisoner's dreams, and had seen other signs of truthfulness in what Joseph did or said when he was with him in jail.

It is noticeable that the cupbearer did not tell Joseph that the dream in question was the king's. He asked Joseph for his interpretation so he could take it back to some unspecified "people." Ignoring that important piece of information must have been deliberate. It is not unlikely that the cupbearer refrained from revealing that information at the command of the king, perhaps to test Joseph. We will see in the next three verses that Joseph's interpretation of the dream, nevertheless, had kingdom-wide implications.

The cupbearer's use of the word "may" when speaking to Joseph does not mean that he was unsure of returning to the king with the interpretation. His earlier confident words "I can let you know its interpretation, so send me" show that he was certain of Joseph's ability to interpret the dream. They also reflect his utter confidence in Joseph's forgiving nature, and that this noble prophet would not turn down his request of the interpretation of the dream in retaliation for not mentioning him before the king.[58] He used "may" because of the embarrassment that he felt having forgotten to mention Joseph to the king after leaving prison as Joseph had requested. The cupbearer's use of the word "may," therefore, was out of courtesy and embarrassment.

قَالَ تَزْرَعُونَ سَبْعَ سِنِينَ دَأَبًا فَمَا حَصَدتُّمْ فَذَرُوهُ فِي سُنبُلِهِ إِلَّا قَلِيلًا مِّمَّا تَأْكُلُونَ ﴿٤٧﴾

He said: "You shall sow for seven years diligently, so leave what you reap in its ear, except a little which you eat (47).

Ibn Kathīr has a beautiful comment on the noble character of Joseph. He notes that Joseph interpreted the dream for the cupbearer without rebuking him for not mentioning him before his lord and without setting any preconditions, such as being freed from prison. He even went on to offer advice on how to deal with the forthcoming hardship. Note that this time Joseph did not ask the cupbearer to carry a message to the king about his personal blight, although he almost certainly knew that the dream he was asked to interpret was the king's.

Joseph told the cupbearer that they will have seven consecutive years in which their crops would be in excellent condition. Before moving to the rest of the interpretation regarding the seven years of hardship that would follow, Joseph gave the cupbearer the brilliant advice that they should leave the harvested grain in their ears and not extract them. Exegetes have noted that this would make the grain survive for many years without going off, so they can be stored for use during the years of drought.

Joseph suggested to the cupbearer that they should store all the harvested grain except what they need to eat: "except a little which you eat." The word "little" carries the advice that people should not allocate extravagant quantities of food for their consumption during the good years, so that they can save enough grain for the years of hardship.

It is clear that the seven good years represent the interpretation of the two symbols of "seven fat cows" and "seven green ears of grain."

ثُمَّ يَأْتِي مِن بَعْدِ ذَٰلِكَ سَبْعٌ شِدَادٌ يَأْكُلْنَ مَا قَدَّمْتُمْ لَهُنَّ إِلَّا قَلِيلًا مِّمَّا تُحْصِنُونَ ﴿٤٨﴾

Then there shall come after that seven years of hardship which shall eat away what you prepare for them,[59] except a little which you protect (48).

Joseph interpreted the symbols of the "seven lean cows" and "seven dry ears of grain" as "seven years of hardship," i.e. of little good. The eating of the fat cows by the lean cows, and the following of the green ears with dry ones, were interpreted as meaning that the hard years would follow the good ones.

The hardship Joseph referred to is drought, as we will see in the next verse. Therefore, "protection" in this verse probably means providing water for the plants during the years of drought.

So, the verse means: "after the seven good years, there will be seven years of drought. During the latter, all your plants will die, except a few which could be protected from drought by providing them with water, so they will grow, and you will be able to harvest them."

ثُمَّ يَأْتِى مِنۢ بَعْدِ ذَٰلِكَ عَامٌ فِيهِ يُغَاثُ ٱلنَّاسُ وَفِيهِ يَعْصِرُونَ ﴿٤٩﴾
Then there shall come after that a year in which people shall be helped with rain, and in which they shall press [crops]" (49).

The verb يُغَاثُ "*yughāthu*" means "be helped." It can be used for any kind of help.[60] The related noun غيث "*ghayth*" is often used for "rain," for "*ghayth*" is the help that comes to rescue plants, and consequently people, from death, as we can see in the following verse:

وَهُوَ الَّذِي يُنَزِّلُ الْغَيْثَ مِن بَعْدِ مَا قَنَطُوا وَيَنشُرُ رَحْمَتَهُ وَهُوَ الْوَلِيُّ الْحَمِيدُ ﴿٢٨﴾. (سورة الشورى).

And it is He who sends down the *ghayth* (rain) after they [people] have despaired, and unfolds His mercy; and He is the Guardian, the Praised One (42.28).

Since the previous verses of the sūra of Joseph talk about plants and the years of prosperity and hardship, it is clear that the help that the verb "*yughāthu*" in verse 12.49 refers to is the falling of rain, hence my translation: "be helped with rain." So, Joseph told the cupbearer that the seven years of drought would be followed by a year of abundant rain.[61]

One indication that the help in this context means the sending of rain is Joseph's description of the year of rain as "in which they shall press." Most exegetes think that this refers to the pressing of various crops such as grapes, dates, olives, and sesame seed. It is likely that the pressing of crops used to occur only in years when there is an unusual abundance of harvest, so Joseph's words were a reference to the abundance of rain and, consequently, crops in that year. Some exegetes have indicated that pressing could include milking cattle, but I do not think that the text lends support to this interpretation.[62]

Clearly, Joseph's interpretation that the seven years of hardship will be followed by a year of abundant rain had no *apparent* symbol in the dream of the king. This proves that the interpretation of dreams, which is one form of the interpretation of talks that Allah conferred on Joseph, is not mere matching of explicit symbols in dreams with their referents in the real world. Contrary to what is believed by the overwhelming majority of people, including exegetes of the Qur'an and scholars in various fields, *symbols in dreams do not have fixed meanings, but they have special meanings in each dream*. In other words, it is wrong to say in general that a "fat cow" in a dream represents a "good year," or even that a "cow" refers to a "year." Books on the interpretation of dreams which assign specific referents to symbols are based on a totally flawed assumption.

Every form of the interpretation of talks, including the interpretation of dreams, is a special ability to recognize the meanings that symbols may take in specific contexts. *The meaning of a particular symbol depends on the context in which it appears*, hence it is unlikely for one symbol to have the same meaning in different contexts, such as different dreams. It is almost certain that, for instance, in another dream, a "cow" would not stand for a "year," and a "fat cow" would not refer to a "good year."

This means that it is not possible to learn the interpretation of dreams without having the special talent required for that. Similarly, the person who has this knowledge *cannot teach* it to others, because it is not a mere rational science like most sciences. This is contrary to the belief of most people and authors of books about the interpretation of dreams.[63]

> وَقَالَ ٱلْمَلِكُ ٱئْتُونِى بِهِۦ فَلَمَّا جَآءَهُ ٱلرَّسُولُ قَالَ ٱرْجِعْ إِلَىٰ رَبِّكَ فَسْـَٔلْهُ مَا بَالُ ٱلنِّسْوَةِ ٱلَّـٰتِى قَطَّعْنَ أَيْدِيَهُنَّ إِنَّ رَبِّى بِكَيْدِهِنَّ عَلِيمٌ ﴿٥٠﴾
>
> And the king said: "Bring him [Joseph] to me." So when the messenger came to him [Joseph], he [Joseph] said: "Go back to your lord and ask him what the matter of the women who cut their hands is; certainly my Lord is aware of their guile" (50).

When the cupbearer reported back to his lord Joseph's interpretation of his dream, the king ordered for Joseph to be brought to him. It is clear that Joseph's interpretation made the king at least curious, so he wanted to ask Joseph directly about his dream. The king probably became convinced that Joseph was indeed credible as described by his cupbearer. He wanted to meet Joseph and honor him.

When the messenger of the king came to take Joseph to his lord, Joseph refused to go with him and asked him to return with a message, which is to ask the king about: "the matter of the women who cut their hands." This is a request for the king to intervene and investigate the story of the women who cut their hands. Aṭ-Ṭabaṭabā'ī noted that the king wanted to see Joseph in order to honor him, not only to meet him and then send him back to prison; this is why Joseph was able to ask for a favor from the king before carrying out his order to go and meet him.

Clearly, both Joseph and the messenger of the king were aware that the king had intended good for Joseph. Otherwise, Joseph would not have put a request instead of carrying out the king's order immediately, and the king's messenger would have forced Joseph to go to the king instead of going back to his lord without him.

Joseph requested the enquiry from the king in order to exonerate himself of any charges that his persecutors had leveled at him. No doubt, Joseph's aim here is the same one that made him explain to his prison mates the circumstances of his imprisonment, which I discussed in my interpretation of verse 12.37. Since Joseph was a caller to Allah, he was keen that people would not associate with Allah any misconduct that was unjustly ascribed to him. He worked hard to refute the charges that were unfairly leveled at him and to tell people, in word and deed, that Allah calls people to righteous deeds and noble behavior:

ٱلشَّيۡطَٰنُ يَعِدُكُمُ ٱلۡفَقۡرَ وَيَأۡمُرُكُم بِٱلۡفَحۡشَآءِۖ وَٱللَّهُ يَعِدُكُم مَّغۡفِرَةً مِّنۡهُ وَفَضۡلًاۗ وَٱللَّهُ وَٰسِعٌ عَلِيمٌ ﴿٢٦٨﴾. (سورة البَقَرة).

Satan promises you [O you who believe!] poverty and enjoins on you lewdness, but Allah promises you forgiveness from Himself and favor; and Allah is Encompassing, Knowing (2.268).

وَإِذَا فَعَلُواْ فَٰحِشَةً قَالُواْ وَجَدۡنَا عَلَيۡهَآ ءَابَآءَنَا وَٱللَّهُ أَمَرَنَا بِهَاۗ قُلۡ إِنَّ ٱللَّهَ لَا يَأۡمُرُ بِٱلۡفَحۡشَآءِۖ أَتَقُولُونَ عَلَى ٱللَّهِ مَا لَا تَعۡلَمُونَ ﴿٢٨﴾. (سورة الأعراف).

And when they [the disbelievers] commit a lewd act, they say: "We found our fathers doing this, and Allah has enjoined it on us." Say [O Muhammad!]: "Surely Allah does not enjoin lewdness; do you say against Allah what you do not know?" (7.28).

Aṭ-Ṭabaṭabā'ī acknowledges that Joseph's words "certainly my Lord is aware of their guile" imply a complaint. He also claims, however, that Joseph refrained from accusing those women of anything, restricting himself to requesting the king to investigate what happened. This interpretation is in fact self-contradictory, because Joseph's very request for the king to conduct an investigation into the women's role implies a clear accusation of the latter. In fact, Joseph's words "certainly my Lord is aware of their guile" leave no doubt that he was complaining to the king about the injustice that those women subjected him to.

Additionally, we will see in the next verse that the king started his enquiry by asking the women: "What was your matter when you tried to seduce Joseph?", which clearly indicates that he had information about the injustice of those women toward Joseph even before speaking to them. Obviously, this information would have been revealed by Joseph to the king through his messenger. In fact, Joseph's description of the women as those "who cut their hands" means that he disclosed to the king's messenger what happened at the 'Azīz's house and how those women cut their hands. The cupbearer was aware of at least some if not all the details of how Joseph was put in jail. I have already pointed out that Joseph would have certainly told the two prisoners about his story to emphasize his chastity and the purity of his religion. He could have reminded him of the story or given him more details, to convey to the king, when he visited him in the prison.

Note that Joseph did not attribute the guile that he suffered to the 'Azīz's wife only, but to all "the women who cut their hands." As I have already mentioned in my interpretation of verse 12.35, "then it occurred to them after they had seen the signs that they should certainly imprison him for a while," the plural pronoun indicates that the women were involved in the plot to put Joseph in prison. I have highlighted this also in my comment on verse 12.33: "He said: 'My Lord! The prison is dearer to me than that which they invite me to; and if You do not turn their scheming away from me, I shall incline toward them and become one of the ignorant'."

Clearly, Joseph gave the messenger of the king information about the identity of those women for the king to question them. It may be suggested that the clause "the women who cut their hands" did not include the 'Azīz's wife. Joseph's possible exclusion of the latter could have been to make the king hear what the other women had to say before she intervenes and makes the women lie in their testimonies. It is more likely, however, that Joseph's words included the 'Azīz's wife also. He did not name her explicitly because he did not distinguish between her and the other women, as they all partook in the scheme against him. The details of the story also necessitated calling the 'Azīz's wife, because she was one of the main characters in that story and the lady of the house where everything took place.

Clearly, one reason for Joseph asking for the testimony of the women who cut their hands is that they witnessed the vow of the 'Azīz's wife to put him in prison if he would not obey her. They also wanted to seduce him, i.e. they were involved in putting him in jail.

I have already pointed out in my interpretation of the verse "then it occurred to them after they had seen the signs that they should certainly imprison him for a while" that a man, probably the 'Azīz, was involved in the plot to put Joseph in prison; so why did Joseph not ask for the testimony of the 'Azīz also? Perhaps, the 'Azīz died when Joseph was in jail. Another possibility is that the women were the main culprits in putting him in jail.

قَالَ مَا خَطْبُكُنَّ إِذْ رَٰوَدتُّنَّ يُوسُفَ عَن نَّفْسِهِۦ ۚ قُلْنَ حَٰشَ لِلَّهِ مَا عَلِمْنَا عَلَيْهِ مِن سُوٓءٍ ۚ قَالَتِ ٱمْرَأَتُ ٱلْعَزِيزِ
ٱلْـَٔـٰنَ حَصْحَصَ ٱلْحَقُّ أَنَا۠ رَٰوَدتُّهُۥ عَن نَّفْسِهِۦ وَإِنَّهُۥ لَمِنَ ٱلصَّـٰدِقِينَ ﴿٥١﴾

He [the king] said: "What was your matter when you tried to seduce Joseph?" They said: "Exalted is Allah! We knew of no evil on him." The wife of the 'Azīz said: "Now the truth has become manifest; I tried to seduce him, and he is surely of the truthful ones (51).

When the messenger of the king returned to his lord with Joseph's request to investigate the injustice that occurred to him, the king called the women and asked them: "What was your matter when you tried to seduce Joseph?" Exegetes think that this question means "what happened when you tried to seduce Joseph?" They also agree that the women's reply, "Exalted is Allah! We knew of no evil on him," means: "Exalted is Allah! Joseph has not committed any evil." In other words, the king's question was about what Joseph did when the women tried to seduce him, and the women answered that Joseph did not commit any lewdness. I think that these interpretations of the question and the answer are both completely wrong.

Let us study first the king's question: "What was your matter when you tried to seduce Joseph?" Exegetes have unduly focused on the king's words "when you tried to seduce Joseph," thus failing to notice that the king's question is actually restricted to the phrase "What was your matter." The latter is a question to the women about details of what *they did* when they tried to seduce Joseph, not about *Joseph's reaction* to their attempt. The king's words "when you tried to seduce Joseph" clearly treat the women's attempt to seduce Joseph as an undisputable fact. The occurrence of this phrase after the question is intended to specify the context of the scheming of the women, whereas the question itself was about the details of that scheming. So, the meaning of the king's question is: "what is the story of your scheme when you tried to seduce Joseph?"

We have seen in the previous verse that Joseph informed the king's messenger about the scheming of the women, and asked him to take his complaint to the king to investigate the matter. Calling the woman for an investigation means that the king did respond to Joseph's request. His words "what was your matter when you tried to seduce Joseph?" must be an interrogative question to the women about what they plotted against Joseph, not about Joseph's reaction to their seductive attempt! Thus, quizzing the women was in itself an acceptance by the king of Joseph's claim that the women plotted against him. How could the king, then, ask the women about what Joseph did as if he had any confidence in them? How silly would the king's question have been if it meant "what did

Joseph do when you tried to seduce him?", as if the king was not interested in the fact that the women tried to seduce Joseph, but focused all his attention on learning what Joseph's reaction was, and, on top of that, sought to know that from the accused women themselves!

Let us move now to the women's reply to the king: "Exalted is Allah! We knew of no evil on him." As I have already mentioned, exegetes wrongly think that this is the women's reply to the king's question about Joseph's reaction to their attempt to seduce him. Exegetes think that the women's exonerative phrase "exalted is Allah!" referred to Joseph, and that their reply "we knew of no evil on him" was a declaration that Joseph did not do anything evil. Note that this common misinterpretation of the women's reply is based on the common misinterpretation of the king's question which I discussed above. The king's question, as I have shown, was a quiz to the women which the king instigated in response to Joseph's request and his claim about their scheming; how could the women's reply, then, be praise for Joseph? Additionally, what would the women gain from defending Joseph?

The common interpretation of the women's reply means that instead of defending themselves against Joseph's accusation that they tried to seduce him, which the king has obviously accepted, they defended Joseph against any accusation and praised his character! In fact, this interpretation makes the women's reply imply a clear confession that they did wrong Joseph! Clearly, this does not make sense, so the common interpretation of the women's reply cannot be true, as the common interpretation of the king's question is wrong. What is then the right interpretation of the women's reply?

As I have shown, the king's question to the women was about what they did to Joseph, not what the latter did. Their answer must have been a denial of the charge of plotting against Joseph. In light of this, I can present my interpretation for the women's reply to the king: "Exalted is Allah! We knew of no evil on him." With the negatory and denouncing phrase "exalted is Allah!," the women *did not mean to exonerate Joseph but themselves*. That phrase is a *general* denial of the accusation put to them by the king. The rest of their reply, "we knew of no evil on him," is a *specific* denial of the charge that they were aware of, hence involved in, the subjection of Joseph to any evil. So, the women's reply to the king's accusatory question was to deny that they attempted to seduce Joseph or played any role in putting him in jail.

This logical interpretation agrees completely with this verse in particular and the story in general. It is also consistent with the behavior of those women who never intended good for Joseph. The view that exegetes have agreed on that "we knew of no evil on him" is an exoneration of Joseph from evil is unfounded and not in line with the king's question which carries an accusation to the women. It also contradicts the Qur'an's image of the behavior of those women.

One reason for the exegete's misinterpretation of the women's words مَا عَلِمْنَا عَلَيْهِ مِن سُوءٍ "*mā 'alimnā 'alayhi min sū'* (we knew of no evil on him)" is their failure to understand the meaning of the combination of the noun سُوءٍ "*sū'* (evil)" and the preposition على "*'alā* (on)." The combination of these two words refers to the befalling of evil *on* a person, *not its perpetration by* him.[64]

Let me summarize my interpretation of "He [the king] said: 'What was your matter when you tried to seduce Joseph?'. They said: 'Exalted is Allah! We knew of no evil on him'." This verse starts with the king's investigative question to the women about the scheming they did to Joseph when they tried to seduce him. The king's words reflect his acceptance of Joseph's account of events. The women's answer was to deny doing any evil to Joseph. They started by saying "Exalted is Allah!," exonerating themselves. They followed that by denying any knowledge of the subjection of Joseph to injustice.

Note how this interpretation clarifies the context of the reply of the 'Azīz's wife which followed the women's: "Now the truth has become manifest; I tried to seduce him, and he is surely of the truthful ones." In contrast to the women who denied what had really occurred, the 'Azīz's wife decided to tell the truth. She started with "now the truth has become manifest," which means that the truth has become clear after a period of time during which it remained unknown. Then she said: "I tried to seduce him," as if she wanted to say: "although these women have denied trying to seduce Joseph, I would like to confess to doing that." She followed that with the statement "and he is surely of the truthful ones" which contradicts the women's accusation of Joseph of telling lies, and in which she confesses that Joseph is truthful in accusing them of plotting against him and being involved in his imprisonment.

Clearly, the reply of the 'Azīz's wife sounds as if it followed something that had an opposite meaning. This would not have been the case if the women's reply exonerated Joseph. Understanding the women's reply as exoneration of themselves and accusation for Joseph of telling lies explains the contrasting tone of the reply of the 'Azīz's wife.

Finally, it is worth noting the mistake of some exegetes who think that the king was the 'Azīz himself and that, accordingly, the 'Azīz's wife was in fact the king's wife. The reference of this verse to that woman as "the 'Azīz's wife" combined with the reference of the previous verse to the ruling monarch as the "king" makes it clear that this view is completely wrong. The story itself does not allow for this interpretation.

ذَٰلِكَ لِيَعْلَمَ أَنِّى لَمْ أَخُنْهُ بِٱلْغَيْبِ وَأَنَّ ٱللَّهَ لَا يَهْدِى كَيْدَ ٱلْخَآئِنِينَ ﴿٥٢﴾
That [I said], so that he knows that I have not betrayed him in his absence, and because Allah does not guide the device of the betrayers (52).

Exegetes have differed about the identity of the person who said these words. One group suggested that it was Joseph. Thus, "that" would refer to Joseph's request to the king to investigate the matter of the women. The statement "so that he knows that I have not betrayed him in his absence, and because Allah does not guide the device of the betrayers" would then be a comment on the reply of the women and the 'Azīz's wife to the king's question. According to this view, the implicit singular masculine pronouns in the verb لِيَعْلَمَ "*liya'lama* (so that he knows)" and the explicit one in أَخُنْهُ "*akhunhu* (betrayed him)" refer to the woman's husband, i.e. the 'Azīz. Consequently, Joseph's words "that, so that he knows that I have not betrayed him" mean "I have asked for a probe into what the women did so that the woman's husband would know that I did not betray him with his wife in his absence."

This interpretation has a significant implication. Since the verse "so that he knows that I have not betrayed him" refers to a person without specifying his identity, that identity must have been referred to explicitly in Joseph's earlier speech: "Go back to your lord and ask him what the matter of the women who cut their hands is; certainly my Lord is aware of their guile." This in turn means that the person referred to is "the lord of the messenger of the king," i.e. the king himself. Therefore, the king must be the 'Azīz himself. This is indeed what some exegetes believe, but it is totally wrong as I have already shown. The king who questioned the women cannot be the 'Azīz whom we met early in the sūra and in whose home Joseph lived.

Attributing the words in verse 12.52 to Joseph is based on the assumption that the 'Azīz was unaware of Joseph's innocence from his wife's accusation of him. This assumption can only be wrong. It suffices to remember that the 'Azīz found Joseph trying to run away from his wife, and that the witness testified that it was she who tried to seduce Joseph and that he rejected her advances. The Qur'anic account of what the 'Azīz's wife did to Joseph leaves no doubt that the 'Azīz was fully aware that Joseph was innocent and that it was his wife who was in the wrong. The confession of the 'Azīz's wife in the previous verse that she tried to seduce Joseph could not have been what made the 'Azīz know that Joseph did not betray him with his wife, as assumed by the misinterpretation above.

This interpretation also fails completely to explain the presence of the word بِالْغَيْبِ "*bilghaybi* (in [his] absence)." Naturally, any marital unfaithfulness is bound to happen in the absence of the husband, so that word would obviously be out of context.

The alternative interpretation which has been adopted by the other exegetes, and which I think is the right one, is that "that [I said], so that he knows that I have not betrayed him in his absence, and because Allah does not guide the device of the betrayers" actually represent the words of the 'Azīz's wife, not Joseph. Note that there is no indication that the speaker in this verse is different from the speaker in the previous verse, i.e. the 'Azīz's wife, though this alone does not necessarily mean that the speaker has not changed.

The main point here is that it is clear from the context that this verse is a continuation of the speech of the 'Azīz's wife in the previous verse. The word ذَٰلِكَ "*dhālika* (that [I said])" refers to her confession "now the truth has become manifest; I tried to seduce him, and he is surely of the truthful ones," i.e. as if she is saying that the reason for her confession is "so that he knows that I have not betrayed him in his absence, and because Allah does not guide the device of the betrayers." The pronouns in "*liya'lama* (so that he knows)" and "*akhunhu* (betrayed him)" certainly refer to Joseph. The reason for the woman's use of the word "*bilghaybi* (in [his] absence)" is that Joseph was absent at the time of her confession, as he was still in prison. She emphasized her opposition to betray him "in his absence" by differentiating herself from the other women who denied their attempts to seduce Joseph and any knowledge that he was the victim of injustice: "Exalted is Allah! We knew of no evil on him."

Strangely enough, even exegetes who attribute "that [I said], so that he knows that I have not betrayed him in his absence, and because Allah does not guide the device of the betrayers" to the 'Azīz's wife not Joseph, such as Ibn Kathīr, have failed to interpret it properly. They thought that she meant that she did not betray *her husband* in his absence. The problem with this interpretation is that the woman's husband was well aware that nothing occurred between her and Joseph. Additionally, if the 'Azīz's wife wanted to stress to her husband that she did not have an affair with Joseph, certainly she would not have waited several years until invited by the king to say that! Furthermore, if her husband did not believe all that time that she did not have an affair with Joseph, he would have had no reason to believe her this time!

In fact, taking "that [I said], so that he knows that I have not betrayed him in his absence, and because Allah does not guide the device of the betrayers" to be the words of the 'Azīz's wife *must* mean that the person referred to is Joseph. This is because Joseph is the person mentioned explicitly in the speech of the woman before that, i.e. "I tried to seduce him, and he is surely of the truthful ones," which in turn represents her reply to the king's question that names Joseph explicitly: "What was your matter when you tried to seduce Joseph?" In addition to all of these arguments, we need to remember that the subject of the verses above is Joseph and his innocence, not the woman's husband!

There are observations which some think justify throwing doubts on attributing the words in question to the 'Azīz's wife. I will mention them and give my explanations. The first observation is that if the 'Azīz's wife was really willing to confess that she wronged Joseph and put him in jail, then what made her keep silent all those years and not try earlier to free him from jail? Note that we have no information about what happened to the 'Azīz's wife from the time Joseph entered prison until she was called by the king. It is possible that this woman who was one day able to put Joseph unjustly in jail lost afterward that authority, so when she changed and wanted to release him from jail she could not do it. For instance, it is possible that her husband lost his powerful position, died, or divorced her and did not want to release Joseph.

The way in which the 'Azīz's wife begun her testimony in the previous verse is particularly interesting: "now the truth has become manifest." The word "now" suggests that the woman found speaking directly to the king the first real opportunity to disclose the truth. Convincing the king of Joseph's innocence would certainly result in releasing him from jail.

The second observation is that the statement "and because Allah does not guide the device of the betrayers" could not have been made except by a believer, whereas exegetes think that the 'Azīz's wife was not a believer. Although she was not a believer at the time when she put Joseph in prison, there is no reason to say that she could not have converted to Islam later on, perhaps after seeing Joseph's actions which reflected his utter and uncompromising loyalty and obedience to his Lord. Interestingly, there was no difference between the behavior of the 'Azīz's wife and that of the other women when they tried to seduce Joseph, but her different behavior in the presence of the king does not leave any doubt that she had changed completely and was not like those women anymore. We must not forget here that Joseph lived in the 'Azīz's house a number of years during which he would have talked a lot about his religion, as he did with his prison mates. It is plausible that although Joseph's guiding sermons did not affect the 'Azīz's wife at the time, his following actions, which were applications of his words, had a great impact on her and contributed to her conversion. His preference to enter prison rather than disobey Allah would particularly have affected her.

We come now to the third observation, which was mentioned among others by aṭ-Ṭabaṭabā'ī. These exegetes note that since the statement "Allah does not guide the device of the betrayers" follows the words "that [I said], so that he knows that I have not betrayed him in his absence," it must be linked to the word "*liya'lama* (so that he knows)," i.e. as if the speaker has said: "so that Joseph knows that Allah does not guide the device of the betrayers." Exegetes then go on to argue that the 'Azīz's wife could not have said this because she was not in a position to offer advice to Joseph, as he was the one who told her when she tried to seduce him: "surely the wrongdoers do not prosper."

The flaw in this argument is that it is based on a misreading of the verse. The statement "Allah does not guide the device of the betrayers" is linked to "*dhālika* (that)," which occurs at the beginning of the verse, not to "so that he knows." The woman's words do not mean that she confessed so Joseph could know that "Allah does not guide the device of the betrayers." They, rather, mean that the fact that "Allah does not guide the device of the betrayers" is one reason for her confession, in addition to "not betraying Joseph in his absence."

Thus, all evidence indicates that the words "that [I said], so that he knows that I have not betrayed him in his absence, and because Allah does not guide the device of the betrayers" were said by the 'Azīz's wife about Joseph. They also mean that she had become a believer when she said them.

وَمَآ أُبَرِّئُ نَفْسِيٓ إِنَّ ٱلنَّفْسَ لَأَمَّارَةُۢ بِٱلسُّوٓءِ إِلَّا مَا رَحِمَ رَبِّيٓ إِنَّ رَبِّي غَفُورٞ رَّحِيمٞ ﴿٥٣﴾

And I do not exculpate myself; surely the self commands committing evil, except such as my Lord bestows mercy on; my Lord is Forgiving, Merciful" (53).

Clearly, the person who says "and I do not exculpate myself" confesses to have erred and does not merely intend to exonerate him/herself. The speaker also emphasizes that every soul urges the person to commit evil, except the souls whom Allah confers mercy on: "surely the self commands committing evil, except such as my Lord bestows mercy on." This mercy takes the form of *preventing* the soul from being a source of evil. The speaker then finishes his/her speech by stressing that Allah is forgiving and merciful.

As is the case with the previous verse, exegetes have split over who said these words, with some attributing them to the 'Azīz's wife, and others to Joseph. It seems that the main reason some exegetes have attributed these words to Joseph is that they are obviously the words of a believer, as exegetes do not believe that the 'Azīz's wife could have become a believer. Nevertheless, there is nothing whatsoever in the Qur'an ruling out the possibility that the 'Azīz's wife believed later on. In fact, I have shown in my comment on the previous verse that the analysis of particular verses leads to the conclusion that the 'Azīz's wife did indeed believe. Therefore, attributing this saying to Joseph is baseless.

There is also an irrefutable argument against suggesting that the sayings in this verse and the previous one could have been Joseph's. The speech in both verses was uttered when Joseph was still in prison. That happened after he sent back the king's messenger with a request to his lord to investigate what happened to him, and before the second visit of the king's messenger to him in prison, which we will read about in the next verse: "And the king said: 'Bring him to me to choose him for myself'" (from 12.54).

It is also important to note that the speech in this verse is part of a dialog. The previous verses cited a dialog between the king and the 'Azīz's wife, but there is no indication that Joseph was exchanging a dialog with anyone. For all that, the words in this verse must have been said by the wife of the 'Azīz, in reply to the king.

Attributing the words in this verse to the 'Azīz's wife necessitates ascribing the speech in the previous verse also to her. According to this interpretation, the saying "and I do not exculpate myself" is a confirmation by the 'Azīz's wife that, having confessed to what she did to Joseph, she wanted to tell the truth; she did not want to exonerate herself at any cost.

The end of the speech of the wife of the 'Azīz's with a reference to the "forgiveness" and "mercy" of Allah in "my Lord is Forgiving, Merciful" is significant. She divided the souls into two categories, the first of which represents the souls that command evil. These souls are used to doing evil, hence they are in need of Allah's "forgiveness." The second category includes the souls that Allah has conferred "mercy" on, so they do not command evil. These are souls to which Allah's "mercy" has reached before His "forgiveness."

Note that describing the souls as a commander of evil occurs *first*, and the exceptions are mentioned *second*. This underlines the fact that the majority of souls command evil, and those that Allah shows mercy to so they do not call to evil represent the minority.

Note also that the word "Forgiving" occurs before "Merciful," in line with the order in which the two kinds of souls that each word relates to are mentioned.

But how did the 'Azīz's wife know all that? She reached this analysis of the human soul by virtue of Allah's guidance to her, first, and her personal experience with Joseph, second. Her division of the soul into two categories, the *soul that commands evil* and *the soul that does not do that because of Allah's mercy*, is a true and accurate description of all souls that she saw. Her description of the soul that commands evil as the *general case*, and the soul that does not command evil because of Allah's mercy as the *exception*, also reflects her experience and observation. Her soul, the souls of the women who cut their hands, and the souls of all those who took part in her plan to imprison Joseph were *all* souls that commanded evil. The same applies to all the people she knew. *Only* the soul of Joseph was of the second category.

This magnificent Qur'anic analysis of the soul reveals the truth about the concept of *infallibility*. The latter represents the state of the souls in the second category. Infallibility is a mercy that Allah confers on His servant so he does not fall in disobedience. *The infallible soul is the soul that does not command evil by virtue of Allah's mercy*. Note the agreement between this analysis and Allah's words in verse 12.24: "And surely she set out to do something to him and he set out to do something to her had he not seen the manifest proof of his Lord; thus [it was] so that We turned evil and lewdness away from him; [for] he is one of Our chosen servants." Allah describes His *intervention* to turn "evil and lewdness" away from Joseph. Allah intervened with His mercy, making Joseph's soul infallible and thus protecting him from disobedience. The servants whom Allah describes in verse 12.24 as "chosen" are those whom He shows mercy to by protecting their souls. They are the same servants whom the 'Azīz's wife refers to with the clause "except such as my Lord bestows mercy on." This does not mean that the infallible soul does not err at all, but it means that there are limits to the mistakes it can make.

Infallibility is not a purely internal state within the soul, but rather a state of intervention by Allah in the human soul and its surroundings to protect it from sins. Note, for instance, how Joseph confessed to his Lord that if He would not turn the women away from him, he would obey them: "and if You do not turn their scheming away from me, I shall incline toward them" (from 12.33). This is why Joseph is described with the active participle "*mukhlaṣ* (chosen one)" in "he is one of Our chosen servants," as it was Allah who chose Joseph for Himself.

Note also the following words of the 'Azīz's wife: "I have tried to seduce him, but he has sought protection [from Allah against my seduction]" (from 12.32). The verb أَسْتَعْصَمَ "*ista'ṣama*," which I have translated as "has sought protection [from Allah against my seduction]," means literally to "seek *external* protection against something." Joseph knew that his infallibility was a mercy that Allah conferred on him, and was not an intrinsic or internal characteristic of his soul.

It is clear that the words "and I do not exculpate myself; surely the self commands committing evil, except such as my Lord bestows mercy on; my Lord is Forgiving, Merciful" are not of someone who is infallible, but one with a soul that commands evil. Therefore, they must be the words of the 'Azīz's wife, not Joseph. This agrees with the conclusion that I presented earlier.

7

Prophet Joseph in Power

We saw in the previous chapter what happened to Joseph in prison, how the truth about the injustice that occurred to him became known to the king, and how he was about to be released from jail. In this chapter, we will follow his release from prison to a great favor from his Lord, and then his first meeting with his ten brothers since they cast him in the well. We will also see what he did in his attempt to bring Benjamin to Egypt.

> وَقَالَ ٱلْمَلِكُ ٱئْتُونِى بِهِۦٓ أَسْتَخْلِصْهُ لِنَفْسِى فَلَمَّا كَلَّمَهُۥ قَالَ إِنَّكَ ٱلْيَوْمَ لَدَيْنَا مَكِينٌ أَمِينٌ ﴿٥٤﴾
>
> And the king said: "Bring him to me to choose him for myself." So when he spoke to him, he said: "Surely, today, you are in our presence [a man] with authority, [and who is] trustworthy" (54).

Having heard what the 'Azīz's wife said, and having known the details of putting Joseph in jail, the king realized the amount of injustice that was inflicted on Joseph. He also learned about Joseph's chastity, purity, patience, and credibility, and that he had many noble qualities that made him a really exceptional and unique man. As noted by al-Qurṭubī, although the king asked in verse 12.50 for Joseph to be simply brought to him: "bring him to me," this time he followed those same words with the clause "to choose him for myself."

The king was curious about Joseph's interpretation of his dream, and he probably believed it. He might have asked in the first instance for Joseph to be brought to him in order to learn from him more about his dream and to honor him. After learning about Joseph's story, however, the king became extremely impressed with him. So when he called him this time, he had already decided to honor him generously and even "choose him for himself," i.e. make him one of his closest elite.

Note the wisdom in Joseph's decision not to leave the prison when the king called him earlier, and to first ask the king to investigate the women's unjust action against him. Joseph's decision to delay his own release from prison, where he had already spent several years, reveals also his great patience.

The clause "so when he spoke to him" refers to the king's speech to Joseph, obviously implying that this time Joseph did attend the king's court. It also indicates that this was the first direct contact between the king and Joseph, thus representing another proof to my earlier conclusion that, contrary to what exegetes explicitly or implicitly suggest, the previous two verses do not represent Joseph's speech with the king.

The king's words "today, in our presence" emphasize the fact that *Joseph's status with the king then* was completely different from *his previous status in the house of the 'Azīz and in prison.* Joseph's new status is represented by the king's decision to make him a close aide and "[a man] with authority, [and who is] trustworthy."[65]

Note that the behavior of the king leaves no doubt that he did not know Joseph before the series of events that was triggered by his request for an interpretation of his dream. So, as I have already emphasized, he cannot be the 'Azīz himself.

قَالَ ٱجْعَلْنِى عَلَىٰ خَزَآئِنِ ٱلْأَرْضِ إِنِّى حَفِيظٌ عَلِيمٌ ﴿٥٥﴾

He said: "Put me in charge of the storehouses of the land; surely I am a good keeper, a knowledgeable one" (55).

The king's words to Joseph "surely, today, you are in our presence [a man] with authority, [and who is] trustworthy" did not merely inform Joseph that he has given him a special position and that he sees him as someone who is worthy of being trusted. The full meaning of the king's words is disclosed only by Joseph's request: "Put me in charge of the storehouses of the land; surely I am a good keeper, a knowledgeable one." Note that the meaning of the word "*makīn* (with authority)" remains vague until the said "authority" is clarified. The same applies to the word "*amīn* (trustworthy)" whose meaning remains unclear until the "trust" referred to is identified.

The king's speech to Joseph was actually an *offer* to put him in a high position and to grant him responsibility in his kingdom. The king did not identify the "position" and "trust," which means that he left them to Joseph to specify. It is as if the king said to Joseph: "I would like to make you someone *with authority* and *trusted* in my kingdom, so what position and trust do you want to have?" Thus, Joseph's request to the king to put him in charge of "the storehouses of the land" was not Joseph's initiative, as exegetes think, but a positive reply from Joseph to the king's offer.

The translation "put me in charge of the storehouses of the land" hides one proof, which is clear in the original Arabic text, that Joseph's words cannot be understood but as a reply to the king's request to specify the position that Joseph wanted to occupy and the trust that he would like to be in charge of. The reply does not use the word أمينا "*amīnan* (trustee)" explicitly but *implicitly*, because it is mentioned explicitly in the king's offer.

The term "storehouses of the land" means "the storehouses of the crops of the agricultural lands." It is clear that Joseph's request to the king to put him in charge of the storehouses of the land was linked to future events that were revealed by his interpretation of the king's dream. Joseph asked the king to give him the responsibility of storing and handling grain, having already recommended to the cupbearer who visited him in jail measures that should be taken to lessen the impact of the forthcoming years of drought. It is also clear that Joseph's release from prison occurred when the king's dream had just started to materialize, i.e. at the beginning of the seven good years. Therefore, he became in charge of carrying out his suggested plan for handling the forthcoming drought.

Joseph's description of himself at the end of his speech as a "good keeper" refers to his quality of keeping the trust. In this context, it means protecting the grain — ensuring that they do not run out, get stolen, or destroyed.

The adjective "knowledgeable" has two meanings that differ in their depth and subtlety. The king took Joseph's words to mean that he can discharge the responsibility that he asked for. He understood the "knowledge" that Joseph referred to as one that enables him to be an efficient and capable keeper of the storehouses of the land. The other deeper and more subtle meaning is Joseph's knowledge that this position would cause him to reunite with his father and brothers and bring much good to all of them. The king, of course, would not have known this meaning.

There are more details on the subject of the storehouses of the land in Chapter 11.

> وَكَذَٰلِكَ مَكَّنَّا لِيُوسُفَ فِي ٱلْأَرْضِ يَتَبَوَّأُ مِنْهَا حَيْثُ يَشَآءُ نُصِيبُ بِرَحْمَتِنَا مَن نَّشَآءُ وَلَا نُضِيعُ أَجْرَ ٱلْمُحْسِنِينَ
>
> ﴿٥٦﴾
>
> And thus did We establish Joseph in the land; he lived wherever he liked. We send down Our mercy on whom We please, and We do not waste the reward of the good-doers (56).

The word "thus" refers to the preceding events. This verse tells us indirectly about the king's consent to appoint Joseph in the position that he asked for in reply to the king's offer to him to take a high position of power.

I have already spoken in my interpretation of verse 12.21 about the clause "and thus did We establish Joseph in the land," as it is exactly the same clause that Allah used to describe the status of Joseph after He made him settle in the house of the man who bought him in Egypt. These words, however, are followed in verse 12.56 by the clause "he lived wherever he liked," because this time the "place" that Allah made available to Joseph was not confined to a house or particular area. He made the whole of the kingdom at his disposal, and it was up to Joseph to choose where to settle.

Unlike verse 12.21, Allah's words "and thus did We establish Joseph in the land" in verse 12.56 are not followed by the clause "and so We could teach him a share of the interpretation of talks." The reason is that Allah had already taught Joseph "the interpretation of talks" through the events and circumstances that He put him through. Allah had a completely different aim behind establishing Joseph in the land this time, as the unfolding events will show us.

As noted by aṭ-Ṭabaṭabā'ī, the words "We send down Our mercy on whom We please" in verse 12.56 correspond to "and Allah has full control over His affair" in verse 12.21. The latter, *general* words mean that Allah does what He wants and no one can stop what He wants to happen. But His words "We send down Our mercy on whom We please" refer *specifically* to His mercy for His servants. They stress that Allah shows mercy to whom He wants, and that no one can block His mercy. As beautifully put by aṭ-Ṭabaṭabā'ī, if causes were ever to prevent Allah's mercy from reaching one of His servants, the many causes that gathered against Joseph would have succeeded in blocking His mercy from reaching this noble servant.

Note that Allah's mention of His reward for the good-doers in verse 12.22 occurs after He conferred on Joseph favors that can be called "spiritual," namely "Wisdom and Knowledge": "And when he attained his full strength, We gave him Wisdom and Knowledge; and thus do We reward the good-doers." Allah's mention of His reward for the good-doers in verse 12.56, however, occurs after He conferred on Joseph a favor that can be described as "worldly," namely raising him to a "high position in the land." There is an essential link between the person's mundane life and his spiritual life. The errant servant who does not use his life in this world to progress spiritually will only make his life on earth the cause of his spiritual demise. In contrast, the good servant turns what he gets in this world into means for spiritual development, so his worldly life becomes a permanent source of spiritual nourishment for himself and for others. Note how Joseph's patience at the major tragedies that occurred to him, and his thankfulness for the favors that he was given, were two means for his spiritual journey to Allah. His nearness to Allah was a means that led many who had contact with him to Allah.

The sentence "and We do not waste the reward of the good-doers" is a declaration that Allah does not waste the efforts of the good-doers in this world or the hereafter. This is the second time that Allah describes Joseph as a good-doer; the first was in verse 12.22: "And when he attained his full strength, We gave him Wisdom and Knowledge; and thus do We reward the good-doers."

وَلَأَجْرُ ٱلْأَخِرَةِ خَيْرٌ لِّلَّذِينَ ءَامَنُواْ وَكَانُواْ يَتَّقُونَ ﴿٥٧﴾
And the reward of the hereafter is much better for those who believe and act dutifully (57).

Aṭ-Ṭabaṭabā'ī suggests that this verse applies to saints but not to common believers. He thinks that the clause وَكَانُواْ يَتَّقُونَ "and act dutifully" refers to one group of "those who believe." This view is actually incorrect.

The reward that is second to that of the hereafter is this world's, which was mentioned in the previous verse: "And thus did We establish Joseph in the land; he lived wherever he liked. We send down Our mercy on whom We please, and We do not waste the reward of the good-doers." The phrase "for those who believe" is followed with "and act dutifully" because "faith" without "righteous deeds" is insufficient. The concept of "dutifulness" includes both "faith" and "righteous deeds." These are described in many verses as the two requirements for attaining Allah's mercy, as in the following example:

وَٱلَّذِينَ ءَامَنُواْ وَعَمِلُواْ ٱلصَّٰلِحَٰتِ أُوْلَٰٓئِكَ أَصْحَٰبُ ٱلْجَنَّةِ هُمْ فِيهَا خَٰلِدُونَ ﴿٨٢﴾. (سورة البَقَرة).

> And those who believe and do righteous deeds are the people of paradise, in which they will live forever (2.82).

وَجَآءَ إِخْوَةُ يُوسُفَ فَدَخَلُواْ عَلَيْهِ فَعَرَفَهُمْ وَهُمْ لَهُ مُنكِرُونَ ﴿٥٨﴾
And Joseph's brothers came and entered his place, and he knew them, while they did not recognize him (58).

This verse informs us of the arrival of Joseph's brothers to Egypt, a monumental event that was planned and executed subtly by Allah.

Perhaps, Joseph himself used to supervise the distribution of sustenance, so he met his brothers when they came seeking it. It is also not unlikely that Joseph, who had the ability of interpreting talks, was aware of the imminent arrival of his brothers, so he started receiving those who came asking for sustenance in order to meet them. As noted by Ṭahmāz, the words "and [they] entered his place, and he knew them" show that Joseph recognized his brothers *after* they entered his place, which implies that he did not know that they were outside before they came in.[66]

As we will see in the next verse, only Joseph's half brothers came to Egypt; Benjamin was not with them.

Joseph recognized his brothers, they did not recognize him. Their failure to recognize their brother seems to be due to the fact that he looked completely different from the young boy they cast in the bottom of the well many years before. He was different in appearance and status. Perhaps, he also spoke to them in the local language through an interpreter.

وَلَمَّا جَهَّزَهُم بِجَهَازِهِمْ قَالَ ٱئْتُونِى بِأَخٍ لَّكُم مِّنْ أَبِيكُمْ أَلَا تَرَوْنَ أَنِّىٓ أُوفِى ٱلْكَيْلَ وَأَنَا۠ خَيْرُ ٱلْمُنزِلِينَ

﴿٥٩﴾

And when he furnished them with their provisions, he said: "Bring to me a brother of yours from your father; do you not see that I give full measure and that I am the best of hosts? (59).

After giving food provisions to his brothers, Joseph said to them: "Bring to me a brother of yours from your father." Clearly, during the meeting, Joseph led his brothers to talk about their parents and reveal particular information. Thus, his latter request to them to bring their brother to Egypt did not make them suspicious about how he knew that they had a half brother. That was important so that they would not suspect that he was their brother Joseph, something that he wanted to keep as a secret then.

The Qur'an does not say how Joseph's justified to his brothers his request to bring Benjamin. One possible answer is that he argued that he wanted to ensure that some of the food that he provided them with would reach Benjamin and their step mother.

He also emphasized that he treated his guests with generosity.

﴿فَإِن لَّمْ تَأْتُونِى بِهِۦ فَلَا كَيْلَ لَكُمْ عِندِى وَلَا تَقْرَبُونِ ﴿٦٠﴾

But if you do not bring him to me, you shall have no measure from me, nor shall you come near me" (60).

Joseph's words in the previous verse encouraged his brothers to bring Benjamin to him; the rest of his speech was a warning. Joseph told his brothers that if they were to come to him again for provisions without bringing Benjamin, then he would not give them what they want and that they would not be allowed near to him.

Perhaps, Joseph pretended that he would not believe what his brothers told him about their families and origin unless they brought Benjamin.

Joseph hid his real identity from his brothers and resorted to cunningness when asking them to bring Benjamin to him and in his later dealings with them. Why did he not reveal his identity and ask them to bring their families to live with him in Egypt as he would do at the end? The answer to this question will become clear when we study the coming verses.

﴿قَالُوا۟ سَنُرَٰوِدُ عَنْهُ أَبَاهُ وَإِنَّا لَفَـٰعِلُونَ ﴿٦١﴾

They said: "We shall seek the consent of his father about him; and we shall do so" (61).

It is clear from the reply of Joseph's brothers to his request regarding Benjamin that they had told Joseph that their father favored Benjamin, and that he would not leave him in their company. Even if Joseph was unsure whether his half brothers were still mistreating Benjamin, learning about his father's keenness not to leave him in the company of his brothers would have dispelled any doubts. Obviously, Joseph's brothers were still harboring evil for Benjamin. Indeed, we will see in the next verses clear evidence that Joseph's brothers were still carrying bad feelings toward Joseph and Benjamin.

This is why Joseph did not reveal his real identity to his brothers and ask them to bring their families to live with him in Egypt. Had Joseph done that at that time, his brothers would not have told their father that they had found Joseph and would not have returned to him again, so he would have once more lost contact with his family. In addition to the fact that Joseph's brothers were still harboring bad feelings for him, they would have feared his revenge for what they did to him, now that he occupies a high position in Egypt. These would have been sufficient reasons to convince Joseph's brothers not to return to him and to keep from their father the news about their brother.

By bringing Benjamin to Egypt, Joseph wanted to secure at least another link with his parents other than his ten brothers. Joseph could not ask his brothers to bring their father and families to live in Egypt without revealing his real identity. Probably, without this revelation, Jacob would not have liked the idea of immigrating to a foreign land. Thus, the plan to bring Benjamin to Egypt was the safest way to achieve his ultimate goal of bringing all his family to Egypt.

As noted in my comment on verse 12.12, the verb يَرْتَعْ "*yarta'*," which I have translated as "enjoy himself," indicates that Joseph's brothers were shepherds. They were also bedouins with no fixed living place, as will be made clear later in Joseph's words in verse 12.100: "and He has indeed been kind to me, as He released me from the prison and brought you from the nomad desert." This explains why Joseph did not send someone to look for his family after Allah raised him to a high position in Egypt. His family would have relocated many times since he departed them. He had to depend on his brothers to reunite with his family.

With their words "and we shall do so," Joseph's brothers confirmed that they would try their best to convince their father to allow them to bring Benjamin with them to Egypt. As we will see, Joseph's brothers were truthful in making that promise because they were delighted with, as well as surprised at, the provisions they got from Joseph. They were also keen on getting more.

> وَقَالَ لِفِتْيَٰنِهِ ٱجْعَلُوا۟ بِضَٰعَتَهُمْ فِى رِحَالِهِمْ لَعَلَّهُمْ يَعْرِفُونَهَآ إِذَا ٱنقَلَبُوٓا۟ إِلَىٰٓ أَهْلِهِمْ لَعَلَّهُمْ يَرْجِعُونَ ﴿٦٢﴾
>
> And he said to his servants: "Put their goods in their luggage so that they may recognize them when they return to their family, so that they may come back" (62).

Joseph ordered some of his servants to put the goods that his brothers brought to him in return for grain in their luggage.[67] This action is explained in the second half of the verse: "so that they may recognize them when they return to their family, so that they may come back." Joseph's aim was to make his brothers return to him almost *immediately* after arriving to their families. But how would implanting the goods in the luggage make Joseph's brothers return to him immediately? It seems that they brought all their stock of goods, so this plan would save them the wait to gather new stocks, thus hastening their return.

Indeed, we will see that when Joseph did not return the goods that his brothers exchanged in their second visit, they had to bring "poor goods" in their third visit: "So when they entered his place, they said: 'O 'Azīz! Harm has afflicted us and our family, and we have brought poor goods, so give us full measure and be charitable to us; surely Allah rewards the charitable'" (12.88). This confirms that they were left with a few goods to exchange for food. This, in turn, shows that they did not possess much, so returning their goods to them was crucial to make them come back with something that they could trade with. They brought poor goods in their third visit because they did not really come to trade, but they came to look for Joseph and Benjamin. Bringing those goods was merely an excuse to come to Egypt and meet with Joseph.

One possible translation of the word يَعْرِفُونَهَا "*ya'rifūnaha*" is "they recognize them." The verse would mean that the recognition of Joseph's brothers of their goods would make them realize that they were returned to them on purpose. They would then see this as charitable help from Joseph, so they would come back hoping for more of his favors. Another possible translation of "*ya'rifūnaha*" is "they find them."

It is clear that Joseph wanted his brothers to find the goods *only after* returning to their family. We will discuss this in our study of verse 12.65.[68]

فَلَمَّا رَجَعُوٓا۟ إِلَىٰٓ أَبِيهِمْ قَالُوا۟ يَٰٓأَبَانَا مُنِعَ مِنَّا ٱلْكَيْلُ فَأَرْسِلْ مَعَنَآ أَخَانَا نَكْتَلْ وَإِنَّا لَهُۥ لَحَٰفِظُونَ ﴿٦٣﴾
So when they returned to their father, they said: "O our father! The measure has been withheld from us, so send with us our brother so that we may get the measure; and surely we shall be protective of him" (63).

Upon returning to their father, the ten brothers told him that they had been prevented from getting more provisions in the future unless he sent Benjamin with them to Egypt.

They also promised their father to protect Benjamin: "surely we shall be protective of him." Note that this last clause is the same clause they used in verse 12.12 when they claimed that they would protect Joseph.

قَالَ هَلْ ءَامَنُكُمْ عَلَيْهِ إِلَّا كَمَآ أَمِنتُكُمْ عَلَىٰٓ أَخِيهِ مِن قَبْلُ فَٱللَّهُ خَيْرٌ حَٰفِظًا وَهُوَ أَرْحَمُ ٱلرَّٰحِمِينَ ﴿٦٤﴾
He said: "Should I entrust you with him, would I be doing other than what I did before when I entrusted you with his brother? So, Allah is the best protector, and He is the most Merciful of the merciful ones" (64).

Jacob's reply to his sons was in the form of criticism of what they did to Joseph. He reminded them that he did entrust them with Joseph in the past but they betrayed his trust. Jacob's answer carries also an implicit acknowledgement that his decision to entrust his sons with Joseph has had negative consequences, and that a similar decision with regard to his other son would likely have similar consequences.

Note Jacob's concentration in his speech on his decision, not on his sons' actions. He did not say something such as: "would you protect him more than you protected his brother in the past?" but focused on his own decision to trust his sons: "Should I entrust you with him, would I be doing other than what I did before when I entrusted you with his brother?" When he gave his permission to his sons to take Joseph with them, Jacob was fully aware of their feelings toward Joseph, so his words reflect his belief that what happened to Joseph was down to his decision to leave Joseph in the care of his brothers.

Jacob's words "so, Allah is the best protector" relate to his self-criticism, as if he said: "although you did not protect Joseph but betrayed him, and I did not protect him when I allowed him to go with you, Allah is the best protector of Joseph and everything." Jacob's words also highlight his knowledge that Joseph was safe under the protection of Allah.

Saying "so, Allah is the best protector" in the context of talking about what happened to Joseph indicates that Jacob was then still unwilling to answer his sons' request to take Benjamin with them.

Jacob's reply contains an implicit criticism of *untrustworthiness* of his sons. This untrustworthiness was on display when they betrayed Joseph, and it will show up again when they betray Benjamin later on. The king's opinion on Joseph, however, was the exact opposite. He described Joseph as "trustworthy" and put him in charge of the storehouses of the land.

Following those words with "and He is the most Merciful of the merciful ones" is a confirmation from Jacob that despite all what happened, Allah, the most merciful, is more merciful to Joseph, as more protective of him, than Jacob himself and his sons. Since the time when he was taken away from his father, Joseph was continuously under Allah's protection and divine mercy that raised him to a high status in Egypt.

Some exegetes see in this clause an indication that Jacob knew that Allah would show mercy to him and reunite him with his son.

وَلَمَّا فَتَحُواْ مَتَـٰعَهُمْ وَجَدُواْ بِضَـٰعَتَهُمْ رُدَّتْ إِلَيْهِمْ قَالُواْ يَـٰٓأَبَانَا مَا نَبْغِى هَـٰذِهِۦ بِضَـٰعَتُنَا رُدَّتْ إِلَيْنَا وَنَمِيرُ أَهْلَنَا وَنَحْفَظُ أَخَانَا وَنَزْدَادُ كَيْلَ بَعِيرٍ ذَٰلِكَ كَيْلٌ يَسِيرٌ ﴿٦٥﴾

And when they opened their baggage, they found that their goods had been returned to them. They said: "O our father! What more can we ask for? Our goods have been returned to us, and we shall bring grain for our family, protect our brother, and have an additional measure of a camel load; this is an easy measure to get" (65).

After returning home and opening their luggage, Joseph's brothers were pleasantly surprised to find out that the goods they exchanged for grain in Egypt had been put in their luggage.[69]

As I explained, Joseph's aim of returning his brothers' goods was to encourage them to return to him *immediately*, as they would be able to use the goods again to buy more grain. This move also stressed to them Joseph's kindness and generosity. Joseph, however, did not simply want to return the goods to them. He deliberately concealed the goods so his brothers could not find them until they arrived home; so why did he do that?

The more likely reason is that this plan was going to create at Jacob's house and in his presence the kind of atmosphere that would encourage him to send his youngest son with his half brothers. Note that when Jacob's sons told their father, in verse 12.63, that the provisions were prevented from them unless they take Benjamin with them to Egypt, Jacob refused in verse 12.64 to send him with them. Since Jacob's reply in verse 12.64 was the last thing that was said about this subject at the time, it is clear that the discussion ended with that decision. What Joseph's brothers found, however, changed matters completely.

Finding their goods in their luggage was a big surprise for Jacob's sons, as it was for their father. This encouraged them to try again to convince their father that he should send Benjamin with them to Egypt. Joseph's brothers must have praised Joseph in front of their father for what he did for them. They must have stressed to him that this very high ranking Egyptian official was a good man, so he would keep his word and give them provisions again if Benjamin went with them. Finding the goods in their luggage came as a confirmation of what they said about Joseph, and brought with it a new opportunity to plea to their father to allow them to take Benjamin with them to Egypt.[70]

They said to their father "what more can we ask for? Our goods have been returned to us," i.e. "the goods that we have exchanged for the provisions have been returned to us, so we got the provisions for nothing." They mentioned then the benefits of going again to Egypt with Benjamin for more provisions. These benefits are "bringing grain to their family" and "having an additional measure of a camel load for Benjamin," while protecting him. The statement "this is an easy measure to get" is meant to emphasize the ease of securing as much as eleven camel loads of provisions by simply going with Benjamin to see Joseph again, whereas they would get nothing without Benjamin. Joseph must have promised to give his brothers one camel load to each of them in return for the goods they bring to him.[71]

It is possible that securing more provisions was not the only reason for Joseph's brothers' desire to go with Benjamin to Egypt. They found Joseph's condition of bringing Benjamin with them to get more provisions an excuse to make their father treat Benjamin as he treated them. So, as an exception to his usual protective treatment of Benjamin, Jacob would send his youngest son with his other sons to get provisions. We will see later how accusing Benjamin of a theft exposed the fact that they still held grudge against him.

قَالَ لَنْ أُرْسِلَهُ مَعَكُمْ حَتَّىٰ تُؤْتُونِ مَوْثِقًا مِّنَ ٱللَّهِ لَتَأْتُنَّنِى بِهِۦٓ إِلَّآ أَن يُحَاطَ بِكُمْ فَلَمَّآ ءَاتَوْهُ مَوْثِقَهُمْ قَالَ ٱللَّهُ عَلَىٰ مَا نَقُولُ وَكِيلٌ ﴿٦٦﴾

He said: "I will not send him with you until you give me a firm covenant in Allah's name that you will certainly bring him back to me unless you become completely powerless." And when they gave him their covenant, he said: "Allah is in charge of what we have said" (66).

Verse 12.64 represents Jacob's answer to his sons' request in verse 12.63 to send Benjamin with them to Egypt to bring sustenance. Verse 12.66 has Jacob's reply to his sons' repetition in verse 12.65 of that same request, but after finding the goods in their baggage. Jacob's response changed as he agreed to let Benjamin go with his brothers if they agreed to his condition. This change in Jacob's position was the result of Joseph's plan to put his brothers' goods in their baggage and hide them so that they would not find them until they arrived at their father's home. The success of this plan in achieving its goal indicates that it is the fruit of the special knowledge of the interpretation of talks that Allah conferred on Joseph.

Joseph was aware that Jacob would not let his sons take Benjamin to Egypt, so he worked out a plan to convince his father to do that. It was clear to Jacob that the spontaneousness of the way in which his sons found the goods in their baggage was genuine, and that they did not make that incident up. This reassured Jacob that his sons were not lying when they told him that the high ranking person in Egypt who supplied them with provisions asked them to bring Benjamin the next time, and that he was indeed a good man who could be trusted.

Jacob granted permission to Benjamin to go with his brothers so long as they gave him a covenant in Allah's name that they would return Benjamin safe. Describing the covenant as being "in Allah's name" means making Allah the witness on it, so whoever gives this kind of covenant becomes responsible for adhering to it before Allah. The overall meaning of "I will not send him with you until you give me a firm covenant in Allah's name that you will certainly bring him back to me" is that Jacob's sons must give him a covenant in which they make Allah witness that they will bring back his son safe to him.[72]

The knowledgeable Jacob did not forget to remind his sons that all that he could ask of them in the covenant was to try their best to return Benjamin safe to him, as what happens is ultimately in the hand of Allah. Therefore, he followed his request with the clause "unless you become completely powerless," i.e. genuinely unable to return him.[73]

Note that Jacob agreed to his sons' request only after much persistence, exactly as happened when they wanted to take Joseph with them. This time, however, he asked them to give him a covenant in the name of Allah that they would return his son to him unless this becomes completely out of their hands. Jacob's condition shows that he was aware of the ill feelings that his sons had toward Benjamin, which is something that we saw and will see more references to, and that therefore they would not be really protective of him. His condition also shows Jacob's knowledge that his sons honored any covenant that they made in name of Allah.

When Jacob's sons did what he asked them to do and gave him a covenant in the name of Allah, he said to them: "Allah is in charge of what we have said," stressing that Allah is the witness on their adherence to the covenant.

It is worth noting that the word نَقُولُ "*naqūl* (we have said)" shows that the covenant was *verbal*, not *written*. A covenant that a person takes before Allah carries the same weight whether it is verbal or written.

وَقَالَ يَـٰبَنِيَّ لَا تَدْخُلُواْ مِنۢ بَابٍ وَٰحِدٍ وَٱدْخُلُوا مِنْ أَبْوَٰبٍ مُّتَفَرِّقَةٍ وَمَآ أُغْنِى عَنكُم مِّنَ ٱللَّهِ مِن شَىْءٍ إِنِ
ٱلْحُكْمُ إِلَّا لِلَّهِ عَلَيْهِ تَوَكَّلْتُ وَعَلَيْهِ فَلْيَتَوَكَّلِ ٱلْمُتَوَكِّلُونَ ﴿٦٧﴾

And he said: "O my sons! Do not enter from one gate but enter from different gates; and I can protect you naught against Allah; the judgment is only Allah's; on Him do I rely, and on Him let the reliant ones rely" (67).

After taking from his sons the covenant in the name of Allah, Jacob ordered them not to enter Egypt from one gate, but from different gates. There is almost consensus among exegetes that Jacob issued this instruction to his sons to protect them from becoming the subject of envy, as they were as many as eleven brothers. One proof of the weakness of this interpretation is that Jacob's instruction was clearly new, i.e. one that he did not give to his sons when they went to Egypt the first time round although they were as many as ten at the time, as only Benjamin was not with them.

This leads us to investigate the possibility that Jacob's order is related to the fact that his sons were making their second visit to Egypt. A relevant fact is that his sons' second trip to Egypt occurred immediately after their first visit. Interestingly, Egyptian historical records about the place and time where Joseph lived, which I will discuss in more detail in Chapter 11, show that border guards used to keep a record of those they allowed to enter Egypt to get provisions. Therefore, it is likely that Jacob's instruction to his sons to enter from different gates means that there was more than one border point to enter the country, and that he wanted his sons to be allowed into Egypt without anyone noticing that they were the same group who was allowed in earlier on. They could otherwise find themselves in trouble, or be prevented from entering Egypt.

It is also likely that Jacob wanted to make sure that, should something go wrong while his sons were trying to enter Egypt, they would not all be caught. Those who managed to enter safely would be able to investigate their brothers' problems and try to help them. For instance, they would seek the help of Joseph who treated them with kindness during their first visit.

Note that Jacob's order to his sons was to "enter" Egypt from different gates, not to "stay" in the country separately. Once in Egypt, they would gather again to visit the 'Azīz. Clearly, the separation was to avoid any problem when trying to enter Egypt; getting together afterward would allow them to know if any of them had troubles. This is further evidence of the exegetes' wrong belief that the aim of Jacob's plan was to protect his sons from envy. The dispersal of his sons would only happen when they enter, but they would get together again once in Egypt.

As Jacob qualified his words to his sons in the previous verse with the clause "unless you become completely powerless," he qualified his order to them in this verse with the clause "and I can protect you naught against Allah." He emphasized that precaution and care would not stop what Allah wants to happen. The latter phrase means "I cannot protect you against something that Allah wants to happen to you."

Jacob's words "the judgment is only Allah's" is a reminder to his sons that it is Allah who does whatever He likes in His kingdom. These words are similar to إِنَّ ٱللَّهَ يَحْكُمُ مَا يُرِيدُ "Allah ordains whatever He wants" (from 5.1). Should Allah want, He could bring about something that cannot be avoided even if they entered from different gates.

Jacob finished his words by emphasizing that it is Allah on whom he relies: "on Him do I rely," and inviting his sons and everyone to rely on Him because He is the one worthy of reliance: "and on Him let the reliant ones rely."

وَلَمَّا دَخَلُواْ مِنْ حَيْثُ أَمَرَهُمْ أَبُوهُم مَّا كَانَ يُغْنِى عَنْهُم مِّنَ ٱللَّهِ مِن شَىْءٍ إِلَّا حَاجَةً فِى نَفْسِ يَعْقُوبَ قَضَىٰهَا وَإِنَّهُ لَذُو عِلْمٍ لِّمَا عَلَّمْنَٰهُ وَلَٰكِنَّ أَكْثَرَ ٱلنَّاسِ لَا يَعْلَمُونَ ﴿٦٨﴾

And as they entered wherefrom their father had ordered them, that/he protected them naught against Allah, but it [the safe entry] was only a desire in the soul of Jacob which He satisfied; and surely he is a possessor of knowledge that We taught him, but most people do not know (68).

Jacob's sons did what their father ordered them to do and entered from different gates: "they entered wherefrom their father had ordered them."[74]

There are two main possible identifications for the implied, singular pronoun in the verb يُغْنِى "*yughnī* (protect)" which correspond to "that" and "he" in my translation.[75] So the meaning is that "that" or "he" did not protect them against anything that Allah wanted to do to them.

Then Allah says: "but [it was only] a desire in the soul of Jacob which He satisfied."[76] This means that Jacob's sons were not safe because of the plan to enter from different gates, but because Allah wanted to satisfy Jacob's desire for his sons to safely arrive to Joseph, which was the aim of his plan.

Allah describes Jacob as a "possessor of knowledge." The clause "that We had taught him" emphasizes that the source of that knowledge is Allah. But what is the relation between the subject of the verse and the statement about the knowledge of Jacob? It is possible that the mentioned knowledge is that which underlines Jacob's caution in the statement "and I can protect you naught against Allah." It is likely, however, that the reference to Jacob's knowledge occurs here because it is the knowledge of the interpretation of talks which Allah has conferred on Jacob that made him know that his sons would be exposed to evil if they would not enter from different gates.

It is also possible that the reference to Jacob's knowledge embraces both of these interpretations. In this case, it is Jacob's knowledge of the interpretation of talks, which lies behind his order to his sons to enter from different gates, and also his knowledge of the power and status of Allah, which he referred to when he told his sons that his plan and provision would not protect them against Allah's will.

Allah then concludes this verse by emphasizing that, unlike the knowledgeable Jacob, most people are ignorant. The description of Jacob in this place as knowledgeable has a specific meaning that relates to the context of the story, whereas describing people as ignorant is general.

8

Prophet Joseph Reunites With His Brother Benjamin

We saw in the previous chapter how Joseph began his attempt to bring Benjamin to Egypt. In this chapter, we will see how this attempt succeeded.

> وَلَمَّا دَخَلُواْ عَلَىٰ يُوسُفَ ءَاوَىٰٓ إِلَيْهِ أَخَاهُ قَالَ إِنِّىٓ أَنَا۠ أَخُوكَ فَلَا تَبْتَئِسْ بِمَا كَانُواْ يَعْمَلُونَ ﴿٦٩﴾
>
> And when they entered Joseph's place, he admitted his brother to his private place and said: "I am your brother, so do not be grieved at what they have been doing" (69).

When Joseph's brothers entered his place, accompanying Benjamin, he took the latter into his private room. He wanted to reveal to him that he was Joseph, his brother who had disappeared years earlier as a result of a plot by his half brothers.[77]

We have seen that Joseph's brothers nurtured envy for Benjamin when he was a small boy: "When they said: 'Verily Joseph and his brother are dearer to our father than us, though we are a band; surely, our father is in manifest error'" (12.8). It is clear from Joseph's words "so do not be grieved at what they have been doing" that his brothers were still mistreating Benjamin, something that was also reflected in Jacob's reluctance to allow them to take him away.

Note that the particle فَـ "*fa* (so)" in فَلَا "*fa lā* (so do not)" links Joseph's revelation to Benjamin "I am your brother" to "so do not be grieved at what they have been doing." It seems that Joseph is telling Benjamin not to be saddened by what his brothers have so far done to him, because everything was going to change now that he was with Joseph.

Allah informs us of Joseph's revelation to Benjamin about his identity, but He does not tell us anything about the latter's reaction to this stunning surprise. This is another example on the special style of the Qur'an in relating history, and its omission of details that are given special importance in the writings of man, which I explained in §1.3. Details of Benjamin's astonishment and happiness, and what he said after hearing the revelation, would have been particularly exciting to read about. Sensationalization and excitement, however, are not among the aims of the Qur'anic story, hence it ignores those details.

فَلَمَّا جَهَّزَهُم بِجَهَازِهِمْ جَعَلَ السِّقَايَةَ فِي رَحْلِ أَخِيهِ ثُمَّ أَذَّنَ مُؤَذِّنٌ أَيَّتُهَا الْعِيرُ إِنَّكُمْ لَسَارِقُونَ ﴿٧٠﴾
So when he furnished them with their provisions, he put the drinking cup in his brother's luggage. Then a proclaimer proclaimed: "O camel caravanners![78] You are certainly thieves" (70).

After giving to each of his brothers a camel load of provisions, as he did in their first visit, Joseph ordered for a "drinking cup" to be put in Benjamin's "luggage."[79]

When Joseph wanted to return his brothers' goods after their first visit, he ordered for the goods to be hidden in their luggage. He wanted to ensure that they would not discover the goods until they unpack the luggage back home, and that it would be clear that it was he who ordered the goods to be returned to them. This time, the aim was exactly the opposite. Joseph wanted the drinking cup put in a place where it could be found relatively easily. Additionally, he was keen that his brothers would not have any suspicion about any involvement on his part.

The Qur'an attributes to Joseph hiding the drinking cup in Benjamin's luggage. This does not mean, however, that it was Joseph himself who did all that. It means that the high ranking Joseph ordered one of his servants to do so.

There is consensus among exegetes that Joseph informed Benjamin about his plan to put the drinking cup in his luggage and then accuse him of theft. It is also likely that he told him about the aim of his plan. The Qur'anic verses support this view. We have seen in the previous verse that Joseph called Benjamin to his private room and told him things that he kept secret from their half brothers. Additionally, the information about Joseph carrying out the plan occurs immediately after the information about his admittance of Benjamin to his private place. This is an indirect indication that he told Benjamin what he planned to do.

After being furnished with provisions, and with the drinking cup hidden in Benjamin's luggage, Joseph's brothers set out home. Joseph then sent some of his men after them, accusing them of robbery.[80]

Clearly, Joseph deliberately let his brothers travel some distance before sending someone after them to accuse them of theft. This was intended to make the whole affair look natural and not to raise any suspicion. It looked as if the disappearance of the drinking cup was noticed only some time after the departure of the brothers, and not when they were about to leave.

> قَالُوا۟ وَأَقْبَلُوا۟ عَلَيْهِم مَّاذَا تَفْقِدُونَ ﴿٧١﴾
>
> They said, and moved toward them: "What have you lost?" (71).

Joseph's brothers asked the proclaimer about the things that he accused them of stealing. The verse indicates that the proclaimer was in a group of people.

The fact that Joseph's brothers "moved toward" the group of the proclaimer after the accusation confirms my explanation of the use of the clause "a proclaimer proclaimed" in the previous verse. The caravan of Joseph's brothers had moved some distance away from the place where Joseph was when he sent some of his servants after them.

The occurrence of the verb "said" before "moved toward" shows that Joseph's brothers started to talk to Joseph's servant while moving back toward them.

> قَالُوا۟ نَفْقِدُ صُوَاعَ ٱلْمَلِكِ وَلِمَن جَآءَ بِهِۦ حِمْلُ بَعِيرٍ وَأَنَا۠ بِهِۦ زَعِيمٌ ﴿٧٢﴾
>
> They said: "We have lost the drinking cup of the king; and he who shall bring it shall have a camel load, and I am responsible for delivering that" (72).

Joseph's servants replied to the enquiry of Joseph's brothers saying that they have lost the drinking cup of the king. Note that the drinking cup is referred to in this verse with the word صُوَاع "*ṣuwā'*," which means the same thing as "*siqāya*" which was mentioned in verse 12.70.

It is interesting to note the pronoun of the speaker changed from the plural "We" in the beginning of the verse to the singular "I" at the end of the verse, then changed back to the plural form in the next three verses, before it changed one more time to the singular form in verse 12.76, where it clearly refers to Joseph. The singular pronoun in verse 12.72 probably refers to Joseph. So, at least the latter part of the verse, i.e. the promise, and the following events, happened at Joseph's place.[81]

The clause "I am responsible for delivering that" is a reminder from Joseph to his brothers of his authority and, therefore, his ability to make good his promise. It is clear that Joseph's promise to give a camel load to whoever finds the drinking cup is a cover-up for his role so that his brothers would have no doubt at all that he had set up what happened.

قَالُوا۟ تَٱللَّهِ لَقَدْ عَلِمْتُم مَّا جِئْنَا لِنُفْسِدَ فِى ٱلْأَرْضِ وَمَا كُنَّا سَـٰرِقِينَ ﴿٧٣﴾
They said: "By Allah! You know that we have not come to cause corruption in the land and that we are not thieves" (73).

Joseph's brothers replied, swearing by Allah, that Joseph knew that they had not come to Egypt to commit evil acts, but to seek provisions, and that they were not thieves. Joseph's brothers referred to what they told him about themselves when he entertained them.

Their words "we are not thieves" underline the fact that Joseph was aware that they worked as shepherds, and that their visits to Egypt to seek provisions prove that they were not thieves.

قَالُوا۟ فَمَا جَزَٰٓؤُهُۥٓ إِن كُنتُمْ كَـٰذِبِينَ ﴿٧٤﴾
They said: "So what shall be its punishment if you are liars?" (74).

Joseph and his men replied slyly, asking his brothers to determine the punishment for the theft if it was proven that they lied and that one or more of them had committed it.

It is possible that the attached, singular, masculine pronoun in the word جَزَٰٓؤُهُۥ "*jazā'uhu*" refers to the "thief," in which case the translation would be "his punishment." This would mean that as Joseph's plan approached its climax, he changed the tone of the conversation and started to imply that there was "one" thief. He would have done that to keep Benjamin only with him.

This possibility, however, sounds weak. The more likely interpretation is that the pronoun in "*jazā'uhu*" refers to the "stolen drinking cup" hence my translation "its punishment."

قَالُوا۟ جَزَٰٓؤُهُۥ مَن وُجِدَ فِى رَحْلِهِۦ فَهُوَ جَزَٰٓؤُهُۥ ۚ كَذَٰلِكَ نَجْزِى ٱلظَّـٰلِمِينَ ﴿٧٥﴾
They said: "Its punishment is that the person in whose baggage it is found shall himself pay/be the price; thus we punish the wrongdoers" (75).

The answer of Joseph's brothers may be divided into two parts, the first of which is "its punishment is that the person in whose baggage it is found shall himself pay/be the price." The first occurrence of the word "*jazā'uhu*" in this sentence refers to the same thing as the same word in the previous verse, i.e. it is likely to mean the "punishment of the stolen drinking cup," hence my translation "its punishment." It is clear that the second "*jazā'uhu*" refers to the "punishment of the thief."

The comment of Joseph's brothers "the person in whose baggage it is found" points out that the punishment should be applied only to the thief.

In this specific case, it means that the punishment should be restricted to the person in whose luggage the drinking cup is found and should not be extended to his other ten brothers. Most exegetes agree that the meaning of the clause فَهُوَ جَزَآؤُهُ "*fa huwwa jazā'uhu*" is that the "thief becomes himself the price of his theft," i.e. that the victim of the theft takes the thief as a slave in retribution for the theft.

The second part of the reply of Joseph's brothers, "thus we punish the wrongdoers," is a confirmation of the first part of their answer about the punishment of the thief. Some exegetes think that Joseph's brothers meant that enslaving the thief was the punishment for theft in the divine Law of Jacob's religion. However, if this is what Joseph's brothers really wanted to say, they would not have used the word ظَّـٰلِمِينَ "*ẓālimīn* (wrongdoers)," but a more specific term such as سارقين "*sāriqīn* (thieves)." The term "wrongdoer" covers all people who commit any "wrongdoing," so it is not restricted to those who commit theft. It is unreasonable to assume that the divine Law that was given to Jacob would have stated that the punishment of every "wrongdoer" is to become a slave to the victim. Clearly Joseph's brothers could not have meant that enslaving the thief was a general punishment in their religious legislations. They were simply talking about that specific incident of theft, and there is no indication that they were talking about Jacob's law.

Joseph trapped his brothers into giving their judgment on the thief when he asked them, directly or through one of his men: "So what shall be its punishment if you are liars?" He did that to further conceal his role in what was going on, making the whole situation appear to be developing without any intervention on his part. If his brothers' judgment would not be in line with what he wanted to do to Benjamin, he would not be obliged to accept it anyway. He knew, however, that his brothers' judgment would be at least imprisonment for the thief. This would suit him well, because it would simply mean keeping Benjamin with him. Clearly, Joseph's brothers were not going to suggest setting the thief free.

Note that the verb قَالُوا "*qālū* (they said)" means that all of Joseph's brothers, including Benjamin, agreed on the judgment. The latter knew that this is what Joseph wanted.

فَبَدَأَ بِأَوْعِيَتِهِمْ قَبْلَ وِعَآءِ أَخِيهِ ثُمَّ ٱسْتَخْرَجَهَا مِن وِعَآءِ أَخِيهِ كَذَٰلِكَ كِدْنَا لِيُوسُفَ مَا كَانَ لِيَأْخُذَ أَخَاهُ فِى
دِينِ ٱلْمَلِكِ إِلَّآ أَن يَشَآءَ ٱللَّهُ نَرْفَعُ دَرَجَٰتٍ مَّن نَّشَآءُ وَفَوْقَ كُلِّ ذِى عِلْمٍ عَلِيمٌ ﴿٧٦﴾

So he began with their containers before the container of his brother, then he produced it from his brother's container. Thus did We subtly plan for Joseph; he would not have taken his brother under the king's law had Allah not willed [that to happen]. We raise in degrees whomsoever We will, and above every possessor of knowledge there is a more knowledgeable one (76).

Keen on concealing his plan, Joseph started searching the containers of his half brothers first, before producing the drinking cup from Benjamin's container.[82]

The reference to Joseph's search of his brothers' luggage does not mean that high ranking Joseph himself searched the luggage, but it must have been one of his servants. Referring to Joseph in particular in this verse — although verse 12.74 uses the plural form, i.e. refers to Joseph's men — stresses that searching the luggage of the ten older brothers before Benjamin's was engineered directly by Joseph.

It should be noted that the verse refers to the drinking cup with a feminine pronoun, using the word ٱسْتَخْرَجَهَا "*istakhrajahā* (he produced it)" instead of إستخرجهُ "*istakhrajahu*." The implication seems to be that the drinking cup is referred to with its feminine name "*siqāya*," which is used in verse 70, not with its alternative masculine name "*ṣuwā'*," which is used in verse 72. Note that the word "*ṣuwā'*" was used by Joseph's servants, whereas in the two times in which "*siqāya*" is used it occurs associated with a verb describing an action by Joseph, "he put the drinking cup" in verse 70, and more implicitly in this verse: "he produced it."

Allah says "thus did We subtly plan for Joseph," and then further explains the meaning by saying: "he would not have taken his brother under the king's law had Allah not willed [that to happen]." Exegetes take this to mean that according to the law of that Egyptian kingdom, enslavement was not the punishment for thief, so Allah intervened to make Joseph able to take Benjamin as a slave. I think that this interpretation is incorrect. What Allah made to happen was for "Joseph to take Benjamin *under* the king's law," not for "Joseph to take Benjamin *despite* the king's law." This is discussed further below.

The exegetes' view means that Joseph could not have taken Benjamin had his brothers not said, in reply to his question, that the punishment for theft was enslavement, because the king's law did not allow him to take Benjamin. The simple fact, however, is that Joseph managed to keep Benjamin not because of his brothers' suggestion of that punishment, but because he was in such a powerful position that he could do what he wanted. Had there been a law in the kingdom specifying the punishment of the thief, and had Joseph not been in a position powerful enough to override that law and to do whatever he wanted, he would not have asked his brothers in the first place to specify the punishment for the theft. He would have to abide by the law of the kingdom instead. The very fact that Joseph asked his brothers to specify the punishment means that he was in a position of passing whatever judgment he wanted, and was not obliged to obey a particular law.

I, thus, conclude that Joseph's request to his brothers to specify the punishment of the thief was not the result of his need for a pretext to keep Benjamin with him. He could have used his authority to keep the latter with him without even justifying his decision to his half brothers. Requesting the view of his brothers about the punishment of the thief was a cunning move on Joseph's part to make sure that his role in the unfolding of events remained invisible, as I mentioned earlier.

My interpretation of "he would not have taken his brother under the king's law had Allah not willed [that to happen]" is that had it not been Allah's will, Joseph would not have ascended to a position of power in the kingdom that would allow him to keep Benjamin with him.

The subtle plan that Allah refers to in His words "thus did We subtly plan for Joseph" is not how Joseph tricked his brothers into suggesting that he should take the thief as a slave. The verse is absolutely clear that the subtle plan enabled Joseph to bring Benjamin to Egypt. This description does not apply to the trick that Joseph played on his brothers, because this trick was not what allowed Joseph to keep Benjamin with him. It simply provided a convenient cover-up for his manipulation of events so that his brothers would not suspect that he had any involvement.

The subtle plan that Allah mentions includes, among other things, putting the cupbearer of the king in prison; making him see the dream which Joseph interpreted successfully; reinstating him in his position in the service to the king; making the king see the dream that Joseph interpreted; making Joseph ask the king to put him in charge of the storehouses of the land; and bringing Joseph's brothers to him in the years of hardship asking for provisions. Allah's subtle plan included all things that led, directly or indirectly, to Joseph's promotion to that powerful position in the kingdom, and allowed him to bring Benjamin to Egypt and keep him there.

The verse: "Thus did We subtly plan for Joseph; he would not have taken his brother under the king's law had Allah not willed [that to happen]" means: "thus we worked out a secret plan for Joseph so that he brings Benjamin to him in the land of the king. That would not have happened had We not wanted it to take place."

Many have misunderstood the meaning of the word دَرَجَـٰتٍ "*darajāt* (degrees)" in this verse. The key to understanding the meaning of this word is noticing the link between the verb نَرْفَعُ "*narfa'u* (We raise)" in the sentence "We raise in degrees whomsoever We will" and the preposition فَوْقَ "*fawqa* (above)" in the sentence "above every possessor of knowledge there is a more knowledgeable one." After mentioning that He "raises in degrees" whomever He likes, Allah adds that "above" everyone with knowledge there is someone who is more knowledgeable. This leaves no doubt that the "degrees" in this verse refer to "degrees of knowledge."

There is a direct link between the successive clauses "We raise in degrees whomsoever We will" and "had Allah not willed," both of which mention Allah's will. The latter clause points out that Joseph kept Benjamin with him because Allah *willed* that to happen; the former explains the *way* in which Allah wanted it to happen: raising Joseph in degrees. This agrees with my interpretation of "degrees" as "degrees of knowledge." Joseph's knowledge of the interpretation of talks was vital in his elevation to that prestigious position in the kingdom, and to keeping Benjamin with him. His knowledge of storing and organizing the distribution of grain also played a role in that.

So, "We raise in degrees whomsoever We will" refers to Allah raising Joseph's knowledge. But why is it followed by "and above every possessor of knowledge there is a more knowledgeable one"? Note that "possessor of knowledge" in this verse is the same phrase with which Allah described Jacob in verse 12.68: "And as they entered wherefrom their father had ordered them, that/he protected them naught against Allah, but it [the safe entry] was only a desire in the soul of Jacob which He satisfied; and surely he is a possessor of knowledge that We taught him, but most people do not know." Allah described Jacob as a "possessor of knowledge" in the context of his knowledge of a potential danger to his sons when they enter Egypt and of how to avert it. Through that knowledge, Jacob was able to protect his sons from evil when they entered Egypt, by making them use different gates. The sentence "and above every possessor of knowledge there is a more knowledgeable one" is mentioned after Joseph's success in making his brothers bring Benjamin to him and in keeping him there. So, it is possible to see this as the result of Joseph's knowledge prevailing over his father's. Jacob tried, using his knowledge, to protect his sons and ensure the safe return of *all* of them. By virtue of his knowledge, however, Joseph succeeded in making Jacob agree to send Benjamin to Egypt, in the company of his brothers, where Joseph kept him.

We should also remember that Jacob's consent to allow Benjamin to go to Egypt was influenced by his sons finding their goods in their luggage when they returned home after their first visit to Egypt. Joseph executed that plan because he knew, through divine knowledge, the positive effect that it was going to have on his father's decision.

Having explained the meaning of the sentence "and above every possessor of knowledge there is a more knowledgeable one" in this particular Qur'anic context, I must add that this is a universal statement that is always true. The description "possessor of knowledge" applies to every creature that Allah has conferred knowledge on. Even when there is a "possessor of knowledge" whose knowledge is more than that of any other creature, Allah "*the knowledgeable One*" will still be infinitely more knowledgeable. Note Allah's differentiation between the adjective عَلِيمٌ "*'alīm* (knowledgeable one)," which He uses to describe Himself with in many places in the Qur'an (e.g. 2.29), and the phrase ذِى علم "*dhī 'ilm* (possessor of knowledge)" which implies limitedness of knowledge and so cannot be used to describe Allah.

The statement "and above every possessor of knowledge there is a more knowledgeable one" is one of the great lessons of the story of Joseph. No matter how much knowledge a person acquires — even if he becomes as knowledgeable as Jacob — there will always be someone who is more knowledgeable than him. The excellence of the knowledge of a prophet over his father's who is also a prophet reminds us of a similar event that involved prophet David and his son prophet Solomon:

وَدَاوُدَ وَسُلَيْمَـٰنَ إِذْ يَحْكُمَـانِ فِى ٱلْحَرْثِ إِذْ نَفَشَتْ فِيهِ غَنَمُ ٱلْقَوْمِ وَكُـنَّا لِحُكْمِهِمْ شَـٰهِدِينَ ﴿٧٨﴾ فَفَهَّمْنَـٰهَا سُلَيْمَـٰنَ وَكُلًّا ءَاتَيْنَا حُكْـمًا وَعِلْمًـا وَسَخَّرْنَا مَعَ دَاوُدَ ٱلْجِبَالَ يُسَبِّحْنَ وَٱلطَّيْرَ وَكُنَّا فَـٰعِلِينَ ﴿٧٩﴾. (سورة الأنبيَـاءِ).

And [remember] David and Solomon when they gave judgment concerning the field where the people's sheep pastured therein, and We were a witness to their judgment (21.78). So We made Solomon understand it; and to each one of them We gave wisdom and knowledge; and We made the mountains and the birds celebrate Our praise with David; and We were the doers (thereof) (21.79).

These two verses tell us that David and Solomon delivered their judgments on a particular issue: "concerning the field where the people's sheep pastured therein." Solomon's judgment was the best of the two: "So We made Solomon understand it," although both prophets were knowledgeable: "and to each one of them We gave wisdom and knowledge."

قَالُوٓاْ إِن يَسۡرِقۡ فَقَدۡ سَرَقَ أَخٞ لَّهُۥ مِن قَبۡلُۚ فَأَسَرَّهَا يُوسُفُ فِي نَفۡسِهِۦ وَلَمۡ يُبۡدِهَا لَهُمۡۚ قَالَ أَنتُمۡ شَرّٞ مَّكَانٗاۖ وَٱللَّهُ أَعۡلَمُ بِمَا تَصِفُونَ ﴿٧٧﴾

They said: "If he has stolen, a brother of his did indeed steal before." But Joseph kept it secret within himself and did not disclose it to them. He said: "You are in a worse situation, and Allah knows best [the truth of] what you describe" (77).

When it became clear that the drinking cup was in Benjamin's luggage, his half brothers disavowed him. They distanced themselves from Benjamin by accusing Joseph also of stealing. They suggested that there is a connection between the alleged robberies of Joseph and Benjamin and the fact that they were from a different mother. Note their description of Joseph as a brother "of Benjamin" instead of a brother "of theirs." The ten brothers meant to say something to the effect of "those two thieves are brothers from the same father and mother, whereas we are from a different mother, so we are not thieves."

It is possible that by making this claim, Joseph's brothers wanted to ensure that they would not be harmed because of Benjamin's guilt. Mentioning Joseph and accusing him of robbery, however, show that they were still fostering envy for Joseph and Benjamin, as they were years earlier: "Verily Joseph and his brother are dearer to our father than us, though we are a band" (from 12.8). Their accusation of Joseph indicates that they never suspected that the 'Azīz may be Joseph himself.

Although there is no mention in the Qur'an of the theft that Joseph's brothers claimed he committed, exegetes have come up with a number of stories, whose authenticity and reliability are very much in doubt. The story that is most circulated by exegetes claims that in Joseph's childhood, his aunt cunningly accused him of stealing a belt which she had herself given to him. She did this so that she could tell his father that she should keep him as a punishment for the robbery, as she loved him and did not want to return him to his father. This story is linked to the widespread idea among exegetes that the punishment for theft is enslaving the thief. Another story claims that little Joseph stole an idol kept by his maternal grandfather. There are other stories, but there is no reason to think that any of them have any seed of truth as they lack any supportive reference in the Qur'an.

The obvious explanation of Joseph's brothers' accusation is that it was simply a lie. This was not the first time they lied. They lied when they told their father that they would protect Joseph should he allow them to take him with them to play and enjoy himself. They also lied when they claimed that a wolf had devoured Joseph, and smeared his shirt with fake blood.

After hearing what his brothers had to say, Joseph "kept it secret within himself and did not disclose it to them." Exegetes have disagreed about the referent of the singular feminine pronoun, translated as "it," i.e. about the nature of what Joseph kept secret.[83] I think that what Joseph concealed is the "truth" that he could have revealed to rebuff his brothers' accusation of himself and Benjamin in their statement that "if he has stolen, a brother of his did indeed steal before."

Joseph's words "you are in a worse situation, and Allah knows best [the truth of] what you describe" might be an accusation of his half brothers that they accused him and Benjamin because they were from a different mother. Joseph replied but preferred not to disclose the reality of the whole story at the time. The clause "you are in a worse situation" means "you are in a worse state than your half brothers whom you have accused of robbery and distanced yourselves from."

The sentence "and Allah knows best [the truth of] what you describe" doubts the verity of the claim.[84] It has a close meaning to the words "and it is Allah whose help is sought against what you describe" which Jacob said to his sons when they lied and claimed that Joseph was devoured by a wolf. Therefore, Joseph's words doubt his brothers' claim that "if he has stolen, a brother of his did indeed steal before."

> قَالُواْ يَٰٓأَيُّهَا ٱلۡعَزِيزُ إِنَّ لَهُۥٓ أَبٗا شَيۡخٗا كَبِيرٗا فَخُذۡ أَحَدَنَا مَكَانَهُۥٓۖ إِنَّا نَرَىٰكَ مِنَ ٱلۡمُحۡسِنِينَ ﴿٧٨﴾
>
> They said: "O the 'Azīz! He has a father who is a very old man, therefore retain one of us instead of him; surely we see you to be one of the good-doers" (78).

Once the element of surprise had worn off and they started to think of what happened, Joseph's brothers stopped behaving under the mere influence of envy for their half brothers. They remembered their father and the covenant that they gave him in Allah's name to bring back Benjamin. They started to appeal to Joseph to allow Benjamin to go back with them, suggesting that one of them is kept instead.

It is possible that this dialog is a continuation of the one in the previous verses. It is also possible, and may be more likely, that Joseph's brothers reassessed what happened and changed their position after leaving Joseph, and they returned to him with this suggestion later.

Joseph's brothers cited the old age of their father as a reason for Joseph to release Benjamin, as elderly people have less tolerance for pain and are more entitled to help. They sought to make Joseph feel sorry for their father and allow his son to return to him.

Note that they did not say "our father" or "we have a father," but said "he has a father" in order to stress their father's attachment to Benjamin as if he was his only son. As I mentioned in my interpretation of verse 12.61, Joseph's brothers had already mentioned to Joseph, when he asked them to bring Benjamin to Egypt, that their father had special love for Benjamin: "We shall seek the consent of his father about him; and we shall do so."

In this verse, we find Joseph's brothers calling Joseph for the first time "the 'Azīz." This, of course, is the same title carried by the husband of the woman who tried to seduce Joseph. It is clearly a title with a great deal of authority and power. In fact, it was next to the king.

Note that this event, in which Joseph's brothers used this title, took place at the earliest seven years after his release from jail and his appointment by the king as a keeper of the storehouses of the land. This encounter between Joseph and his brothers took place after the end of the good years and during the years of hardship.

When the king released him from jail, Joseph did not ask the king to make him "the 'Azīz," but "the keeper of the storehouses of the land." This means that the position of "the 'Azīz" is different from that of the keeper of the storehouses of the land. Clearly, the latter was also a prominent position, but it is also clear that the title of "the 'Azīz" that Joseph carried involved also the responsibility of keeping the storehouses. Perhaps, the position of the "keeper of the storehouses" is what Joseph occupied immediately after his release from jail, and that "the 'Azīz" is a higher position that he was promoted to afterward and to which he annexed the responsibility of keeping the storehouses, thus combining both responsibilities.

Some might see more likely the possibility that "the 'Azīz" was a title that was carried by any person who reaches a particular level of responsibility. This means that there could have been more than one "Azīz" at the same time, as there are more than one minister, for example. I think, however, that the context of the story stands against this suggestion. The linguistic use of the "'Azīz" in the sūra also rules out this possibility. For instance, the women used the phrase "the wife of the 'Azīz" without specifying a particular 'Azīz. Had there been more than one 'Azīz, the phrase would have been "the wife of 'Azīz so and so."

After citing the old age of their father in order to convince Joseph to let Benjamin go back with them, Joseph's brothers suggested to him taking one of them as a slave instead of Benjamin. Perhaps, Joseph's brothers were not really serious about that offer. It could have been intended only to convince him to release Benjamin, but it is more likely that they were genuinely willing to do that because of the covenant they gave to their father. When what happened had sunk in, Joseph's brothers' reaction changed from the way they reacted at the time of finding the drinking cup in Benjamin's luggage.

We will see later in verse 12.80 that after Joseph's rejection of his brothers' offer, the oldest brother decided to stay in Egypt and not go back until his father permitted him to do so, or until something that justifies his return happens. It is possible that it was this brother who offered to replace Benjamin.

Joseph's brothers ended their appeal to him by praising him: "surely we see you to be one of the good-doers." They meant that "you are a good and kind man so we hope that you will agree to our request and show kindness toward our father." This is the same commendatory clause that the two prisoners used when addressing Joseph. This is a subtle Qur'anic reference to Allah's favor upon Joseph. He changed his state from a prisoner to one with power and authority to imprison people. Allah described Joseph in verse 12.22 as "one of the good-doers," made his prison mates describe him so in verse 12.36, and has now made his brothers also call him "one of the good-doers."

The accusation of theft that Joseph's brothers leveled at Joseph and Benjamin shows that they still had envy for the two, and that they were unsatisfied with their father's preference of their half brothers over them. Their behavior, however, had now become different from their behavior when they put Joseph in the bottom of the well many years earlier. At the time, they did not give any attention to the pain that they would cause to their father, and were only focused on removing Joseph from the scene. This time, we see them try their best so that their other half brother would not end up away from their father. This behavior is in complete contrast to their behavior during the episode of Joseph. This is a remarkable improvement in the behavior of Joseph's brothers.

Additionally, their betrayal of Joseph was a *premeditated* action. They spent days waiting to carry out their plan until they managed to convince their father to send Joseph with them. On the contrary, while their behavior in Benjamin's case showed envy, it was a *spontaneous* reaction. When they thought carefully about the matter, they appealed to Joseph to change his decision and let Benjamin return with them. They even went as far as suggesting to him that he keeps one of them instead.

We must also remember that Joseph's brothers tried their best to help Benjamin despite their belief that he had indeed committed a robbery, as they were unaware of the reality of that charge. In contrast, they treated Joseph with aggression when they threw him in the well although they knew very well that he had not done anything wrong.

Clearly, the way Joseph's brothers thought of their half brothers and their behavior toward them improved markedly.

> قَالَ مَعَاذَ ٱللَّهِ أَن نَّأْخُذَ إِلَّا مَن وَجَدْنَا مَتَـٰعَنَا عِندَهُۥٓ إِنَّآ إِذًا لَّظَـٰلِمُونَ ﴿٧٩﴾
>
> He said: "Allah forbid that we should seize other than the person with whom we found our property, otherwise we would certainly be unjust" (79).

The phrase مَعَاذَ ٱللَّه "*ma'ātha Allah*," which I have translated as "Allah forbid," is used to wish that something does not happen. Joseph used this phrase here to argue that it would be unfair to retain any of his brothers instead of the one in whose luggage the cup was found. In his reply, Joseph overlooked his brothers' comment about their father's attachment to Benjamin. Clearly, he wanted to reject the request of his brothers and keep Benjamin with him.

One beautiful comment made by some exegetes, including al-Jalālayn, is that Joseph did not call his brother a thief. He did not say, for instance, "the person who stole our property," but said "the person with whom we found our property." He was well aware that Benjamin did not steal the king's drinking cup, but it was placed in his luggage according to his plan.

9

Prophet Joseph Reunites With His Father Prophet Jacob

Joseph brought Benjamin to Egypt and kept him there to achieve the greater goal of bringing his father and all of his family to Egypt. In this chapter, we will accompany Joseph as he accomplishes that.

> فَلَمَّا ٱسْتَيْـَٔسُوا۟ مِنْهُ خَلَصُوا۟ نَجِيًّا قَالَ كَبِيرُهُمْ أَلَمْ تَعْلَمُوٓا۟ أَنَّ أَبَاكُمْ قَدْ أَخَذَ عَلَيْكُم مَّوْثِقًا مِّنَ ٱللَّهِ وَمِن قَبْلُ مَا فَرَّطتُمْ فِى يُوسُفَ فَلَنْ أَبْرَحَ ٱلْأَرْضَ حَتَّىٰ يَأْذَنَ لِىٓ أَبِىٓ أَوْ يَحْكُمَ ٱللَّهُ لِى وَهُوَ خَيْرُ ٱلْحَٰكِمِينَ ﴿٨٠﴾
>
> So, when they despaired of [convincing] him, they conferred privately. The eldest among them said: "Do you not know that your father has taken from you a covenant in Allah's name, and how you gave away Joseph before? Therefore I will not depart from this land until my father permits me or Allah judges for me, and He is the best of judges (80).

Joseph's brothers failed in their appeal to convince him to let Benjamin return with them. The clause "when they despaired of [convincing] him" suggests that Joseph's brothers tried their best to make Joseph agree to their request, but in vain.

After losing hope of convincing Joseph, his brothers went into an isolated place and discussed what to do next, having promised their father to bring back Benjamin.[85] The oldest one reminded his brothers that they had given their father a covenant in Allah's name that they would do everything they could to make sure that Benjamin returns with them. He also reminded them of their previous betrayal of their father when they cast Joseph in the well. He seems to be saying that their failure to keep Benjamin resembles their previous act of betrayal with regard to Joseph. The eldest brother then concluded by saying that, since he cannot bring Benjamin back with him, he would not leave Egypt unless his father gives him permission to return or "Allah decides for him."

Some exegetes think that the eldest brother meant by the latter clause that "Allah enables him to go back with Benjamin." It is also possible, however, that it has the more general meaning that "Allah would work something out for him," without specifying what that thing would be. He ended his speech by stating that Allah "is the best of judges."

This verse gives another piece of evidence that Joseph's brothers had changed remarkably. The eldest brother did not only denounce their failure to keep their covenant with their father, but also clearly acknowledged that they all made a mistake with what they did to Joseph.

> ٱرْجِعُوٓا۟ إِلَىٰٓ أَبِيكُمْ فَقُولُوا۟ يَـٰٓأَبَانَآ إِنَّ ٱبْنَكَ سَرَقَ وَمَا شَهِدْنَآ إِلَّا بِمَا عَلِمْنَا وَمَا كُنَّا لِلْغَيْبِ حَـٰفِظِينَ ﴿٨١﴾
>
> Go back to your father and say: 'O our father! Your son has committed theft, and we did not bear witness except to what we have known, and we did not know the unseen'" (81).

Some exegetes think that this speech is part of what Joseph's brothers were saying to each other, i.e. as though they said "let us go back to our father and say....." It is more likely, however, that this speech is a continuation of the oldest brother's words in the previous verse. In this case, "go back to your father" refers to his decision to stay in Egypt, whereas the latter part of the verse represents what he instructed his nine younger brothers to say to their father: "Your son has committed theft, and we did not bear witness except to what we have known, and we did not know the unseen."

These words of Joseph's brothers to their father have been interpreted in a number of different ways by exegetes. Some have suggested that they mean "your son has committed theft. When we gave you the covenant to return him to you, we had no knowledge of the unseen — that he was going to steal from the 'Azīz and that the latter would, therefore, arrest and keep him." Thus, exegetes interpreted the act of "bearing witness" as that of "giving the covenant." The problem with this interpretation is that the sentence "we did not bear witness except to what we have known" refers to "an act of bearing witness that is based on relevant knowledge." This description does not apply to the act of giving a covenant to their father.

The majority of exegetes have adopted one of two main interpretations. The first is that "your son has committed theft, and we did not bear witness except to what we have known" means "Benjamin has committed theft, and in saying this, we only bear witness to what we know." This refers to their presence when the king's drinking cup was produced from Benjamin's luggage. Therefore, the act of "bearing witness" here refers to "informing" their father of the news of what happened. In this case, "and we did not know the unseen" means "but we do not know if he has indeed stolen, as we do not know the unseen." The fact that the verb شَهِدْنَا "*shahidnā* (bore witness)" is in the past tense, however, makes this interpretation unlikely. Had that verb been in the present tense, i.e. as نشهد "*nashhad* (bear witness)," this interpretation would have been likely.

According to the second common interpretation, the words of Joseph's brothers mean: "when we bore witness that the punishment of the thief is enslavement, we did not know the unseen, that our brother had stolen and that he would end up a slave."

I agree with the latter view, but I think that "what we have known" refers to the knowledge of Joseph's brothers that "none of them was a thief." The meaning of their words is: "when we told the 'Azīz that he should take the thief as a slave in punishment for his theft, we did not believe that the thief could be one of us." This interpretation of the act of "bearing witness" is further supported by the fact that it is used in this same meaning in verse 12.26: "and a witness from her own folk bore witness." In both cases, "to bear witness" means "to testify" after being asked to do so.

It is interesting to note that both instances of bearing witness were requested by the 'Azīz, though the identity of the 'Azīz was different on the two occasions.[86]

> وَسْـَٔلِ ٱلْقَرْيَةَ ٱلَّتِى كُنَّا فِيهَا وَٱلْعِيرَ ٱلَّتِىٓ أَقْبَلْنَا فِيهَا وَإِنَّا لَصَـٰدِقُونَ ﴿٨٢﴾
>
> And ask the town in which we were and the camel caravan with which we came, and surely we are truthful" (82).

Whether or not this was a continuation of the instructions given by Joseph's eldest brothers, the next verse shows that Joseph's brothers said the words in this and the previous verses to their father.

Because of what they did to Joseph and of their father's awareness of the ill feelings they had for Benjamin, Jacob's nine sons were expecting their father to have doubts about their account of what happened to their half brother. Emphasizing the accuracy of their account, they suggested to him checking it with the town in which they were, i.e. the place in which Benjamin stayed, and with the caravan in which they came.

Obviously, the suggestion of Jacob's sons to their father to "ask the town in which we were" was symbolic. They did not mean that Jacob should go to Egypt to enquire about what happened. They meant that if their father would be able to go to the town where the events took place, he would discover the truthfulness of their account.

As for the caravan, it is possible that when Jacob's sons came back they were still in the company of caravanners who were in Egypt and who were aware of what happened to Benjamin. It is equally possible that this is also symbolic, suggesting that Jacob may catch the caravan and enquire about what took place.

قَالَ بَلْ سَوَّلَتْ لَكُمْ أَنفُسُكُمْ أَمْرًا فَصَبْرٌ جَمِيلٌ عَسَى ٱللَّهُ أَن يَأْتِيَنِى بِهِمْ جَمِيعًا إِنَّهُۥ هُوَ ٱلْعَلِيمُ ٱلْحَكِيمُ ﴿٨٣﴾

He said: "[No,] rather your souls have suggested to you [doing] something [evil]; so, [my course is] perfect patience; may Allah bring them all together to me. Surely He is the Knowing, the Wise" (83).

Jacob's comment on what his sons told him resembles his response to them when they told him that a wolf had devoured Joseph: "[No,] rather your souls have suggested to you [doing] something [evil]; so, [my course is] perfect patience. And it is Allah whose help is sought against what you describe" (from 12.18). In both cases, Jacob accused his sons of giving in to some evil suggestions from their lower selves, and said that he would keep patient and not complain about the calamity that hit him.

Jacob's sons unjustly accused Joseph of theft and falsely suggested that their half brothers were thieves because they were from a different mother, instead of defending Benjamin. This confirms Jacob's belief that his sons harbored evil: "[No,] rather your souls have suggested to you [doing] something [evil]."

It should be noted, however, that even if Jacob's sons did not level those charges at Benjamin and tried instead to defend him, they would not have influenced Joseph's decision to keep his brother. He had already decided to do that anyway, so the evil that was suggested by the lower selves of Jacob's sons did not play any role in making Joseph retain Benjamin.

Although Jacob's responses to his sons' accounts after Joseph's and Benjamin disappearances share significant similarities, they also have significant differences. In the aftermath of throwing Joseph in the well, Jacob threw doubts on his sons' claims that *they went racing with one another, leaving Joseph alone with their belongings, so he was devoured by a wolf.* He commented on their claims: "it is Allah whose help is sought against what you describe," asking Allah to disclose the truth of what happened. Indeed, Jacob's sons had given their father a completely false account.

On the contrary, when Jacob's sons failed to return Benjamin, their account about the events was accurate. They did indeed think that Benjamin committed a theft and that he became a slave because of that robbery. Remarkably, Jacob did not doubt the truthfulness of their account. He did not say something to the effect of "it is Allah whose help is sought against what you describe" which would have indicated his rejection of the story about the alleged death of Joseph.

Jacob was therefore accurate not to accuse his sons of giving a false account of the events, and he was equally right to accuse their lower selves of having suggested something evil to them. This reflects the degree of knowledge that Allah bestowed on him.

Jacob then added "may Allah bring them all together to me." Speaking in the plural rather than in the dual means that he was referring to Joseph also, not only to Benjamin and his oldest son. This a clear confirmation that Jacob was totally aware that Joseph was still alive and that he was going to reunite with him at some point. This is in line with my earlier observation that Jacob knew the interpretation of talks and knew from Joseph's dream the future that Allah had ordained for him, Joseph, and the rest of his sons.

It is also likely that the marked improvement in the behavior of Joseph's brothers made them confess to their father the truth of what happened to Joseph — that they threw him in the well and that a wolf did not really devour him. This is supported by the fact that they were aware that their father did not believe for a moment their fake story about Joseph, as I indicated in my interpretation of verse 12.18. This does not mean, nevertheless, that Joseph's brothers shared their father's unshaken belief throughout the long years that their brother was still alive.

It is clear from Jacob's words "may Allah bring them all together to me" that he was not aware, at least until then, of the nature of his future reuniting with his sons. Jacob prayed to Allah to "bring" his sons to him, whereas Allah would make him "go" to the place of his three sons, i.e. Egypt, as we will see later.

After praying to Allah to make it possible for him to reunite with his sons, Jacob says: "surely He is the Knowing, the Wise." This highlights Jacob's acceptance that the loss of his sons, his future reuniting with them, its time, and the way in which it would happen are all decided by the knowledge of Allah who brings about events as He pleases. As I mentioned, Jacob was not aware that his reuniting with his sons was not going to be in the form of "them coming to him" but "him going to them." How beautiful, therefore, are his words "surely He is the Knowing, the Wise" that follow his prayer! They are an acknowledgment that it is Allah "the Knowing, the Wise" who ultimately decides what happens. They also represent surrender to Allah's decision and choice.

How good is that which Allah chose for Jacob and his sons! Jacob asked Allah to reunite him with his sons by making them return home.

Allah's answer to Jacob's prayer, however, was much better than the request. He took Jacob and his sons to where Joseph was living, and gathered them together in a place where they enjoyed a much better life.

وَتَوَلَّىٰ عَنْهُمْ وَقَالَ يَٰٓأَسَفَىٰ عَلَىٰ يُوسُفَ وَٱبْيَضَّتْ عَيْنَاهُ مِنَ ٱلْحُزْنِ فَهُوَ كَظِيمٌ ﴿٨٤﴾

And he turned away from them, and said: "Alas, my grief for Joseph!" And his eyes became white because of the grief, for he kept within him lots of grief (84).

After his reaction in the previous verse to the news about his two sons staying in Egypt, Jacob stopped talking to his sons about what happened.

It is interesting to note that despite his sadness for missing his other two sons, Jacob's permanent sorrow was mainly for Joseph: "Alas, my grief for Joseph!". Jacob specially cared for Benjamin also, but his care for Joseph was exceptional because he was aware of the high status of this prophet and his nearness to Allah. Losing Joseph when he was still a small child, and the long years of separation, would have also played a role in establishing that sorrowfulness in Jacob's heart.

Jacob's sadness was enormous to the extent that it caused him to lose his sight: "And his eyes became white because of the grief." If there is any doubt that the *whitening of the eye* means *blindness*, Joseph's speech to his brothers in verse 12.93 dispels that: "Go with this shirt of mine and cast it on my father's face. He will come sighted [to Egypt]."

It is interesting to discuss how the expression *whitening of the eye* acquired the sense of *blindness*. The human eye consists of two parts, white and colored. The white part has nothing to do with sight, which is the function of the central, colored part. Therefore, the expression *whitening of the eye* implies that the eye lost its colored part with which it sees and was left with the white part only, hence referring to blindness. Obviously, the expression is symbolic and does not mean that the eye becomes physically white.

It is worth noting that Jacob's loss of sight is mentioned right after his sorrowful utterance: "Alas, my grief for Joseph!". This clearly indicates that it was his sadness for Joseph in particular, not for his other two sons who were in Egypt, which caused his blindness. Joseph's plan to keep Benjamin in Egypt had no role in his father's loss of sight. Jacob's sadness for losing Joseph was so great that his sorrow for Benjamin was almost negligible.

After mentioning Jacob's sadness for Joseph and his consequent loss of sight, Allah ends this verse by stressing the enormous grief that Jacob kept within himself.[87]

قَالُواْ تَٱللَّهِ تَفْتَؤُاْ تَذْكُرُ يُوسُفَ حَتَّىٰ تَكُونَ حَرَضًا أَوْ تَكُونَ مِنَ ٱلْهَٰلِكِينَ ﴿٨٥﴾
They said: "By Allah! You will not cease to remember Joseph until you are about to die or be one of the dead" (85).

This verse cites something that was addressed to Jacob, but it does not identify the speakers, referring to them only with the plural verb قَالُوا "*qālū* ([they] said)." It is possible that the plural form here refers to some of Jacob's family other than his sons, such as the families of his sons, but it is more likely that the reference is to the same group mentioned in the previous verse, i.e. Jacob's sons.

The occurrence of this verse after the clause "and he turned away from them" in the previous verse means that this verse does not describe a particular event, but simply summarizes the speakers' unease with Jacob's unceasing concern over Joseph.

Exegetes have suggested a number of meanings for the term حَرَضًا "*ḥaraḍan*" all of which have the sense of "frailness" and "poor health." It seems to me that the most accurate meaning is "close to death," as it fits better in the verse, and in particular with the phrase "one of the dead" which follows. Note that this speech reflects the concern of the speakers, who are likely to be Jacob's sons, about his health. They thought that Jacob's continued thinking of Joseph and his sorrow for him were damaging his health, as he had already lost his sight.

The claim of Jacob's sons that their father's undiminished remembrance of Joseph would bring him close to death or kill him means that they believed that Jacob was not going to see Joseph again. Jacob's sons had ruled out the possibility of their father meeting Joseph again, even in the remote possibility that their brother was still alive.

قَالَ إِنَّمَا أَشْكُواْ بَثِّى وَحُزْنِىٓ إِلَى ٱللَّهِ وَأَعْلَمُ مِنَ ٱللَّهِ مَا لَا تَعْلَمُونَ ﴿٨٦﴾
He said: "I only complain of my grief and sorrow to Allah, and I know from Allah what you do not know (86).

Jacob's reply to his sons' criticism implied a refutation of their denunciation of his remembrance of Joseph, and an explanation of the mistake they made in their judgment. In the first half of his reply, "I only complain of my grief and sorrow to Allah," Jacob drew his sons' attention to the fact that he was not complaining about his sorrowfulness to anyone other than Allah. Perfect patience means not to complain *of* Allah, whether within one's self or to other people, but it does not mean not to complain *to* Allah. Complaining to Allah is an act of worship, because it is one form of praying, so it can only be good. It is as if Jacob is saying to his critics: "How can you criticize my complaint of sadness when I am complaining to Allah only?"

There is some disagreement among exegetes about the meaning of بَثِّى "*baththī*." Some think that it means "my need," but the more likely interpretation seems to be "the grief that is so great that the person cannot help but talk about it." Note that the verb بَثَّ "*baththa*" means "voiced," "broadcast"...etc.

Jacob knew that Joseph was still alive and that he was going to reunite with him. This is the knowledge he refers to in the second half of his reply to his sons' criticism of his continued mention of Joseph: "I know from Allah what you do not know." This sūra told us early on that Jacob had knowledge of the interpretation of talks, which enabled him to interpret Joseph's dream about his future and the future of Jacob's family. It is also likely that Allah later revealed to Jacob more information about Joseph.

Note that Jacob did not disclose to his sons the nature of the knowledge that he received from Allah and which they were ignorant of. He did not want the bad feelings they were still carrying for Joseph to prevent them from doing what he was going to ask them to do: look for Joseph and Benjamin. Had Jacob told his sons that he knew that Allah had conferred on Joseph great favors and established him in a land, it is unlikely that they would go to search for Joseph, partly because of their envy for him, and partly because of their fear that he might take revenge on them.

The nature of Jacob's complaint to Allah was different from what his sons thought. Jacob did not complain to Allah about his concern over Joseph; he knew that Allah had ordained great favors for his son. He was complaining to his Lord about his sorrowfulness for missing Joseph and longing to see him.

> يَٰبَنِيَّ ٱذْهَبُوا۟ فَتَحَسَّسُوا۟ مِن يُوسُفَ وَأَخِيهِ وَلَا تَا۟يْـَٔسُوا۟ مِن رَّوْحِ ٱللَّهِ إِنَّهُۥ لَا يَا۟يْـَٔسُ مِن رَّوْحِ ٱللَّهِ إِلَّا ٱلْقَوْمُ
> ٱلْكَٰفِرُونَ ﴿٨٧﴾
>
> O my sons! Go and trace Joseph and his brother, and do not despair of Allah's mercy; surely no one despairs of Allah's mercy except the disbelieving people" (87).

This verse informs us of Jacob's decision at some point to send his sons to look for Joseph and Benjamin. Since Benjamin was in Egypt, it is clear that Jacob sent his sons to that land. We will see a clear reference to this in the next verse.

Jacob's instruction to his sons to look for "Joseph and his brother" means that he knew that Joseph also was in Egypt. Mentioning Joseph before his brother stresses the fact that Jacob's instruction to his sons to go to Egypt was as much about looking for Joseph as looking for Benjamin. It is even likely that Jacob knew that his sons were at the same place or at least in places near to each other.

Note that the clause "trace Joseph and his brother" might mean that tracing one of the two brothers would eventually lead to the other, suggesting that the brothers were near to each other.[88]

We have seen in verse 12.67 that Jacob ordered his sons to enter Egypt from different gates. As explained earlier, Jacob wanted to make sure that the border guards would not notice that his sons revisited Egypt within a short period of time, and also to avoid the possibility of something evil happening to all of them. It is clear that these two possibilities were present during the third visit of Jacob's sons to Egypt, so why does the verse not indicate that Jacob ordered his sons to enter from different gates this time also? Based on my interpretation above, Jacob would certainly have done that. The reason for omitting any reference to that is the Qur'anic style of choosing shorter clauses and sentences, thus at times not stating explicitly what can be concluded from the context.

After instructing them to go to Egypt to look for Joseph and Benjamin, Jacob reminded his sons not to despair of the mercy of Allah. He then finished his speech to them with a reminder that despairing of Allah's mercy is the work of the disbelievers. The explanation of this is that losing hope that Allah might change things to the better amounts to believing in limits to His power. Jacob's advice to his sons "do not despair of Allah's mercy; surely no one despairs of Allah's mercy except the disbelieving people" is equivalent to the older words of his grandfather Abraham: وَمَن يَقْنَطُ مِن رَّحْمَةِ رَبِّهِۦٓ إِلَّا ٱلضَّآلُّونَ "and who loses hope of the mercy of his Lord but those who have gone astray?" (from 15.56).

One aspect of beauty in Jacob's words is to see him — he who had lost his sight because of his grief over Joseph — instruct his sighted, healthy, and young sons not to fall in the trap of disbelief of despairing of the mercy of Allah. The terrible combination of sorrow for Joseph, frailness of old age, and losing his sight could not make the elderly Jacob fall into despair of Allah's mercy. In contrast, his sons, who had not suffered anything that is even remotely close to their father's ordeal, had lost hope of returning Benjamin to their father.

Note how each episode of the story of Joseph has lessons and sermons to each of its characters. These are living lessons that continue to pour their wisdom to the reader of this fascinating story.

فَلَمَّا دَخَلُوا۟ عَلَيْهِ قَالُوا۟ يَـٰٓأَيُّهَا ٱلْعَزِيزُ مَسَّنَا وَأَهْلَنَا ٱلضُّرُّ وَجِئْنَا بِبِضَـٰعَةٍ مُّزْجَىٰةٍ فَأَوْفِ لَنَا ٱلْكَيْلَ وَتَصَدَّقْ عَلَيْنَآ إِنَّ ٱللَّهَ يَجْزِى ٱلْمُتَصَدِّقِينَ ﴿٨٨﴾

So when they entered his place, they said: "O the 'Azīz! Harm has afflicted us and our family, and we have brought poor goods, so give us full measure and be charitable to us; surely Allah rewards the charitable" (88).

In response to their father's order, Jacob's sons went to Egypt and met the 'Azīz Joseph for the third time.

A large number of exegetes have suggested that Jacob's sons brought a letter to Joseph from their father pleading with him to let his son come back with his brothers. There is actually no reference in the verse to the alleged letter. Had that really happened, it would have been mentioned in the speech of Jacob's sons to Joseph. They told Joseph that they brought "poor goods." They did not mention bringing anything else.

Exegetes have not only reiterated the unfounded story of the alleged letter, but also claimed that Allah reprimanded Jacob for writing that letter of complaint to the 'Azīz! Note how contradictory this claim is to Jacob's words and behavior which show his great patience and refusal to complain to anyone other than Allah. This unjustified accusation of Jacob is similar to the exegetes' unfair accusation of Joseph that he erred when he asked one of his prison mates to mention his story to his lord.

Clearly, Jacob's sons did not know where and how to start looking for Joseph, in obedience to their father's order. Therefore, they went to look for Benjamin whom they had left with the 'Azīz. Asking for provisions seems to be a pretext used by Jacob's sons to get close to the 'Azīz again, to check on Benjamin and explore the possibility of bringing him back.

Keeping secret the real goal of their visit is another proof that Jacob's sons did not convey a message from their father to Joseph. They would not present such a letter to Joseph unless they were going to talk to him openly about Benjamin.

The "harm" that Jacob's sons mentioned is the lack of provisions, as they followed that by saying that they had brought with them poor goods and requested Joseph to give them full measure and be charitable to them.[89]

Some exegetes think that asking Joseph to be charitable means that Joseph's brothers asked Joseph to let Benjamin come back with them. This is an unlikely interpretation, as there is nothing in the verse to suggest that. In fact, they deliberately refrained from mentioning Benjamin and mentioned only their lack of provisions. It is likely, however, that they used that tone of humility to subtly influence Joseph that he may release Benjamin.

قَالَ هَلْ عَلِمْتُم مَّا فَعَلْتُم بِيُوسُفَ وَأَخِيهِ إِذْ أَنتُمْ جَـٰهِلُونَ ﴿٨٩﴾

He said: "Do you know how you treated Joseph and his brother when you were ignorant?" (89).

Joseph has decided that the time has come for him to reveal his real identity to his brothers.

Despite the evil nature of what his brothers did to him and to Benjamin, Joseph reminded his brothers of what they did in a kind way that reflects his merciful and forgiving nature. This is the same nature of his father Jacob and his grandfathers Isaac and Abraham. The inquiring style, "do you know," is the lightest form of reminding someone of their guilt.

Note also the link in Joseph's reminder to his brothers between the verb "know" and the adjective "ignorant" which have opposite meanings, and how they refer to two different times. It is as if Joseph had told his brothers: "you did that in the *past* when you were *ignorant*, so do you *know today* the evil reality of what you did?" In his gentle criticism of his brothers, Joseph differentiated between their past and present. He attributed the evil that they did to the past, and implied in his question that their present is different from their past, and that they were no longer the same ignorant people who mistreated him and Benjamin.

We have seen that although Joseph's brothers were still harboring ill feelings for Joseph and Benjamin at the time when Joseph kept him in Egypt, they had actually changed remarkably. The 'Azīz's stunning revelation to Jacob's sons that he is Joseph, their brother, changed them completely and irreversibly. Allah transformed Joseph's brothers gradually and prepared them for the moment when Joseph revealed his real identity to them, at which point He completed His transformation of their character. He continued His preparation of them for the time when He was going to make them like their brother Joseph and their fathers: prophets. As I showed in my interpretation of verse 12.6 in Chapter 3, the Qur'anic term "*Asbāṭ*" refers to prophets, and these prophets are Joseph and his eleven brothers.

The situation described in this verse represents the fulfillment of Allah's promise to Joseph when his brothers threw him in the well: "You will certainly inform them of this affair of theirs while they are unaware" (from 12.15). Throughout their three visits to the 'Azīz and up to the moment when Joseph reminded them of what they did to him, Joseph's brothers were unaware of his identity. He also mentioned their ill treatment of Benjamin.

قَالُوٓاْ أَءِنَّكَ لَأَنتَ يُوسُفُ قَالَ أَنَا۠ يُوسُفُ وَهَٰذَآ أَخِى قَدْ مَنَّ ٱللَّهُ عَلَيْنَآ إِنَّهُۥ مَن يَتَّقِ وَيَصْبِرْ فَإِنَّ ٱللَّهَ لَا يُضِيعُ أَجْرَ ٱلْمُحْسِنِينَ ﴿٩٠﴾

They said: "Are you indeed Joseph?" He said: "I am Joseph, and this is my brother; Allah has indeed conferred on us favors; surely, as for he who acts dutifully and patiently, Allah does not waste the reward of the good-doers" (90).

When Joseph's brothers heard the 'Azīz's words, they realized that he was Joseph. The surprise, however, was so stunning that their reply was in the form of a question: "Are you indeed Joseph?" as if to say: "can it be true that you are Joseph?" They could not understand or even imagine how the little child whom they threw in the well somewhere very far from Egypt could have reached the prestigious position of the 'Azīz in Egypt. They were equally unable to understand how the 'Azīz, whom they visited and talked to on three different occasions, could have been Joseph without them discovering that.

Joseph answered "I am Joseph," in reply to the question of his stunned brothers, confirming his identity, as if he said: "Yes, it is me, the 'Azīz, Joseph himself."

Joseph's answer contains something intriguing that, although exegetes have failed to notice, reveals interesting details. Although his brothers' question was about his identity, Joseph included Benjamin in his reply. He did not say "I am Joseph" and continued with "Allah has indeed conferred on me favors," but he referred to Benjamin also saying: "I am Joseph, and this is my brother; Allah has indeed conferred on us favors." So, why did he do that?

Note that Joseph's words "I am Joseph" revealed his identity to his brothers, so the second part of his reply, "and this is my brother," must have revealed Benjamin's identity. This in turn means that, as they failed to recognize Joseph, Joseph's brothers did not recognize Benjamin. The demonstrative pronoun هَٰذَا "*hādhā* (this)" is used for things and people that are *near*. Using it to refer to Benjamin means that he was also present during Joseph's conversation with his brothers. But how do we explain the failure of Joseph's brothers to recognize Benjamin?

It seems that Joseph had made Benjamin wear Egyptian clothes which completely changed the way he looked. He had also made him a high ranking person in his office, thus further hiding his identity from his brothers. Joseph met on three different occasions with his brothers without allowing them to recognize him, and planned and executed the plan to keep Benjamin with him without raising any doubt in his brothers' minds about his role. He was certainly able to change Benjamin's appearance so that his brothers would not recognize him.

Thus, as they failed to see Joseph in the 'Azīz, Joseph's brothers failed to realize that the other Egyptian looking high ranking officer was in fact Benjamin.

This explains Joseph's declaration "and this is my brother." This interpretation explains Joseph's reference to Allah's favors not only on himself but on Benjamin also: "Allah has indeed conferred on us favors." As Joseph had become the 'Azīz, Benjamin had also been given a high position. It is as if Joseph has said to his brothers: "you mistreated me and my brother and intended evil for us, but Allah wanted for us good, and He does what He wants."

Joseph went on to stress that dutifulness and patience are the way to attain Allah's favor: "surely, as for he who acts dutifully and patiently, Allah does not waste the reward of the good-doers." Allah has assigned rewards in this world and in the hereafter for the dutiful and patient person. We have seen that dutifulness and patience were two qualities that never departed Joseph at any stage of his life, including the times of hardship and calamity. The story suggests that Benjamin was also a righteous person. Thus, after revealing his and Benjamin's identity and the favors that Allah had conferred on them, Joseph explained to his brothers that dutifulness and patience, not deceit and perfidy, are the way to Allah's favors.

There is a contrast in this situation that shows that Allah promotes and demotes people as He wants, and that no one can challenge His will. Joseph was in a prestigious status of power, and Benjamin in a state of honor and respect. On the contrary, his half brothers were in his office in a state of need and humiliation, as clearly shown in the humble tone of their words. They spoke about the hard times that they and their families were having, explained that they could only bring poor goods, and asked Joseph to show generosity and charity toward them: "So when they entered his place, they said: 'O 'Azīz! Harm has afflicted us and our family, and we have brought poor goods, so give us full measure and be charitable to us; surely Allah rewards the charitable'."

﴿قَالُواْ تَٱللَّهِ لَقَدْ ءَاثَرَكَ ٱللَّهُ عَلَيْنَا وَإِن كُنَّا لَخَٰطِـِٔينَ ﴿٩١﴾﴾

They said: "By Allah! Allah has indeed preferred you over us, and we have been sinners" (91).

The reply of Joseph's brothers was an acknowledgment, supported by an oath, that Allah has preferred Joseph over them, and that they were sinners in what they did to Joseph, Benjamin, and their father. They mistreated Joseph and Benjamin, caused their father so much pain because of what they did to Joseph, and accused him of unfairly preferring Joseph to them: "Verily Joseph and his brother are dearer to our father than us, though we are a band; surely, our father is in manifest error" (12.8). They accepted now that it was Allah, not their father, who had preferred Joseph over them, so they surrendered to Allah's will.

This situation in which they acknowledged their guilt resembles the acknowledgment of the wife of the former 'Azīz of her guilt. This supports my view that she genuinely repented and became righteous.

قَالَ لَا تَثْرِيبَ عَلَيْكُمُ الْيَوْمَ يَغْفِرُ اللَّهُ لَكُمْ وَهُوَ أَرْحَمُ الرَّاحِمِينَ ﴿٩٢﴾

He said: "You shall not be rebuked today. [May] Allah forgive you, and He is the most Merciful of the merciful ones" (92).

Joseph's brothers would have expected from Joseph some retaliation for what they did to him, particularly as he was in a state of power that allowed him to exert any kind of revenge he would have wanted. The reaction of the merciful and forgiving Joseph to his brothers' acknowledgement of their guilt was a reassurance that he had no intention of even criticizing them for what happened in the past: "You shall not be rebuked today."

Joseph followed his words "You shall not be rebuked" with the word "today" to stress that *now* his brothers were not as they were in the past, and that he was not going to criticize them for the evil that they had committed. Joseph's discernment between his brothers' past and their present re-enforced the implication of his earlier speech to them: "Do you know how you treated Joseph and his brother when you were ignorant?", as I pointed out in my comment on that verse. This discernment is thus another confirmation that they completely changed. This is consistent with the fact that Joseph's brothers later became prophets.

Joseph's noble treatment of his brothers was mentioned by Prophet Muhammad after his peaceful conquer of Mecca. The tribe of Quraysh, who used to control Mecca, had tortured and killed Muslims and put them under social and economic sanctions when they were in Mecca, and continued to wage war against them after they immigrated to al-Madīna. The Prophet asked the Qurayshites about what they thought he was going to do to them. They answered: "Good! You are a generous brother and a generous cousin, with power." The Messenger replied: "And I say as my brother Joseph said: 'You shall not be rebuked today'." What mercy is this that made this honorable Prophet forgive, while in a state of power, those who subjected him, his family, and followers, when they were weak, to all forms of extreme suffering!

In fact, the companion ‘Umar bin al-Khattāb had already told the people of Mecca after it was conquered by the Muslims: “Today we will take revenge on you and do so and so.” He later said: “I sweated in embarrassment as a result of the words of the Messenger of Allah.” Allah revealed that he put in Prophet Muhammad mercy from Him:

فَبِمَا رَحْمَةٍ مِنَ اللَّهِ لِنتَ لَهُمْ وَلَوْ كُنتَ فَظًّا غَلِيظَ الْقَلْبِ لَانفَضُّوا مِنْ حَوْلِكَ فَاعْفُ عَنْهُمْ وَاسْتَغْفِرْ لَهُمْ وَشَاوِرْهُمْ فِي الْأَمْرِ فَإِذَا عَزَمْتَ فَتَوَكَّلْ عَلَى اللَّهِ إِنَّ اللَّهَ يُحِبُّ الْمُتَوَكِّلِينَ ﴿١٥٩﴾. (سورة آل عمران).

“It is due to mercy from Allah that you [O Muhammad!] are so gentle with them [those who believe]; and had you been rough, hard-hearted, they would have certainly dispersed from around you. So, pardon them, ask forgiveness for them, and consult with them [on various matters]. So, when you have decided [on an action], then rely on Allah. Surely, Allah loves those who rely [on Him]” (3.159).

It is no surprise that the Last Prophet should be merciful, having been described as a mercy for people:

وَمَا أَرْسَلْنَاكَ إِلاَّ رَحْمَةً لِلْعَالَمِينَ ﴿١٠٧﴾. (سورة الأنبياء).

And We have not sent you [O Muhammad!] but as a mercy to the people (21.107).

Joseph did not only avoid criticizing his brothers, but also prayed to Allah to forgive them: “[may] Allah forgive you.”[90] He made it clear to his brothers that he held no grudge against them and would not even ask for an apology, but that it is Allah whom they should apologize to and ask for forgiveness from. Joseph then ended his speech by saying “and He is the most Merciful of the merciful ones,” stressing the case to always hope for forgiveness from Allah.[91]

اذْهَبُوا بِقَمِيصِي هَـٰذَا فَأَلْقُوهُ عَلَىٰ وَجْهِ أَبِي يَأْتِ بَصِيرًا وَأْتُونِي بِأَهْلِكُمْ أَجْمَعِينَ ﴿٩٣﴾

Go with this shirt of mine and cast it on my father’s face. He will come sighted [to Egypt]; and bring to me all your families” (93).

The Qur’anic text does not say how Joseph came to know about the blindness of his father. He could have known about that from Allah or through his brothers. No doubt, after Joseph revealed his real identity to his brothers, they spoke for long, and the state of his father would have been the first thing they would have talked about. The verse tells us that Joseph gave his shirt to his brothers to put over his father’s face to restore his sight. Note the tone of confidence in Joseph's words that the miracle will happen: "He will come sighted [to Egypt]."

One aspect of the eloquence of the Qur'an in this verse is the use of the verb يَـأْتِ "*ya'ti* (come)" to replace two clauses with one. Instead of having one clause for the restoration of Jacob's sight and another for Joseph's request for his father to come to Egypt, the single clause يَـأْتِ بَصِـيرًا "*ya'ti baṣīran* (he will come sighted [to Egypt])" conveys both meanings.

There is another aspect of the fascinating eloquence of the Qur'anic clause "he will come sighted [to Egypt]," which reveals Joseph's noble prophetic manners. Joseph wanted his brothers to bring all of their families to Egypt, so he said to them: "bring to me all your families." He also wanted his father to come to Egypt. However, the politeness and courtesy that Allah taught him would not allow him to use that instructive request when referring to his father. He did not therefore say something such as "and let my father come." He used instead the informative clause "he will come sighted [to Egypt]," which has a verb in the present tense. In other words, he *informed of*, not *requested*, the coming of his father.

These are the kind of good manners that Allah confers on His chosen servants. He praised Prophet Muhammad saying وَإِنَّـكَ لَعَـلَىٰ خُلُـقٍ عَظِيمٍ "and you have great manners" (68.4). The Messenger of Allah said about the noble manners that Allah has conferred on him: أدّبني ربّي فأحسن تأديبي "Allah has brought me up. He brought me up with the best manners."

The sublime manners of prophets are a special gift from Allah to those chosen servants. We often fail even to recognize signs and allusions of good manners in the behavior and speech of the prophets, such as Joseph's words in verse 12.93, let alone have manners close to theirs.

Almost all exegetes agree that the shirt that is mentioned in this verse is the same shirt that Allah made Abraham, Joseph's great grandfather, wear to protect him from the fire in which his disbelieving people threw him. They think that Abraham left this shirt to his son Isaac, who passed it to his son Jacob, who then gave it to his son Joseph. The source of this interpretation is a false saying that some attribute to Prophet Muhammad and others to his grandson al-Ḥusayn. The Qur'an explicitly contradicts this inauthentic saying and stresses that the shirt was Joseph's, as we will see below.

Let us start first with the story of Allah's rescue of Abraham from the fire in which his disbelieving people threw him:

قَالُوا۟ حَرِّقُوهُ وَٱنصُرُوٓا۟ ءَالِـهَتَكُمْ إِن كُنـتُمْ فَـٰعِلِينَ ﴿٦٨﴾ قُلْنَا يَـٰنَارُ كُونِى بَرْدًا وَسَلَـٰمًا عَلَىٰٓ إِبْرَٰهِيمَ ﴿٦٩﴾. (سورة الأنبيَـاء).

They said: "Burn him and stand by your gods; do that" (21.68). We said:

"O fire! Be coolness and peace for Abraham" (21.69).

Note that Allah did not say that He changed the properties of Abraham's body making him fireproof, or that He covered him with something to protect him from the fire. He rather ordered the "fire" to be "coolness and peace for Abraham." Allah changed the properties of that fire and made it unable to harm the body of His prophet. Allah is the Creator of everything, including natural laws, and He is capable of changing those laws whenever and in whatever way He wants. In this miracle, He made the fire incapable of burning Abraham's body, so Abraham was not in need for a cover to protect him from the fire.

Let us now see what the Qur'an says about the shirt. Joseph described the shirt as: "this shirt of mine." If that shirt really belonged to his grandfather Abraham, as claimed by exegetes, Joseph would not have attributed it to himself. Joseph was too polite, well mannered, and respectful of his grandfather to do that.

We will also see in the next verse that when Joseph's brothers headed to Jacob's land, their father smelt the "scent of Joseph" not the "scent of Abraham" or any other prophet.

Additionally, it is very difficult to understand how Abraham's shirt could have ended up in the possession of Joseph in Egypt. First, Abraham was a "young man" when the miracle of the cold fire occurred, whereas Joseph was a "young boy" when he was thrown in the well by his brothers.[92] Obviously, that shirt was too large for him, so Joseph could not have worn it. Second, after throwing him into the well, Joseph's brothers smeared Joseph's shirt with fake blood and brought it home to their father: "And they came with false blood on his shirt." So, even if Joseph had worn that shirt, it was taken from him by his brothers before they cast him into the well.

It is thus clear that the shirt Joseph sent to his father was his, and that his father's cure by that shirt was a divine miracle that Allah conferred on Joseph and Jacob. The miracle of Joseph's restoration of his father's sight was no different from a miracle such as Jesus' healing the blind from birth:

إِذْ قَالَ ٱللَّهُ يَـٰعِيسَى ٱبْنَ مَرْيَمَ ٱذْكُرْ نِعْمَتِى عَلَيْكَ وَعَلَىٰ وَٰلِدَتِكَ إِذْ أَيَّدتُّكَ بِرُوحِ ٱلْقُدُسِ تُكَلِّمُ
ٱلنَّاسَ فِى ٱلْـمَهْدِ وَكَهْلاً وَإِذْ عَلَّمْتُكَ ٱلْكِتَـٰبَ وَٱلْحِكْمَةَ وَٱلتَّوْرَاةَ وَٱلإِنجِيلَ وَإِذْ تَخْلُقُ مِنَ ٱلطِّينِ
كَهَيْئَةِ ٱلطَّيْرِ بِإِذْنِى فَتَنفُخُ فِيهَا فَتَكُونُ طَيْرًۢا بِإِذْنِى وَتُبْرِئُ ٱلأَكْمَهَ وَٱلْأَبْرَصَ بِإِذْنِى وَإِذْ تُخْرِجُ
ٱلْـمَوْتَىٰ بِإِذْنِى وَإِذْ كَفَفْتُ بَنِىٓ إِسْرَٰٓءِيلَ عَنكَ إِذْ جِئْتَهُم بِٱلْبَيِّنَـٰتِ فَقَالَ ٱلَّذِينَ كَفَرُواْ مِنْهُمْ إِنْ
هَـٰذَآ إِلَّا سِحْرٌ مُّبِينٌ ﴿١١٠﴾. (سورة المَائِدَة).

> When Allah said: "O Jesus, son of Mary! Remember My favor on you and on your mother, that I have supported you with the *Rūḥ al-Qudus* (Spirit of al-Qudus), [and made you] speak to people in the cradle and when of old age; and that I taught you the Book, Wisdom, and the Torah and the Injīl; and that you create out of clay the figure of a bird by My permission, then you breath into it and it becomes a bird by My permission, and heal he who was born blind and the leprous by My permission; and that you raise the dead by My permission; and that I withheld the Children of Israel from you when you came to them with clear proofs, but those who disbelieved among them said: 'This is nothing but clear magic'" (5.110).

Perhaps, Jesus cured the blind by touching them directly, such as touching them by his hand or blowing on their eyes, or indirectly, such as touching them by personal objects that have acquired blessings from him, such as his clothes. Similarly, Joseph restored his father's sight with his shirt that had contact with his body and had thus acquired blessings from him. The blessings that Allah conferred on Joseph enabled him to restore his father's sight, as the blessings that Allah bestowed on Jesus enabled this prophet to cure the blind from birth and perform other miracles. The sources of such miracles and religious paranormal phenomena are blessings that Allah confers on prophets and righteous people, making the blessed person a source of blessings. The originator and maintainer of the blessings is Allah.

The fact that Allah made the fire in which Abraham was thrown cool and peaceful for him does not mean that this fire could was harmless to others also. This is something that Abraham's people who witnessed the miracle experienced first hand. Similarly, Joseph's shirt would not "necessarily" cure every blind person. All that can be concluded from the Qur'anic text is that Joseph was aware that casting his shirt on the face of his father was going to restore his sight.

> وَلَمَّا فَصَلَتِ ٱلْعِيرُ قَالَ أَبُوهُمْ إِنِّى لَأَجِدُ رِيحَ يُوسُفَ لَوْلَآ أَن تُفَنِّدُونِ ﴿٩٤﴾
>
> And when the camel caravan had departed, their father said: "I perceive the scent of Joseph; may you not disbelieve me!" (94).

The fact that Jacob smelt the scent of Joseph when the caravan left Egypt means that he did so from a very far distance. Clearly, this is one of Jacob's miracles.

Jacob smelt the scent of his son after the departure of the caravan but when it was still in the same land where Joseph lived for years. Why did he smell the scent of Joseph then but not at any earlier time in the previous years? Allah made this miracle a sign to Jacob that his reuniting with his son Joseph was about to happen. The fact that Jacob only said "I perceive the scent of Joseph," however, means that he did not reveal the significance of that miracle.

Jacob asked not to be disbelieved because his sons, and their families also, used to doubt his undying hope to reunite with Joseph one day, as they told him previously: "By Allah! You will not cease to remember Joseph until you are about to die or be one of the dead" (12.85).

Most exegetes think that not all of Jacob's sons went to see Joseph in the third visit, but that some of them stayed with him, and that those are the ones whom Jacob spoke to in this verse. Perhaps, what made exegetes incline toward this interpretation is the phrase "their father." The word "father," however, is not used for the father only, but also for any "grandfather," as I have already shown in my comment on verse 12.6.

Jacob sent all of his sons in the first two visits, so there is no reason to assume that he sent only some of them this time, particularly given that he wanted them to trace Joseph and Benjamin: "Go and trace Joseph and his brother" (from 12.87). Therefore, I think that Jacob sent all of his nine sons in their third visit to Egypt, and that those whom Jacob is seen speaking to in this verse are his grandsons. This possibility has also been pointed out by some exegetes, such as Ibn Kathīr and al-Qurṭubī.

قَالُوا۟ تَٱللَّهِ إِنَّكَ لَفِى ضَلَـٰلِكَ ٱلْقَدِيمِ ﴿٩٥﴾
They said: "By Allah, you are surely still in your old error" (95).

Clearly, these are the words of those whom Jacob spoke to in the previous verse and are referred to in the phrase "their father." As already mentioned, I believe that these are members of Jacob's family other than his sons, namely his grandsons.

The speakers in the verse swear that Jacob was still living in his old error. Exegetes believe that the speakers meant by Jacob's error his preference of Joseph over the rest of his sons. Aṭ-Ṭabaṭabā'ī, who also thinks that the speakers are some of Jacob's sons, has linked the aforementioned illusion to the following words which they said when Joseph was still a little child: "Verily Joseph and his brother are dearer to our father than us, though we are a band; surely, our father is in manifest error" (12.8).

This interpretation, however, is incorrect. Jacob did not speak about his preference of Joseph over his other sons for his grandsons to refer to it as the "old error." He mentioned that he smelt Joseph's scent and that his grandsons disbelieved him. Jacob mentioned what he thought to be proof of the verity of the belief he never abandoned: Joseph was still alive and they would reunite one day. This is what his grandsons referred to as the "old error." We have already seen how Jacob's sons criticized their father for his continued remembrance of Joseph: "by Allah! You will not cease to remember Joseph until you are about to die or be one of the dead."

As Jacob spoke of Joseph's scent when the caravan was still very far, a relatively long period of time must have passed before the materialization of his claim. No doubt, such a long passage of time would have further convinced Jacob's grandsons that their grandfather was wrong when he said: "I perceive the scent of Joseph." They must have been stunned when Joseph's shirt arrived, as their fathers were stunned earlier on by the revelation of Joseph's identity.

> فَلَمَّآ أَن جَآءَ ٱلْبَشِيرُ أَلْقَىٰهُ عَلَىٰ وَجْهِهِۦ فَٱرْتَدَّ بَصِيرًا قَالَ أَلَمْ أَقُل لَّكُمْ إِنِّىٓ أَعْلَمُ مِنَ ٱللَّهِ مَا لَا تَعْلَمُونَ ﴿٩٦﴾
>
> So when the bearer of good news came he cast it on his face, so he regained his sight. He said: "Did I not say to you that I know from Allah what you do not know?" (96).

The "bearer of good news" was one of Jacob's sons who brought the shirt and cast it on his father's face. Jacob then regained his sight immediately.

Jacob then said to his sons "did I not say to you that I know from Allah what you do not know?" reminding them of what he had told them on previous occasions, including the time when he responded to their criticism of him for mentioning Joseph so often: "I only complain of my grief and sorrow to Allah, and I know from Allah what you do not know." Jacob referred again to that knowledge after it became clear to all that Joseph was still alive and that he would see him. This supports the view which I expressed in my comment on verse 12.86 that the knowledge in question refers to Jacob's knowledge that Joseph was still alive and that he would reunite with him.

Note how Jacob mentioned Allah immediately after regaining his sight.

It is notable that Jacob mentioned the knowledge that he received from Allah without specifying its nature: "I know from Allah what you do not know." He did not say, for instance, that he knew from Allah that Joseph was still alive. That is because Jacob knew much more from Allah; that Joseph was alive is only a part of that knowledge.

Exegetes have highlighted the role played by "Joseph's shirt" in his story. First, Joseph's brothers smeared his shirt with fake blood to show it to their father as evidence that a wolf had devoured Joseph. Second, Joseph's shirt and the cut that was made to it by the 'Azīz's wife played a role in vindicating him from the charge that she unfairly leveled at him. Finally, here is Joseph's shirt again, this time restoring the sight of his father. Clearly, three different shirts featured in these three different events.

Note the fascinating contrast between the two events when Joseph's brothers' brought his shirt to their father after throwing him in the well and when they brought it from Egypt. The first event ultimately led to Jacob's loss of sight, whereas the second event restored it. In the first event, Jacob's sons used Joseph's shirt as proof of his death, whereas bringing the shirt from Egypt was a proof that Joseph was still alive.

قَالُواْ يَٰٓأَبَانَا ٱسْتَغْفِرْ لَنَا ذُنُوبَنَآ إِنَّا كُنَّا خَٰطِـِٔينَ ﴿٩٧﴾
They said: "O our father! Ask forgiveness for our sins. We have certainly been sinners" (97).

Here Jacob's sons acknowledge their guilt in the presence of their father, as they did earlier in front of Joseph.[93]

Note their request to their father to ask Allah to forgive them. Were they not able to ask directly for forgiveness from Allah? They were certainly able to pray to Allah directly for forgiveness, and there is no doubt that each one of them did that. They asked their father to ask Allah to forgive them because they were aware of Jacob's special status in the sight of Allah, and that Allah answers the prayer of His close servants more often. Jacob's sons asked their father to act as an intermediary to their Lord to forgive them.

One proof that the request of Jacob's sons to their father to ask Allah to forgive them was absolutely sound religiously is Jacob's consent to the request. Jacob was well aware that he was unable to protect his sons from any harm or bring them any good if Allah had wanted something different. This knowledge is embodied in Jacob's words in verse 12.67: "I can protect you naught against Allah." Nevertheless, Jacob, and his sons also, knew that his nearness to Allah meant that Allah might answer his prayers more than his sons'.

Note also, for instance, how Allah instructed Prophet Muhammad to ask for forgiveness for the believers: وَٱسْتَغْفِرْ لِذَنۢبِكَ وَلِلْمُؤْمِنِينَ وَٱلْمُؤْمِنَٰتِ "and ask for forgiveness for your sin and for the believing men and believing women" (from 47.19). Had the request for forgiveness by the Prophet had no special blessing and no more responsiveness from Allah, He would not have ordered the Prophet to ask for forgiveness for the believers.

﴿قَالَ سَوْفَ أَسْتَغْفِرُ لَكُمْ رَبِّيٓ إِنَّهُۥ هُوَ ٱلْغَفُورُ ٱلرَّحِيمُ ﴿٩٨﴾﴾

He said: "I shall ask for forgiveness for you from my Lord; certainly He is the Forgiving, the Merciful" (98).

Jacob's response to his sons' acknowledgement of their sins and request to him to pray to Allah to forgive them was full of mercy, like Joseph's response to his brothers' acknowledgment of their sins.

Exegetes have suggested that Jacob promised his sons to ask for forgiveness for them "later" because he wanted to pray for them at the time of dawn or on a Friday night when prayers are more answered. It is clear, however, that Jacob meant that he was going to dedicate a particular time to pray for forgiveness for his sons. Jacob's postponement of the request for forgiveness means that he was not going to say something brief such as "may Allah forgive you." He wanted to pray to Allah at length for his sons at a time in which he will be alone with his Lord.

﴿فَلَمَّا دَخَلُوا۟ عَلَىٰ يُوسُفَ ءَاوَىٰٓ إِلَيْهِ أَبَوَيْهِ وَقَالَ ٱدْخُلُوا۟ مِصْرَ إِن شَآءَ ٱللَّهُ ءَامِنِينَ ﴿٩٩﴾﴾

Then when they entered Joseph's place, he admitted his parents to his private place and said: "Enter into Egypt, Allah willing, secure" (99).

As requested by Joseph, his parents and brothers and their families all came to Egypt. When they entered in Joseph's place, he admitted his parents to his private room. This is a special honor that Joseph offered his parents, as he did to Benjamin when he came with the rest of his brothers. Note how Joseph differentiated between his brothers in their second visit to him, inviting Benjamin but not his other brothers to his private residence. Now, Jacob's sons have become true brothers, and the oldest ten no longer plan evil for Joseph and Benjamin, so Joseph did not differentiate between them. As for inviting his parents to his private residence, that was to further honor them.

Joseph told his parents and brothers that they will have a safe life in Egypt, Allah willing: "Enter into Egypt, Allah willing, secure." Many exegetes thought that it is not possible that Joseph would have said that to his family after they had already entered the country. They suggested, therefore, that Joseph's "admittance of his parents to his private place" would have occurred outside Egypt when he went out to receive them. There he wished them and the rest of his family to enter Egypt safely when they enter the country in his company.

Joseph's words to his family here, however, are similar to what a host would say to guests he receives at his home, as he continues to welcome them even after coming in and taking seats, to stress how much he values them and appreciates their visit. The exegetes' view above is in fact unwarranted. Additionally, that view is based on a complete misunderstanding of the meaning of the verb ءَاوَىٰ "*āwā*," which I have translated as "admit to one's private place," as I explained in my comment on verse 12.69. In the latter verse also, we saw this separation between "entering to Joseph's place" and "Joseph's admittance of whom he wants to his private place." That event did definitely take place in Egypt, in the place where Joseph was living.

وَرَفَعَ أَبَوَيْهِ عَلَى ٱلْعَرْشِ وَخَرُّوا۟ لَهُۥ سُجَّدًا وَقَالَ يَـٰٓأَبَتِ هَـٰذَا تَأْوِيلُ رُءْيَـٰىَ مِن قَبْلُ قَدْ جَعَلَهَا رَبِّى حَقًّا وَقَدْ
أَحْسَنَ بِىٓ إِذْ أَخْرَجَنِى مِنَ ٱلسِّجْنِ وَجَآءَ بِكُم مِّنَ ٱلْبَدْوِ مِنۢ بَعْدِ أَن نَّزَغَ ٱلشَّيْطَـٰنُ بَيْنِى وَبَيْنَ إِخْوَتِىٓ إِنَّ
رَبِّى لَطِيفٌ لِّمَا يَشَآءُ إِنَّهُۥ هُوَ ٱلْعَلِيمُ ٱلْحَكِيمُ ﴿١٠٠﴾

And he raised his parents on the throne, and they fell down in prostration before him, and he said: "O my father! This is the interpretation of my vision of old; my Lord has indeed made it come true; and He has indeed been kind to me, as He released me from the prison and brought you from the nomad desert after Satan had sown seeds of dissent between me and my brothers; surely my Lord is subtle in making what He wants come true; surely He is the Knowing, the Wise" (100).

For some reason, most exegetes think that the "throne" in this verse means "bed." All that the story makes clear is that the mentioned "throne" is the place where the king, or perhaps the high ranking 'Azīz, sits, regardless of whether or not that had the form of a bed. Joseph raised his parents on the throne to honor them.[94]

Allah then informs us that "they fell down in prostration before him." The verse does not reveal when exactly this event took place. It is clear that it was separate from the event when Joseph raised his parents on the throne, and that it occurred after the latter event, though this does not mean that it occurred "immediately" after it. In fact, the following analysis of this verse will show that the event of prostration occurred in a place other than Joseph's private residence.

It is clear from the story, Joseph's dream, and the used plural pronoun that those who prostrated to Joseph were his brothers and parents. A number of exegetes think that this prostration was to thank Allah for His favor on Joseph. Exegetes liken this act of prostration to the prostration of the angels to Adam: وَإِذْ قُلْنَا لِلْمَلَـٰٓئِكَةِ ٱسْجُدُوا۟ لِـَٔادَمَ فَسَجَدُوٓا۟ إِلَّآ إِبْلِيسَ أَبَىٰ "And when We said to the angels: 'Prostrate before Adam', they prostrated save for Iblīs (Satan) who refused" (20.116). I do not agree with the exegetes' view and likening the prostration of Joseph's parents and brothers to the angels' prostration before Adam.

The angels prostrated to Adam because Allah commanded them to do that, so their prostration was in obedience to a divine command. There is no reference in the sūra of Joseph that Allah ordered Joseph's parents and family to prostrate to him. Therefore, this act of prostration was certainly for a reason different from that of the angels' prostration to Adam.

I think the prostration of Joseph's parents and brothers before him followed an established tradition of greeting kings and people in high positions; this is still used in some parts of the world today. Therefore, that event is likely to have happened, probably in Joseph's official residence, when he came out to a crowd of people that included his parents and brothers. The latter prostrated before him as the other people did.

It is clear that while it was *Joseph* who "raised" his parents to the throne, it was *his brothers and parents* who chose to prostrate to him. This is in line with my interpretation that the prostration of Joseph's parents and brothers emulated the way Joseph was received by the present people.

After the event of prostration, Joseph said to his father: "O my father! This is the interpretation of my vision of old," referring to the dream that he recounted to him when was a child: "When Joseph said to his father: 'O my father! I saw eleven stars, the sun, and the moon; I saw them prostrating to me'" (12.4). Note that Joseph's speech is only addressed to his father which indicates that he was the only one whom he told about that dream. As instructed by his father at the time, Joseph did not talk to any of his brothers about that dream: "O my son! Do not relate your vision to your brothers, otherwise they would scheme against you a scheme; Satan is a manifest enemy to man" (from 12.5).

According to my interpretation above, Joseph's brothers must have prostrated to him in their previous three visits. In their second visit, all of the eleven brothers would have prostrated to Joseph. This conclusion explains why the eleven stars are mentioned before the sun and moon in the description of Joseph's dream. When the sun, the moon, and the planets are mentioned, it is common to mention the two luminaries first, and then the planets. Additionally, the fact that the two luminaries represented Jacob and Joseph's mother whereas the stars stood for Joseph's brothers, would lead one to expect the sun and the moon to be mentioned first. This order, however, is reversed in Joseph's description of his dream, reflecting the fact that his brothers would prostrate to him before they would do again with his parents. Note the fascinating and amazing subtle consistency between the different parts of the Qur'anic text.

Joseph then continues his speech and remembers Allah's favor to him when He released him from jail. There is immense politeness in Joseph's words which the Qur'an teaches us to adhere to in our relationship with Allah. Joseph attributed to Allah the favor of rescuing him from prison, but he did not ascribe to Him his term in jail. Allah is certainly the ultimate doer in both cases. The lesson that Joseph's politeness teaches us here is to be satisfied with whatever Allah does to us, be patient with His will, and thank and praise Him for His favors. We do not deserve any of Allah's favors, nor is He obliged to give any of them to us.

Joseph saw that freeing him from prison was a favor that is worth thanking Allah for, but he did not consider putting him in jail anything other than a test that required obedience and patience. This is the same prophetic politeness seen in the words of his grandfather Abraham when he described Allah to his people as follows:

وَٱلَّذِى هُوَ يُطْعِمُنِى وَيَسْقِينِ ﴿٧٩﴾ وَإِذَا مَرِضْتُ فَهُوَ يَشْفِينِ ﴿٨٠﴾. (سورة الشعراء).

And [He is the One] who feeds me and gives me water (26.79). And when I am sick, it is He who cures me (26.80).

Abraham attributed to Allah the favor of providing him with food and drink, but did no ascribe to Him making him feel hungry and thirsty. He attributed to Allah the favor of curing him, but he did not impute to Him making him ill.

Man can increase the favor that Allah confers on him, and can turn it into a misfortune. He can also aggravate any misfortune that Allah tests him with. Thanking Allah for a favor doubles it and makes it have positive worldly and spiritual effects, whereas being ungrateful to Him has negative worldly and spiritual effects on the person. Similarly, adhering to patience at any misfortune converts it into a worldly and spiritual merit for the person, and showing impatience at afflictions exacerbates them, thus negatively affecting the person spiritually and in the life of this world.

Joseph continues to mention Allah's favors on him and his family, pointing out how Allah brought his parents from the nomad desert to Egypt, after Satan had caused dissent between him and his brothers. Note the kindness of Joseph who saw in Allah's favor to his parents and brothers, having brought them from the nomad desert to Egypt, a favor to *himself*.

Now that his brothers have acknowledged their guilt and prayed to

Allah for forgiveness, Joseph deliberately avoids criticizing them as he says: "after Satan had sown seeds of dissent between me and my brothers." He ignores the fact that the influence of Satan was *on his brothers in particular* which stresses their shortcomings and the fact that they were the cause of the dissent that took place.

After mentioning what he and his family went through, Joseph went on to say: "surely my Lord is *laṭīf* (subtle) in making what He wants come true." The Arabic term لُطْف "*luṭf*" means "subtlety" and "being non-detectable by the senses."[95] Joseph's words mean that Allah guides matters to their ultimate ends without anyone recognizing how He does that. While all of Allah's Beautiful Names can be seen in the story of Joseph, اللَّطِيفُ "*al-Laṭīf* (the Subtle)" is the most manifested.

One of the greatest lessons of this fascinating story is that Allah does what He wants and no one can stand in the face of His will. Allah wanted much good for Joseph and Jacob's family, as He revealed to little Joseph in the dream. The immense and complicated schemes of Joseph's brothers, the wife of the 'Azīz, and his persecutors all failed to prevent that good from coming Joseph's way. In fact, Allah turned that very scheming into "means" to drive things to the ends He wanted. This is something that Joseph's brothers realized when he revealed to them his identity, so they said: "By Allah! Allah has indeed preferred you over us." They acknowledged that their scheming could not have resulted in the exact opposite of what they intended unless Allah Himself had intervened.

Allah preferred Joseph over his brothers, wanted to teach him the interpretation of talks and give him a share of kingship, so He turned every plot against him into a means that drew him further toward these favors. Throwing Joseph into the well by his brothers was what took him to Egypt, specifically, to the house of the 'Azīz. Allah made the latter a school for Joseph in which He taught him the interpretation of talks. Similarly, throwing Joseph in jail by the 'Azīz's wife was ultimately the cause for the news about him reaching the king and, consequently, for him to leave prison to a state of honor and power.

Through its revelation of subtle links between events that appear to be unrelated and random, the sūra of Joseph shows that Allah's creation is free of any randomness and meaninglessness. This is one great lesson that is beautifully illustrated in this great sūra. No one looking at little Joseph lying helplessly *at the bottom of a well* in the desert could have imagined how this event could be the beginning of his *rise to a high position* in the hierarchy of power in Egypt, which was at an enormous distance from that well. Divine subtlety links all those events to each other, giving them meanings that are visible only to those whom Allah chooses. For the rest, these meanings remain invisible until the appointed time of their appearance. Beautiful Names such as ٱللَّطِيفُ "*al-Laṭīf* (the Subtle)," ٱلْعَلِيم "*al-'Alīm* (the Knowledgeable)," and ٱلْحَكِيم "*al-Ḥakīm* (the Wise)" imply that the universe is void of any randomness and full of meanings. Some of these meanings can be recognized by any person, whereas others are visible only to those who Allah has chosen them to see.

After saying "surely my Lord is subtle in making what He wants come true," Joseph concluded his speech by describing Allah as "the Knowledgeable, the Wise." This means that Allah drives things subtly with His knowledge and wisdom, and brings about whatever He wishes to happen. Note that "the Knowledgeable" and "the Wise" are the same Beautiful Names that Jacob mentioned in his interpretation of the dream to his son Joseph: "And thus your Lord will choose you, teach you a share of the interpretation of talks, and perfect His favor on you and on the lineage of Jacob, as He perfected it before on your fathers Abraham and Isaac; your Lord is Knowledgeable, Wise" (12.6). Everything that happened, including the realization of the dream, confirms that Allah "is the Knowledgeable, the Wise." These are the most occurring Beautiful Names in the sūra of Joseph after "Allah."

رَبِّ قَدْ ءَاتَيْتَنِى مِنَ ٱلْمُلْكِ وَعَلَّمْتَنِى مِن تَأْوِيلِ ٱلْأَحَادِيثِ فَاطِرَ ٱلسَّمَـٰوَٰتِ وَٱلْأَرْضِ أَنتَ وَلِىِّۦ فِى ٱلدُّنْيَا وَٱلْآخِرَةِ تَوَفَّنِى مُسْلِمًا وَأَلْحِقْنِى بِٱلصَّـٰلِحِينَ ﴿١٠١﴾

"My Lord! You have given me a share of kingship and taught me a share of the interpretation of talks. Originator of the heavens and the earth! You are my guardian in this world and the hereafter; make me die as a Muslim and join me with the righteous" (101).

This is the last verse of the story of Joseph, but it is not the last verse in the sūra of Joseph.

In the previous verse, Joseph was addressing his family, but now he is praying to his Lord. Clearly, this prayer took place at a later time when Joseph was worshipping Allah. Note how Joseph passed over the difficulties that he went through on his way to learn the interpretation of talks and rise to kingship, mentioning only Allah's favors to him. The knowledgeable and wise Joseph believed that all hardships that happened to him were in reality favors and a grace from Allah that helped him attain to what he achieved spiritually and in this world.

As he did in his speech in the previous verse, Joseph starts his speech in this verse by mentioning some of Allah's favors to him. He mentions "a share of kingship" and "a share of the interpretation of talks." As I pointed out in my comment on verse 12.6, the phrase "a share of the interpretation of talks" means "some" of the huge knowledge to interpret talks. Similarly, "a share of kingship" refers to the limitedness of Joseph's kingship.[96]

It is interesting to note how Joseph thanks Allah for giving him مِنَ ٱلْمُلْكِ "*min al-mulk* (a share of kingship)" in this verse, and how he raised his parents on "the throne" in the previous verse. There are two possible interpretations for those two Qur'anic references. First, Joseph was still occupying the position of the 'Azīz at the time of his brothers' last visit when he revealed to them his real identity, as his brothers called him the 'Azīz: "So when they entered his place, they said: 'O 'Azīz! Harm has afflicted us and our family, and we have brought poor goods, so give us full measure and be charitable to us; surely Allah rewards the charitable'" (12.88). Then he became king sometime between that visit and receiving his parents in Egypt and raising them to "the throne."

The other interpretation, which I find more likely, is that Joseph was still occupying the position of the 'Azīz when he met his father. Joseph used the humble phrase "a share of kingship" instead of "kingship" to stress the limitedness of what he controlled, as he was not a "true king" in the full meaning of the word.[97]

In this case, there are two possible meanings for "the throne." First, it refers to the throne of the powerful 'Azīz. The position that combined the responsibility of the 'Azīz and that of managing the storehouses must have been very high, almost certainly next to the king. The second possible meaning is that Joseph was indeed deputy to the king and stood for him in his absence. This interpretation explains how Joseph was not a full king yet was at the same time sitting on the throne of the king when his parents came to see him. This particular interpretation also explains how Joseph accused Benjamin of stealing the king's drinking cup. That would have been so easy for Joseph to arrange if he had received his brothers in the king's court.[98]

Most exegetes think that Joseph's prayer "make me die as a Muslim" is a request for death. They have even suggested that Joseph was the first prophet to ask for death. In fact, this is a complete misunderstanding of Joseph's prayer. Joseph's words "make me die as a Muslim" are a prayer to Allah to make him adhere to Islam until he dies. "Islam" here means *the complete surrender to Allah*. Joseph was a living example of the perfect Muslim in his complete surrender to Allah's command and in his acceptance with patience all of what was ordained for him.

Joseph's last prayer was "join me with the righteous." Exegetes think that "the righteous" are Joseph's fathers, namely Abraham, Isaac, and Jacob. Although those great prophets are among the righteous, there is no indication in the prayer that Joseph only referred to them with the term "the righteous." Joseph meant by the word "Muslim" in his prayer "make me die as a Muslim" every true Muslim. Similarly, the term "the righteous" in his prayer "join me with the righteous" refers to all righteous people.

The word ٱلصَّـٰلِحِينَ "*aṣ-ṣāliḥīn* (the righteous)" concludes the last verse of one of the Qur'an's best stories — the story of the righteous prophets of Allah, Joseph, his father Jacob, and his brothers the "*Asbāṭ*."

10

The Epilogue of the Sūra of Joseph

The story of Joseph concluded with verse 101. In this chapter, we will study the last ten verses in the sūra of Joseph. Some of these verses refer to the story of Joseph.

ذَٰلِكَ مِنْ أَنۢبَآءِ ٱلْغَيْبِ نُوحِيهِ إِلَيْكَ وَمَا كُنتَ لَدَيْهِمْ إِذْ أَجْمَعُوٓاْ أَمْرَهُمْ وَهُمْ يَمْكُرُونَ ﴿١٠٢﴾
These are some tidings of the unseen which We reveal to you [O Muhammad!]. And you were not with them when they agreed on their course of action, when they were scheming (102).

After recounting the story of Joseph, Allah stressed that the details He revealed to Prophet Muhammad were "tidings of the unseen." The word غَيْب "*ghayb* (the unseen)," which we already have come across in verse 12.81 and in the commentary on verse 12.3, encompasses the meanings of "unknown," "hidden" ...etc. For example, the tidings of the Day of Resurrection are tidings of the unseen, because no one can know them without revelation from Allah.

The story of Joseph represented "tidings of the unseen" for Prophet Muhammad because it referred to events that took place in the past and which could not be observed directly or indirectly. After recounting the story of Joseph to him, Allah reminds Prophet Muhammad that he was "not with them when they agreed on their course of action, when they were scheming." The group meant in this verse is Joseph's brothers, whereas the event of scheming is their agreement to cast Joseph in the well. In fact, the verb أَجْمَعُوا "*ajma'ū* (agreed)" in this verse is the same verb used in verse 12.15 which talks about the plot of Joseph's brothers: "So when they took him away and agreed that they should throw him to the bottom of the well, and We revealed to him: 'You will certainly inform them of this affair of theirs while they are unaware'." Allah mentioned in verse 12.102 this particular event because it was the one that triggered what was to follow in the story of Joseph; it was the starting point of the story.

This verse is one of a number of verses that refer to ancient events that

Prophet Muhammad did not know, and tell him that he came to know about them only as a result of being chosen to be a Messenger and given the Qur'an. I have already discussed this in Chapter 2 in my comment on verse 12.3:

نَحْنُ نَقُصُّ عَلَيْكَ أَحْسَنَ ٱلْقَصَصِ بِمَآ أَوْحَيْنَا إِلَيْكَ هَـٰذَا ٱلْقُرْءَانَ وَإِن كُنتَ مِن قَبْلِهِ لَمِنَ ٱلْغَـٰفِلِينَ ﴿٣﴾. (سورة يوسف).

We narrate to you [O Muhammad!] the best of narratives, by revealing this Qur'an to you; and before it you were one of the unaware (12.3).

Interestingly, the verses that relate the story of Joseph (12.4-12.101) fall between verse 12.3 which ends with a reference to the fact that the Prophet did not know that story before it was revealed to him in the Qur'an, "before it you were one of the unaware," and verse 12.102 which starts with a similar reference: "These are some tidings of the unseen."

The Qur'an also refutes several accusations directed at Prophet Muhammad that he did not receive the Qur'an from Allah. For instance, the Qur'an responds to the disbelievers' claim that the Messenger of Allah authored the Qur'an himself or that he copied it from other books. It points out the well known fact that the Prophet was illiterate: وَمَا كُنتَ تَتْلُو مِن قَبْلِهِ مِن كِتَابٍ وَلَا تَخُطُّهُ بِيَمِينِكَ إِذًا لَّٱرْتَابَ ٱلْمُبْطِلُونَ "And you [O Muhammad!] did not recite before it [the Qur'an] any book, nor did you write one with your hand, for the deniers [of the verity of the Qur'an] to have doubts" (29.48).

Additionally, a story such as that of prophet Joseph was not known to those who were not Jews or Christians. Jewish and Christian religious authorities who had authentic copies of the Torah of Moses and the Injīl of Jesus deliberately concealed those books so that lay people and those who did not share their religions had no access to them:

وَمَا قَدَرُواْ ٱللَّهَ حَقَّ قَدْرِهِ إِذْ قَالُواْ مَآ أَنزَلَ ٱللَّهُ عَلَىٰ بَشَرٍ مِّن شَىْءٍ قُلْ مَنْ أَنزَلَ ٱلْكِتَـٰبَ ٱلَّذِى جَآءَ بِهِ مُوسَىٰ نُورًا وَهُدًى لِّلنَّاسِ تَجْعَلُونَهُ قَرَاطِيسَ تُبْدُونَهَا وَتُخْفُونَ كَثِيرًا وَعُلِّمْتُم مَّا لَمْ تَعْلَمُوٓاْ أَنتُمْ وَلَآ ءَابَآؤُكُمْ قُلِ ٱللَّهُ ثُمَّ ذَرْهُمْ فِى خَوْضِهِمْ يَلْعَبُونَ ﴿٩١﴾. (سورة الأنعام).

And they do not appreciate the real status of Allah when they say: "Allah has not sent down anything to a human being." Say [O Muhammad!]: "Who sent down the Book which Moses brought as a light and a guidance to people, which you have made into parchments some of which you show and much of which you conceal? And you were taught that which you and your fathers did not know." Say: "Allah," then leave them sporting in their vain discourses (6.91).

وَإِذْ أَخَذَ ٱللَّهُ مِيثَـٰقَ ٱلَّذِينَ أُوتُواْ ٱلْكِتَـٰبَ لَتُبَيِّنُنَّهُ لِلنَّاسِ وَلَا تَكْتُمُونَهُ فَنَبَذُوهُ وَرَآءَ ظُهُورِهِمْ

وَٱشْتَرَوْا۟ بِهِۦ ثَمَنًا قَلِيلًا فَبِئْسَ مَا يَشْتَرُونَ ﴿١٨٧﴾. (سورة آل عِمْرَان).

And when Allah took a covenant from those who were given the Book: "You shall certainly make it available to the people and you shall not conceal it"; but they cast it behind their backs and took a small price for it; therefore, damn is that which they buy (3.187).

إِنَّ ٱلَّذِينَ يَكْتُمُونَ مَآ أَنزَلْنَا مِنَ ٱلْبَيِّنَٰتِ وَٱلْهُدَىٰ مِنۢ بَعْدِ مَا بَيَّنَّٰهُ لِلنَّاسِ فِى ٱلْكِتَٰبِ أُو۟لَٰٓئِكَ يَلْعَنُهُمُ ٱللَّهُ وَيَلْعَنُهُمُ ٱللَّٰعِنُونَ ﴿١٥٩﴾. (سورة البَقَرَة).

Surely those who conceal what We have sent down of clear proofs and guidance after We made them clear in the Book for people, these Allah curses, and those who curse curse them too (2.159).

Some disbelievers claimed that one of the People of the Book was teaching Prophet Muhammad the Qur'an. Allah has refuted this argument by pointing out that the purported teacher was not a native Arabic speaker, so he could not have authored the immaculate and fascinating Arabic Qur'an:

وَلَقَدْ نَعْلَمُ أَنَّهُمْ يَقُولُونَ إِنَّمَا يُعَلِّمُهُۥ بَشَرٌ لِّسَانُ ٱلَّذِى يُلْحِدُونَ إِلَيْهِ أَعْجَمِىٌّ وَهَٰذَا لِسَانٌ عَرَبِىٌّ مُّبِينٌ ﴿١٠٣﴾. (سورة النحل).

And We know well that they [the disbelievers] say: "Only a man teaches him [Muhammad]." The tongue of him at whom they falsely hint is foreign, whereas this [the Qur'an] is manifest Arabic tongue (16.103).

There are many verses in which Allah stresses that He is the one who revealed the Qur'an and that He is the source of the knowledge that reached the Prophet through that Book:

وَلَوْلَا فَضْلُ ٱللَّهِ عَلَيْكَ وَرَحْمَتُهُۥ لَهَمَّت طَّآئِفَةٌ مِّنْهُمْ أَن يُضِلُّوكَ وَمَا يُضِلُّونَ إِلَّآ أَنفُسَهُمْ وَمَا يَضُرُّونَكَ مِن شَىْءٍ وَأَنزَلَ ٱللَّهُ عَلَيْكَ ٱلْكِتَٰبَ وَٱلْحِكْمَةَ وَعَلَّمَكَ مَا لَمْ تَكُن تَعْلَمُ وَكَانَ فَضْلُ ٱللَّهِ عَلَيْكَ عَظِيمًا ﴿١٣٣﴾. (سورة النساء).

And were it not for Allah's favor upon you [O Muhammad!] and His mercy, a party of them [the disbelievers] would surely have set out to lead you astray, and they lead no one astray but themselves, and they shall not harm you in the least. And Allah has sent down to you the Book and Wisdom, and He has taught you what you did not know; and Allah's favor on you has been great (4.113).

وَمَآ أَكْثَرُ ٱلنَّاسِ وَلَوْ حَرَصْتَ بِمُؤْمِنِينَ ﴿١٠٣﴾

And most people will not believe no matter how keen you are [that they should do] (103).

By referring to the keenness of the Prophet on calling people to Islam, this verse emphasizes the strenuous efforts that he exerted.

Allah reminds the Prophet here that *most people* would not believe in His Message regardless of his efforts to convince them to do so. The occurrence of this reminder in various suwar of the Qur'an highlights the Prophet's hardship in inviting people to the true religion. It is also a reminder to the Messenger not to be saddened by people's rejection of his call, that he is not to blame for that, and that this was the same experience that the previous messengers had with their people. These are some verses on this matter:

قَدْ نَعْلَمُ إِنَّهُ لَيَحْزُنُكَ ٱلَّذِى يَقُولُونَ فَإِنَّهُمْ لَا يُكَذِّبُونَكَ وَلَٰكِنَّ ٱلظَّٰلِمِينَ بِـَٔايَٰتِ ٱللَّهِ يَجْحَدُونَ ﴿٣٣﴾. (سورة الأنعام).

We know indeed that what they say certainly saddens you [O Muhammad!]; but in truth they are not calling you a liar, but the wrongdoers are denying the verses of Allah (6.33).

لَعَلَّكَ بَٰخِعٌ نَّفْسَكَ أَلَّا يَكُونُوا۟ مُؤْمِنِينَ ﴿٣﴾. (سورة الشُّعَرَاءِ).

It may be that you [O Muhammad!] torment yourself because they have not become believers (26.3).

وَإِن يُكَذِّبُوكَ فَقَدْ كَذَّبَ ٱلَّذِينَ مِن قَبْلِهِم جَآءَتْهُمْ رُسُلُهُم بِٱلْبَيِّنَٰتِ وَبِٱلزُّبُرِ وَبِٱلْكِتَٰبِ ٱلْمُنِيرِ ﴿٢٥﴾. (سورة فَاطِر).

And if they call you [O Muhammad!] a liar, so did those before them indeed [call their messengers liars]; their messengers came to them with clear arguments, with Scriptures, and with the illuminating Book (35.25).

إِنَّآ أَنزَلْنَا عَلَيْكَ ٱلْكِتَٰبَ لِلنَّاسِ بِٱلْحَقِّ فَمَنِ ٱهْتَدَىٰ فَلِنَفْسِهِ وَمَن ضَلَّ فَإِنَّمَا يَضِلُّ عَلَيْهَا وَمَآ أَنتَ عَلَيْهِم بِوَكِيلٍ ﴿٤١﴾. (سورة الزّمَر).

Surely We have sent down to you [O Muhammad!] the Book for the people, with truth; so whoever follows the right way, it is for his own soul, and whoever goes astray, he goes astray only to its detriment; and you have not been put in charge of them (39.41).

فَتَوَلَّ عَنْهُمْ فَمَآ أَنتَ بِمَلُومٍ ﴿٥٤﴾. (سورة الذارِيَاتِ).

So turn away from them [O Muhammad!], for you are not to blame (51.54).

فَذَكِّرْ إِنَّمَآ أَنتَ مُذَكِّرٌ ﴿٢١﴾ لَّسْتَ عَلَيْهِم بِمُصَيْطِرٍ ﴿٢٢﴾. (سورة الغاشية).

Therefore do [O Muhammad!] remind them [with the Message that We have revealed to you], for you are only a reminder (88.21). You have no control over them (88.22).

There is a special reason for Allah's reminder to Prophet Muhammad that most people would not believe regardless of how much efforts he would exert, to appear in this particular place. Allah referred in the previous verse to one miraculous aspect of the Qur'anic story of Joseph: it is tidings of the unseen which could not have reached the Prophet through any means other than Allah. For any sound mind, the story of Joseph represents proof of the divine origin of the Qur'an. Nevertheless, most people who hear the story of Joseph, and the other Qur'anic suwar in general, would not become believers. In order for the Prophet not to grieve and blame himself, Allah reminded him that no matter how great the miracles of Allah, they would not force people to embrace Islam. Even the Qur'an, the greatest miracle, would not force those who are not interested in truth to believe in the Message of the Prophet. Allah, therefore, instructed the Prophet not to blame himself for people's rejection of his call.

Allah referred more explicitly in other verses to the fact that His miracles would not force people to believe. These are some examples:

وَلَقَدْ أَرْسَلْنَا مِن قَبْلِكَ فِى شِيَعِ ٱلْأَوَّلِينَ ﴿١٠﴾ وَمَا يَأْتِيهِم مِّن رَّسُولٍ إِلَّا كَانُوا۟ بِهِۦ يَسْتَهْزِءُونَ
﴿١١﴾ كَذَٰلِكَ نَسْلُكُهُۥ فِى قُلُوبِ ٱلْمُجْرِمِينَ ﴿١٢﴾ لَا يُؤْمِنُونَ بِهِۦ وَقَدْ خَلَتْ سُنَّةُ ٱلْأَوَّلِينَ
﴿١٣﴾ وَلَوْ فَتَحْنَا عَلَيْهِم بَابًا مِّنَ ٱلسَّمَآءِ فَظَلُّوا۟ فِيهِ يَعْرُجُونَ ﴿١٤﴾ لَقَالُوٓا۟ إِنَّمَا سُكِّرَتْ
أَبْصَـٰرُنَا بَلْ نَحْنُ قَوْمٌ مَّسْحُورُونَ ﴿١٥﴾. (سورة الحجر).

And surely We sent messengers before you [O Muhammad!] to the nations of old (15.10). But no messenger would come to them but they would mock him (15.11). Thus do We make the hearts of the guilty react to it [the Qur'an] (15.12). That they do not believe in it; and indeed the example of the former people has already passed (15.13). And even if We open out to them a gateway to heaven, so that they keep ascending through it (15.14). They would certainly say: "It is only that our eyes have been intoxicated; nay, we are rather a bewitched people" (15.15).

Here Allah stresses that people's rejection of the Qur'an is similar to their predecessors' accusation of the messengers of lying. He then emphasizes that should He perform another great miracle, such as opening out a gateway in heaven for people to ascend through, it would not make someone who is bent on denial turn into a believer. This message is also mentioned in this verse:

وَلَوْ نَزَّلْنَا عَلَيْكَ كِتَٰبًا فِى قِرْطَاسٍ فَلَمَسُوهُ بِأَيْدِيهِمْ لَقَالَ ٱلَّذِينَ كَفَرُوٓا۟ إِنْ هَٰذَآ إِلَّا سِحْرٌ مُّبِينٌ ﴿٧﴾. (سورة الأنعام).

And if We had sent down to you [O Muhammad!] a book [written] on paper and they touched it with their hands, the disbelievers would have said: "This is nothing but manifest enchantment" (6.7).

The Qur'an was inspired to the Prophet who then read it to people. Some of these people wrote it down. Allah makes it clear in verse 6.7 that even if His revelation of the Qur'an was in the form of sending it down from heaven as a written book that people would be able to touch, the disbelievers would still have said that they were bewitched by what they saw, so they would not believe.

وَمَا تَسْـَٔلُهُمْ عَلَيْهِ مِنْ أَجْرٍ إِنْ هُوَ إِلَّا ذِكْرٌ لِّلْعَٰلَمِينَ ﴿١٠٤﴾

And you do not ask them for a reward for it [the Qur'an]; it is only a reminder for the people (104).

After confirming in the previous verse that most people would not believe in the Qur'an although it is a miraculous Book, Allah continues in this verse His rebuke of the disbelievers. He stresses that the Prophet did not ask people for any wage or reward for delivering the Qur'an to them. Muhammad was only a Messenger sent by Allah to deliver the Qur'an to people. The Messenger shared with people the knowledge that Allah bestowed on him so they may draw near to Allah:

كَمَآ أَرْسَلْنَا فِيكُمْ رَسُولًا مِّنكُمْ يَتْلُوا۟ عَلَيْكُمْ ءَايَٰتِنَا وَيُزَكِّيكُمْ وَيُعَلِّمُكُمُ ٱلْكِتَٰبَ وَٱلْحِكْمَةَ وَيُعَلِّمُكُم مَّا لَمْ تَكُونُوا۟ تَعْلَمُونَ ﴿١٥١﴾. (سورة البقرة).

As We have sent to you [O people!] a Messenger from among you, who recites to you Our verses, purifies you, teaches you the Book and Wisdom, and teaches you that which you did not know (2.151).

Allah has, thus, provided people with reasons to believe, and made sure that there are no real reasons not to believe in the Qur'an. Nevertheless, most people reject Allah's call. Allah specifically mentions the fact that the Prophet does not ask people for a wage for delivering the Qur'an for them to see that as a reason for hesitating to answer his call. He makes this point elsewhere in the Qur'an, as in this verse:

أَمْ تَسْـَٔلُهُمْ أَجْرًا فَهُم مِّن مَّغْرَمٍ مُّثْقَلُونَ ﴿٤٠﴾. (سورة الطور).

Or do you [O Muhammad!] ask them for a reward, so that they are overburdened by a debt? (52.40).

Note Allah's description of the Qur'an as a "reminder for the people." The Qur'an is a "reminder" because it reminds people of Allah, the Day of Resurrection, and what Allah wants from them. The Arabic word الْعَالَمِين "*al-'ālamīn*," translated as "the people," includes both humans and jinn.[99] This emphasizes the fact that the Qur'an is a universal Message that Allah has sent to all creation. Since the Qur'an is a "reminder for the people," it is natural that the Prophet of the Qur'an, Muhammad, is a Messenger to all people:

وَمَا أَرْسَلْنَاكَ إِلاَّ رَحْمَةً لِلْعَالَمِينَ ﴿١٠٧﴾. (سورة الأنبياء).

And We have not sent you [O Muhammad!] but as a mercy to the people (21.107).

وَكَأَيِّن مِّنْ ءَايَةٍ فِى ٱلسَّمَـٰوَٰتِ وَٱلْأَرْضِ يَمُرُّونَ عَلَيْهَا وَهُمْ عَنْهَا مُعْرِضُونَ ﴿١٠٥﴾

And like any sign in the heavens and the earth which they pass by while turning away from it (105).

The word كَأَيِّن "*ka'aiin*," which is translated as "any," is used to imply large numbers. Allah identifies here the fundamental problem that people have: they simply do not care about religion. He stresses that people see the countless signs everywhere, in the heavens and the earth, that point to Him, yet they turn away from them instead of studying and thinking about them. These signs include all creation in the heavens and the earth — such as the sun, moon, stars, humans, animals, and plants — which Allah specifies in many places in the Qur'an. Allah's signs also include the relics of previous nations that He destroyed for their disbelief.

Aṭ-Ṭabaṭabā'ī has noticed that the verb يَمُرُّون "*yamurrūna* (pass by)" implies moving from one sign to another. This means that wherever the person goes, there are visible divine signs in the heavens and the earth.

Aṭ-Ṭabaṭabā'ī has another observation that is worth discussing. It is clear how living on earth means passing by divine signs on the plant; but how can that represent passing by divine signs in the heavens? Aṭ-Ṭabaṭabā'ī thinks that this can be a subtle reference to the motion of the earth around the sun. This motion makes the person indirectly move through the heavenly divine signs because it allows him to see different parts of the sky. According to this interpretation, passing through the earthly signs means moving from one place on earth to another. Passing through the signs of heavens represents the earth's motion around the sun, and thus man's ability to witness different parts of the sky as it does so. In fact, the motion of earth around itself can also be incorporated into this interpretation.

Aṭ-Ṭabaṭabā'ī's interpretation assumes that verse 12.105 addresses only the human beings on the earth. This assumption would be logical if "them" in verse 12.104 and "they" in 12.105 refer to humans only. We have to remind ourselves, however, that much of the Qur'anic speech is addressed to both humans and jinn. Note Allah's description of the Qur'an as a "reminder for the people" and Prophet Muhammad as a "mercy to the people," where "the people" include both humans and jinn, as I have shown in my interpretation of verse 12.104. For instance, the phrase أُوْلِى ٱلْأَلْبَٰبِ "those of understanding" in the verse إِنَّ فِى خَلْقِ ٱلسَّمَٰوَٰتِ وَٱلْأَرْضِ وَٱخْتِلَٰفِ ٱلَّيْلِ وَٱلنَّهَارِ لَءَايَٰتٍ لِّأُوْلِى ٱلْأَلْبَٰبِ "Surely, the creation of the heavens and the earth, and the alternation of the night and the day are signs for those of understanding" (3.190) includes every human and jinn of understanding. There are also verses that stress explicitly that the Qur'an has been sent as much to the jinn as to the humans.[100]

Since the ending of the previous verse (12.104) with "the people" is a generalization of the speech in that verse to include both humans and jinn, the current verse must also be speaking about humans and jinn. In this case, the heavenly signs include both those that the human eye can reach and those that only the jinn can see. It is also possible that the use of "heavens" instead of "heaven" indicates that the signs meant are not confined to the celestial phenomena that the human being can see from the surface of the earth.

وَمَا يُؤْمِنُ أَكْثَرُهُم بِٱللَّهِ إِلَّا وَهُم مُّشْرِكُونَ ﴿١٠٦﴾
And most of them do not believe in Allah without associating others [with Him] (106).

This verse points out that most of those who believe in Allah still associate other gods with Him. It includes anyone who believes in Allah but also worships other gods. Examples of such polytheists are worshippers of idols besides Allah, such as the Arabs of the Arabian Peninsula before Islam, or believers who say Allah has a son. Allah responds to all such false claims in many verses, such as the following:

قُل لِّمَنِ ٱلْأَرْضُ وَمَن فِيهَآ إِن كُنتُمْ تَعْلَمُونَ ﴿٨٤﴾ سَيَقُولُونَ لِلَّهِ قُلْ أَفَلَا تَذَكَّرُونَ ﴿٨٥﴾
قُلْ مَن رَّبُّ ٱلسَّمَٰوَٰتِ ٱلسَّبْعِ وَرَبُّ ٱلْعَرْشِ ٱلْعَظِيمِ ﴿٨٦﴾ سَيَقُولُونَ لِلَّهِ قُلْ أَفَلَا تَتَّقُونَ
﴿٨٧﴾ قُلْ مَنۢ بِيَدِهِۦ مَلَكُوتُ كُلِّ شَىْءٍ وَهُوَ يُجِيرُ وَلَا يُجَارُ عَلَيْهِ إِن كُنتُمْ تَعْلَمُونَ ﴿٨٨﴾

سَيَقُولُونَ لِلَّهِ قُلْ فَأَنَّىٰ تُسْحَرُونَ ﴿٨٩﴾ بَلْ أَتَيْنَـٰهُم بِٱلْحَقِّ وَإِنَّهُمْ لَكَـٰذِبُونَ ﴿٩٠﴾ مَا ٱتَّخَذَ
ٱللَّهُ مِن وَلَدٍ وَمَا كَانَ مَعَهُۥ مِنْ إِلَـٰهٍ إِذًا لَّذَهَبَ كُلُّ إِلَـٰهٍۭ بِمَا خَلَقَ وَلَعَلَا بَعْضُهُمْ عَلَىٰ بَعْضٍ
سُبْحَـٰنَ ٱللَّهِ عَمَّا يَصِفُونَ ﴿٩١﴾. (سورة المؤمنون).

Say [O Muhammad!]: "Do you know whose the earth and what is therein are?" (23.84). They [the disbelievers] will say: "Allah's." Say: "Will you not then remember?" (23.85). Say: "Who is the Lord of the seven heavens and the Lord of the mighty throne?" (23.86). They will say: "[They are] Allah's." Say: "Will you not then act dutifully?" (23.87). Say: "Who is it in whose hand is the kingdom of all things and who gives help but against whom help cannot be given, if you do know?" (23.88). They will say: "[It is] Allah's." Say: "How are then you bewitched [that you do not believe in the Qur'an]?" (23.89). Nay! We have brought to them the truth, and surely they are liars (23.90). Allah has not chosen for Himself offspring, and there was never with him any [other] god; otherwise, each god would have certainly taken away what he created, and some of them would certainly have overpowered others; glory be to Allah above what they describe (23.91).

أَفَأَمِنُوٓا۟ أَن تَأْتِيَهُمْ غَـٰشِيَةٌ مِّنْ عَذَابِ ٱللَّهِ أَوْ تَأْتِيَهُمُ ٱلسَّاعَةُ بَغْتَةً وَهُمْ لَا يَشْعُرُونَ ﴿١٠٧﴾

Do they then feel secure that a torment from Allah would not cover them or [that] the Hour [of Judgment] would not come to them suddenly while they are unaware? (107).

Allah continues in this verse His denouncement of the disbelievers' behavior. He criticizes how they feel secure from Allah's torment or from the sudden arrival of the Day of Judgment while there are unaware. This sense of security is false and unjustified because the person must not feel secure from Allah's torment if Allah has not granted him that security:

أَفَأَمِنَ أَهْلُ ٱلْقُرَىٰٓ أَن يَأْتِيَهُم بَأْسُنَا بَيَـٰتًا وَهُمْ نَآئِمُونَ ﴿٩٧﴾ أَوَ أَمِنَ أَهْلُ ٱلْقُرَىٰٓ أَن يَأْتِيَهُم
بَأْسُنَا ضُحًى وَهُمْ يَلْعَبُونَ ﴿٩٨﴾ أَفَأَمِنُوا۟ مَكْرَ ٱللَّهِ فَلَا يَأْمَنُ مَكْرَ ٱللَّهِ إِلَّا ٱلْقَوْمُ ٱلْخَـٰسِرُونَ
﴿٩٩﴾. (سورة الأعراف).

Do the people of the towns then feel secure that Our wrath would not come upon them by night while they are asleep? (7.97). Or do the people of the towns feel secure that Our wrath would not come upon them by day while they are playing about? (7.98). Do they then feel secure from Allah's scheme? But no one feels secure from Allah's scheme except the losing people (7.99).

أَفَأَمِنَ ٱلَّذِينَ مَكَرُواْ ٱلسَّيِّئَاتِ أَن يَخْسِفَ ٱللَّهُ بِهِمُ ٱلْأَرْضَ أَوْ يَأْتِيَهُمُ ٱلْعَذَابُ مِنْ حَيْثُ لَا

يَشْعُرُونَ ﴿٤٥﴾ أَوْ يَأْخُذَهُمْ فِى تَقَلُّبِهِمْ فَمَا هُم بِمُعْجِزِينَ ﴿٤٦﴾ أَوْ يَأْخُذَهُمْ عَلَىٰ تَخَوُّفٍ فَإِنَّ

رَبَّكُمْ لَرَءُوفٌ رَّحِيمٌ ﴿٤٧﴾. (سورة النَّحْـل).

Do then those who devise evil feel secure that Allah would not cause the
earth to swallow them or that punishment would not overtake them from
whence they do not perceive? (16.45). Or that He would not seize them in
the course of their goings to and fro? They shall not frustrate Him (16.46).
Or that He would not seize them after frightening them? Lo! Your Lord is
surely Compassionate, Merciful (16.47).

Man must never feel secure that the Day of Resurrection will not come
suddenly. Allah has not promised to let us know about it before it arrives.
In fact, He makes it clear that it will come suddenly:

يَسْـُٔلُونَكَ عَنِ ٱلسَّاعَةِ أَيَّانَ مُرْسَىٰهَا قُلْ إِنَّمَا عِلْمُهَا عِندَ رَبِّى لَا يُجَلِّيهَا لِوَقْتِهَآ إِلَّا هُوَ ثَقُلَتْ فِى

ٱلسَّمَـٰوَاتِ وَٱلْأَرْضِ لَا تَأْتِيكُمْ إِلَّا بَغْتَةً يَسْـُٔلُونَكَ كَأَنَّكَ حَفِىٌّ عَنْهَا قُلْ إِنَّمَا عِلْمُهَا عِندَ ٱللَّهِ

وَلَـٰكِنَّ أَكْثَرَ ٱلنَّاسِ لَا يَعْلَمُونَ ﴿١٨٧﴾. (سورة الأَعْراف).

They ask you [O Muhammad!] about the appointed time of the Hour [of
Judgment]. Say: "The knowledge of it is only with my Lord; no one but He
shall manifest it at its time; it will be momentous in the heavens and the
earth; it will not come on you but suddenly." They ask you as if you knew
about that. Say: "The knowledge of it is only with Allah," but most people
do not know (7.187).

وَلَا يَزَالُ ٱلَّذِينَ كَفَرُواْ فِى مِرْيَةٍ مِّنْهُ حَتَّىٰ تَأْتِيَهُـمُ ٱلسَّاعَةُ بَغْتَةً أَوْ يَأْتِيَهُمْ عَذَابُ يَوْمٍ عَقِيمٍ

﴿٥٥﴾. (سورة الـحَج).

And those who disbelieve shall not cease to be in doubt concerning it
[the Qur'an] until the Hour [of Judgment] overtakes them suddenly, or
there comes on them the torment of a disastrous day (22.55).

هَلْ يَنظُرُونَ إِلَّا ٱلسَّاعَةَ أَن تَأْتِيَهُمْ بَغْتَةً وَهُمْ لَا يَشْعُرُونَ ﴿٦٦﴾. (سورة الزّخْرُف).

Do they wait for aught but the Hour [of Judgment] which will come upon
them suddenly while they do not perceive? (43.66).

يَسْـُٔلُكَ ٱلنَّاسُ عَنِ ٱلسَّاعَةِ قُلْ إِنَّمَا عِلْمُهَا عِندَ ٱللَّهِ وَمَا يُدْرِيكَ لَعَلَّ ٱلسَّاعَةَ تَكُونُ قَرِيبًا

﴿٦٣﴾. (سورة الأَحْزَاب).

People ask you [O Muhammad!] about the Hour [of Judgment]; say:
"The knowledge of it is only with Allah"; and for all you know, the Hour
may be nigh (33.63).

ٱللَّهُ ٱلَّذِىٓ أَنزَلَ ٱلْكِتَٰبَ بِٱلْحَقِّ وَٱلْمِيزَانَ وَمَا يُدْرِيكَ لَعَلَّ ٱلسَّاعَةَ قَرِيبٌ ﴿١٧﴾. (سورة الشّورَىٰ).

It is Allah who sent down the Book with truth, and the Balance; and for all you know, the Hour [of Judgment] may be nigh (42.17).

قُلْ هَٰذِهِۦ سَبِيلِىٓ أَدْعُوٓا۟ إِلَى ٱللَّهِ عَلَىٰ بَصِيرَةٍ أَنَا۠ وَمَنِ ٱتَّبَعَنِى وَسُبْحَٰنَ ٱللَّهِ وَمَآ أَنَا۠ مِنَ ٱلْمُشْرِكِينَ ﴿١٠٨﴾

Say [O Muhammad!]: "This is my way. I call to Allah, with clear evidence, I and those who follow me; and glory be to Allah, and I am not one of the polytheists" (108).

Here Allah instructs the Prophet to say to people "This is my way," in reference to the Qur'anic way to Allah. He then commands the Messenger to explain that his way is to: "call to Allah, with clear evidence." Calling to worshipping and surrendering to Allah represents the best of words, as Allah says:

وَمَنْ أَحْسَنُ قَوْلًا مِّمَّن دَعَآ إِلَى ٱللَّهِ وَعَمِلَ صَٰلِحًا وَقَالَ إِنَّنِى مِنَ ٱلْمُسْلِمِينَ ﴿٣٣﴾. (سورة فُصِّلَت).

And who is better in speech than he who calls to Allah, does righteous deeds, and says: "I am one of the Muslims [those who surrender to Allah]"? (41.33).

The phrase "with clear evidence" emphasizes that the call of the Messenger and his followers is based on evidence from Allah and is not something that they devised.

Allah also orders the Prophet to declare that Allah has no peer or partner, and to proclaim that he is not a polytheist, but a believer in the one God, Allah.

This verse sums up the essence of the call of each and every prophet and messenger sent by Allah.

وَمَآ أَرْسَلْنَا مِن قَبْلِكَ إِلَّا رِجَالًا نُّوحِىٓ إِلَيْهِم مِّنْ أَهْلِ ٱلْقُرَىٰٓ أَفَلَمْ يَسِيرُوا۟ فِى ٱلْأَرْضِ فَيَنظُرُوا۟ كَيْفَ كَانَ عَٰقِبَةُ ٱلَّذِينَ مِن قَبْلِهِمْ وَلَدَارُ ٱلْءَاخِرَةِ خَيْرٌ لِّلَّذِينَ ٱتَّقَوْا۟ أَفَلَا تَعْقِلُونَ ﴿١٠٩﴾

And We have not sent [messengers] before you [O Muhammad!] but men to whom We gave revelations, [who were] from the people of the towns. Have they [the disbelievers] not then traveled in the land and seen what was the end of those before them? And surely the abode of the hereafter is better for those who act dutifully; do you [O people!] not understand? (109).

Allah says that *all* the messengers that He sent before Prophet

Muhammad, such as prophet Joseph, were men from various towns, to whom He revealed the Message. In describing the "men to whom We gave revelations" as being "from the people of the towns," Allah emphasizes that those messengers were human beings who were known to their people. They were not "jinn" men, who are also mentioned in the Qur'an:

وَأَنَّهُ كَانَ رِجَالٌ مِّنَ ٱلْإِنسِ يَعُوذُونَ بِرِجَالٍ مِّنَ ٱلْجِنِّ فَزَادُوهُمْ رَهَقًا ﴿٦﴾. (سورة الجن).

And that human men used to seek refuge with jinn men, so they increased them in tiredness (72.6).

The statement "We have not sent [messengers] before you [O Muhammad!] but men to whom We gave revelations, [who were] from the people of the towns" stresses that sending Muhammad, who was a man from the people of the town of Mecca, as a Messenger was not an innovation that had no precedent:

قُلْ مَا كُنتُ بِدْعًا مِّنَ ٱلرُّسُلِ وَمَآ أَدْرِى مَا يُفْعَلُ بِى وَلَا بِكُمْ إِنْ أَتَّبِعُ إِلَّا مَا يُوحَىٰٓ إِلَىَّ وَمَآ أَنَا۠ إِلَّا نَذِيرٌ مُّبِينٌ ﴿٩﴾. (سورة الأحقاف).

Say [O Muhammad!]: "I am no new thing among the messengers [of Allah], and I do not know what will be done to me or to you. I do not follow anything but that which is revealed to me, and I am but a manifest warner" (46.9).

These are some of the verses that stress the human nature of all the messengers that Allah sent to people, and that they were men from the people of the towns:

وَمَآ أَرْسَلْنَا قَبْلَكَ إِلَّا رِجَالًا نُّوحِىٓ إِلَيْهِمْ فَسْـَٔلُوٓا۟ أَهْلَ ٱلذِّكْرِ إِن كُنتُمْ لَا تَعْلَمُونَ ﴿٧﴾ وَمَا جَعَلْنَـٰهُمْ جَسَدًا لَّا يَأْكُلُونَ ٱلطَّعَامَ وَمَا كَانُوا۟ خَـٰلِدِينَ ﴿٨﴾. (سورة الأنبياء).

And We did not send before you [O Muhammad!] but men to whom We gave revelations, so ask [O people!] the people of the revelations [those who know about the messengers of Allah] if you do not know (21.7). And We did not give them bodies that would not eat food, and they were not immortal (21.8).

وَمَآ أَرْسَلْنَا قَبْلَكَ مِنَ ٱلْمُرْسَلِينَ إِلَّآ إِنَّهُمْ لَيَأْكُلُونَ ٱلطَّعَامَ وَيَمْشُونَ فِى ٱلْأَسْوَاقِ وَجَعَلْنَا بَعْضَكُمْ لِبَعْضٍ فِتْنَةً أَتَصْبِرُونَ وَكَانَ رَبُّكَ بَصِيرًا ﴿٢٠﴾. (سورة الفرقان).

And We have not sent before you [O Muhammad!] any messengers but they surely ate food and went about in the markets. And We made some of you a test for others whether you will have patience. And your Lord is ever Seeing (25.20).

وَمَا قَدَرُوا۟ ٱللَّهَ حَقَّ قَدْرِهِۦٓ إِذْ قَالُوا۟ مَآ أَنزَلَ ٱللَّهُ عَلَىٰ بَشَرٍ مِّن شَىْءٍ قُلْ مَنْ أَنزَلَ ٱلْكِتَٰبَ ٱلَّذِى
جَآءَ بِهِۦ مُوسَىٰ نُورًا وَهُدًى لِّلنَّاسِ تَجْعَلُونَهُۥ قَرَاطِيسَ تُبْدُونَهَا وَتُخْفُونَ كَثِيرًا وَعُلِّمْتُم مَّا لَمْ تَعْلَمُوٓا۟
أَنتُمْ وَلَآ ءَابَآؤُكُمْ قُلِ ٱللَّهُ ثُمَّ ذَرْهُمْ فِى خَوْضِهِمْ يَلْعَبُونَ ﴿٩١﴾. (سورة الأنعام).

And they do not appreciate the real status of Allah when they say: "Allah has not sent down anything to a human being." Say [O Muhammad!]: "Who sent down the Book which Moses brought as a light and a guidance to people, which you have made into parchments some of which you show and much of which you conceal? And you were taught that which you and your fathers did not know." Say: "Allah," then leave them sporting in their vain discourses (6.91).

The following verses respond to the disbelievers' misguided belief that Allah did not send human messengers:

وَمَا مَنَعَ ٱلنَّاسَ أَن يُؤْمِنُوٓا۟ إِذْ جَآءَهُمُ ٱلْهُدَىٰٓ إِلَّآ أَن قَالُوٓا۟ أَبَعَثَ ٱللَّهُ بَشَرًا رَّسُولًا ﴿٩٤﴾.
(سورة الإسراء).

And nothing prevented people from believing when guidance came to them except that they said: "What! Has Allah sent a human as a messenger?" (17.94).

قَالَتْ رُسُلُهُمْ أَفِى ٱللَّهِ شَكٌّ فَاطِرِ ٱلسَّمَٰوَٰتِ وَٱلْأَرْضِ يَدْعُوكُمْ لِيَغْفِرَ لَكُم مِّن ذُنُوبِكُمْ
وَيُؤَخِّرَكُمْ إِلَىٰٓ أَجَلٍ مُّسَمًّى قَالُوٓا۟ إِنْ أَنتُمْ إِلَّا بَشَرٌ مِّثْلُنَا تُرِيدُونَ أَن تَصُدُّونَا عَمَّا كَانَ يَعْبُدُ
ءَابَآؤُنَا فَأْتُونَا بِسُلْطَٰنٍ مُّبِينٍ ﴿١٠﴾ قَالَتْ لَهُمْ رُسُلُهُمْ إِن نَّحْنُ إِلَّا بَشَرٌ مِّثْلُكُمْ وَلَٰكِنَّ ٱللَّهَ يَمُنُّ
عَلَىٰ مَن يَشَآءُ مِنْ عِبَادِهِۦ وَمَا كَانَ لَنَآ أَن نَّأْتِيَكُم بِسُلْطَٰنٍ إِلَّا بِإِذْنِ ٱللَّهِ وَعَلَى ٱللَّهِ فَلْيَتَوَكَّلِ
ٱلْمُؤْمِنُونَ ﴿١١﴾. (سورة إبراهيم).

Their messengers said: "Can there be doubt about Allah, the Originator of the heavens and the earth? He invites you to forgive you your sins, and He reprieves you till an appointed term." They said: "You are nothing but humans like us seeking to turn us away from what our fathers used to worship. Bring us therefore some clear authority" (14.10). Their messengers said to them: "We are not but humans like you, but Allah bestows favors on whom He pleases of His servants. And it is not for us to bring to you an authority except by Allah's permission; and on Allah let the believers rely" (14.11).

وَقَالُوا۟ لَوْلَآ أُنزِلَ عَلَيْهِ مَلَكٌ وَلَوْ أَنزَلْنَا مَلَكًا لَّقُضِىَ ٱلْأَمْرُ ثُمَّ لَا يُنظَرُونَ ﴿٨﴾. (سورة
الأنعام).

And they [the disbelievers] say: "Only if an angel has been sent down to him [Prophet Muhammad]!" And had We sent down an angel, the matter would have certainly been settled, and then they would not have been given a respite (7.8).

It is important to realize that these verses talk *specifically* about Allah's Messenger to "all people" for the purpose of "bringing the good news and warning about the Day of Resurrection." Allah also has non-human messengers, such as the angels, whom He sends to "particular individuals" on "special assignments":

ٱلْحَمْدُ لِلَّهِ فَاطِرِ ٱلسَّمَـٰوَٰتِ وَٱلْأَرْضِ جَاعِلِ ٱلْمَلَـٰٓئِكَةِ رُسُلًا أُو۟لِىٓ أَجْنِحَةٍ مَّثْنَىٰ وَثُلَـٰثَ وَرُبَـٰعَ يَزِيدُ فِى ٱلْخَلْقِ مَا يَشَآءُ إِنَّ ٱللَّهَ عَلَىٰ كُلِّ شَىْءٍ قَدِيرٌ ﴿١﴾. (سورة فاطر).

Praise be to Allah, the Originator of the heavens and the earth, the Maker of the angels as messengers who have two, three, and four routes; He increases the creation as He pleases; surely Allah has power over all things (35.1).

One task that Allah assigned to angels is conveying His messages to righteous people, such as informing those who surrender to Allah and follow the straight path that they will go to paradise:

إِنَّ ٱلَّذِينَ قَالُوا۟ رَبُّنَا ٱللَّهُ ثُمَّ ٱسْتَقَـٰمُوا۟ تَتَنَزَّلُ عَلَيْهِمُ ٱلْمَلَـٰٓئِكَةُ أَلَّا تَخَافُوا۟ وَلَا تَحْزَنُوا۟ وَأَبْشِرُوا۟ بِٱلْجَنَّةِ ٱلَّتِى كُنتُمْ تُوعَدُونَ ﴿٣٠﴾ نَحْنُ أَوْلِيَآؤُكُمْ فِى ٱلْحَيَوٰةِ ٱلدُّنْيَا وَفِى ٱلْـَٔاخِرَةِ وَلَكُمْ فِيهَا مَا تَشْتَهِىٓ أَنفُسُكُمْ وَلَكُمْ فِيهَا مَا تَدَّعُونَ ﴿٣١﴾. (سورة فُصِّلت).

As for those who say: "Our Lord is Allah," and follow the right way, angels descend upon them, saying: "Fear not, nor be grieved, and here is the good news about paradise which you were promised (41.30). We are your guardians in this life and in the hereafter, and you shall have therein that which your souls desire, and you shall have therein what you ask for" (41.31).

Another example is informing prophet Zachariah that he was going to have prophet John as a son:

هُنَالِكَ دَعَا زَكَرِيَّا رَبَّهُۥ قَالَ رَبِّ هَبْ لِى مِن لَّدُنكَ ذُرِّيَّةً طَيِّبَةً إِنَّكَ سَمِيعُ ٱلدُّعَآءِ ﴿٣٨﴾ فَنَادَتْهُ ٱلْمَلَـٰٓئِكَةُ وَهُوَ قَآئِمٌ يُصَلِّى فِى ٱلْمِحْرَابِ أَنَّ ٱللَّهَ يُبَشِّرُكَ بِيَحْيَىٰ مُصَدِّقًۢا بِكَلِمَةٍ مِّنَ ٱللَّهِ وَسَيِّدًا وَحَصُورًا وَنَبِيًّا مِّنَ ٱلصَّـٰلِحِينَ ﴿٣٩﴾. (سورة آل عِمْران).

There did Zachariah pray to his Lord; he said: "My Lord! Grant me from You good offspring; surely You are the Hearer of prayers" (3.38). Then the angels called him as he stood praying in the pulpit: "Allah gives you the good news of [the birth of] John, who will confirm with a Word from Allah [the previous messengers], be honorable, chaste, and a prophet from among the righteous" (3.39).

One special assignment that Allah gives to angels is the infliction of revenge on wrongdoing people, as in the angels' destruction of the people of prophet Lot:

فَلَمَّا جَآءَ ءَالَ لُوطٍ ٱلْمُرْسَلُونَ ﴿٦١﴾ قَالَ إِنَّكُمْ قَوْمٌ مُّنكَرُونَ ﴿٦٢﴾ قَالُوا۟ بَلْ جِئْنَـٰكَ بِمَا
كَانُوا۟ فِيهِ يَمْتَرُونَ ﴿٦٣﴾ وَأَتَيْنَـٰكَ بِٱلْحَقِّ وَإِنَّا لَصَـٰدِقُونَ ﴿٦٤﴾ فَأَسْرِ بِأَهْلِكَ بِقِطْعٍ مِّنَ ٱلَّيْلِ
وَٱتَّبِعْ أَدْبَـٰرَهُمْ وَلَا يَلْتَفِتْ مِنكُمْ أَحَدٌ وَٱمْضُوا۟ حَيْثُ تُؤْمَرُونَ ﴿٦٥﴾ وَقَضَيْنَآ إِلَيْهِ ذَٰلِكَ ٱلْأَمْرَ
أَنَّ دَابِرَ هَـٰٓؤُلَآءِ مَقْطُوعٌ مُّصْبِحِينَ ﴿٦٦﴾ وَجَآءَ أَهْلُ ٱلْمَدِينَةِ يَسْتَبْشِرُونَ ﴿٦٧﴾ قَالَ إِنَّ هَـٰٓؤُلَآءِ
ضَيْفِى فَلَا تَفْضَحُونِ ﴿٦٨﴾ وَٱتَّقُوا۟ ٱللَّهَ وَلَا تُخْزُونِ ﴿٦٩﴾ قَالُوٓا۟ أَوَلَمْ نَنْهَكَ عَنِ ٱلْعَـٰلَمِينَ
﴿٧٠﴾ قَالَ هَـٰٓؤُلَآءِ بَنَاتِىٓ إِن كُنتُمْ فَـٰعِلِينَ ﴿٧١﴾ لَعَمْرُكَ إِنَّهُمْ لَفِى سَكْرَتِهِمْ يَعْمَهُونَ ﴿٧٢﴾
فَأَخَذَتْهُمُ ٱلصَّيْحَةُ مُشْرِقِينَ ﴿٧٣﴾ فَجَعَلْنَا عَـٰلِيَهَا سَافِلَهَا وَأَمْطَرْنَا عَلَيْهِمْ حِجَارَةً مِّن سِجِّيلٍ
﴿٧٤﴾. (سورة الحِجْر).

So when the messengers came to Luṭ's family (15.61). He said: "Surely you are an unknown people" (15.62). They said: "We have rather come to you with that which they have rejected (15.63). And we have come to you with the truth; and we are surely truthful (15.64). Therefore, go forth with your household in a part of the night, and follow their rear, and let not any one of you turn round, and go to where you are commanded" (15.65). And We revealed to him this decree: the roots of these [his people] shall be cut off in the morning (15.66). And the people of the town came [to him] with joyful expectations (15.67). He said: "These are my guests, so do not disgrace me (15.68). And act dutifully toward Allah, and do not put me to shame" (15.69). They said: "Have we not forbidden you from [talking to] people?" (15.70). He said: "These are my daughters [to marry], if you must do so" (15.71). Verily! They are blindly wandering on in their intoxication (15.72). So the blast overtook them at sunrise (15.73). Thus, We turned it upside down, and rained down upon them stones of Sijjīl (15.74).

There are non-human messengers who are sent on other special missions, such as Gabriel who delivered the Message of Allah to Prophet Muhammad to guide the human beings and jinn:

قُلْ مَن كَانَ عَدُوًّا لِّجِبْرِيلَ فَإِنَّهُۥ نَزَّلَهُۥ عَلَىٰ قَلْبِكَ بِإِذْنِ ٱللَّهِ مُصَدِّقًا لِّمَا بَيْنَ يَدَيْهِ وَهُدًى وَبُشْرَىٰ
لِلْمُؤْمِنِينَ ﴿٩٧﴾. (سورة البقرة).

Say [O Muhammad!]: 'Who is an enemy of Gabriel?' For he brought it down to your heart by Allah's command, confirming that [the Book] which was before it, and as guidance and good news for the believers (2.97).

Allah also aided prophet Jesus with Gabriel (*Rūḥ al-Qudus*):

وَلَقَدْ ءَاتَيْنَا مُوسَى ٱلْكِتَـٰبَ وَقَفَّيْنَا مِنۢ بَعْدِهِۦ بِٱلرُّسُلِ وَءَاتَيْنَا عِيسَى ٱبْنَ مَرْيَمَ ٱلْبَيِّنَـٰتِ وَأَيَّدْنَـٰهُ بِرُوحِ ٱلْقُدُسِ ﴿٨٧﴾. (سورة البقرة).

And certainly We gave Moses the Book and sent messengers after him one after another; and We gave Jesus, the son of Mary, clear proofs and strengthened him with the Rūḥ al-Qudus (from 2.87).

Allah, therefore, has non-human messengers whom He sends to elite individuals, not common people, in order to deliver a particular message, or whom He sends to execute a particular task. The messengers that Allah sent to common people to deliver the good news and warning about the Day of Resurrection, such as the messengers that are referred to in verse 12.109, however, were all human beings.

Let us get back to the verse under discussion and turn our attention to the words "have they not then traveled in the land and seen what was the end of those before them?" This is also an indirect criticism of the polytheists and disbelievers. It is a denouncement of their adherence to polytheism and disbelief despite the fact that they have seen the relics and heard the stories of Allah's punishment of past polytheistic and disbelieving nations.

Allah's words "surely the abode of the hereafter is better for those who act dutifully" stress, implicitly, that the dutiful servants will have good in this world and, explicitly, that their reward in the hereafter will be even greater. They encourage people to seek the path of dutifulness.

Allah concludes the verse saying "do you [O people!] not understand?" emphasizing that His words and His other signs should convince every person with sound mind. Anyone who does not believe in Allah's signs is therefore failing to understand properly.

حَتَّىٰٓ إِذَا ٱسْتَيْـَٔسَ ٱلرُّسُلُ وَظَنُّوٓا۟ أَنَّهُمْ قَدْ كُذِبُوا۟ جَآءَهُمْ نَصْرُنَا فَنُجِّىَ مَن نَّشَآءُ وَلَا يُرَدُّ بَأْسُنَا عَنِ ٱلْقَوْمِ ٱلْمُجْرِمِينَ ﴿١١٠﴾

When the messengers despaired and thought that they were given an untrue promise, Our help came to them, so those whom We pleased were saved; and Our punishment cannot be warded off the guilty people (110).

Exegetes have disagreed in their interpretation of this verse. Some have gone with its apparent meaning, whereas others have adopted alternative interpretations to what the verse appears to say. The reason that made the majority of exegetes look for alternatives to the apparent meaning is their perception that this meaning depreciates Allah's messengers and contradicts their own understanding of the concept of the infallibility of prophets. Let us study first the apparent meaning of this verse.

The controversial part of this verse is "when the messengers despaired and thought that they were given an untrue promise." This verse appears to mean that the hardship that prophets faced became so difficult at times that they went through periods of despair during which they began to doubt Allah's promise to aid them. Aṭ-Ṭabarī cited an opinion for Ibn 'Abbās in which the latter adopts this interpretation. Al-'Ayyāshī and al-Qummī have also ascribed to Imām al-Ḥusayn bin 'Alī a saying that is in line with this interpretation. This saying indicates that this weakness occurred to messengers at moments when Allah left them alone in control of themselves.

According to Al-Qurṭubī, Abū Naṣr al-Qushayrī has said that if this is indeed the correct interpretation of this verse, then it means that these negative feelings and doubts "occurred to the messengers' hearts, but the messengers did not allow them to materialize in their souls." He refers to the following saying that is attributed to Prophet Muhammad: "Allah ignores for my nation their bad thoughts as long as they do not get spoken or turned into action."

Al-Qurṭubī has also reported that ath-Tha'labī and an-Naḥḥās have quoted Ibn 'Abbās saying: "they [the messengers] were humans who were weakened by the length of the period of calamity, so they forgot and thought that the promise given to them had been broken," and then cited the following verse: حَتَّىٰ يَقُولَ ٱلرَّسُولُ وَٱلَّذِينَ ءَامَنُواْ مَعَهُۥ مَتَىٰ نَصْرُ ٱللَّهِ "[such] that the messenger and those who believed with him said: 'When will Allah's help come?'" (from 2.214). The situation described in the latter verse, however, differs from the one mentioned in verse 12.110. This is verse 2.214 in full:

أَمْ حَسِبْتُمْ أَنْ تَدْخُلُوا الْجَنَّةَ وَلَمَّا يَأْتِكُمْ مَثَلُ الَّذِينَ خَلَوْا مِنْ قَبْلِكُمْ مَسَّتْهُمُ الْبَأْسَاءُ وَالضَّرَّاءُ وَزُلْزِلُواْ حَتَّىٰ يَقُولَ ٱلرَّسُولُ وَٱلَّذِينَ ءَامَنُواْ مَعَهُۥ مَتَىٰ نَصْرُ ٱللَّهِ أَلَآ إِنَّ نَصْرَ ٱللَّهِ قَرِيبٌ ﴿٢١٤﴾. (سورة البقرة).

Or do you think that you [O you who believe!] would enter paradise before the like of that which came to those who passed away before you has come to you? Affliction and adversity befell them, and they were so shaken that the messenger and those who believed with him said: 'When will Allah's help come?' Verily, Allah's help is nigh! (2.214).

The messengers' words "when will Allah's help come?" may be an expression of their "despair" that help will ever arrive. It may alternatively reflect the "expiry of their patience" for the belatedness of that help, as though they were complaining for having to wait that long for the help from Allah.

Al-Qurṭubī has reported that at-Tirmidhī al-Ḥakīm suggested that the messengers thought that their souls might have committed something that nullified Allah's promise to them, so when their wait for Allah's help was prolonged, despair and doubts crept inside them. The word كُذِبُوْا "*kudhibū*," which I have translated as "given an untrue promise," however, makes this interpretation difficult to accept. Had the messengers thought that their souls were the reason that Allah's help was never going to arrive, they would not have called that "being given an untrue promise."

Let us now look at alternative interpretations for the verse under study. One view is attributed to 'Ā'ishā, one of the Prophet's wives, who read the word "*kudhibū*" as كُذِّبوا "*kudhdhibū* (were accused of lying)." This is a different reading from that in the printed Qur'an and to the reading of Ibn 'Abbās and Ibn Mas'ūd, both of whom read it as "*kudhibū*," as pointed out by Ibn Kathīr. The suggested alternative reading changes the meaning completely. It now means that the messengers despaired of their people ever believing because the latter accused them of lying, not that the messengers developed doubts about Allah's fulfillment of His promise to them.

One objection that has been made to this interpretation is that it is in contradiction with the use of the verb ظَنُّوْا "*ẓannū*" which, although translated as "thought," implies an undertone of "guessing" and "uncertainty." Certainly, the messengers must have known whether they were accused of lying or not by their people. This kind of certain knowledge cannot be described with the verb "*ẓannū*." Additionally, according to this interpretation, the messengers' despair developed because people accused them of lying; but how could they despair when they are uncertain that people accused them of lying? One possible response to this objection is that the verb ظَنَّ "*ẓanna*" (noun: *ẓann*) could also mean "knew with certainty," as I explain in my comment on the same verb in verse 12.42 in Chapter 6. The crucial point here, however, is that the verb "despaired" occurs in the verse before the verb "thought." It is, therefore, wrong to suggest that this "thinking" was the cause of the "despair," regardless of what is referred to by the verb "thought" and what was "despaired" of.

There is a large number of exegetes who read "*kudhibū*" as "*kudhdhibū*," but still agree with the view that the messengers' despair was of their people believing in their Messages, not of Allah's promise to aid them. One form that this view has taken is the suggestion that the verb "*ẓannū*" refers to the people of the prophets not to the prophets themselves. This would mean that it is those people, not the prophets, who thought that Allah broke his promise to the prophets. This opinion has been mentioned by aṭ-Ṭabarī, al-Ḥuwayzī, al-Jalālayn, aṭ-Ṭūsī, and others.

These are the most common alternatives to the apparent meaning of the verse. They aim to interpret the verse in such a way so that it does not mean that the prophets despaired of Allah's mercy and thought that He broke His promise to help them. There are other similar, though less popular, views. It is clear, however, that these unjustified interpretations are called upon to deny the interpretation that the verse apparently suggests, because exegetes think that the latter interpretation undermines the prophets' status.

The verbs ٱسْتَيْـَٔسَ "*istay'asa* ([they] despaired)" and "*ẓannū* (thought)," which are linked with the conjunction "and," refer to one subject. Since ٱلرُّسُلُ "*ar-rusulu* (the messengers)" is undoubtedly the subject of the verb "despaired," then it must also be the subject of "thought." Additionally, since both verbs "despaired" and جَآءَهُمْ "*jā'ahum* ([it] came to them)" refer explicitly to "the messengers," then it is not possible for the verb "thought," which falls between those two verbs, to refer to any subject other than "the messengers." We will also see in the next verse that the pronoun in the word قَصَصِهِمْ "*qaṣaṣihim* (their stories)" also refers to "the messengers," thus leaving no doubt that there is one subject in this verse: "the messengers." Therefore, the verb "*kudhibū* (given an untrue promise)" must refer to "the messengers," and the said "promise" is Allah's promise of help to the messengers.

The verb "*istay'asa* ([they] despaired)" occurs in one other place in the Qur'an, which describes Joseph's brothers' despair of convincing Joseph to let Benjamin return with them: "So, when they despaired of [convincing] him, they conferred privately" (from 12.80). Note that this verse mentions explicitly what Joseph's brothers despaired of: "convincing him." Therefore, it is logical to expect what the messengers despaired of to be mentioned explicitly in verse 12.110, in which case it must be "Allah's help."

The situation described in this verse does not derogate in any way the mentioned messengers of Allah. This verse simply mentions particular moments that those messengers went through, but it does not indicate that they stayed in that state for a long time. The main point that the verse emphasizes is the enormous calamity that the messengers met. It is not meant to derogate messengers.

We must not forget the very important point that the messengers of Allah went through those moments of despair because of difficulties that they faced *while discharging their responsibilities in conveying the Message of Allah.* It is certain that those instances of despair were very brief and transient, as proved by their failure to weaken the adherence of the messengers to their Messages and their determination to convey it to people. One proof that those instances of weakness were transient is that Allah honored His messengers and gave them His support.

As mentioned earlier, some exegetes have cited the following verse which also talks about messengers and their followers waiting for the help from Allah: "Or do you think that you [O you who believe!] would enter paradise before the like of that which came to those who passed away before you has come to you? Affliction and adversity befell them, and they were so shaken that the messenger and those who believed with him said: 'When will Allah's help come?' Verily, Allah's help is nigh!" (2.214). Their words "when will Allah's help come?" show the escalation of the hardship and describe a situation in which those who were waiting for Allah's help lost their patience. This verse also, however, does not derogate the messengers. It does exactly the opposite. It shows that despite the graveness of the hardship that the messengers experienced, they did not give up their duty of delivering the Message. This verse and verse 12.110 teach us to have patience at any difficulty that we go through. They remind us that Allah has ordained hardships even for the servants who are very close to Him. The calamities that He sent to those honorable servants were so difficult that at times the messengers despaired of Allah's promise to them, and lost patience while waiting for His help.

Allah's exposure of hidden shortcomings in one's soul is a great spiritual experience that guides the righteous servant to a stronger and deeper faith and to higher spiritual states. Allah uses both calamity and favor to differentiate between the righteous and wrongdoing servants, leading each to his ultimate state of righteousness or disbelief. The patience of the righteous person at times of calamity, and his thankfulness for any favor he receives, strengthen him spiritually and draw him closer Allah. Conversely, being impatient when calamity strikes and not offering thanks at times of prosperity take the disbeliever away from Allah, leading him ultimately to hell.[101]

لَقَدْ كَانَ فِي قَصَصِهِمْ عِبْرَةٌ لِّأُوْلِي ٱلْأَلْبَٰبِ مَا كَانَ حَدِيثًا يُفْتَرَىٰ وَلَٰكِن تَصْدِيقَ ٱلَّذِي بَيْنَ يَدَيْهِ وَتَفْصِيلَ
كُلِّ شَيْءٍ وَهُدًى وَرَحْمَةً لِّقَوْمٍ يُؤْمِنُونَ ﴿١١١﴾

There is a lesson in their stories for the people of understanding. It is not a narrative which could be forged, but a confirmation of what was before it, an explanation of all things, and a guidance and a mercy to people who believe (111).

Allah referred to the stories of the Qur'an at the start of this sūra before recounting the story of Joseph: "We narrate to you [O Muhammad!] the best of narratives, by revealing this Qur'an to you; and before it you were one of the unaware" (12.3). He ended the sūra of Joseph by referring to the Qur'anic stories again.

The pronoun "their" in "their stories" refers to the messengers who were mentioned in the previous two verses. Most of the verses of the sūra of Joseph talk about some of those messengers, namely Jacob his sons. Allah stresses that the stories of the messengers contain lessons and sermons for anyone with sound thinking.

The clause "it is not a narrative which could be forged" is a confirmation that the Qur'an could not have been authored by any creature. The miraculous aspects of the Qur'an and the knowledge it contains are clear evidence that it was authored by Allah.

Allah mentions in this verse three goals for revealing the Qur'an. First, it is "a confirmation of what was before it," i.e. proof of the divine origin of the Books that He revealed before the Qur'an, such as the Torah and the Injīl. It is another proof to those who rejected the previous divine Books that those Books were indeed revealed by Allah. It is also proof to the believers in those Books that the Qur'an has come from the same divine source that revealed the Books that they believed in, hence they must believe in the Qur'an.

Second, it explains to people religion and matters about this world and thereafter: "an explanation of all things." Third, it is "a guidance and a mercy to people who believe." Allah uses the Qur'an to guide the believers and to show mercy toward them.

With this verse ends the sūra which contains one of "the best of narratives": the story of prophet Joseph.

11

Prophet Joseph In History

We have already seen that the Qur'an says explicitly that Joseph lived in Egypt. In this chapter, we will investigate the possibility of identifying the part of Egypt and the era in which he lived.

11.1 Among the Hyksos in the Eastern Delta?

Archaeological excavations have so far failed to uncover any ancient Egyptian text or artifact that refers explicitly to prophets Jacob, Joseph, or Moses. This is attributed to a number of reasons, the most important of which is the limited archaeological finds.

Some historians, archaeologists, and Biblical scholars, however, think that there are pieces of circumstantial evidence indicating that Joseph's entry into Egypt took place during the rule of the Hyksos, and that he settled in the eastern Delta in the northern part of Egypt. This region was under the rule of the Semite Hyksos between 1663-1555 BCE.[102] This circumstantial evidence comes from linking historical references in the Old Testament with independent historical and archaeological information.

In this section, we will study the researchers' main reasons for linking the era and place in which Joseph lived in Egypt with the time and place of the rule of the Hyksos. In the next section, we will study the conclusions that can be drawn from the Qur'an about this theory.

The Egyptians used papyrus for writing. Some Egyptian papyri found show that Semitic herdsmen were often allowed into the eastern Delta during times of famine. One such example is Papyrus Anastasi VI,[103] which is thought to have come from the city of Memphis in northern Egypt. This papyrus contains a report from an official on the eastern Egyptian frontier on the entry of Asiatic Bedouins from the region of Edom to the Nile Delta escaping a drought and looking for pasturage. This is dated during the reign of Pharaoh Merneptah, i.e. around the end of the 13th century BCE.

The entry of Semitic shepherds to the eastern Delta during times of famine has been linked with the Old Testament's claim that Jacob sent his sons to Egypt to buy grain because of the famine that struck the land of Canaan. Researchers concluded that the area to which Joseph's brothers went to seek provisions, and the land where Joseph lived and met them, must have been the eastern Delta in the north of Egypt.

Additionally, the Old Testament states the following about Jacob's sons and his descendants who were contemporaries of Moses who lived about four centuries after Joseph:[104]

> *Now these are the names of the Children of Israel, which came into Egypt; every man and his household came with Jacob. Reuben, Simeon, Levi, and Judah, Issachar, Zebulun, and Benjamin, Dan, and Naphtali, Gad, and Asher. And all the souls that came out of the loins of Jacob were seventy souls: for Joseph was in Egypt already. And Joseph died, and all his brethren, and all that generation. And the Children of Israel were fruitful, and increased abundantly, and multiplied, and waxed exceeding mighty; and the land was filled with them.*
>
> *Now there arose up a new king over Egypt, which knew not Joseph. And he said unto his people, Behold, the people of the Children of Israel are more and mightier than we: Come on, let us deal wisely with them; lest they multiply, and it come to pass, that, when there falleth out any war, they join also unto our enemies, and fight against us, and so get them up out of the land. Therefore they did set over them taskmasters to afflict them with their burdens. And they built for Pharaoh treasure cities, Pithom and Raamses.*
>
> *But the more they afflicted them, the more they multiplied and grew. And they were grieved because of the Children of Israel. And the Egyptians made the Children of Israel to serve with rigour: And they made their lives bitter with hard bondage, in morter, and in brick, and in all manner of service in the field: all their service, wherein they made them serve, was with rigour. (Exodus, 1:1-14).*

Researchers think that the Biblical city of *Pithom* is now possibly identified with Tell el-Maskhuta or the nearby Tell el-Retabe. As for the Biblical city of "Raamses," it is known today to be the Egyptian city of "Pi-Ramesse A-nakhtu (Domain of Ramesses-Great-of-Victories)"; it is sited at Tell el-Dab'a in Avaris in the eastern Delta, near modern Qantir. There are a number of ancient Egyptian texts that describe Pi-Ramesse as a store city for food.[105] If the Children of Israel, who are the descendants of Jacob, at the time of Moses were living in the Delta region in Egypt, then it is likely that Jacob and his sons also lived there.

Researchers also think that Joseph entered Egypt during the period when the eastern Delta was under the control of the Hyksos. The latter assumed power after the 14th Pharaonic Dynasty, around 1663 BCE, confining the authority of the Pharaohs in Egypt to Thebes. Researchers incline toward this possibility because they see the fact that the Hyksos were not Egyptian but Semitic as a factor that would have facilitated the migration of other Semitics, including Jacob and his sons, to the eastern Delta. This fact makes it also likely that the rising of a non-Egyptian person such as Joseph to prominence happened during the role of the Hyksos rather than Egyptians.

Another observation that should be mentioned is the use of the name "Jacob" by the Hyksos, as their second king was called "Ya'qub-her." This also makes it likely that Jacob and his sons were contemporary to the Hyksos, lived in the place that they ruled, and were close to them.

The sparseness of preserved records from the Hyksos period in general has contributed to the absence of references to Joseph in Egyptian records. The scarceness of these records is attributed to two factors. First, the Hyksos had little influence in regions beyond the Delta and northern parts of Egypt, so their relics were confined to the Delta region. Second, because of their resentment to being under the rule of foreigners, the Egyptians wanted to forget this unpleasant period of their history. After their expulsion of the Hyksos, they launched an active campaign to obliterate and destroy the monuments erected by the Hyksos, as excavation tells us.[106]

11.2 The Theory in the Light of the Qur'an

Having explained the most popular theory among researchers about the place and time in which Joseph lived, I will try in this section to show whether the Qur'an supports or rejects this view. Western scholars have studied extensively the story of Joseph in the Old Testament, but they have neglected completely its Qur'anic counterpart.

We have already seen that the Qur'an calls the land where Joseph lived "Egypt" (12.21, 99). The Book of Allah tells us that the land in which Moses lived was also called "Egypt":

وَأَوْحَيْنَآ إِلَىٰ مُوسَىٰ وَأَخِيهِ أَن تَبَوَّءَا لِقَوْمِكُمَا بِمِصْرَ بُيُوتًا وَٱجْعَلُوا۟ بُيُوتَكُمْ قِبْلَةً وَأَقِيمُوا۟ ٱلصَّلَوٰةَ وَبَشِّرِ ٱلْمُؤْمِنِينَ ﴿٨٧﴾. (سورة يونس).

And We revealed to Moses and his brother [saying]: "Have for your people houses in Egypt, make your houses a *qiblā*, keep up prayer, and give good news to the believers" (10.87).

وَنَادَىٰ فِرْعَوْنُ فِى قَوْمِهِۦ قَالَ يَٰقَوْمِ أَلَيْسَ لِى مُلْكُ مِصْرَ وَهَٰذِهِ ٱلْأَنْهَٰرُ تَجْرِى مِن تَحْتِىٓ أَفَلَا تُبْصِرُونَ ﴿٥١﴾. (سورة الزّخْرُف).

And Pharaoh proclaimed amongst his people: "O my people! Is the kingship of Egypt not mine? And these rivers flow beneath me; do you not then see?" (43.51).

Additionally, there is a verse that shows someone from Pharaoh's people who believed in the Message of Moses say to his people:

وَلَقَدْ جَآءَكُمْ يُوسُفُ مِن قَبْلُ بِٱلْبَيِّنَٰتِ فَمَا زِلْتُمْ فِى شَكٍّ مِّمَّا جَآءَكُم بِهِۦ حَتَّىٰٓ إِذَا هَلَكَ قُلْتُمْ لَن يَبْعَثَ ٱللَّهُ مِنۢ بَعْدِهِۦ رَسُولًا ﴿٣٤﴾. (سورة غَافِر).

And surely Joseph came to you [O my people!] in times gone by with clear proofs, but you ever remained in doubt about what he brought to you. When he died, you said: "Allah will not send a messenger after him" (from 40.34).

This verse in particular clearly shows that the "Egypt" which Joseph and his family entered was the same Egypt in which Moses lived. This leads us to another observation that is detailed below.

The Qur'an always refers to the monarch in the story of Moses with the title of فِرعون "Pharaoh," and never calls him مَلِك "king" or "king of Egypt." Equally significant is the fact that the ruler of Egypt in the story of Joseph is never referred to as "Pharaoh" but "king" in the five verses that mention his title (12.43, 50, 54, 72, 76). The Qur'an uses the title "king" to refer to various monarchs, including the one in the story of Joseph, but it uses the title "Pharaoh" only for the ruler of Egypt during the life of Moses. Why, then, does the Qur'an clearly distinguish between the "Pharaoh" and the "king" of Egypt?

This actually underlines a fundamental difference between the monarch who was a contemporary of Joseph and the one who lived at the time of Moses. The term "Pharaoh" was a special title for the native monarchs of Egypt who ruled it for about 3,000 years. Not using the title "Pharaoh" for the ruler in the Qur'anic story of Joseph reflects the fact that this king was not one of those Egyptian "Pharaohs." This strongly suggests that this ruler was one of the Semitic Hyksos kings who were not ethnically related to the Egyptians.

The Old Testament calls the ruler during the time of Joseph "Pharaoh" (e.g. Genesis, 20:13, 14, 17) at times, and "king" (e.g. Genesis,

39:20, 40:1, 5) at others. It does the same with the monarch of Egypt who was a contemporary of Moses, calling him "Pharaoh" (Exodus, 1:11, 19, 22) and "king" of Egypt (e.g. Exodus, 1:8, 15, 17). The Old Testament uses the terms "Pharaoh" and "king" interchangeably. Clearly, the writers and editors of the Old Testament were unaware of the ethnic difference between the ruler of Egypt during the life of Joseph and that at the time of Moses. Henceforth, I will follow the Qur'anic use of the title "Pharaoh," applying it only to the ruler of Egypt during the time of Moses.

Let's now examine an indirect proof, from the story of Moses, that Joseph lived in the eastern Delta when it was under the rule of the Hyksos. When Moses showed Pharaoh his first two miracles, Pharaoh accused him and his brother, prophet Aaron, of aiming to *drive the people out of their land*:

وَلَقَدْ أَرَيْنَـٰهُ ءَايَـٰتِنَا كُلَّهَا فَكَذَّبَ وَأَبَىٰ ﴿٥٦﴾ قَالَ أَجِئْتَنَا لِتُخْرِجَنَا مِنْ أَرْضِنَا بِسِحْرِكَ يَـٰمُوسَىٰ ﴿٥٧﴾. (سورة طَـهَ).

And verily We showed him [Pharaoh] all Our signs, but he rejected [them] and refused [to believe] (20.56). He Said: "Have you come to us to drive us out of our land by your magic, O Moses?" (20.57).

قَالُوٓاْ إِنْ هَـٰذَٰنِ لَسَـٰحِرَٰنِ يُرِيدَانِ أَن يُخْرِجَاكُم مِّنْ أَرْضِكُم بِسِحْرِهِمَا وَيَذْهَبَا بِطَرِيقَتِكُمُ ٱلْـمُثْلَىٰ ﴿٦٣﴾. (سورة طَـهَ).

They [Pharaoh and his chiefs] said: "These are surely two magicians who wish to drive you out of your land by their magic and take away your ideal tradition" (20.63).

فَأَلْقَىٰ عَصَاهُ فَإِذَا هِىَ ثُعْبَانٌ مُّبِينٌ ﴿٣٢﴾ وَنَزَعَ يَدَهُ فَإِذَا هِىَ بَيْضَآءُ لِلنَّـٰظِرِينَ ﴿٣٣﴾ قَالَ لِلْمَلَإِ حَوْلَهُ إِنَّ هَـٰذَا لَسَـٰحِرٌ عَلِيمٌ ﴿٣٤﴾ يُرِيدُ أَن يُخْرِجَكُم مِّنْ أَرْضِكُم بِسِحْرِهِ فَمَـاذَا تَأْمُرُونَ ﴿٣٥﴾. (سورة الشُّعَراء).

So he [Moses] flung down his staff and it became a manifest serpent (26.32). And he took his hand out and lo! It was white to the beholders (26.33). He [Pharaoh] said to the chiefs around him: "This is verily an accomplished magician (26.34). Who would like to drive you out of your land by his magic; so what is your advice?" (26.35).

فَأَلْقَىٰ عَصَاهُ فَإِذَا هِىَ ثُعْبَانٌ مُّبِينٌ ﴿١٠٧﴾ وَنَزَعَ يَدَهُ فَإِذَا هِىَ بَيْضَآءُ لِلنَّـٰظِرِينَ ﴿١٠٨﴾ قَالَ ٱلْمَلَأُ مِن قَوْمِ فِرْعَوْنَ إِنَّ هَـٰذَا لَسَـٰحِرٌ عَلِيمٌ ﴿١٠٩﴾ يُرِيدُ أَن يُخْرِجَكُم مِّنْ أَرْضِكُمْ فَمَـاذَا تَأْمُرُونَ ﴿١١٠﴾. (سورة الأَعْراف).

So he flung his staff down and it became a manifest serpent (7.107).

> And he took his hand out and lo! It was white to the beholders (7.108). The chiefs of Pharaoh's people said: "Surely this is an accomplished magician (7.109). Who would like to drive you out of your land; so what is your advice?" (7.110).

Verse 7.123 sheds more light on the "land" mentioned in these verses. Having seen the miracles of Moses, Pharaoh asked him to prove the superiority of his miracles by competing with the best magicians that Pharaoh could gather from various Egyptian cities. The magicians lost the contest and witnessed what they knew for sure could not have been magic. So, they declared their embracement of the religion of Moses. This action prompted Pharaoh to extend his accusation of Moses and Aaron of trying to *drive the people out of the land* to the magicians as well:

وَأُلْقِىَ ٱلسَّحَرَةُ سَـٰجِدِينَ ﴿١٢٠﴾ قَالُوٓاْ ءَامَنَّا بِرَبِّ ٱلْعَـٰلَمِينَ ﴿١٢١﴾ رَبِّ مُوسَىٰ وَهَـٰرُونَ ﴿١٢٢﴾ قَالَ فِرْعَوْنُ ءَامَنتُم بِهِۦ قَبْلَ أَنْ ءَاذَنَ لَكُمْ إِنَّ هَـٰذَا لَـمَكْرٌ مَّكَرْتُمُوهُ فِى ٱلْـمَدِينَةِ لِتُخْرِجُواْ مِنْهَآ أَهْلَهَا فَسَوْفَ تَعْلَمُونَ ﴿١٢٣﴾. (سورة الأعراف).

> And the magicians were thrown down in prostration (7.120). They said: "We believe in the Lord of the people (7.121). The Lord of Moses and Aaron" (7.122). Pharaoh Said: "You believe in Him before I give you permission? This is but a scheme which you have devised in the city, that you may drive its people out of it, but you shall know [what I will do to you] (7.123).

Verse 7.123 makes it clear that the "land" referred to in the verses above was a *particular* "city." The Qur'an also tells us that Pharaoh had brought the magicians from *several cities*:

قَالُوٓاْ أَرْجِهْ وَأَخَاهُ وَٱبْعَثْ فِى ٱلْـمَدَآئِنِ حَـٰشِرِينَ ﴿٣٦﴾ يَأْتُوكَ بِكُلِّ سَحَّارٍ عَلِيمٍ ﴿٣٧﴾. (سورة الشُّعَرَاء).

> They [the chiefs of Pharaoh's people] said [to Pharaoh]: "Put him and his brother off [for a while], and send callers into the cities (26.36). To bring to you every skillful magician" (26.37).

قَالُوٓاْ أَرْجِهْ وَأَخَاهُ وَأَرْسِلْ فِى ٱلْـمَدَآئِنِ حَـٰشِرِينَ ﴿١١١﴾ يَأْتُوكَ بِكُلِّ سَـٰحِرٍ عَلِيمٍ ﴿١١٢﴾. (سورة الأَعْراف).

> They [the chiefs of Pharaoh's people] said [to Pharaoh]: "Put him and his brother off [for a while], and send callers into the cities (7.111). To bring to you every accomplished magician" (7.112).

The word "city" in verse 7.123 could not have been equivalent to the whole of "the country," i.e. upper and lower Egypt, which consisted of a *number of cities*.

Moses simply asked Pharaoh to allow him to take the Israelites and leave Egypt, so why would Pharaoh and his court think of the rather bizarre accusation that Moses and Aaron, and later the magicians as well, had planned to drive the inhabitants of "the city" out of it? The answer has a lot to do with the painful memories of the Hyksos.

The city that Pharaoh and his chiefs were talking about is Pi-Ramesse, the same city where Moses and Aaron met Pharaoh and where the contest with the magicians took place. Ramesses II (1279-1212 BCE), who is the Pharaoh of the story of Moses, built Pi-Ramesse on the same site of Avaris, which was the capital of the Hyksos a few centuries earlier. Pharaoh did not believe Moses' claim that he wanted to take the Israelites out of Egypt for good. He thought that this was only the first step of a re-run of a disturbing episode in the history of the Egyptians, when the Semitic Hyksos, who came from the east, took over the eastern Delta. Pharaoh and his court believed that Moses would take the Israelites out simply to use them as a nucleus to build around it an army of Semitics. He would then invade Lower Egypt to re-establish the Semitic kingdom in the city that is now Pi-Ramesse, and which Ramesses II had made his capital.

But what has all this to do with our investigation of the city in which Joseph lived? Pharaoh and his men would not have thought of this scenario had the people involved in Moses' request not been the Israelites, the descendants of Joseph and his brothers. They were well aware, of course, that the Israelites were the descendants of those forefathers who settled in the eastern Delta and built strong relations with the Hyksos. They also knew Joseph quite well, which means that they knew that one of those Israelite forefathers rose to a very prominent position in the Hyksos kingdom. This can be clearly seen in the following words of one believer from Pharaoh's people to his people: "And surely Joseph came to you [O my people!] in times gone by with clear proofs, but you ever remained in doubt about what he brought to you. When he died, you said: 'Allah will not send a messenger after him'. Thus does Allah cause to err him who is extravagant, a doubter" (40.34). Pharaoh and his men's miscalculations about the ultimate purpose of the mission of Moses represent another indication that Joseph, and the early fathers of the Israelites, lived in the eastern Delta when it was under the control of the Hyksos.

Another significant piece of information in the Qur'anic story of Joseph is putting him in charge of the "storehouses of the land." This is another strong indication that Joseph lived in the Delta part of Egypt. It is well known today from ancient Egyptian documents, as already explained, that the fertile Delta was often a sought destination at times of famine even by people from outside Egypt. It must have been full of food stores, as clear from the description of Pi-Ramesse that we read earlier.

It is possible, of course, that some food stores were already in use in Lower Egypt before Joseph took charge. But when asking the king to put him in charge of the storehouses of the land, it is likely that Joseph was not referring only to the already existing storehouses, but also to considerably larger storehouses which he advised the king to build. These would store the harvest of the seven prosperous years which was to be used in the following seven years of poor harvest. Joseph successfully established a large and organized grain storage system in the eastern Delta.

It is very interesting to recall here that Ramesses II built his store city in Pi-Ramesse which itself was built on the same site of ancient Avaris where Joseph established his storehouses. Does this indicate something more than a *coincidence*? According to the Old Testament, the answer is negative; the Pharaoh who enslaved the Israelites in building his store cities, "*Pithom and Raamses*," had no knowledge of Joseph: "*Now there arose up a new king over Egypt, which knew not Joseph*" (Exodus, 1:8). We have seen, however, that the Qur'an refutes the Biblical claim; it stresses that Joseph was known to and still remembered by the court of Ramesses II. This strongly suggests that there was no creativity in Ramesses II's decision to build storehouses in Pi-Ramesse. He simply copied Joseph's creative idea. This is another strong Qur'anic indication that Joseph indeed lived in the eastern Delta during the Hyksos reign who had their capital at Avaris.

It is clear that the Qur'an implies that Joseph's entry into Egypt must have happened in the Delta region when it was under the rule of the Hyksos. I have also already mentioned that the presence of the name "Jacob" as part of the name of the second king of the Hyksos is likely to have been influenced by the name of prophet Jacob. The Hyksos must have heard of the name Jacob, from his son Joseph, before he came to live in the eastern Delta. This means that Joseph's entry into Egypt must have happened during the rule of the first or second king of the Hyksos.

Note that the speech of the believer from the people of Pharaoh "and surely Joseph came to you in times gone by with clear proofs, but you ever remained in doubt about what he brought to you. When he died, you said: 'Allah will not send a messenger after him'" *may imply* that Joseph was the last prophet there before Moses, but it *certainly mean* that he left the biggest impact until Moses' time. Jacob was very old when he entered Egypt, so no doubt he lived for a relatively short period. The influence of Joseph's brothers also was relatively very limited. In addition to having a higher spiritual status than his brothers, Joseph lived in Egypt since his childhood, and rose to a high position that gave him a considerable influence. Joseph remained by far the most famous among the other prophets of that era.

11.3 The Age of Prophet Joseph

I will now try to roughly estimate the age of Joseph at different stages of his life. I need to emphasize that these are only rough calculations.

The Qur'an tells us that Joseph was a "young boy" when his brothers cast him in the well and was later found by the caravanners: "They said: 'O our father! Why do you not entrust us with Joseph? Surely we seek good for him (12.11). Send him with us in the early morning to enjoy himself and play, and surely we shall be protective of him'" (12.12), "And there came a caravan. They [the caravanners] sent someone to draw some water, and he let down his bucket; he said: 'O good news! Here is a young boy'; and they concealed him as an article of merchandise, and Allah was aware of what they were doing" (12.19). It can be assumed that he was 6-10 years old.

He then lived in the house of his master until he became a youth: "And when he attained his full strength, We gave him Wisdom and Knowledge; and thus do We reward the good-doers" (12.22). This age could be estimated between 16-18, which means that he lived at the house of the 'Azīz for 6-12 years.

Then the wife of his master tried to seduce him, and when he turned her down, she put him in jail, where he stayed for several years: "So he remained in the prison several years" (from 12.42), say 4-6 years, though it may have been longer.

When the king released him from jail and put him in charge of the storehouses of the land, Joseph must have been 20-24 years old. Thus, possibly Joseph's rise to power happened 10-18 years after his entry into Egypt.

Joseph had been in charge of the storehouses for at least the seven prosperous years when his brothers came to him at some point in the following seven years of hardship asking for provisions. Therefore, when Joseph met his brothers in Egypt, he was not younger than 27-31 years old. We do not know in which of the famine years this meeting took place.

Joseph's reuniting with his father took place after the third visit of his brothers to him. It is possible, therefore, that Joseph's separation from his father lasted 17-25 years.

How great this test was for Jacob, Joseph, and his brothers, and how great their reward was!

12

Prophet Joseph in the Qur'an and the Old Testament

In this chapter, I will take a different approach in studying the Qur'anic text from that of previous chapters. I will compare the Qur'anic account of the story of Joseph with its Biblical counterpart. Such a study can shed further light on the miraculous aspects of the Qur'anic text.

12.1 Comparative Religious Studies and the Divine Source of the Qur'an

There are two main approaches in the study of the Qur'an each of which can continuously unveil proofs of the divine origin of the Qur'an. The first is *studying the Qur'anic text alone, with no reference to any other text or external source of information.* This has been the approach that I followed in particular in Chapters 2-10 in which I studied the text of the sūra of Joseph. Among the miraculous aspects of the Qur'anic text that this approach of research can reveal is its stunning, apparent and subtle consistency; paranormal eloquence; and unparalleled beauty. This approach can also reveal complicated mathematical relations between various parts of the Qur'anic text which could not have been made by humans.

The other research methodology that reveals miracles of the Qur'an is *the comparative study of the Qur'anic text, i.e. comparing the Qur'an with external sources.* This approach can take various forms. First, Qur'anic miracles can be discovered by *comparing information from this Book with knowledge reached and discoveries made by man through various means.* Such miracles show that this Book was not only ahead of its time, but that it is ahead of all time. For instance, archaeological and historical findings in ancient Egypt and Palestine have revealed miraculous aspects in the Qur'anic story of prophet Moses, as shown in our book *History Testifies to the Infallibility of the Qur'an,*[107] and in the story of prophet

Joseph, as we saw in Chapter 11. Scholars have found in the Qur'an references to scientific facts that were unknown and could not have been known at the time of the revelation of the Book, and which were discovered only in modern times.

Second, proofs of the divine origin of the Qur'anic text can be seen when *comparing its intellectual depth and the quality of its values and principles with their equivalents in the society in which the Qur'an was revealed.* Note, for instance, its prohibition of female infanticide; its treatment of people as equal, regardless of their color, race, or social status; its differentiation between people's spiritual status in the sight of Allah only in terms of their dutifulness toward Him; and its non-inclusion of any of the many myths and legends of that time and place. In addition to the consistency it shows and the absolute justice it promotes, the Qur'an's values and principles show no influence by any cultural and societal biases, unlike any philosophy and book created by man. This emphasizes the transcendence of this unique Book over any thought produced by man. Such comparison reveals that this noble Book was not the creation of and does not represent any human culture. This pure divine work represents a radical intellectual and cultural revolution that cannot be attributed to a particular place or time.

The third form of comparative study of the Qur'anic text that reveals its divine source is *comparing it with human books.* Apart from the Qur'an, any book that is in existence today was written by man. Naturally, religious books are the most relevant books for the purpose of such comparison. This kind of comparative study of the Qur'anic text is the subject of this chapter.

Contrary to what happens with the Qur'an, the deeper a religious book is examined, the more its shortcomings are exposed. Even if they contain traces from old divine Scriptures or were originally derived from such Scriptures, the fact that these religious books were written and edited by man means that they are bound to contain inconsistencies, contradictions, mistakes, weaknesses, and so forth.

Problems in any of these religious books can be seen even when they are investigated independently of external sources. Examining them in the light of the developing knowledge of man exposes more incorrect and inaccurate information. The advancement of this knowledge means an increase in the ability of man to identify shortcomings in these books.

In fact, the main reason for the decline of religion in the developed, Christian world is the disappearance of the aura of infallibility that surrounded the Old and New Testaments for centuries, and the disclosure of their flaws. These shortfalls are not only difficult to hide, but equally hard to fully count. The abundance of incorrect and inaccurate scientific and historical information in these two books has made them in the eyes of many associated with backwardness.

Contrary to this Biblical ebb, Islam is spreading fast, because of the nature of the Qur'an and its stunning accuracy. In fact, Islam is the fastest growing religion in the world. Significantly, the religion of the Qur'an has been growing in the very countries where the religion of the Bible has been declining. One telling observation is that most intellectuals, thinkers, and scientists who experience religious conversion convert to Islam. *Islam is the religion of knowledge and the knowledgeable, of thought and thinkers.*

In addition to revealing that the Old and New Testaments were written by man and could not have been inspired by Allah, the shortcomings of the Biblical text disclose the simple-mindedness of their writers and editors. They reflect the influence of the authors of the Bible by the culture and values of the places and times in which they lived. First, *weaknesses and naivety permeate these books*, reflecting the very simple minds and limited knowledge of the Biblical writers and editors.

Second, like many *human writings that glorify the people of their respective authors*, the Old Testament is based on the assumption that the Israelites are "the chosen people of God." That is why it is a book on the history of the Children of Israel more than anything else. One natural consequence of this is the biased attitude of this book toward the Israelites in a way that contradicts divine justice, and contravenes even human justice as understood by the majority of people. For instance, this is what the Old Testament says to its believers: "*Thou shalt not lend upon usury to thy brother; usury of money, usury of victuals, usury of any thing that is lent upon usury: Unto a stranger thou mayest lend upon usury; but unto thy brother thou shalt not lend upon usury: that the LORD thy God may bless thee in all that thou settest thine hand to in the land whither thou goest to possess it*" (Deuteronomy, 23:19-20). On the contrary, the true divine justice in the Qur'an prevents the Muslim from taking usury from all people, without discriminating between Muslims and non-Muslims:

ٱلَّذِينَ يَأْكُلُونَ ٱلرِّبَوٰا۟ لَا يَقُومُونَ إِلَّا كَمَا يَقُومُ ٱلَّذِى يَتَخَبَّطُهُ ٱلشَّيْطَٰنُ مِنَ ٱلْمَسِّ ذَٰلِكَ
بِأَنَّهُمْ قَالُوٓا۟ إِنَّمَا ٱلْبَيْعُ مِثْلُ ٱلرِّبَوٰا۟ وَأَحَلَّ ٱللَّهُ ٱلْبَيْعَ وَحَرَّمَ ٱلرِّبَوٰا۟ فَمَن جَآءَهُۥ مَوْعِظَةٌ مِّن رَّبِّهِۦ
فَٱنتَهَىٰ فَلَهُۥ مَا سَلَفَ وَأَمْرُهُۥٓ إِلَى ٱللَّهِ وَمَنْ عَادَ فَأُو۟لَٰٓئِكَ أَصْحَٰبُ ٱلنَّارِ هُمْ فِيهَا خَٰلِدُونَ
﴿٢٧٥﴾ يَمْحَقُ ٱللَّهُ ٱلرِّبَوٰا۟ وَيُرْبِى ٱلصَّدَقَٰتِ وَٱللَّهُ لَا يُحِبُّ كُلَّ كَفَّارٍ أَثِيمٍ ﴿٢٧٦﴾ إِنَّ ٱلَّذِينَ

ءَامَنُوا۟ وَعَمِلُوا۟ ٱلصَّٰلِحَٰتِ وَأَقَامُوا۟ ٱلصَّلَوٰةَ وَءَاتَوُا۟ ٱلزَّكَوٰةَ لَهُمْ أَجْرُهُمْ عِندَ رَبِّهِمْ وَلَا خَوْفٌ
عَلَيْهِمْ وَلَا هُمْ يَحْزَنُونَ ﴿٢٧٧﴾ يَٰٓأَيُّهَا ٱلَّذِينَ ءَامَنُوا۟ ٱتَّقُوا۟ ٱللَّهَ وَذَرُوا۟ مَا بَقِىَ مِنَ ٱلرِّبَوٰٓا۟ إِن كُنتُم
مُّؤْمِنِينَ ﴿٢٧٨﴾ فَإِن لَّمْ تَفْعَلُوا۟ فَأْذَنُوا۟ بِحَرْبٍ مِّنَ ٱللَّهِ وَرَسُولِهِۦ وَإِن تُبْتُمْ فَلَكُمْ رُءُوسُ أَمْوَٰلِكُمْ
لَا تَظْلِمُونَ وَلَا تُظْلَمُونَ ﴿٢٧٩﴾ وَإِن كَانَ ذُو عُسْرَةٍ فَنَظِرَةٌ إِلَىٰ مَيْسَرَةٍ وَأَن تَصَدَّقُوا۟ خَيْرٌ لَّكُمْ إِن
كُنتُمْ تَعْلَمُونَ ﴿٢٨٠﴾. (سورة البَقَرَة).

Those who swallow usury do not move except as one whom Satan has touched and sent astray. That is because they say, "trading is like usury"; and Allah has permitted trading but forbidden usury. Therefore, he who desisted after an admonition from his Lord has come to him shall have what has already passed, and his affair is in the hands of Allah; and whoever returns [to it], these are the people of the Fire; they shall abide in it for ever (2.275). Allah deprives money gained by usury of all blessing, and He causes charitable alms to prosper; and Allah does not love any ungrateful sinner (2.276). Those who believe, do righteous deeds, keep up prayer, and pay the obligatory alms shall have their reward from their Lord, and they shall have no fear, nor shall they grieve (2.277). O you who believe! Be dutiful toward Allah and relinquish what has remained [due to you] of usury, if you are believers (2.278). But if you do not, then be apprised of war from Allah and His Messenger; and if you repent, then you shall have your capitals; neither shall you wrong [someone] nor shall you be wronged (2.279). And if he [the debtor] is in straitened circumstances, then let there be a postponement until there is ease; and if you remit [the debt] as charitable alms then that is better for you, if only you know (2.280).

Significantly, the New Testament completely ignores the ethnic concept of "the chosen people of God" which is the very foundation of the Old Testament. Therefore, the claim of the believers in the New Testament that it is a continuation of the Old Testament lacks any basis.

Third, the *Old Testament degrades holy characters*, showing clearly that the writers and editors of that book lacked understanding of what it meant for a human being to be a "prophet." Prophets of the Old Testament behave like common people, showing almost no distinction as recipients of divine inspiration, as if divine revelation does not develop and change the personality of its recipient.

The prophets of the Qur'an are very different from their equivalent characters of the Old Testament in thought and behavior. As an example of the Old Testament's distortion of the image of a prominent righteous figure whom it describes as a "man of God," I have already cited in §1.3 the claim of that book that prophet David committed adultery. Of course, the writers of the Old Testament did not forget to emphasize at the end of that story that what they alleged David to have done was detestable in the sight of Allah!

It is not my aim here to review or study in detail the shortcomings of the Old Testament. This falls outside the scope of this book.[108] This brief introduction was necessary to study the story of Joseph in the Old Testament.

I have already mentioned that one approach to studying the miraculous nature of the Qur'an is to compare it with human writings, particularly religious ones. No doubt, the most appropriate comparison of this nature to undertake in this book is between the story of Joseph in the Qur'an and its version in the Old Testament. This story occupies chapters 37-50, which are the last chapters, of the book of Genesis. Scholars believe that the attempts to write down this text started a few centuries after the events it describes, and that this start was about three thousand years ago.

Having studied the Qur'anic story of Joseph and seen its beauty that captures the heart and knowledge that intrigues the intellect, I will examine comparatively later in the chapter some of the shortcomings in the structure and content of the Biblical story. These deficiencies show the huge difference between the weak Biblical account and the marvelous structure and fascinating content of the Qur'anic story.

First, however, it is necessary to touch, at least briefly, on a fundamental difference between the Qur'anic text and the text of the Old Testament.

12.2 One Qur'an Versus Many Bibles

The Qur'an describes itself as a Book that Allah revealed to all people through one Messenger, Muhammad. This Book was revealed over little more than two decades. In contrast, the Old Testament, which recounts a history that spans many centuries, cannot be tied in its entirety, nor can any of its books, to one particular prophet.[109] Even when a Biblical book could be related to a particular prophet, it still contains texts that imply that the book cannot be related to that prophet in the same way that the Qur'an is related to Prophet Muhammad. The book cannot be described as a Message that was delivered in that exact textual form to the mentioned prophet.

For instance, although the first five Biblical books are known as "the five books of Moses," as well as the "Pentateuch," those books relate in the third person a history that starts with Allah's creation of the universe and ends with the death of Moses himself! It is impossible, therefore, to suggest that those books were revealed by Allah to Moses and that they are totally divine scriptures. The books of the Old Testament in general are closer to being historical books than anything else. This very fact imposes strict limits on what claims can be made about the Biblical text.

There is another essential difference between the Qur'an and the Old Testament which concerns us here. The authenticity of the Qur'an means that each letter and word in it has been inspired by Allah. Indeed, there is only "one" Qur'anic text; it is the same text that Allah revealed to the Messenger of the Qur'an, Muhammad. Allah has declared in the Qur'an that He will protect it against any change:

إِنَّا نَحْنُ نَزَّلْنَا ٱلذِّكْرَ وَإِنَّا لَهُۥ لَحَـٰفِظُونَ ﴿٩﴾. (سورة الحِجْر).

Surely it is We who revealed the *Dhikr* [Qur'an], and surely, We are its Guardian (15.9).

إِنَّ ٱلَّذِينَ كَفَرُوا۟ بِٱلذِّكْرِ لَمَّا جَآءَهُمْ وَإِنَّهُۥ لَكِتَـٰبٌ عَزِيزٌ ﴿٤١﴾ لَّا يَأْتِيهِ ٱلْبَـٰطِلُ مِنۢ بَيْنِ يَدَيْهِ وَلَا مِنْ خَلْفِهِۦ تَنزِيلٌ مِّنْ حَكِيمٍ حَمِيدٍ ﴿٤٢﴾. (سورة فُصِّلَت).

Surely those who disbelieved in the *Dhikr* when it came to them [were wrong]; and surely it is an impregnable Book (41.41). Falsehood cannot come to it from anywhere; [it is] a revelation from One who is Wise and Praised (41.42).

Analyzing the Qur'anic text, as I did with the story of Joseph, proves the accuracy of what the Qur'an says about itself. It brings one proof after another that every letter, word, verse, and sūra in this Book has been revealed by Allah. Any translation of the Qur'an does not represent the Qur'an in the target language, but an interpretation of the Qur'an in that language. A translation reflects the translator's understanding of the Qur'anic text. Even if that understanding was correct, it would be limited and incapable of comprehending all meanings of the deep Qur'anic text. Translations are also constrained by limitations of the target language and the linguistic competence of the translator.

In the case of the Old Testament, it cannot be claimed that every letter and word in it was authored by Allah. In fact, even those who believe in the divine origin of the Old Testament are themselves split into groups as to whether some books belong to the Old Testament or not! Let us, however, put that aside because there is no disagreement that the text of the story of Joseph, which is what concerns us here, is a genuine part of the Old Testament. Nevertheless, there are many manuscripts of books that the believers in the Old Testament agree are genuine parts of the

Bible, which differ little or much from each other. This fact means that there is not "one" text that the believers in the divine origin of the Old Testament can claim to be a text that was revealed by Allah as is the case with the Qur'an. The most that the believers in the Old Testament can claim is that the text of the Old Testament is *in general* or *in spirit* the words of Allah, but they cannot claim that the Biblical text is *literally* Allah's words. The "divine origin of the Qur'an" as a concept, therefore, has a totally different meaning from the concept of the "divine origin of the Old Testament." In fact, the "divine origin" in the latter case is one form of "human origin" in the Qur'anic perspective.

The Qur'an that we have today is exactly the same Arabic text that was revealed to Prophet Muhammad, about fourteen centuries ago. The same cannot be said of the Bible. The believers in the divine origin of the Old Testament do not have any evidence that, for instance, the present text of the book of Genesis, which includes the story of Joseph, is the same text that Allah revealed, regardless of what the clause "Allah revealed" means in this context. In fact, there is no evidence that the language of the oldest manuscript of the book of Genesis that exists today is *exactly* the same language of the original text! If the original text of that book was in Hebrew, this does not necessarily mean that this very old Hebrew was *exactly* the same Hebrew of the oldest manuscripts of the book of Genesis that exist today.

We may describe this particular difference between the Qur'an and the Old Testament by noting that the Qur'an is a book "without history," because it did not go through development phases, and its text has not changed. The Old Testament, in contrast, has a "long history" during which it went through different phases of change, as happens to other books.

This essential difference between the authentic Qur'an and the inauthentic Old Testament has immense consequences when interpreting these texts. The authenticity of the Qur'anic text means that it is "one entity" whose different parts can be used to interpret each other. This is a well known method in Qur'anic exegesis which I have tried to follow in interpreting the story of Joseph. This divine authenticity also means that everything in the Qur'an was intentionally chosen and has a deep meaning. Conclusions can therefore be drawn even from observing the presence of one particular letter rather than an alternative, or from the occurrence of a particular word in a particular place rather than another, as I have shown in my analysis of the text of the sūra of Joseph.

As for the Old Testament, the lack of its text of divine authenticity means that it is not "one entity," so it cannot be used to interpret itself.

Even if some of that text has a divine origin, this is not the case with the rest of the book. Because of the inauthenticity of the Biblical text, it is also not possible to presume that everything in that text has a deep meaning. The exegete of the Old Testament cannot claim with confidence that the use of a particular word instead of one of its synonyms was intentional and then draw conclusions from that. The human writers of the Old Testament were not omniscient. It cannot be assumed that their writings are fully interlinked and consistent at all levels, or that their use of a specific word in a particular position reflects deep meanings.

In fact, it is wrong to talk about "one writer" of the story of Joseph in the Old Testament, because it is certain that the text that exists today is the product of a number of people who edited and changed it through the centuries. This very fact means that it is natural that this text cannot be talked about as if it was one entity.

I had to touch on this topic in order to emphasize that any attempt to analyze the Biblical text with the same accuracy and specificity that can be used for analyzing the Qur'anic text represents an unwarranted and misleading methodology. The shortcomings and deficiencies in the Biblical story of Joseph, which I will address in the next section, are mainly contradictions and weaknesses in the structure of the narrative. They are not the result of a linguistic analysis of the Biblical text.

12.3 Shortcomings in the Biblical Story of Prophet Joseph

As already mentioned, disclosing deficiencies that show that the Old Testament was written by man is an indirect way of proving the divine origin of the Qur'an. The flaws in the Biblical story of Joseph clearly highlight the huge difference between a text that was written by man and the divine Qur'anic text.

Talking the Qur'anic story of Joseph as the basis of comparison, the story of Joseph in the Old Testament shows that its writers were aware of many of its details. The Biblical text also contains shortcomings that suggest that those writers were ignorant of many other events. This suggests that the Biblical story of Joseph must have been derived from a text of divine origin, and that its current version is the final product of editorial processes that were applied to that original text. This conclusion is very significant, because it is in line with the Qur'an's explicit assertion that the Israelites tampered with the Books that Allah revealed to them before the Qur'an. This implies that the Old Testament is among the texts that were written by people and based on what Allah had revealed to prophets and prophetic teachings.

It is worth noting that Biblical scholars today believe, on the basis of numerous studies and findings, that the current version of the Bible has resulted from editing older texts, over centuries. This fact, whose historical and archaeological proofs started to emerge only in the nineteenth century, was mentioned in the Qur'an fourteen centuries ago!

We have seen in our study of the Qur'anic story of Joseph that it contains many allusions which, although subtle, are important to observe for understanding details of that story. The story of the Old Testament ignores such allusions and their significance. These two facts point to two conclusions. First, the original divine text from which the story of Joseph was derived, which could be the Torah that Allah revealed to prophet Moses, had this same Qur'anic characteristic. It contained subtle allusions to significant details in the story. Second, the writers of the Bible, or those who had direct access to the original text and through whom the story found its way to the writers of the Bible, failed to notice those allusions and understand them.

Instead of generally referring to the shortcomings in the Bible, let us identify flaws in the story of Joseph specifically. The following flaws differ in their significance. Some of them may be seen as weaknesses, but the majority are fundamental flaws. The order in which they are listed here does not reflect their relative significance, but often the order in which they occur in the text of the Old Testament.

1) The Old Testament claims that seventeen-year old Joseph was well aware of his brothers' envy of him, yet that did not prevent him from recounting his dreams to them. Even their bad reaction to hearing the details of the first dream did not make him refrain from relating the second dream to them!

2) When describing Joseph's dream, the Qur'an mentions the eleven stars before the sun and moon: "O my father! I saw eleven stars, the sun, and the moon; I saw them prostrating to me." I have mentioned in my comment on verses 12.4 and 12.100 that this reflects the fact that the prostration of Joseph's brothers' before him was going to happen before his parents', as shown in the Qur'anic story. Having failed to notice this subtle reference, the writers of the Old Testament used the traditional style of mentioning the two luminaries before the planets: "*Behold, I have dreamed a dream more; and, behold, the sun and the moon and the eleven stars made obeisance to me*" (Genesis, 37:9). They did that despite their explicit statement that Joseph's brothers prostrated before him in the two visits

they made to Egypt to buy corn, i.e. before the arrival of Jacob to Egypt: "*and Joseph's brethren came, and bowed down themselves before him with their faces to the earth*" (Genesis, 42:6), "*And when Joseph came home, they brought him the present which was in their hand into the house, and bowed themselves to him to the earth*" (Genesis, 43:26).

3) The Old Testament states that Jacob reprimanded Joseph for his dream, as if he was responsible for seeing it: "*And he told it to his father, and to his brethren: and his father rebuked him, and said unto him, What is this dream that thou hast dreamed? Shall I and thy mother and thy brethren indeed come to bow down ourselves to thee to the earth?*" (Genesis, 37:10)! This accuses Jacob, implicitly, of being ignorant of the fact that such dreams are divine visions, and that the person has no control over seeing them. At the same, the Bible points out that Jacob understood from the dream that the sun stood for himself and the moon for Joseph's mother; he realized the truthfulness of that dream and knew its interpretation. The Biblical writers have fallen in an obvious contradiction.

4) One major weakness in the Biblical account of the story of Joseph is its complete omission of the prostration of Jacob and Joseph's mother to their son, although it is mentioned in the dream and in Jacob's successful interpretation! This omission has great significance, because dreams play such a major role in the story of Joseph; the failure of the Biblical writers to mention the realization of one of them represents a failure to recount essential details of the original story.

5) In my comment on verse 12.10, I point out that the decision of Joseph's brothers to cast him down the well represented a rejection of the suggestion to kill Joseph. They adopted the alternative plan of abandoning him in a land far from where his father lived, as some caravanners would pick him and take him away. Joseph's brothers cast him in the well instead of trying to give or sell him directly to those travelers because Joseph was bound to resist such a plot and expose his brothers in front of the potential buyers. This was going to undermine Joseph's brothers' plan, and perhaps land them in trouble. The Qur'anic story is absolutely consistent.

In the Old Testament, we find one of Joseph's brothers convince his brothers not to kill Joseph and to cast him in the well instead: "*And Reuben heard it, and he delivered him out of their hands; and said, Let us not kill him. And Reuben said unto them, Shed no blood, but cast him into this pit that is in the wilderness, and lay no hand upon him; that he might rid him out of their hands, to deliver him to his father again*" (Genesis, 37:21-22). The Old Testament claims that Reuben's aim was to rescue Joseph and return him to his father; it does not explain why the rest of Joseph's brothers agreed to that suggestion. When a group of merchants passed by that place, one of Joseph's brothers said: "*What profit is it if we slay our brother, and conceal his blood?*" which indicates that although they threw Joseph in the well, they were still thinking of killing him. This clear contradiction prompts the question about their consent to cast Joseph in the well in the first place!

Joseph's brothers then sold him to Midianite merchants. This is another contradiction with the fact that they threw him in the well.

The cause of these contradictions and weaknesses is simple. The Biblical writers knew from the original story that Joseph was put in the well, and that he was picked up by the caravanners. They did not understand, however, the causes of these events and their connection with each other. When they mentioned them and tried to link them to each other as they thought fit, the narrative came out weak and discrepant.

6) According to the Qur'an, this was Jacob's reaction to seeing the blood-stained shirt: "[No,] rather your souls have suggested to you [doing] something [evil]; so, [my course is] perfect patience. And it is Allah whose help is sought against what you describe" (from 12.18). In contrast, this was Jacob's reaction according to the Old Testament: "*And he knew it, and said, It is my son's coat; an evil beast hath devoured him; Joseph is without doubt rent in pieces. And Jacob rent his clothes, and put sackcloth upon his loins, and mourned for his son many days. And all his sons and all his daughters rose up to comfort him; but he refused to be comforted; and he said, For I will go down into the grave unto my son mourning. Thus his father wept for him*" (Genesis, 37:33-35). The immense difference between the Qur'anic account and its Biblical counterpart reflects the great difference between the images of Jacob in the two books.

As I have already mentioned in §1.3 and §12.1, the Old Testament portrays the prophets of Allah in a way that often does not distinguish them from ordinary people, ignores their revered status, and shows little respect toward them. Note how Jacob's reaction in the Qur'an reflects his *knowledge* that his sons have plotted an evil scheme and that their account was untrue: "[No,] rather your souls have suggested to you [doing] something [evil]"; his perfect, prophetic *patience*: "[my course is] perfect patience"; and his *reliance* on Allah to reveal the truth: "And it is Allah whose help is sought against what you describe."

Conversely, the Old Testament portrays Jacob as being *ignorant* of the truth of what his sons claimed. It even claims that Jacob did not believe his sons at the beginning when they came back from Egypt with the news that Joseph was still alive: "*And they went up out of Egypt, and came into the land of Canaan unto Jacob their father, And told him, saying, Joseph is yet alive, and he is governor over all the land of Egypt. And Jacob's heart fainted, for he believed them not. And they told him all the words of Joseph, which he had said unto them: and when he saw the wagons which Joseph had sent to carry him, the spirit of Jacob their father revived: And Israel said, It is enough; Joseph my son is yet alive: I will go and see him before I die*" (Genesis, 45:25-28).

In addition to accusing Jacob of ignorance, the Old Testament portrays Jacob as *lacking any patience* at Allah's tests. Jacob's behavior makes one wonder about the difference, if any, between this prophet and any other person! The Bible claims that Joseph himself doubted his father's knowledge when he blessed his two sons. He was displeased to see his father bless his younger son before the elder, so he tried to move his father's hand from his younger to the older son: "*And when Joseph saw that his father laid his right hand upon the head of Ephraim, it displeased him: and he held up his father's hand, to remove it from Ephraim's head unto Manasseh's head. And Joseph said unto his father, Not so, my father: for this is the firstborn; put thy right hand upon his head. And his father refused, and said, I know it, my son, I know it: he also shall become a people, and he also shall be great: but truly his younger brother shall be greater than he, and his seed shall become a multitude of nations*" (Genesis, 48:17-19).

Note also the Old Testament's claim that it was Jacob who sent Joseph to his brothers. The Qur'an, on the other hand, stresses that Jacob was reluctant to allow Joseph to go with his brothers because he was concerned over his sons' attitude toward Joseph, as clear in his sons' words to him: "Why do you not entrust us with Joseph?" (from 12.11). He agreed to his sons' request to take Joseph only after much persistence from them. He hoped that this would improve their relationship with Joseph, as I have explained in my interpretation of verse 12.15.

7) The Qur'an is absolutely clear about the reason behind the 'Azīz's wife's complaint to her husband that Joseph tried to seduce her. Her husband arrived to the house when she was trying to seduce Joseph. He saw how his wife and Joseph looked, and noticed that Joseph was trying to escape from the house with a torn shirt. This exposed what was

happening, so the 'Azīz's wife rushed to accuse Joseph in order to repel the charge away from herself: "And they raced with one another to the door, and she tore his shirt from behind; and they met her lord at the door. She said: 'What is the punishment of he who intends evil for your wife other than imprisonment or a painful torment?'" (12.25).

The imprisonment of Joseph was mainly intended to force him to obey the evil calls of the wife of the 'Azīz and the other women: "Then it occurred to them after they had seen the signs that they should certainly imprison him for a while" (12.35). The 'Azīz himself had an interest in putting Joseph in prison, as I explained in my commentary on verse 12.35.

The Biblical account does not explain at all why the wife of the 'Azīz accused Joseph of making advances toward her. It only says that the wife of the 'Azīz tried one day to seduce Joseph when "*there was none of the men of the house there within*" (Genesis, 39:11), and that he fled the house leaving his shirt in her hands. Unlike her role in the Qur'anic story, the wife of the 'Azīz was not under any pressure to explain away a situation that involved her and Joseph to have to accuse him in defense of herself. She looks to have accused him with no reason!

Unlike the Qur'an, the Old Testament does not say that the injustice that caused the imprisonment of Joseph was exposed later on.

8) The Qur'an explains why Joseph returned to his brothers their goods in the following verse: "And he said to his servants: 'Put their goods in their luggage so that they may recognize them when they return to their family, so that they may come back'" (12.62). As explained in my comment on verse 12.65, Joseph had two goals. First, he wanted to give his brothers goods that they can exchange for grain to enable them to return to him quickly. Second, he used that to influence his father so that he would allow his sons to take Benjamin to Egypt. Witnessing the unplanned situation of his sons finding their goods gave Jacob more confidence in them and in their description of the kindness of the 'Azīz. This made him overturn his earlier decision and agree to let Benjamin go with his brothers: "And when they opened their baggage, they found that their goods had been returned to them. They said: 'O our father! What more can we ask for? Our goods have been returned to us, and we shall bring grain for our family, protect our brother, and have an additional measure of a camel load; this is an easy measure to get' (12.65). He said: 'I will not send him with you until you give me a firm covenant in Allah's name that you will certainly bring him back to me unless you become completely powerless'. And when they gave him their covenant, he said: 'Allah is in charge of what we have said' (12.66)."

The Old Testament says: "*Then Joseph commanded to fill their sacks with corn, and to restore every man's money into his sack, and to give them provision for the way*" (Genesis, 42:25), but without explaining why Joseph did that! Note also the following Biblical statement "*And it came to pass as they emptied their sacks, that, behold, every man's bundle of money was in his sack: and when both they and their father saw the bundles of money, they were afraid*" (Genesis, 42:35). This means that the writers were aware that there was a link between Joseph's return of the goods to his brothers and the latter finding the goods at home in the presence of their father. It is equally clear that the Biblical writers did not know Joseph's aim, so they did not say that Joseph wanted his brothers to find the goods at home. Joseph's decision to return his brothers' goods stayed in the text, but in the absence of any mention of the fact that it was part of Joseph's plan and of its role in that plan.

9) The Bible claims that Joseph kept one of his brothers as a hostage so that his brothers would bring Benjamin to him: "*and [Joseph] took from them Simeon, and bound him before their eyes*" (Genesis, 42:24). It also mentions Jacob's sorrow for losing that son: "*And Jacob their father said unto them, Me have ye bereaved of my children: Joseph is not, and Simeon is not, and ye will take Benjamin away: all these things are against me*" (Genesis, 42:36). The Biblical writers, however, ignored this major event completely afterward!

Genesis 43 starts as follows "*And the famine was sore in the land. And it came to pass, when they had eaten up the corn which they had brought out of Egypt, their father said unto them, Go again, buy us a little food. And Judah spake unto him, saying, The man did solemnly protest unto us, saying, Ye shall not see my face, except your brother be with you*" (Genesis, 43:1-3). Note how Jacob and his sons, or more appropriately the Biblical writers, overlooked the fact that Simeon was kept as a hostage by Joseph! In fact, Jacob ordered his sons to go to Egypt only to bring more provisions after they finished their stock!

10) Jacob sent his sons again to Egypt because "*the famine was sore in the land*" (Genesis, 43:1), yet the presents that he sent to Joseph indicate that they had anything but a famine: "*take of the best fruits in the land in your vessels, and carry down to the man a present, a little balm, and a little honey, spices, and myrrh, nuts, and almonds*" (Genesis, 43:11)!

11) I have said that the following two verses indicate that Joseph had a private place to which he admitted special guests: "And when they entered Joseph's place, he admitted his brother to his private place and said: 'I am your

brother, so do not be grieved at what they have been doing'" (12.69), and "then when they entered Joseph's place, he admitted his parents to his private place and said: 'Enter into Egypt, Allah willing, secure'" (12.99).

This private room is referred to in the Biblical account, but in a different context: "*And they answered, Thy servant our father is in good health, he is yet alive. And they bowed down their heads, and made obeisance. And he lifted up his eyes, and saw his brother Benjamin, his mother's son, and said, Is this your younger brother, of whom ye spake unto me? And he said, God be gracious unto thee, my son. And Joseph made haste; for his bowels did yearn upon his brother: and he sought where to weep; and he entered into his chamber, and wept there. And he washed his face, and went out, and refrained himself, and said, Set on bread*" (Genesis, 43:28-31). The Biblical writers knew that Joseph's private room played a role in the story, but they had no clue what that role was. They assigned to it the completely insignificant role of being the place in which Joseph wept.

12) In the Qur'anic story, Joseph's plan to keep Benjamin with him aimed at ensuring that he would not lose contact with his father and brothers should the latter discover his identity and decide not to come back to him. In the Biblical story also, Joseph carries out the plan of accusing Benjamin of robbery. The whole plot, however, ends up with him revealing his real identity to his brothers during the same visit! The Bible portrays Joseph's plan to accuse Benjamin as completely goalless. This is yet another real event which the Biblical writers knew of but did not know its role and significance, so they ended up mentioning it as a goalless event!

13) The Qur'an points out that Joseph's brothers asked him to take one of them as a slave instead of Benjamin, so that they could return the latter to their father and not break their covenant with him: "They said: 'O 'Azīz! He has a father who is a very old man, therefore retain one of us instead of him; surely we see you to be one of the good-doers'" (12.78). The Old Testament indicates that Joseph's brothers asked him to take them "all" as slaves "in addition to Benjamin": "*And Judah and his brethren came to Joseph's house; for he was yet there: and they fell before him on the ground. And Joseph said unto them, What deed is this that ye have done? wot ye not that such a man as I can certainly divine? And Judah said, What shall we say unto my lord? what shall we speak? or how shall we clear ourselves? God hath found out the iniquity of thy servants: behold, we are my lord's servants, both we, and he also with whom the cup is*

found" (Genesis, 44:14-16)! The offer of Joseph's brothers was not only of no benefit whatsoever for them, but was also an invitation to Joseph to harm them!

The Old Testament then refers to a later event in which Judah asked Joseph to take him as a slave instead of Benjamin so that the latter can return to his father: "*Now therefore, I pray thee, let thy servant abide instead of the lad a bondman to my lord; and let the lad go up with his brethren*" (Genesis, 44:33). This is clearly closer to the real event than the earlier account.

14) The Biblical story does not mention at all Jacob's loss of sight and Joseph's miracle of restoring it. There are references in the Old Testament, however, that could have originated from that ignored part of the original story. These references are the Lord's promise to Jacob: "*and Joseph shall put his hand upon thine eyes*" (Genesis, 46:4); Jacob's words to Joseph after they met: "*now let me die, since I have seen thy face*" (Genesis, 46:30); and the clause "*now the eyes of Israel were dim for age*" (Genesis, 48:10).

There are many more contradictions and inaccuracies in the Biblical story of Joseph. Its feeble structure is also all too evident to require highlighting. One example is the silly details in Genesis 47 about how Joseph bought the Egyptians and all their properties and lands in return for the grain that he provided them with. Another instance is the Bible's reference to Joseph giving seeds to people to plant and give a fifth of the harvest to Pharaoh when the years of the famine had not yet elapsed (Genesis, 47:24).

There are also excessive details about the names of Jacob's descendants and how long they lived. This kind of information, which permeates much of the Old Testament, reflects the special interest of this race-focused book in the Israelites whom it promotes as "the chosen people of God."[110] There are many details in the Bible that make it more of a book of history than one of religion, and show its similarity to the kind of historical records that ancient civilizations used to keep of their history and daily life.

The discussion above shows that the Biblical story of Joseph contains many, substantial shortcomings. More important, comparing that weak and contradictory story with the consistent Qur'anic story of prophet Joseph sheds more light on miraculous aspects of the Qur'an. This comparison exposes the preposterous suggestion that the Qur'an was copied from the Old Testament. It also proves the Qur'an's implicit claim that religious books such as the Old Testament have been written by people who made use of some authentic information but much more inauthentic details:

يَـٰٓأَيُّهَا ٱلرَّسُولُ لَا يَحْزُنكَ ٱلَّذِينَ يُسَـٰرِعُونَ فِى ٱلْكُفْرِ مِنَ ٱلَّذِينَ قَالُوٓا۟ ءَامَنَّا بِأَفْوَٰهِهِمْ وَلَمْ تُؤْمِن
قُلُوبُهُمْ وَمِنَ ٱلَّذِينَ هَادُوا۟ سَمَّـٰعُونَ لِلْكَذِبِ سَمَّـٰعُونَ لِقَوْمٍ ءَاخَرِينَ لَمْ يَأْتُوكَ يُحَرِّفُونَ ٱلْكَلِمَ
مِنۢ بَعْدِ مَوْضِعِهِۦ يَقُولُونَ إِنْ أُوتِيتُمْ هَـٰذَا فَخُذُوهُ وَإِن لَّمْ تُؤْتَوْهُ فَٱحْذَرُوا۟ ﴿٤١﴾. (سورة
المَائِدَة).

O Messenger! Do not be saddened by those who hasten to disbelief from among those who have said “We believe” with their mouths yet their hearts have not believed, and those from among the Jews who listen to lies and to other people who have not come to you who alter the Words from their contexts and say [to the Jews]: “If you are given [a text similar to] this, accept it, but if you are not given this, be cautious” (from 5.41).

مِّنَ ٱلَّذِينَ هَادُوا۟ يُحَرِّفُونَ ٱلْكَلِمَ عَن مَّوَاضِعِهِۦ وَيَقُولُونَ سَمِعْنَا وَعَصَيْنَا وَٱسْمَعْ غَيْرَ مُسْمَعٍ
وَرَٰعِنَا لَيًّۢا بِأَلْسِنَتِهِمْ وَطَعْنًا فِى ٱلدِّينِ ﴿٤٦﴾. (سورة النِّسَاء).

Of the Jews [there are those who] alter words from their contexts and say: “We hear and we disobey” and: “Hear [what we have to say]; you will not be heard,” and: “Do take our interests into consideration,” distorting [the Word] with their tongues and undermining religion (from 4.46).

وَمِنْهُمْ أُمِّيُّونَ لَا يَعْلَمُونَ ٱلْكِتَـٰبَ إِلَّآ أَمَانِىَّ وَإِنْ هُمْ إِلَّا يَظُنُّونَ ﴿٧٨﴾ فَوَيْلٌ لِّلَّذِينَ يَكْتُبُونَ
ٱلْكِتَـٰبَ بِأَيْدِيهِمْ ثُمَّ يَقُولُونَ هَـٰذَا مِنْ عِندِ ٱللَّهِ لِيَشْتَرُوا۟ بِهِۦ ثَمَنًا قَلِيلًا فَوَيْلٌ لَّهُم مِّمَّا كَتَبَتْ أَيْدِيهِمْ
وَوَيْلٌ لَّهُم مِّمَّا يَكْسِبُونَ ﴿٧٩﴾. (سورة البَقَرَة).

And among them [the People of the Book] are illiterates who do not know the Book but only imagine it in line with their wishes, and they only guess (2.78). Woe, then, to those who write the book with their hands and then say “This is from Allah” to get a small price for it; therefore woe to them for what their hands have written, and woe to them for what they earn (2.79).

وَإِنَّ مِنْهُمْ لَفَرِيقًا يَلْوُۥنَ أَلْسِنَتَهُم بِٱلْكِتَـٰبِ لِتَحْسَبُوهُ مِنَ ٱلْكِتَـٰبِ وَمَا هُوَ مِنَ ٱلْكِتَـٰبِ وَيَقُولُونَ
هُوَ مِنْ عِندِ ٱللَّهِ وَمَا هُوَ مِنْ عِندِ ٱللَّهِ وَيَقُولُونَ عَلَى ٱللَّهِ ٱلْكَذِبَ وَهُمْ يَعْلَمُونَ ﴿٧٨﴾ مَا كَانَ
لِبَشَرٍ أَن يُؤْتِيَهُ ٱللَّهُ ٱلْكِتَـٰبَ وَٱلْحُكْمَ وَٱلنُّبُوَّةَ ثُمَّ يَقُولَ لِلنَّاسِ كُونُوا۟ عِبَادًا لِّى مِن دُونِ ٱللَّهِ وَلَـٰكِن
كُونُوا۟ رَبَّـٰنِيِّـۧنَ بِمَا كُنتُمْ تُعَلِّمُونَ ٱلْكِتَـٰبَ وَبِمَا كُنتُمْ تَدْرُسُونَ ﴿٧٩﴾. (سورة آل عِمْرَان).

And surely there is among them [the People of the Book] a party who distort the Book with their tongue that you [O you who believe!] may consider it to be [part] of the Book, when it is not [part] of the Book, and they say: "It is from Allah," while it is not from Allah, and they tell lies about Allah whilst they know (3.78). It is not possible that a human being is given the Book, Wisdom, and prophethood by Allah then he says to people: "Be my servants rather than Allah's"; but rather [he would say]: "Be faithful servants of the Lord by virtue of your constant teaching of the Book and of your constant study thereof" (3.79).

أَفَتَطْمَعُونَ أَن يُؤْمِنُوا۟ لَكُمْ وَقَدْ كَانَ فَرِيقٌ مِّنْهُمْ يَسْمَعُونَ كَلَـٰمَ ٱللَّهِ ثُمَّ يُحَرِّفُونَهُۥ مِنۢ بَعْدِ مَا عَقَلُوهُ وَهُمْ يَعْلَمُونَ ﴿٧٥﴾. (سورة البَقَرَة).

Do you [O you who believe!] hope that they [the Children of Israel] would believe with you when a party from among them used to hear the Word of Allah and then alter it after they had understood it, knowingly? (2.75).

فَبِمَا نَقْضِهِم مِّيثَـٰقَهُمْ لَعَنَّـٰهُمْ وَجَعَلْنَا قُلُوبَهُمْ قَـٰسِيَةً يُحَرِّفُونَ ٱلْكَلِمَ عَن مَّوَاضِعِهِۦ وَنَسُوا۟ حَظًّا مِّمَّا ذُكِّرُوا۟ بِهِۦ وَلَا تَزَالُ تَطَّلِعُ عَلَىٰ خَآئِنَةٍ مِّنْهُمْ إِلَّا قَلِيلًا مِّنْهُمْ فَٱعْفُ عَنْهُمْ وَٱصْفَحْ إِنَّ ٱللَّهَ يُحِبُّ ٱلْمُحْسِنِينَ ﴿١٣﴾. (سورة المَائِدَة).

But because they [the Children of Israel] broke their covenant We cursed them and made their hearts hard, so they altered Words from their contexts, and they forgot a part of what they were reminded of; and you [O Muhammad!] will continue to discover treachery from them, save a few of them; so pardon them and overlook [their misdeeds]; surely Allah loves those who do righteous deeds [to others] (5.13).

The Qur'an revealed facts about the inauthenticity of the Bible that Biblical scholars came to know and accept only in the past two centuries or so. Comparing the Qur'anic story of Joseph with its Biblical counterpart shows clearly the difference between an authentic divine text and one that is only partly based on authentic divine revelation and was written and edited by man.

Epilogue

In this book, we have studied various miraculous aspects of the Qur'anic story of prophet Joseph. We journeyed through fascinating eloquence, gripping narrative styles, great lessons and sermons, and stunning consistency between the various parts of this sūra, and between it and the rest of the Qur'an.

When the Qur'an is studied with sincerity, seriousness, and studiousness, one miraculous attribute that becomes particularly and increasingly visible is the depth of the meanings of this text. There is no text that matches the richness and depth in meaning of the divine text. The more the person discovers meanings of the Qur'an, the more he becomes certain of the infinity of the knowledge that Allah put in this unique Book. Allah has differentiated the Qur'an even from other divine Books and made it superior:

وَأَنزَلْنَآ إِلَيْكَ ٱلْكِتَـٰبَ بِٱلْحَقِّ مُصَدِّقًا لِّمَا بَيْنَ يَدَيْهِ مِنَ ٱلْكِتَـٰبِ وَمُهَيْمِنًا عَلَيْهِ ﴿٤٨﴾. (سورة المَائِدَة).

And We have revealed to you [O Muhammad!] the Book with truth, confirming what was before it of the Book and having authority over it (from 5.48).

Studying the Qur'an is a fascinating experience that has a unique and inimitable taste.

This absorbing spiritual journey with the Qur'an is a reminder that the Book of Allah is deeper than any erudite exegete can interpret or an intelligent thinker can comprehend. The Qur'an is an eternal spring of knowledge for the studious seeker of true knowledge. The keen student of the Qur'an sees in it meanings and information that others cannot see, and derives from this unique Book knowledge that is unreachable to others. The knowledge of the Qur'an, however, is unlimited and fathomless. This Book remains a source of new knowledge for its student regardless of how high he or she climbs on the ladder of knowledge.

No doubt, my interpretation of the sūra of Joseph has missed many lessons and so much knowledge of this great Qur'anic story. I have also consciously avoided touching on particular aspects of the sūra of Joseph, such as its intriguing numerical relationships. Note that this sūra speaks about Joseph and his *11* brothers, it consists of *111* verse, the phrase أَحَدَ عَشَرَ كَوْكَبًا "eleven stars" consists of *11* letters, the story of Joseph ends in verse *101*, and the order of this sūra in the Qur'an is 12th, which may be written as *11+1*. Allah knows best the meaning and significance of these references.

Finally, I pray to Allah that He accepts this modest contribution to the study of His great Book, and that He forgives me for all that I have misinterpreted or misrepresented.

Prayer and Peace be upon the Messenger of the Qur'an, his family, and his companions.

Appendix A

Transliteration Conventions

The following romanization conventions are used in the book:

Arabic Letter	Latin Character	Arabic Letter	Latin Character
أ	Ā	ظ	Ẓ
ب	B	ع	‘
ت	T	غ	Gh
ث	Th	ف	F
ج	J	ق	Q
ح	Ḥ	ك	K
خ	Kh	ل	L
د	D	م	M
ذ	Dh	ن	N
ر	R	ه	H
ز	Z	و	Ū
س	S	ي	Ī
ش	Sh	َ	A
ص	Ṣ	ِ	I
ض	Ḍ	ُ	U
ط	Ṭ		

Appendix B

Qur'anic Terms and Names

This is a list of Qur'anic terms and names of prophets that are used in the book.

English	Qur'anic (Arabic)	English	Qur'anic (Arabic)
Aaron	Hārūn	Joseph	Yūsuf
Abraham	Ibrāhīm	Lot	Lūṭ
David	Dāwūd	Moses	Mūsā
Goliath	Jālūt	Muhammad	Muḥammad
Isaac	Isḥāq	Noah	Nūḥ
Ishmael	Ismā'īl	Qur'anic chapter	Sūra
Israel	Isrā'īl	Qur'anic chapters	Suwar
Jacob	Jacob	Qur'anic Exegesis	Tafsīr
Jesus	'Īsā	Qur'anic verse	āya
Jesus' divine Book	Injīl	Qur'anic verses	āyāt
Job	Ayyūb	Solomon	Sulaymān
John (the Baptist)	Yaḥyā	Torah[111]	Tawrāt
Jonah	Yūnus	Zachariah	Zakariyyā

Notes

1. This Prophetic saying has been reported by Abū al-Faḍl ar-Rāzī al-Qāri' in his book *Faḍā'il al-Qur'an wa tilāwatih (The Virtues of the Qur'an and its Recitation).*

2. Ṣaḥīḥ al-Bukhārī, saying 1.

3. It should be noted that "*idh*" which is used in the Qur'an to start recounting an event in the past differs from the conditional إِذَا "*idhā* (when/if)."

4. This city was originally known as "Yathrib." It became known as "*al-Madīna al-Munawarra* (the illuminated city)" after the arrival of the Prophet. For brevity, it is usually referred to as "al-Madīna (the city)."

5. Note that the Qur'an does not reveal the name of any of Joseph's brothers. Muslim exegetes, nevertheless, have used their Biblical names in their writings, thus referring to Joseph's full brother with "Benjamin." As the term "Joseph's brothers" occurs numerous times in this book, I will also refer to Joseph's full brother with the name "Benjamin" for clarity and easier read. There is no evidence, however, to confirm or deny that this was the name of Joseph's brother.

6. The name "al-Jalālayn" means "the two Jalāl's," as the first name of both authors of this book of exegesis is "Jalāl."

7. Note that there is a major difference between the use of the term "prophet" in the Qur'an and the Bible. Prophethood in the Qur'an refers to the state of receiving revelations from Allah and acting as His messenger to teach people the true religion. Biblical prophethood, on the other hand, is associated with prophecies. A Qur'anic prophet, such as David, might be described as a "man of God" in the Bible (II Chronicles, 8:14).

8. II Samuel, 11.

9. *Ṣaḥīḥ al-Bukhārī*, saying 5079.

10. This is a complete list of the combinations of separate letters and the suwar that start with them:

Separate Letters			Sura
Number	**Arabic**	**Transliteration**	
1	ص	*Ṣād*	38
1	ق	*Qāf*	50

1	ن	*Nūn*	68
2	طه	*Ṭā', hā'*	20
2	طس	*Ṭā', sīn*	27
2	يس	*Yā', sīn*	36
2	حم	*Ḥā', mīm*	40, 41, 43, 44, 45, 46
3	الم	*Alif, lām, mīm*	2, 3, 29, 30, 31, 32
3	الر	*Alif, lām, rā'*	10, 11, 12, 14, 15
3	طسم	*Ṭā', sīn, mīm*	26, 28
4	المص	*Alif, lām, mīm, ṣād*	7
4	المر	*Alif, lām, mīm, rā'*	13
5	حم عسق	*Ḥā', mīm, 'ayn, sīn, qāf*	42
5	كهيعص	*Kāf, hā', yā', 'ayn, ṣād*	19

11. In aṭ-Ṭabrasī's book *Majma' al-Bayān (The Collection of Clarification).*

12. اسم الله الأعظم or the "greatest name of Allah" is believed to be the Beautiful Name that if prayed to, Allah is guaranteed to answer the call.

13. This is similar to the clause وَلَـٰكِنَّا كُنَّا مُرْسِلِينَ "but We have sent [you as] a Messenger" in the following verses which also describe historical events that Prophet Muhammad could not have come to know had he not been receiving knowledge from Allah:

وَلَقَدْ ءَاتَيْنَا مُوسَى ٱلْكِتَـٰبَ مِنۢ بَعْدِ مَآ أَهْلَكْنَا ٱلْقُرُونَ ٱلْأُولَىٰ بَصَآئِرَ لِلنَّاسِ وَهُدًى وَرَحْمَةً لَّعَلَّهُمْ
يَتَذَكَّرُونَ ﴿٤٣﴾ وَمَا كُنتَ بِجَانِبِ ٱلْغَرْبِىِّ إِذْ قَضَيْنَآ إِلَىٰ مُوسَى ٱلْأَمْرَ وَمَا كُنتَ مِنَ ٱلشَّـٰهِدِينَ ﴿٤٤﴾
وَلَـٰكِنَّآ أَنشَأْنَا قُرُونًا فَتَطَاوَلَ عَلَيْهِمُ ٱلْعُمُرُ وَمَا كُنتَ ثَاوِيًا فِىٓ أَهْلِ مَدْيَنَ تَتْلُوا۟ عَلَيْهِمْ ءَايَـٰتِنَا وَلَـٰكِنَّا كُنَّا
مُرْسِلِينَ ﴿٤٥﴾ وَمَا كُنتَ بِجَانِبِ ٱلطُّورِ إِذْ نَادَيْنَا وَلَـٰكِن رَّحْمَةً مِّن رَّبِّكَ لِتُنذِرَ قَوْمًا مَّآ أَتَىٰهُم مِّن نَّذِيرٍ
مِّن قَبْلِكَ لَعَلَّهُمْ يَتَذَكَّرُونَ ﴿٤٦﴾. (سورة القَصَص).

And We gave Moses the Book, after We destroyed the generations of old, as clear testimonies for people, a guidance, and a mercy, that they might remember (28.43). And you [O Muhammad!] were not on the western side [of the Mount] when We handed to Moses the matter, and you were not one of the witnesses (28.44). But We brought forth generations, and their lives dragged on for them; and you were not dwelling with the people of Midian, reciting to them Our verses, but We have sent [you as] a Messenger (28.45). And you were not on the side of the Mount when We called [Moses], but this [knowledge that We have revealed to you] is a mercy from your Lord for you to warn a people to whom no warner before you came, that they may give heed (28.46).

We will study the relation between the knowledge of Prophet Muhammad and his Message in more detail when we look into the interpretation of verse 12.3 in this chapter and verse 12.102 in Chapter 10.

14. Note that the adjectives "manifest" and "wise" which precede the word "Book" in the English translations of these verses occur actually after the Arabic word for "Book" in the original text, as the adjective follows the noun in Arabic.

15. Allah has given the Qur'an unique attributes that distinguish it even from previous divine Books, as He explained in the following verses:

وَأَنزَلْنَآ إِلَيْكَ ٱلْكِتَـٰبَ بِٱلْحَقِّ مُصَدِّقًا لِّمَا بَيْنَ يَدَيْهِ مِنَ ٱلْكِتَـٰبِ وَمُهَيْمِنًا عَلَيْهِ فَٱحْكُم بَيْنَهُم بِمَآ أَنزَلَ ٱللَّهُ وَلَا تَتَّبِعْ أَهْوَآءَهُمْ عَمَّا جَآءَكَ مِنَ ٱلْحَقِّ لِكُلٍّ جَعَلْنَا مِنكُمْ شِرْعَةً وَمِنْهَاجًا وَلَوْ شَآءَ ٱللَّهُ لَجَعَلَكُمْ أُمَّةً وَٰحِدَةً وَلَـٰكِن لِّيَبْلُوَكُمْ فِى مَآ ءَاتَىٰكُمْ فَٱسْتَبِقُوا۟ ٱلْخَيْرَٰتِ إِلَى ٱللَّهِ مَرْجِعُكُمْ جَمِيعًا فَيُنَبِّئُكُم بِمَا كُنتُمْ فِيهِ تَخْتَلِفُونَ ﴿٤٨﴾. (سورة المائدة).

And We have sent down to you [O Muhammad!] the Book with truth, confirming what was before it of the Book and having authority over it. Therefore, adjudicate between them with what Allah has sent down, and do not follow their low desires instead of the truth that has come to you. For every one [nation] of you We have prescribed a law and a way. Had Allah willed, He would have made you [all] a single nation, but He wanted to try you with what He has given you. Therefore, vie with one another to virtuous deeds; to Allah is your return, all of you, so He will tell you the truth about what you used to differ on (5.48).

This verse stresses the fact that Allah revealed other Books before the Qur'an, and that the latter has come to be "confirming what was before it of the Book," i.e. those earlier Books. The Qur'an carried the same Message of the Torah and the Injīl which were still available at the time when the Qur'an was revealed:

وَكَيْفَ يُحَكِّمُونَكَ وَعِندَهُمُ ٱلتَّوْرَىٰةُ فِيهَا حُكْمُ ٱللَّهِ ثُمَّ يَتَوَلَّوْنَ مِنۢ بَعْدِ ذَٰلِكَ وَمَآ أُو۟لَـٰٓئِكَ بِٱلْمُؤْمِنِينَ ﴿٤٣﴾. (سورة المائدة).

And how do they [The Children of Israel] make you [O Muhammad!] a judge when they have the Torah wherein is Allah's judgment? Yet they turn back after that, and these are not the believers (5.43).

قُلْ يَـٰٓأَهْلَ ٱلْكِتَـٰبِ لَسْتُمْ عَلَىٰ شَىْءٍ حَتَّىٰ تُقِيمُوا۟ ٱلتَّوْرَىٰةَ وَٱلْإِنجِيلَ وَمَآ أُنزِلَ إِلَيْكُم مِّن رَّبِّكُمْ وَلَيَزِيدَنَّ كَثِيرًا مِّنْهُم مَّآ أُنزِلَ إِلَيْكَ مِن رَّبِّكَ طُغْيَـٰنًا وَكُفْرًا فَلَا تَأْسَ عَلَى ٱلْقَوْمِ ٱلْكَـٰفِرِينَ ﴿٦٨﴾. (سورة المائدة).

Say [O Muhammad!]: "O People of the Book! You follow no good until you observe the Torah, the Injīl, and that which has been sent down to you from your Lord"; and surely, that which has been sent down to you from your Lord shall make many of them increase in insolence and disbelief, so do not be sad for the disbelieving people (5.68).

Additionally, the revelation of the Qur'an and the appearance of Prophet Muhammad confirmed what was mentioned in those Books about the Prophet who would come and the Book that he would be given. Verse 5.48 mentions also one of the unique attributes of the Qur'an: its *higher authority and status in comparison with the previous Books.*

Note also the reference of verse 5.48 to the Qur'an with the term "the Book" as the Qur'an is one of the forms in which the Book has been revealed: "And We have revealed to you [O Muhammad!] the Book with truth."

In §12.1 I will touch on another attribute that differentiates the Qur'an from other divine Books: Allah's protection of this text against any attempt to change it, thus preserving its integrity.

16. The Qur'anic Arabic term that I have translated as "the unseen" here is الْغَيْبِ "*al-ghayb*." Words that share the same root with "*ghayb*" include غاب "*ghāba* (became absent; disappeared)" and غائِب "*ghā'ib* (absent)." This should shed more light on the meaning of "*ghayb*."

17. The Arabic word كَوْكَب "*kawkab*" (plural: *kawākib*) is used technically in modern Arabic to mean "planet." This word, however, is used in the Qur'an to refer to a "star," hence my translation of the word كَوْكَبًا "*kawkaban*" in verse 12.4 as "star." The following comparison which shows that the word كَوَاكِب "*kawākib*" is equivalent to مَصَٰبِيح "*maṣābīḥ* (lamps)" justifies this translation:

إِنَّا زَيَّنَّا ٱلسَّمَآءَ ٱلدُّنْيَا بِزِينَةٍ ٱلْكَوَاكِبِ ﴿٦﴾. (سورة الصّافاتِ).

Surely We have adorned the nearest heaven with the adornment of *kawākib* (stars) (37.6).

وَزَيَّنَّا ٱلسَّمَآءَ ٱلدُّنْيَا بِمَصَٰبِيحَ ﴿١٢﴾. (سورة فُصِّلَت).

And We adorned the nearest heaven with *maṣābīḥ* (lamps) (from 41.12).

18. These are the relevant verses:

فَلَمَّا بَلَغَ مَعَهُ ٱلسَّعْىَ قَالَ يَٰبُنَىَّ إِنِّىٓ أَرَىٰ فِى ٱلْمَنَامِ أَنِّىٓ أَذْبَحُكَ فَٱنظُرْ مَاذَا تَرَىٰ قَالَ يَٰٓأَبَتِ ٱفْعَلْ مَا تُؤْمَرُ سَتَجِدُنِىٓ إِن شَآءَ ٱللَّهُ مِنَ ٱلصَّٰبِرِينَ ﴿١٠٢﴾ فَلَمَّآ أَسْلَمَا وَتَلَّهُۥ لِلْجَبِينِ ﴿١٠٣﴾ وَنَٰدَيْنَٰهُ أَن يَٰٓإِبْرَٰهِيمُ ﴿١٠٤﴾ قَدْ صَدَّقْتَ ٱلرُّءْيَآ إِنَّا كَذَٰلِكَ نَجْزِى ٱلْمُحْسِنِينَ ﴿١٠٥﴾ إِنَّ هَٰذَا لَهُوَ ٱلْبَلَٰٓؤُا۟ ٱلْمُبِينُ ﴿١٠٦﴾ وَفَدَيْنَٰهُ بِذِبْحٍ عَظِيمٍ ﴿١٠٧﴾. (سورة الصّافاتِ).

And when he [Abraham's son, Ishmael] was old enough to work with him [his father Abraham], he [Abraham] said: "O son! I see in a dream that I am sacrificing you, so let me know what you think." He [Ishmael] said: "O father! Do what you are commanded to do; Allah-willing, you will find me one of those with patience" (37.102). So when they submitted [to Allah's command], and he [Abraham] laid him

[Ishmael] on his forehead (37.103). And We called to him saying: "O Abraham! (37.104). You have fulfilled the vision." Indeed, this is how we reward the good-doers (37.105). Surely this was a manifest trial (37.106). And we ransomed him [Ishmael] with a tremendous sacrifice (37.107).

19. According to aṭ-Ṭūsī, there are two purposes for the repetition of the verb "saw." First, "for emphasis, because the speech had become lengthy," i.e. because the first verb "saw" is separated from "prostrating to me" by a relatively long clause. This explanation, which is mentioned by aṭ-Ṭabaṭabā'ī also, is actually baseless. Following the sentence "I saw eleven stars, the sun, and the moon" with "prostrating to me" without repeating the verb "saw" would not have left any ambiguity about the meaning. Additionally, the sentence is not really long anyway, contrary to what aṭ-Ṭūsī and aṭ-Ṭabaṭabā'ī suggest. Aṭ-Ṭabarī also mentions the view of some that the aim of the repetition is emphasis, though he does not link that to the length of the sentence.

Aṭ-Ṭūsī's second purpose for the repetition is to "indicate that he [Joseph] saw them and saw their prostration." According to this interpretation, which may seem plausible, Joseph's vision was first seeing "eleven stars, the sun, and the moon," and then seeing them prostrating to him. One possible objection to this interpretation is that if this was the reason for repeating the verb "saw," the second "saw" would have been preceded by "and," so the wording would have been "and I saw" rather than "I saw." The structure of the verse suggests that it describes one scene, not two, and that the sentence "I saw them prostrating to me" *details* the state of the mentioned eleven stars and two luminaries.

Aṭ-Ṭabaṭabā'ī adds a third cause for the repetition of the verb "saw," which is "to indicate that he saw them prostrating together, not separately." This interpretation is also unjustified, because the clause "I saw them prostrating to me" does not necessarily mean that Joseph saw them "prostrating together."

20. The word آباء "*ābā'* (fathers)" refers to grandfathers and forefathers as well as immediate fathers. Another example on this use of the word "*ābā*" is found in Moses' following words to Pharaoh: لَا إِلَـٰهَ إِلَّا هُوَ يُحْيِ وَيُمِيتُ رَبُّكُمْ وَرَبُّ ءَابَآئِكُمُ ٱلْأَوَّلِينَ "There is no god but He; He gives life and causes death; [He is] your Lord and the Lord of your ancient *ābā'* (fathers)" (44.8).

21. According to al-Jalālayn, Ibn Kathīr, and views cited by aṭ-Ṭabarī, يَجْتَبِيكَ "*yajtabīka*" means "[He] chooses you"; I agree with this view. Aṭ-Ṭūsī thinks that إجتباء "*ijtibā'*," the noun of that verb, means "choosing the best things for the chosen one..... It is derived from the verb جَبَيت "*jabayt*" which means 'collected', as in 'collected the water in the basin'." He draws the meaning closer to what al-Jalālayn say as he interprets the verse to mean: "Allah will choose you, elect you, select you, and honor you with that, as he honored you when he showed you that dream in your sleep." Aṭ-Ṭabaṭabā'ī expresses a similar view:

"*Ijtibā'*" is derived from جباية "*jibāya*" which means "collecting." "*Jabayt*" water in the basin means "collect" it there. The "*jibāya*" of taxes means collecting them, and as in Allah's words يُجْبَىٰٓ إِلَيْهِ ثَمَرَٰتُ كُلِّ شَىْءٍ "to which [Al-Ḥarām Mosque which embraces the Ka'ba] all kinds of fruit are brought" (from 28.57). The meaning of "*ijtibā'*" involves collecting the different parts of something and protecting it from separation and dispersion. It implies a movement from the collector toward the collected. The "*ijtibā'*" of Allah of a servant means targeting him with His mercy, preferring him with much honor, protecting him from dispersing in different Satanic paths that send man astray, leading him to His straight path, taking control of him, and making him totally dedicated and devoted to Him, as Allah said about Joseph: إِنَّهُۥ مِنْ عِبَادِنَا ٱلْمُخْلَصِينَ "he is one of Our chosen servants" (from 12.24).

22. Ṣalāḥ al-Khālidī studied in detail the concept of تَأْوِيل "*ta'wīl*" in the Qur'an in his book *Tafsīr and Ta'wīl in the Qur'an* (Jordan: Dar Al-Nafā'is, 1996). He agrees with the view that ar-Rāghibī al-Aṣfahānī expressed in his book *Al-Mufradāt (Vocabularies)* that "*ta'wīl*" is "to attribute something to its intended purpose, should that be knowledge or action." If that thing was "knowledge," "*ta'wīl*" would mean "interpreting/interpretation"; and if the thing was an "action," "*ta'wīl*" would mean "fulfillment."

In his comment on verse 100 of the sūra of Joseph, Ibn Kathīr suggests that the word "*ta'wīl*" refers to what something يؤول "*ya'ūl*" or "develops to." This opinion is also mentioned by aṭ-Ṭabarī in his interpretation of verse 12.6.

In some of the contexts in which the word "*ta'wīl*" occurs in the Qur'an, its meaning *must* be "interpretation/explanation," as in verse 18.78, in the phrase "*ta'wīl al-aḥādīth*," and in other relevant verses in the sūra of Joseph:

قَالَ هَٰذَا فِرَاقُ بَيْنِى وَبَيْنِكَ سَأُنَبِّئُكَ بِتَأْوِيلِ مَا لَمْ تَسْتَطِع عَّلَيْهِ صَبْرًا ﴿٧٨﴾. (سورة الكهف).

He [Moses' companion] said: "This is the parting between me and you! I will inform you of the *ta'wīl* (explanation) of that which you could not bear with patience" (18.78).

I think that it is possible to take all occurrences of all variations of the word "*ta'wīl*" in the Qur'an to mean "interpreting/interpretation" or "clarifying/clarification."

Note also that the linguistic category of the word "*ta'wīl*" is تفعيل "*taf'īl*." This refutes the suggestion that this word means "what things develop to." The word "*ta'wīl*" in "*ta'wīl al-aḥādīth*" refers to an action taken by the person who has that ability, something that agrees with my assertion that "*ta'wīl*" means "interpreting/interpretation."

23. Note that "*al*" in "*al-aḥādīth*" is the Arabic equivalent of the English definite article "the," so the word we are interested in is actually "*aḥādīth*."

24. See more on this in the commentary on verse 12.43 in Chapter 6.

25. Note, for instance, the similar use of "*min*," but in association with the word مُلْك "*mulk* (property)," in this verse which talks about the Children of Israel: أَمْ لَهُمْ نَصِيبٌ مِّنَ ٱلْمُلْكِ فَإِذًا لَّا يُؤْتُونَ ٱلنَّاسَ نَقِيرًا "Or have they a share of property, in which case they would not give a farthing to people?" (4.53). I will discuss this point in more detail in Chapter 9 when I comment on verse 12.101.

26. The particle لَ "*lām* (l)" which precedes the name of Joseph in the word لَيُوسُفُ "*la Yūsuphu*" is known as لام التأكيد "the affirmative l"; it is used in the response to an oath. It is as if Joseph's brothers said: "By Allah, verily Joseph....etc."

27. My interpretation of "and after him you will be a righteous people" differs from that accepted by exegetes such as al-Qurṭubī, Ibn Kathīr, al-Jalālayn, aṭ-Ṭūsī, aṭ-Ṭabaṭabā'ī, and aṭ-Ṭabarī. According to the traditional interpretation, the phrase مِن بَعْدِهِ "*min ba'dihi*" which I have read as meaning "after him" is read as "after it," meaning "after the sin of removing Joseph"; and the word صَٰلِحِينَ "*sāliḥīn* (righteous)" it taken by exegetes to refer to the repentance of Joseph's brothers from their sin.

One flaw in this interpretation is that it ignores the presence of the clause "so that your father pays attention exclusively to you," i.e. it reads the verse as if it says: "kill Joseph or cast him to a land faraway, and after it you will be a righteous people." This interpretation renders Joseph's brothers' reference to "making their father pay attention exclusively to them" meaningless in the context of that verse. The truth is that the clause "so that your father pays attention exclusively to you" stresses that Joseph's brothers wanted to be the only focus of their father's attention so that they would acquire from him the blessings that Joseph used to get, as I explained.

28. The word غَيَٰبَتِ "*ghayābati*" means in general the "place where things disappear from sight," so it means the "bottom" of "the well" in this instance. It shares the same root with the word "*ghayb*" which we came across in verse 12.3 and which I have translated as "the unseen."

29. This latter view seems to be based on verse 12.80 which shows the eldest son taking a good stance. He refused to leave Egypt and head home without Benjamin, unless his father gives him his permission to do so or something happens: "So, when they despaired of [convincing] him, they conferred privately. The eldest among them said: 'Do you not know that your father has taken from you a covenant in Allah's name, and how you gave away Joseph before? Therefore I will not depart from this land until my father permits me or Allah judges for me, and He is the best of judges'."

30. Some exegetes have referred to the absence of the answer to لَمَّا "*lammā* (when)" from the verse. It looks as if Allah said: "and when Joseph's brothers took him away and agreed to cast him at the bottom of the well," but then instead of going on to talk about what happened, He diverted to talk about His revelation to Joseph. Exegetes have suggested a number of reasons for the omission of the answer of "*lammā*" from this verse. For instance, this is what aṭ-Ṭabaṭabā'ī has to say:

> The answer to "*lammā*" has been omitted to highlight the horrendous and terrible nature of the matter, which is a common usage in language. You may find a speaker describing a heinous matter, such as the killing of an innocent person, that makes the heart burn with pain and which the ear cannot bear to hear. He then starts to detail the causes and circumstances that led to it. When he reaches the event itself, he goes into deep silence, before starting to talk about events that followed the killing. This indicates that the murder was such heinous that the speaker would not be able to describe it and the listener would not bear hearing it.
>
> The situation here is as if when the story teller, glory be to His name, said: "So when they took him away and agreed that they should throw him to the bottom of the well," He went silent and refrained from describing what Joseph's brothers did to him in sadness and regret, because the ear would not bear hearing what they did to this wronged, infallible prophet and son of prophets. He did not commit anything that deserves what his brothers did to him while in full knowledge of how much his father, the noble prophet, loved him.

Aṭ-Ṭūsī thinks that "the answer to '*lammā*' is' omitted and that it is equivalent to the clause 'their plot was so grave or that what they intended to do was so serious'." He also refers to an opinion of linguists of the school of the Iraqi city of Kūfa that the particle و "*wa* (and)" in وَأَجْمَعُوٓاْ "*wa ajma'ū* (and [they] agreed)" has been "forced in," and that the meaning is أجمعوا "[they] agreed." The linguists of the school of the Iraqi city of Baṣra have rejected this view. Aṭ-Ṭabarī is one exegete who adopted the view of the linguists of Kūfa. The problem with this interpretation is that it suggests that Joseph's brothers agreed to cast him in the well *after* they took him away, when in fact they took him in order to cast him in the well.

The interpretation of al-Jalālayn states that the omission of the answer of "*lammā*" means that they did throw Joseph in the well. Al-Qurṭubī mentions the view of some that the answer of "*lammā*" is the sentence قَالُواْ يَـٰٓأَبَانَآ إِنَّا ذَهَبْنَا نَسْتَبِقُ "They said: 'O our father! We went to race with one another'" in verse 12.17, which we will study later. He indicates that according to the Baṣra linguists, the implied answer of "*lammā*" is جعلوه فيها "they cast him in it." He also mentions an opinion of the Kūfa linguists that there is a "forced in" "*wa* (and)," though he refers to "*wa*" in

وَأَوْحَيْنَآ "*wa awḥaynā* (and We revealed)" not in وَأَجْمَعُوٓاْ "*wa ajmaʿū* (and [they] agreed)." Al-Qurṭubī points out that the Kūfa linguists think that "*wa*" can be added superfluously to "*lammā*" and حَتَّى "*ḥattā* (until)." He cites some examples from the Qur'an, including the following use of *ḥattā*:

وَسِيقَ ٱلَّذِينَ ٱتَّقَوْاْ رَبَّهُمْ إِلَى ٱلْجَنَّةِ زُمَرًا حَتَّىٰٓ إِذَا جَآءُوهَا وَفُتِحَتْ أَبْوَٰبُهَا وَقَالَ لَهُمْ خَزَنَتُهَا سَلَٰمٌ عَلَيْكُمْ طِبْتُمْ فَٱدْخُلُوهَا خَٰلِدِينَ ﴿٧٣﴾. (سورة الزّمَر).

> And those who were dutiful toward their Lord shall be driven to paradise in groups; until when they come to it, and its doors shall be opened, and its keepers shall say to them: "Peace be on you, you shall be happy; therefore enter it to abide thereinto for ever" (39.73).

He indicates that "*wa*" in وَفُتِحَتْ "*wa futiḥat* (and [its doors] shall be opened)" is زائدة "superfluous" and that the implied meaning is فُتِحَتْ "*futiḥat* ([its doors] shall be opened)," as in the following very similar verse from the same sūra:

وَسِيقَ ٱلَّذِينَ كَفَرُوٓاْ إِلَىٰ جَهَنَّمَ زُمَرًا حَتَّىٰٓ إِذَا جَآءُوهَا فُتِحَتْ أَبْوَٰبُهَا وَقَالَ لَهُمْ خَزَنَتُهَآ أَلَمْ يَأْتِكُمْ رُسُلٌ مِّنكُمْ يَتْلُونَ عَلَيْكُمْ ءَايَٰتِ رَبِّكُمْ وَيُنذِرُونَكُمْ لِقَآءَ يَوْمِكُمْ هَٰذَا قَالُواْ بَلَىٰ وَلَٰكِنْ حَقَّتْ كَلِمَةُ ٱلْعَذَابِ عَلَى ٱلْكَٰفِرِينَ ﴿٧١﴾. (سورة الزّمَر).

> And those who disbelieved shall be driven to hell in groups; until when they come to it, its doors shall be opened, and its keepers shall say to them: "Did messengers from among yourselves not come to you, recite the verses of your Lord, and warn you about the meeting of this day of yours?" They shall say: "Yes." But the word of punishment is due against the disbelievers (39.71).

As another example on the presence of a superfluous "*wa*" in the answer of "*lammā*," al-Qurṭubī mentions verses 37.103-104, stressing that the word وَنَٰدَيْنَٰهُ "*wa nādaynāhu* (and We called him)" is equivalent to نَادَيْنَاهُ "*nādaynāhu* (We called him)":

فَلَمَّآ أَسْلَمَا وَتَلَّهُۥ لِلْجَبِينِ ﴿١٠٣﴾ وَنَٰدَيْنَٰهُ أَن يَٰٓإِبْرَٰهِيمُ ﴿١٠٤﴾ قَدْ صَدَّقْتَ ٱلرُّءْيَآ إِنَّا كَذَٰلِكَ نَجْزِى ٱلْمُحْسِنِينَ ﴿١٠٥﴾. (سورة الصافّات).

> So when they submitted [to Allah's command], and he [Abraham] laid him [Ishmael] on his forehead (37.103). And We called to him saying: "O Abraham! (37.104). You have fulfilled the vision." Indeed, this is how we reward the good-doers (37.105).

It is clear that there are many verses, of which I have cited only a few, in which the answer of "*lammā*" and "*ḥattā*" is absent. Therefore, an interpretation such as that advocated by aṭ-Ṭabaṭabā'ī does not seem plausible, because it tries to explain the absence of the answer of "*lammā*" from verse 12.15 as if it was a phenomenon that is unique to that verse, rather than seen in many Qur'anic verses.

I find more acceptable the view of the linguistic school of Kūfa that the answer to "*lammā*" and "*ḥattā*" is not actually absent from those verses, but that it looks that way because of the presence of a superfluous "*wa* (and)" in the answer, causing it to look absent. In the case of verse 12.15, the superfluous "and" could be the one in "*wa ajma'ū* (and [they] agreed)" or "*wa awḥaynā* (and We revealed)." We have already ruled out the former; the latter possibility means that the superfluous "and" separates between the description of the acts of Joseph's brothers, "so when they took him away and agreed that they should throw him to the bottom of the well," and that of the divine act, "and We revealed to him: 'You will certainly inform them of this affair of theirs while they are unaware'." This, in turn, means that Allah's act is the answer of "*lammā*," and represents the response to the acts of Joseph's brothers. The reason for the presence of the superfluous "and" may be for stressing the verb in "*awḥaynā* (We revealed)," thus ultimately emphasizing Allah's act.

31. In addition to verse 12.17, the verb إستَبَق "*istabaqa* (raced)" occurs four times in the Qur'an. It occurs twice in the clause فَٱسْتَبِقُوا۟ ٱلْخَيْرَٰتِ "so race with one another to [do] good deeds" (from 2.148; from 5.48), once in وَٱسْتَبَقَا ٱلْبَابَ "and they [Joseph and the 'Azīz's wife] raced with one another to the door" (from 12.25), and once in the clause فَٱسْتَبَقُوا۟ ٱلصِّرَٰطَ "so they would race with one another to the way" (from 36.66). It is clear that the kind of race that the verb in all of those verses is associated with is not spontaneous, but planned. There is an important difference, however, between the grammatical use of the verb in verse 12.17 and its use in the other four verses, as it is not associated with an object in the former. My interpretation of this is that the verb "race" in verse 12.17 refers to racing for the sake of it, not for a specific goal, hence the absence of the object. The verse means that Joseph's brothers went away to race with one another.

32. This use of the adjective جَمِيلٌ "*jamīl* (beautiful)" suggests that it shares the same root with كامل "*kāmil* (perfect)," and the same applies to the nouns of these two adjectives, جمال "*jamāl* (beauty)" and كمال "*kamāl* (perfection)." Patience that is *Jamīl* is one that is *kamil*, and something can be "perfect" only if it is free of any flaw. The flaw of patience is complaint.

33. The word سَيَّارَةٌ "*sayyāra*" is derived from سَيْر "*sayr*" which means "movement," "travel" ...etc. Some exegetes have suggested that the word "*sayyāra*" means *pedestrian* travelers. This opinion could be supported by the fact that the Qur'an uses the word عِيرٌ "*'īr*" for traveling caravans of camels in three verses of the sūra of Joseph (70, 82, and 94).

The word "*sayyāra*" occurs in the sūra of Joseph in verse 12.10 as a masculine noun and in verse 12.19 as both masculine and feminine. The reason for this is that this word has two slightly different meanings: the masculine "caravanners" and the feminine "caravan."

In verse 12.10, where "*sayyāra*" is treated as masculine, it is translated as "caravanners." In verse 12.19, in the sentence وَجَآءَتْ سَيَّارَةٌ فَأَرْسَلُوا۟ وَارِدَهُمْ "and there came a caravan. They sent someone to draw some water," the same word is used as feminine and masculine, hence it is translated as "caravan" and "caravanners." The latter is referred to with the pronoun "they."

The Qur'an's use of "*sayyāra*" in two meanings is identical to its use of the word عِير "*'īr*," which is very close in meaning to "*sayyāra*," as pointed out above. In the following two verses, the word "*'īr*" has the feminine meaning of "caravan" of camels:

وَسْـَٔلِ ٱلْقَرْيَةَ ٱلَّتِى كُنَّا فِيهَا وَٱلْعِيرَ ٱلَّتِىٓ أَقْبَلْنَا فِيهَا ﴿٨٢﴾. (سورة يوسف).

And ask in the town in which we were and the caravan with which we came (from 12.84).

وَلَمَّا فَصَلَتِ ٱلْعِيرُ ﴿٩٤﴾. (سورة يوسف).

And when the caravan had departed (from 12.94).

Then there is the verse أَيَّتُهَا ٱلْعِيرُ إِنَّكُمْ لَسَـٰرِقُونَ "O caravanners! You are certainly thieves" (from 12.70). The word عِير "*'īr*" is first used as meaning the feminine "caravan," as obvious from the attached, feminine pronoun in أَيَّتُهَا "O you!". It is then used to mean "caravanners" in إِنَّكُمْ لَسَـٰرِقُونَ "you are certainly thieves."

Thus, the two sentences وَجَآءَتْ سَيَّارَةٌ فَأَرْسَلُوا۟ وَارِدَهُمْ "and there came a caravan and they sent their water drawer" and أَيَّتُهَا ٱلْعِيرُ إِنَّكُمْ لَسَـٰرِقُونَ "O caravanners! You are certainly thieves" have exactly the same structure as far as the use of the two words سَيَّارَةٌ "*sayyāra*" and عِير "*'īr*" is concerned.

34. It is possible that this verse refers to *one particular group of the caravanners, not all of them*, who sent one of them to get water for them. In other words, the caravan consisted of more than one group of travelers. It was common for different groups of travelers with the same route to travel as one caravan for a number of reasons, such as safety. Perhaps, those travelers hid Joseph with their goods so that no other travelers would claim to have a share in him. It is also possible that the group who found Joseph would have to pay extra fees for any additional traveler; this explains why they hid him as "an article of merchandise." Another possible reason for the travelers hiding Joseph is so that his family would not find him, if they were looking for him, so they can sell him later on as an article of merchandise. The reason could also be none of these, as it is not possible to verify any of these hypotheses.

35. This sheds the light on the use in Arabic of words such as إمكانية "*Imkāniyya*" to mean "ability" and مكانة "*makāna*" to mean "status." The word منزلة

"*manzila*," which also means "status," shares the same root with منزل "*manzil* (house)." Obviously, the place that the person occupies is directly related to his status.

36. These are two such verses:

وَإِن يَمْسَسْكَ ٱللَّهُ بِضُرٍّ فَلَا كَاشِفَ لَهُۥٓ إِلَّا هُوَ وَإِن يُرِدْكَ بِخَيْرٍ فَلَا رَآدَّ لِفَضْلِهِۦ يُصِيبُ بِهِۦ مَن يَشَآءُ مِنْ عِبَادِهِۦ وَهُوَ ٱلْغَفُورُ ٱلرَّحِيمُ ﴿١٠٧﴾. (سورة يونس).

And if Allah should afflict you [O Muhammad!] with harm, then there is no one to remove it but He. And if He intends good for you, there is no one to repel His favor. He brings it to whom He pleases of His servants. And He is the Forgiving, the Merciful (10.107).

إِنَّ رَبَّكَ فَعَّالٌ لِّمَا يُرِيدُ ﴿١٠٧﴾. (سورة هُود).

Your Lord [O Muhammad!] is the capable doer of what He wishes (from 11.107).

37. The "attainment of full strength" occurs in different forms in eight verses, including the following verse which occurs twice in the Qur'an: وَلَا تَقْرَبُوا۟ مَالَ ٱلْيَتِيمِ إِلَّا بِٱلَّتِى هِىَ أَحْسَنُ حَتَّىٰ يَبْلُغَ أَشُدَّهُۥ "and do not approach the property of the orphan except in the best manner until he attains his full strength" (from 6.152; from 17.34). It is possible to know the age meant in this verse by comparing it with the following verse on the same subject:

وَابْتَلُوا الْيَتَامَى حَتَّى إِذَا بَلَغُوا النِّكَاحَ فَإِنْ آنَسْتُمْ مِنْهُمْ رُشْدًا فَادْفَعُوا إِلَيْهِمْ أَمْوَالَهُمْ وَلَا تَأْكُلُوهَا إِسْرَافًا وَبِدَارًا أَنْ يَكْبَرُوا ﴿٦﴾. (سورة النساء).

And test the orphans; so when they attain puberty see if you find them of sound judgment, [in which case] make over to them their property, and do not consume it extravagantly and hastily lest they grow up (from 4.6).

This verse specifies two conditions for handing over properties to their orphan owners: reaching the age of puberty and acquiring mental maturity.

It is clear, therefore, that the clause "attained his full strength" which occurs in verses 6.152 and 17.34 refers to an age after that of puberty when the person becomes able to make sound and responsible decisions about his life. In other words, the clause "attained his full strength" refers to a specific age that is not determined by physical maturity only, but by mental maturity also. In fact, the other five verses which include the different variations of "attaining full strength" (18.82; 22.5; 28.14; 40.67; 46.15) show that the age range during which the person is in full strength extends from the time of attaining physical and mental maturity to the time when the person's physical, and perhaps also mental, abilities start to deteriorate.

38. The use of the emphatic verb غَلَّقَتِ "*ghallaqat* ([she] made fast)" instead of غلقتْ "*ghalaqat*" seems to stress the woman's meticulousness in locking up the doors in preparation for her plan.

39. Aṭ-Ṭabaṭabā'ī draws attention to the fact that Joseph ended his words by saying "surely the wrongdoers do not prosper." He notes that had Joseph been talking about the lord of the house earlier, he would have used the word خائنون "*khā'inūn* (traitors)" rather than ظَّـٰلِمُونَ "*ẓālimūn* (wrongdoers)." Aṭ-Ṭabaṭabā'ī's point is that committing fornication with the wife of the lord of the house would have been an act of betrayal to the lord of the house, whereas the term "wrongdoers" has a religious meaning here because it indicates that every person who gets involved in fornication is a "wrongdoer" because he/she wrongs him/herself. It could also be argued, however, that "wrongdoers" is a universal term that includes "traitors" because treason is one form of wrongdoing, hence Joseph's use of the term "wrongdoers" does not necessarily mean that he was not referring to the lord of the house. It is the arguments that I made earlier which show that Joseph was referring to Allah.

40. For more details on such claims of exegetes see, for instance, those that al-Qurṭubī and aṭ-Ṭabarī have compiled in their respective commentaries on verse 12.24, and those compiled by the latter in his commentary on 12.53. Some of those interpretations mention excessive, defamatory details that have absolutely no foundations whatsoever.

41. Let us look at sample verses where either the passive participle "*mukhlaṣīn*" or the active participle "*mukhliṣīn*" are used. The following verses refer to people *taking action*, so it is natural to describe them with "*mukhliṣīn*":

قُلْ أَمَرَ رَبِّى بِٱلْقِسْطِ وَأَقِيمُوا۟ وُجُوهَكُمْ عِندَ كُلِّ مَسْجِدٍ وَٱدْعُوهُ مُخْلِصِينَ لَهُ ٱلدِّينَ كَمَا بَدَأَكُمْ تَعُودُونَ ﴿٢٩﴾. (سورة الأعراف).

> Say [O Muhammad!]: "My Lord has enjoined justice." And set upright your faces [O you who believe!] at every time of prayer and call on Him, being *mukhliṣīn* (sincere) to Him. As He brought you forth in the beginning, so shall you also return (7.29).

فَإِذَا رَكِبُوا۟ فِى ٱلْفُلْكِ دَعَوُا۟ ٱللَّهَ مُخْلِصِينَ لَهُ ٱلدِّينَ فَلَمَّا نَجَّىٰهُمْ إِلَى ٱلْبَرِّ إِذَا هُمْ يُشْرِكُونَ ﴿٦٥﴾. (سورة العَنكَبوتِ).

> So when they board ships they call upon Allah, being *mukhliṣīn* (sincere) to Him. But when He has brought them safe to the land, lo! they associate others [with Him] (29.65).

In the following verse, Allah speaks about servants that *He saves* from the torment, hence the passive participle "*mukhlaṣīn*" is used:

إِنَّكُمْ لَذَآئِقُواْ ٱلْعَذَابِ ٱلْأَلِيمِ ﴿٣٨﴾ وَمَا تُجْزَوْنَ إِلَّا مَا كُنتُمْ تَعْمَلُونَ ﴿٣٩﴾ إِلَّا عِبَادَ ٱللَّهِ ٱلْمُخْلَصِينَ ﴿٤٠﴾ أُوْلَٰٓئِكَ لَهُمْ رِزْقٌ مَّعْلُومٌ ﴿٤١﴾. (سورة الصّافات).

Surely you [O people!] will taste the painful punishment (37.38). And you will not be punished but for what you did (37.39). Save the *mukhlaṣīn* (sincere) servants of Allah (37.40). For those there is a determined sustenance (37.41).

Similarly, in the following verse, Allah speaks about the servants that *He has chosen and saved* from the torture, so He refers to them as "*mukhlaṣīn*":

فَٱنظُرْ كَيْفَ كَانَ عَٰقِبَةُ ٱلْمُنذَرِينَ ﴿٧٣﴾. إِلَّا عِبَادَ ٱللَّهِ ٱلْمُخْلَصِينَ ﴿٧٤﴾. (سورة الصّافات).

So see [O Muhammad!] how was the end of those warned (37.73). Save the *mukhlaṣīn* (sincere) servants of Allah (37.74).

42. "Witness" is my translation of the noun شَاهِدٌ "*shāhidun*," and "bore witness" of the verb شَهِدَ "*shahida*." These Arabic terms do not necessarily imply that the person *witnessed* the even with his eyes. The verb "*shahida*" can mean seeing an event or being present at it, as in the following verse:

قَالُواْ تَقَاسَمُواْ بِٱللَّهِ لَنُبَيِّتَنَّهُۥ وَأَهْلَهُۥ ثُمَّ لَنَقُولَنَّ لِوَلِيِّهِۦ مَا شَهِدْنَا مَهْلِكَ أَهْلِهِۦ وَإِنَّا لَصَٰدِقُونَ ﴿٤٩﴾. (سورة النّمل).

They said: "Swear to each other by Allah that we will certainly ambush him and his family by night, then we will say to his heir: 'We did not *shahidnā* (witness) the destruction of his family, and we are most surely truthful" (27.49).

This is a *special* use of the verb "*shahida*." The more general meaning of this verb, nevertheless, is "stated," "declared," or "testified" something on the basis of whatever the testifier finds convincing, including circumstantial evidence and rational arguments. This is, in fact, the sense in which this verb is used in *most* of its occurrences in the Qur'an. These are two sample verses:

قُلْ هَلُمَّ شُهَدَآءَكُمُ ٱلَّذِينَ يَشْهَدُونَ أَنَّ ٱللَّهَ حَرَّمَ هَٰذَا فَإِن شَهِدُواْ فَلَا تَشْهَدْ مَعَهُمْ وَلَا تَتَّبِعْ أَهْوَآءَ ٱلَّذِينَ كَذَّبُواْ بِـَٔايَٰتِنَا وَٱلَّذِينَ لَا يُؤْمِنُونَ بِٱلْأَخِرَةِ وَهُم بِرَبِّهِمْ يَعْدِلُونَ ﴿١٥٠﴾. (سورة الأنعام).

Say [O Muhammad!]: "Bring your *shuhadā'ikum* (witnesses) who *yashhadūn* (bear witness) that Allah has forbidden this [eating particular kinds of food]." Then if they *shahidū* (bear witness), do not *tashhad* (bear witness) with them; and do not follow the low desires of those who reject Our signs and those who do not believe in the hereafter and who make others equal to their Lord (6.150).

حَتَّىٰٓ إِذَا مَا جَآءُوهَا شَهِدَ عَلَيْهِمْ سَمْعُهُمْ وَأَبْصَٰرُهُمْ وَجُلُودُهُم بِمَا كَانُواْ يَعْمَلُونَ ﴿٢٠﴾. (سورة فُصِّلَت).

Until when they come to it [hell], their ears, their eyes, and their skins *shahida* (shall bear witness) against them as to what they did (41.20).

Thus, the words "*shahida* (bore witness)" and "*shāhid* (witness)" in verse 12.26 do not mean that the person had witnessed the event which he was consulted about. They, rather, refer to his role of "testifying" about the event after studying its circumstances. The word "testified" can be used for "*shahida*," and "testifier" for "*shāhid*."

The witness is partially performing the role of a "judge." The Qur'an, however, calls that person a "*shāhid* (witness/testifier)," rather than a word that corresponds to "judge." The reason for this is that the final judgment about what really happened lied with the husband, not the consulted testifier.

Some may argue that this person was called "*shāhid*" in the clause "*shahida shāhid*," which I have translated as "*a witness [from her own folk] bore witness [saying]*," because he was with the husband when he returned home. However, there are more than one reason to reject this suggestion. First, the verb "*shahida*" undoubtedly refers to the role of that person in giving his "testimony" on the implications and significance of the way the shirt was torn. This testimony follows the clause above, with half of it in verse 12.26 and the other half in 12.27. Therefore, the active participle "*shāhid*" must also be derived from the same sense of the verb "*shahida*"; the latter refers to the person's role in testifying regarding his conclusions from the way the shirt was torn; it does not suggest that he "saw" the event.

Second, it is clear from verses 12.26-28, and particularly 12.28, that the "*shāhid*" did not know which side of the shirt was torn. Therefore, the verb "*shahida*" cannot mean "saw."

43. Exegetes have noted that the verse uses the masculine plural word خَاطِئِينَ "*khāṭi'īna* (sinners)" instead of the feminine خاطئات "*khāṭi'āt*." They explain this as a reference to "sinners" in general, not only female ones, as the masculine word includes both male and female sinners. It is clear, as I have already noted, that any reference to "sins" in this verse does not carry any religious meaning.

Perhaps, the witness used the more general term "*khāṭi'īna*" instead of "*khāṭi'āt*" for the same reason that made him use the plural form when talking about the women's guile in the previous verse, i.e. to water down the tone of his criticism of the woman.

The use of the word "sinners" indicates that promiscuity was considered to be bad behavior even though it was common.

44. One opinion claims that "*muttaka*" means something that is "leaned on." The later context of the verse, however, shows that there was a meal, or some kind of food, without a reference to the preparation of that food other than the sentence "and she prepared for them a *muttaka'*." This means that the term "*muttaka*" implies the presence of food, hence the meaning of this term is "a gathering where people sit or lean to have food." I have, therefore, translated this term to

"banquet." Nevertheless, it could also be argued that the absence of an explicit reference to the preparation of the food is due to the fact that it is implied in the text that follows. This would invalidate the conclusion above.

45. The use of the over-stressed verb قَطَّعْنَ "*qaṭṭa'na*" instead of قطعْنَ "*qaṭa'na*," both of which mean "[they] cut," indicates that each woman cut her hand more than once.

46. The particle ل "*lām*" with which لَيُسْجَنَنَّ "*layusjananna* (he shall certainly be imprisoned)" starts and the letter ن "*nūn*" with which it ends are used for an oath.

47. The "Beautiful Names," which the Qur'an calls ٱلْأَسْمَآءُ ٱلْحُسْنَىٰ "*al-Asmā' al-ḥunsā*," are 99 attributes of Allah. This term is mentioned in verses 7.180, 17.110, 20.8, and 59.24.

48. Similar to the suggestion in their comments on verse 12.30 that فَتَىٰهَا "*fatāhā* (her *fatā*)" means "her slave," exegetes have suggested that فَتَيَانِ "*fatayān*" in this verse means "two slaves." I mentioned in my interpretation of 12.30, however, that this is only one of the possible meanings, because the word فتى "*fatā*" can also mean "male servant" in general whether free or slave. This word also means "young man."

49. My translation of the clause إِنِّيٓ أَرَىٰنِي "*innī arānī*" is "I see myself"; it means "I have seen myself in a dream." I have already talked about using the verb أَرَىٰ "*arā* (see)" in this context in my comment on verse 12.4.

50. Aṭ-Ṭabaṭabā'ī cites a wrong and uncommon view about the referent of the attached pronoun in the word بِتَأْوِيلِهِ "*bita'wīlihī*" which impacts the interpretation of the first part of the verse. Although aṭ-Ṭabaṭabā'ī himself classifies this view as unlikely given the context of the Qur'anic text, it is useful to discuss this view to expose its weaknesses, which some might overlook.

According to that view, the pronoun in بِتَأْوِيلِهِ "*bita'wīlihī*" in this verse has the same referent of the pronoun of the same word in the previous verse, i.e. "the two dreams." This means that the meaning of "*bita'wīlihī*" is "of its interpretation," i.e. "of the interpretation of the account of the two dreams." This, in turn, implies that لَا يَأْتِيكُمَا طَعَامٌ تُرْزَقَانِهِۦٓ إِلَّا نَبَّأْتُكُمَا بِتَأْوِيلِهِۦ قَبْلَ أَن يَأْتِيَكُمَا means "no food will come as sustenance for you before I inform you of the interpretation of the two dreams," or "I shall inform you of the interpretation of the two dreams before any food comes to you as sustenance." Nevertheless, there are obvious errors in this interpretation.

First, it makes the structure of the sentence, namely the way in which the word يَأْتِيكُمَا "*ya'tīkumā* ([it] comes to you)" is repeated, rather odd. Second, this interpretation assumes that Joseph was not going to interpret the two dreams immediately, yet the following verses refute this assumption, as they show him interpret the two dreams immediately with no mention of serving of food. Third, the alleged link between interpreting the two dreams and the arrival of the food would be meaningless unless we assume that Joseph was unable to interpret the two dreams immediately, and that he set for himself a deadline by which he would tell the two men the interpretation of their dreams. Jacob's interpretation of Joseph's dream and, later, Joseph's interpretation of the king's dream, however, were both done immediately, and did not require asking for time.

For all these reasons, that interpretation of the pronoun in "*bita'wīlihi*," and the subsequent conclusion about the meaning of the first part of the verse, must both be wrong.

51. Abd al-Ḥamīd Maḥmūd Ṭahmāz, "*Al-waḥi, wan-nubuwwa, wal-'ilm fī sūrat Joseph (Revelation, Prophethood, and Knowledge in the sūra of Joseph)* (Damascus: Dār al-Qalam, 1990).

52. Islam, the Qur'an tells us, is the one religion that Allah, the One and only God, revealed to every prophet that He sent to people since the time of the first man and prophet, Adam. Noah, Abraham, Ishmael, Isaac, Jacob, Joseph, Moses, Aaron, David, Solomon, Zachariah, John, Jesus, and all other prophets were Muslims who taught Islam to people. For instance, the following verse describes Israelite prophets as "Muslims":

إِنَّآ أَنزَلْنَا ٱلتَّوْرَىٰةَ فِيهَا هُدًى وَنُورٌ يَحْكُمُ بِهَا ٱلنَّبِيُّونَ ٱلَّذِينَ أَسْلَمُوا۟ لِلَّذِينَ هَادُوا۟ ﴿٤٤﴾. (سورة المَائِدَة).

Surely We sent down the Torah in which there was guidance and light; using it, the prophets who *aslamū* [became Muslims] guided the Jews (from 5.44).

Prophet Muhammad is the last Prophet of Islam, and the Qur'an is the last Book from Allah:

مَّا كَانَ مُحَمَّدٌ أَبَآ أَحَدٍ مِّن رِّجَالِكُمْ وَلَـٰكِن رَّسُولَ ٱللَّهِ وَخَاتَمَ ٱلنَّبِيِّـۧنَ وَكَانَ ٱللَّهُ بِكُلِّ شَىْءٍ عَلِيمًا ﴿٤٠﴾. (سورة الأَحْزَاب).

[O people!] Muhammad is not the father of any of your men, but he is the Messenger of Allah, and the last of the prophets; and Allah is aware of everything (33.40).

53. The use of the over-stressed قَهَّارُ "*qahhār* (Conqueror)" instead of the active participle قاهر "*qāhir*" emphasizes the conquering power of Allah.

54. Some might think that the verb ظَنَّ "*ẓanna*," which I have translated as "knew," in verse 12.42 means that Joseph was not sure of the accuracy of his interpretation. The reason is that forms of this verb occur in the Qur'an in the sense of "guess," "surmise," "opine" and such meanings which reflect uncertain knowledge and information that could be wrong. These are sample verses:

وَمِنْهُمْ أُمِّيُّونَ لَا يَعْلَمُونَ ٱلْكِتَٰبَ إِلَّآ أَمَانِيَّ وَإِنْ هُمْ إِلَّا يَظُنُّونَ ﴿٧٨﴾. (سورة البَقَرة).

And among them [the People of the Book] are illiterates who know not the Book but only imagine it in line with their wishes, and they only *yaẓinnūn* (guess) (2.78).

وَقَوْلِهِمْ إِنَّا قَتَلْنَا ٱلْمَسِيحَ عِيسَى ٱبْنَ مَرْيَمَ رَسُولَ ٱللَّهِ وَمَا قَتَلُوهُ وَمَا صَلَبُوهُ وَلَٰكِن شُبِّهَ لَهُمْ وَإِنَّ
ٱلَّذِينَ ٱخْتَلَفُوا۟ فِيهِ لَفِى شَكٍّ مِّنْهُ مَا لَهُم بِهِۦ مِنْ عِلْمٍ إِلَّا ٱتِّبَاعَ ٱلظَّنِّ وَمَا قَتَلُوهُ يَقِينًۢا ﴿١٥٧﴾. (سورة
النِّساءِ).

And because of their [the People of the Book] saying: "We killed the Messiah, Jesus son of Mary, the messenger of Allah." And they did not kill nor crucify him, but so it appeared to them. And surely those who have disagreed about him are in doubt thereof; they have no knowledge thereof save pursuit of *aẓ-ẓan* (a guess); and they did not kill him for certain (4.157).

The word "*ẓanna*," however, must mean something else in verse 12.42. There are a number of reasons why Joseph could not have been uncertain of his interpretation. First, he had already described it as divine knowledge: "that is of what my Lord has taught me." Second, Joseph could not have attributed his interpretation to divine knowledge and used it as proof in calling the two prisoners to the true religion when he himself had doubts about the verity of the interpretation. Third, Joseph's words "the matter which you have inquired about is done" clearly reflect his absolute confidence that things will happen in accordance with his interpretation of the dreams.

Indeed, the word "*ẓanna*" in the Qur'an has another meaning that is totally different from how it is used in verses 2.78 and 4.157. The verb "*ẓanna*" can mean "knew," implying the certainty of belief, as in the following verses that talk about the believers' certainty of the Day of Resurrection:

وَٱسْتَعِينُوا۟ بِٱلصَّبْرِ وَٱلصَّلَوٰةِ وَإِنَّهَا لَكَبِيرَةٌ إِلَّا عَلَى ٱلْخَٰشِعِينَ ﴿٤٥﴾ ٱلَّذِينَ يَظُنُّونَ أَنَّهُم مُّلَٰقُوا۟ رَبِّهِمْ
وَأَنَّهُمْ إِلَيْهِ رَٰجِعُونَ ﴿٤٦﴾. (سورة البَقَرة).

And seek [O Children of Israel!] help through patience and prayer; and surely it is hard except for the Allah-fearing (2.45). Who *yaẓinnūn* (know) that they shall meet their Lord and that they shall return to Him (2.46).

فَلَمَّا فَصَلَ طَالُوتُ بِٱلْجُنُودِ قَالَ إِنَّ ٱللَّهَ مُبْتَلِيكُم بِنَهَرٍ فَمَن شَرِبَ مِنْهُ فَلَيْسَ مِنِّى وَمَن لَّمْ يَطْعَمْهُ فَإِنَّهُۥ
مِنِّىٓ إِلَّا مَنِ ٱغْتَرَفَ غُرْفَةًۢ بِيَدِهِۦ فَشَرِبُوا۟ مِنْهُ إِلَّا قَلِيلًا مِّنْهُمْ فَلَمَّا جَاوَزَهُۥ هُوَ وَٱلَّذِينَ ءَامَنُوا۟ مَعَهُۥ قَالُوا۟ لَا طَاقَةَ
لَنَا ٱلْيَوْمَ بِجَالُوتَ وَجُنُودِهِۦ قَالَ ٱلَّذِينَ يَظُنُّونَ أَنَّهُم مُّلَٰقُوا۟ ٱللَّهِ كَم مِّن فِئَةٍ قَلِيلَةٍ غَلَبَتْ فِئَةً كَثِيرَةًۢ بِإِذْنِ ٱللَّهِ
وَٱللَّهُ مَعَ ٱلصَّٰبِرِينَ ﴿٢٤٩﴾. (سورة البَقَرة).

So when Saul departed with the soldiers, he said: "Surely Allah will try you with a river; whoever then drinks from it, he is not with me, and whoever does not taste of it, he is surely with me, except he who takes with his hand as much of it as fills the hand." So, they drank from it except a few of them. So when he and those who believed with him crossed it, they said: "We have today no power against Goliath and his soldiers." Those who *yaẓinnūn* (know) that they will meet their Lord said: "How often a small force overcame a big one by Allah's permission! And Allah is with the patient" (2.249).

It is clear, thus, that the meaning of "*ẓanna*" depends on the context in which it occurs.

Note that these two occurrences of the verb "*ẓanna*" relate to the Day of Resurrection which is a future event, like the release of the prisoner which was a future event at the time when Joseph interpreted the dreams. Therefore, the verb "*ẓanna*" in the clause "and he said to that of the two whom he *ẓanna* would be saved" means "knew," as I have translated it, which in turn means that Joseph was certain of the prisoner's future release from prison.

55. The plural verb in verse 12.43 that I have translated as "interpret" is تَعْبُرُونَ "*ta'burūn*," which also means "cross." Aṭ-Ṭabaṭabā'ī thinks that the former meaning of "*ta'burūn*" is derived from "crossing a river and the like, as if the person crosses from the dream to the interpretation that lies behind it." It is more likely, however, that "*ta'burūn*" means "to describe with *'ibārāt* (phrases)." So, in the context of dreams, this verb means "interpret a dream" because it involves describing the meaning of dream imageries with phrases.

56. But why did the king not ask for a dream interpretation during the previous years that Joseph spent in prison? There is the unlikely possibility that the king did not see any dream that attracted his attention during that period, or that this particular dream affected him, perhaps because of its recurrence, so he asked for an interpretation. More likely, however, is that the king used to have someone who would interpret his dreams for him, as there has been rarely a time or place where there was not someone who claims to be able to interpret dreams, but that this person was no more available for one reason or another when the king told his court about his dream.

57. The Qur'anic word that I have translated as "a period of time" is أُمَّةٍ "*ummatin*." This is another verse which uses this word in the same sense:

وَلَئِنْ أَخَّرْنَا عَنْهُمُ ٱلْعَذَابَ إِلَىٰٓ أُمَّةٍ مَّعْدُودَةٍ لَّيَقُولُنَّ مَا يَحْبِسُهُۥٓ أَلَا يَوْمَ يَأْتِيهِمْ لَيْسَ مَصْرُوفًا عَنْهُمْ وَحَاقَ بِهِم مَّا كَانُوا۟ بِهِۦ يَسْتَهْزِءُونَ ﴿٨﴾. (سورة هود).

And if We delay for them the torment until a stated *ummatin* (period of time), they [the disbelievers] will certainly say: "What withholds it?". Surely, on the day when it comes to them, it shall not be averted from them, and that which they derided shall surround them (11.8).

58. The semi-verb لَعَلَّ "*la'alla*" means "may or might." It is used for events that are *possible* but not certain to happen. The cupbearer's words "*la'allī* (that I may) go back to the people" do not mean that he was not sure of "going back to the people," but that he was unsure of "going back to the people with the interpretation." People's learning of the interpretation depended on the cupbearer returning to them with that interpretation. Given that the likelihood of the latter event was described with "*la'alla*," the occurrence of the former was also described with "*la'alla*": "*la'allahum* (so they may) know." So, the meaning of the cupbearer's words is: "if you would give me your opinion about the dream then I shall go back to the people with the interpretation so they know."

59. Some exegetes — including al-Qummī, aṭ-Ṭabaṭabā'ī, aṭ-Ṭabarī, and al-Jalālayn — have pointed out that the clause يَأْكُلْنَ مَا قَدَّمْتُمْ لَهُنَّ, which I have translated as "eat away what you prepare for them," means that the years of hardship would eat away all that people had saved for them in the prosperous years. Exegetes have overlooked the fact that this interpretation cannot be reconciled with the clause "except a little which you protect." If "what you prepare for them" refers to the food that people had saved for the years of hardship, then "protecting" that food can only mean "preventing themselves from eating it"; this is clearly nonsense.

Exegetes' failure to properly understand this is the result of their misunderstanding of the verb قَدَّمْتُم "*qaddamtum* ([you] prepare(d))" followed by the particle ل "*lām* (for)" in this verse. In several verses, the Qur'an uses the verb قدّم ل "*qaddama li*" in the sense "do in preparation for a future purpose," as in the following two verses, for example:

وَأَقِيمُوا۟ ٱلصَّلَوٰةَ وَءَاتُوا۟ ٱلزَّكَوٰةَ وَمَا تُقَدِّمُوا۟ لِأَنفُسِكُم مِّنْ خَيْرٍ تَجِدُوهُ عِندَ ٱللَّهِ إِنَّ ٱللَّهَ بِمَا تَعْمَلُونَ بَصِيرٌ ﴿١١٠﴾. (سورة البَقَرة).

And keep up prayer, and pay the obligatory alms; and whatever good *tuqaddimū li* (you prepare for) yourselves, you will find it with Allah; surely Allah sees what you do (2.110).

يَٰٓأَيُّهَا ٱلَّذِينَ ءَامَنُوا۟ ٱتَّقُوا۟ ٱللَّهَ وَلْتَنظُرْ نَفْسٌ مَّا قَدَّمَتْ لِغَدٍ وَٱتَّقُوا۟ ٱللَّهَ إِنَّ ٱللَّهَ خَبِيرٌۢ بِمَا تَعْمَلُونَ ﴿١٨﴾. (سورة الحَشر).

O you who believe! Fear Allah, and let every soul consider what *qaddamat li* (it has prepared) for the morrow, and be dutiful toward Allah; surely Allah is Aware of what you do (59.18).

Therefore, exegetes have thought that "what you prepare for them" refers to what people prepared in advance for the years of hardship, and concluded that this would be the stored "grain."

It is clear, however, that the years of drought would not affect the grain that people had stored but that which they plant during those years. My interpretation, which agrees with the apparent meaning of "what you prepare for them," is that this clause refers to what people plant during the hard years. The drought in those years would destroy everything that people plant during them, except a little that they manage to protect: "except a little which you protect."

According to this interpretation, the reason for using the verb قدَّمَ لـ "prepare for" is that planting *precedes* harvesting, of course. What people prepare for the years of famine is whatever they plant hoping to reap its harvest later. In other words, "what you prepare for them" means "what you prepare to harvest in those years."

60. These are some verses that use variations of the verb يُغَاثُ "*yughāthu*" for various kinds of help:

وَدَخَلَ ٱلْمَدِينَةَ عَلَىٰ حِينِ غَفْلَةٍ مِّنْ أَهْلِهَا فَوَجَدَ فِيهَا رَجُلَيْنِ يَقْتَتِلَانِ هَٰذَا مِن شِيعَتِهِ وَهَٰذَا مِنْ عَدُوِّهِ فَٱسْتَغَٰثَهُ ٱلَّذِى مِن شِيعَتِهِ عَلَى ٱلَّذِى مِنْ عَدُوِّهِ فَوَكَزَهُ مُوسَىٰ فَقَضَىٰ عَلَيْهِ قَالَ هَٰذَا مِنْ عَمَلِ ٱلشَّيْطَٰنِ إِنَّهُ عَدُوٌّ مُّضِلٌّ مُّبِينٌ ﴿١٥﴾. (سورة القَصَص).

And he [Moses] entered the city at a time of unawareness on the part of its people, and he found therein two men fighting, one of his own people and the other of his enemies. And he who was of his people *istaghāthahu* (asked him for help) against him who was of his enemies; So Moses struck him [the latter] and killed him. He said: "This is of Satan's doing; he is a manifest misleading enemy" (28.15).

إِذْ تَسْتَغِيثُونَ رَبَّكُمْ فَاسْتَجَابَ لَكُمْ أَنِّى مُمِدُّكُم بِأَلْفٍ مِّنَ ٱلْمَلَٰٓئِكَةِ مُرْدِفِينَ ﴿٩﴾. (سورة الأنفال).

When you [O you who believe!] *tastaghīthūna* (sought help from) your Lord, so He answered you: "I will assist you with a thousand of angels following one another" (8.9).

وَقُلِ ٱلْحَقُّ مِن رَّبِّكُمْ فَمَن شَآءَ فَلْيُؤْمِن وَمَن شَآءَ فَلْيَكْفُرْ إِنَّآ أَعْتَدْنَا لِلظَّٰلِمِينَ نَارًا أَحَاطَ بِهِمْ سُرَادِقُهَا وَإِن يَسْتَغِيثُواْ يُغَاثُواْ بِمَآءٍ كَٱلْمُهْلِ يَشْوِى ٱلْوُجُوهَ بِئْسَ ٱلشَّرَابُ وَسَآءَتْ مُرْتَفَقًا ﴿٢٩﴾. (سورة الكَهفِ).

And say [O Muhammad!]: "[This is] the truth from your Lord, so let he who wants believe, and let he who wants disbelieve." Surely, We have prepared for the wrongdoers a fire, the curtains of which shall surround them; and if they *yastaghīthū* (seek help), they *yughāthū* (shall be helped) with water which is like molten brass which will scald their faces; how dreadful a drink, and how dreadful a resting place! (18.29).

61. Aṭ-Ṭabaṭabā'ī has made an interesting observation that is worth mentioning. In his interpretation of the king's dream, Joseph used the plural

pronoun "you" in verses: "you shall sow for seven years diligently, so leave what you reap in its ear, except a little which you eat," and "then there shall come after that seven years of hardship which shall eat away what you prepare for them, except a little which you protect." In contrast, Joseph used the word "people" in the following verse: "then there shall come after that a year in which people shall be helped with rain, and in which they shall press [crops]," i.e. he did not say "in which *you* shall be helped with rain, and in which *you* shall press [crops]." Aṭ-Ṭabaṭabā'ī thinks that this is a reference to the fact that in that year "people" would not be in need of state aids from the stored grain, because rain would help them directly.

62. Some exegetes read يَعْصِرُونَ "*ya'ṣirūna* (press)" in the passive voice, i.e. يُعصَرون "*yū'ṣaruna* (be helped to press)," or even يُعصِرون "*yū'ṣīruna*," in reference to:

وَأَنزَلْنَا مِنَ ٱلْـمُعْصِرَٰتِ مَآءً ثَجَّاجًا ﴿١٤﴾ لِّنُخْرِجَ بِهِۦ حَبًّا وَنَبَاتًا ﴿١٥﴾. (سورة النّبأ).

And We sent down from the *mu'ṣirāti* (clouds) water in abundance (78.14). So that We bring with it grain and plant (78.15).

It seems that this opinion has originated from the fact that the verb "*yughāthu*" is in the passive voice. I believe, however, that the reading of most exegetes of the verb in question as "*ya'ṣirūna*" is the right one, because the word "*yū'ṣaruna*" has the same meaning as "*yughāthu*," and thus would add nothing to the sentence.

Additionally, it is natural for the verb "*yughāthu*" to be in the passive voice, because people *receive* that help, *not offer* it. It is also natural for the verb "*ya'ṣirūna*" to be in the active voice, because it is the people themselves who do the pressing.

63. This complex subject is outside the scope of this book. Interested readers may consult our Arabic book *Paranormalogy: Readings in the Science of the Paranormal* (Lebanon: World Book Publishing, 1999) which discusses this complicated subject in detail.

64. In addition to verse 51 of the sūra of Joseph, the word "*sū*" occurs in combination with "*'alā*" in this verse:

ثُمَّ يَوْمَ ٱلْقِيَٰمَةِ يُخْزِيهِمْ وَيَقُولُ أَيْنَ شُرَكَآءِىَ ٱلَّذِينَ كُنتُمْ تُشَٰٓقُّونَ فِيهِمْ قَالَ ٱلَّذِينَ أُوتُوا۟ ٱلْعِلْمَ إِنَّ ٱلْـخِزْىَ ٱلْيَوْمَ وَٱلسُّوٓءَ عَلَى ٱلْكَٰفِرِينَ ﴿٢٧﴾. (سورة النّحل).

Then on the Day of Resurrection He will bring them [the polytheists] to disgrace and say: "Where are My associates [whom you claimed to exist], for whose sake you became hostile [to My Message]?" Those who were given knowledge will say: "Surely the disgrace and the *sū'* (evil) are today *'alā* (on) the disbelievers" (16.27).

Note how the evil mentioned in this verse is something that "*happens to*" the disbelievers, *not* something they "*do*." There are also the following two verses in which the phrase دَائِرَةُ السَّوْءِ "*dā'iratu as-sū'* (evil turn of fortune)" is used with "*'alā* (on)" in the word عَلَيْهِمْ "*'alayhim* (on them)":

وَمِنَ ٱلْأَعْرَابِ مَن يَتَّخِذُ مَا يُنفِقُ مَغْرَمًا وَيَتَرَبَّصُ بِكُمُ ٱلدَّوَائِرَ عَلَيْهِمْ دَآئِرَةُ ٱلسَّوْءِ وَٱللَّهُ سَمِيعٌ عَلِيمٌ ﴿٩٨﴾. (سورة التوبة).

And of the wandering Arabs are those who take what they spend [in the cause of Allah] to be a fine; and they await for [bad] turns of fortune for you [O you who believe!]. The *Dā'iratu as-sū'* (evil turn of fortune) will fall *'alayhim* (on them). And Allah is hearer, knower (9.98).

وَيُعَذِّبَ ٱلْمُنَٰفِقِينَ وَٱلْمُنَٰفِقَٰتِ وَٱلْمُشْرِكِينَ وَٱلْمُشْرِكَٰتِ ٱلظَّآنِّينَ بِٱللَّهِ ظَنَّ ٱلسَّوْءِ عَلَيْهِمْ دَآئِرَةُ ٱلسَّوْءِ وَغَضِبَ ٱللَّهُ عَلَيْهِمْ وَلَعَنَهُمْ وَأَعَدَّ لَهُمْ جَهَنَّمَ وَسَآءَتْ مَصِيرًا ﴿٦﴾. (سورة الفتح).

And that He might torment the hypocritical men and the hypocritical women, and the polytheistic men and the polytheistic women, who entertain evil thoughts about Allah. *'Alayhim* (on them) will be the *dā'iratu as-sū'* (evil turn of fortune), and Allah is wroth with them. Allah has cursed them and prepared for them hell, and evil it is for a destination (48.6).

Here also Allah talks about evil that *happens to, not caused by*, wandering Arabs, hypocrites, and polytheists. All of this proves unquestionably that the clause "*mā 'alimnā 'alayhi min sū*" means "we knew of no evil on him," not "we knew of no evil *from* him." It means that the women denied any knowledge of Joseph's subjection to injustice, because such knowledge would have implied their involvement in the matter in one way or another.

65. The adjective مَكِينٌ "*makīn*" is derived from مكان "*makān* (place or position)"; it means "having a special and established position," i.e. being someone "with authority." The adjective أَمِينٌ "*amīn* (trustworthy)" occurs in the Qur'an in two different meanings. When used as an adjective for a place, "*amīn*" is derived from أمان "*amān* (safety)," and means "safe." It denotes a place whose population live in peace, as in the following verses:

إِنَّ ٱلْمُتَّقِينَ فِى مَقَامٍ أَمِينٍ ﴿٥١﴾. (سورة الدخان).

The dutiful ones shall be in an *amīn* (safe) abode (44.51)

وَهَٰذَا ٱلْبَلَدِ ٱلْأَمِينِ ﴿٣﴾. (سورة التين).

And this *amīn* (safe) city (95.3).

When "*amīn*" describes people, then its root is أمانة "*amāna* (trustworthiness)," in which case it refers to the quality of "carefully looking after a trust." For instance, Allah uses the word "*amīn*" several times to describe His messengers, referring to the fact that He entrusted the Message with them and that they proved trustworthy. They conveyed the Message to whom Allah intended without slacking or tampering with it, as in the following verses:

إِذْ قَالَ لَهُمْ أَخُوهُمْ نُوحٌ أَلَا تَتَّقُونَ ﴿١٠٦﴾ إِنِّي لَكُمْ رَسُولٌ أَمِينٌ ﴿١٠٧﴾. (سورة الشُّعَرَاء).

When their brother Noah said to them [his people]: "Will you not act dutifully? (26.106). I am an *amīn* (trustworthy) messenger to you" (26.107).

وَإِنَّ رَبَّكَ لَهُوَ ٱلْعَزِيزُ ٱلرَّحِيمُ ﴿١٩١﴾ وَإِنَّهُۥ لَتَنزِيلُ رَبِّ ٱلْعَـٰلَمِينَ ﴿١٩٢﴾ نَزَلَ بِهِ ٱلرُّوحُ ٱلْأَمِينُ ﴿١٩٣﴾ عَلَىٰ قَلْبِكَ لِتَكُونَ مِنَ ٱلْـمُنذِرِينَ ﴿١٩٤﴾. (سورة الشُّعَرَاء).

And most surely your Lord [O Muhammad!] is the Invincible, the Merciful One (26.191). And most surely this is a revelation from the Lord of the people (26.192). The *ar-Rūḥ al-Amīn* (the trustworthy Spirit) has descended with it (26.193) upon your heart so that you be of the warners (26.194).

So addressing Joseph with "*amīn*" means that the king drew Joseph close to him to the extent of making him one of those whom he trusted.

66. Abd al-Ḥamīd Maḥmūd Ṭahmāz, *Al-waḥi, wan-Nubuwwa, wal-'Ilm fī Sūrat Joseph (Revelation, Prophethood, and Knowledge in the sūra of Joseph)* (Damascus: Dar al-Qalam, 1990).

67. The word رِحال "*riḥāl*" refers to the "luggage" of the راحِلين "*rāḥilīn* (travelers)." The singular of "*riḥāl*" is رَحْل "*raḥl*"; it is the luggage of the راحِل "*rāḥil* (traveler)." It is not surprising, therefore, to find the word "*raḥl*" used to refer to the things that are put on transport animals.

68. It is worth noting that the semi-verb لَعَلَّ "*la'alla* (may)" does not refer to "*ya'rifūnaha* (they recognize them)," for it is natural that Joseph's brothers would know their goods when they find them. It rather refers to the whole clause يَعْرِفُونَهَا إِذَا ٱنقَلَبُوٓاْ إِلَىٰٓ أَهْلِهِمْ "recognize them when they return to their family." So, the meaning is "that they may find the goods when they return to their family."

The second "may" in the clause "they may come back" is linked to the same word in the earlier clause "they may recognize them when they return to their family." In other words, the return of Joseph's brothers depended on their recognition of their goods when they return home, and since the later is qualified by "may," then their return to him is also qualified by that word. We have already seen the same double use of the semi-verb "*la'alla* (may)" in verse 12.46 also.

69. Note first that Joseph ordered his servants in verse 12.62 to put his brothers' goods in رِحَالِهِم "*riḥālihim* (their luggage)," whereas Joseph's brothers found their goods in مَتَـٰعَهُمْ "*matā'ihim* (their baggage)." As explained earlier, the word رَحْل "*raḥl*" refers to the traveler's luggage in general, whereas the word مَتَـٰع "*matā*" means "belongings" in general, so I have translated it as "baggage." Some exegetes, however, think that "*matā*" in this context means merchandize.

We have seen in verse 12.62 that Joseph asked his servants to put the goods of his brothers in their luggage so they can find them "when they return to their family."

In other words, Joseph wanted to *hide* the goods in his brothers' luggage so that they would not find them until they arrive to their family. The best hidden place in the luggage was chosen by Joseph's servants who decided that the goods should be put in the "*matā'* (baggage)"; the latter is part of the "*riḥāl*," but it is difficult to determine exactly which part it represents. It is possible that Joseph's servants put the goods of his brothers with the "provisions" that he gave to them because they were not going to open the latter until they arrive home.

70. Some exegetes think that Joseph put the goods in his brothers' luggage in order to make them and their father feel morally obliged to return them, as they were no more theirs after exchanging them for provisions. That would make them come back to Joseph. The statement of Joseph's brothers that "their goods have been returned to them," however, shows that they did not see the matter as suggested by those exegetes. They considered it as an act of generosity and charity from Joseph toward them. It is clear from the verses above and the interpretations that I gave, that Joseph's plan to make his brothers come back had nothing to do with making them feel morally obliged to return the goods because they were not theirs anymore. By returning the goods to his brothers, Joseph encouraged them to come back to him and, most important, encouraged their father to permit them to take Benjamin with them to Egypt.

71. The conjunction "and" at the beginning of "and we shall bring grain for our family" means that the latter clause is linked to "our goods have been returned to us." So, Joseph's brothers considered "returning their goods to them" to be a benefit like "bringing grain to their family" and "having an additional camel load."

72. The Arabic word مَوْثِق "*mawthiq*," which I have translated as "covenant," is a variation of the word وثيقة "*wathīqa* (document)," whose verb is وَثَّق "*waththaq* (to document)."

73. The literal translation of the clause which I have translated as "unless you become completely powerless" is "unless you are surrounded." The verb يُحَاط "*yuḥāṭ* (be surrounded)" in this verse means to be surrounded from all sides that the person becomes unable to do anything, hence my translation "completely powerless."

74. It is possible to argue that the use of the phrase مِنْ حَيْثُ "*min ḥaythu* (wherefrom)" instead of a word that means "as," such as كما "*kamā*" and مثلما "*mithlamā*," means that Jacob also specified for his sons the different gates that he ordered them to use. The word "wherefrom" would then refer to Jacob's identification of the points of entry, not only to how the entry should happen. It is also possible that the order to enter from different gates meant, directly or indirectly, the entry from specific points and did not require Jacob to specify them.

75. First, the pronoun may refer to the action of entering Egypt with which the verse starts: "And as they entered wherefrom their father had ordered them." In this case, the sentence would mean: "*that entry* protected them naught against Allah." This possible interpretation is represented by the use of "that" in my translation.

Second, the pronoun may refer to Jacob himself, in which case the sentence "he protected them naught against Allah" would be a confirmation, using an implicit pronoun, of Jacob's words in the previous verse: "and I can protect you naught against Allah." In this case, the pronoun would refer to the word أَبُوهُم "their father," and the verse would mean: "their father did not provide them with any protection against Allah." This possible interpretation is represented by the use of "he" in the translation.

No matter which interpretation is the right one, the meaning of "that/he protected them naught against Allah" would be almost the same: "Jacob" or the "entry according to Jacob's plan" did not prevent Allah from doing whatever He wanted to do to Jacob's sons.

76. The use of the word حَاجَةً "desire" preceded by إِلَّا "but" makes the implicit pronoun in "that/he protected them naught against Allah" more likely to refer to the act of *entering* than to *Jacob*.

It is worth pointing out that the word إِلَّا "*illā*" may be used for exclusion. This is not, however, how it is used in his verse, for the clause "protected them naught against Allah" is always true. "*Illā*" can also mean "but"; this is how it is used in this verse.

77. Exegetes say that the transitive verb ءَاوَى "*āwā*" here means "embraced." This interpretation is actually incorrect. I have translated "*āwā*" as "admitted to his private place." Supporting evidence for this interpretation is found in the Qur'an. In the following verse, Allah reminds Prophet Muhammad of His favor to him: أَلَمْ يَجِدْكَ يَتِيمًا فَـَٔاوَىٰ "Did He not find you an orphan so He *āwā* (gave you shelter?)" (93.6). In another verse about "the people of the cave," the intransitive version أَوَى "*awā*" is used: إِذْ أَوَى ٱلْفِتْيَةُ إِلَى ٱلْكَهْفِ "When the young men *awā* (resorted) to the cave" (from 18.10). It is clear that "*āwā*" means to "admit to" a مأوى "*ma'wā* (shelter)," and "*awā*" to "go to" a shelter.

Joseph's brothers entered to the official place where Joseph receives visitors. Then, he invited Benjamin only to his private room. Something similar will happen when Joseph's family comes to him in Egypt. All of them will enter his formal place, but then he will only admit his parents to his private place: فَلَمَّا دَخَلُوا۟ عَلَىٰ يُوسُفَ ءَاوَىٰٓ إِلَيْهِ أَبَوَيْهِ "Then when they entered Joseph's place, he admitted his parents to his private place."

78. As mentioned in my note on the word "caravan" in verse 12.19, "camel caravanners" is the translation of the word عِيرٌ "*īr*." It seems that the words "*īr*" and بعير "*ba'īr* (camel)" share the same linguistic root.

79. Exegetes are in agreement that سِقَايَة "*siqāya*" is a drinking cup. This noun obviously shares the same root with the verb سَقَى "*saqā* (water, give drink)."

80. Al-Qurṭubī thinks that the verb أَذَّنَ "*adhdhana*," which I have translated as "proclaimed," means "shouted many times." I think that أذان "*adhān*," a noun of "*adhdhana*," has the more general meaning of proclaiming and making the announcement reach the targeted people, who are usually present at different distances from the place of the "*adhān*." Therefore, the "*adhān*" involves shouting loudly to get the message to far distances, to as many people as possible. It also involves repetition. Note, for instance, that the "*adhān*" of the five daily prayers is used to announce that the time of prayer has come, and that it involves the use of loud voice and repetition to make the announcement reach as many people who observe prayer as possible. Clearly, there is a link between the words "*adhān*" and أُذُن "*udhun*," which means "ear."

The verb "*adhdhana*" occurs also in the following verse in which the verb نَادَى "*nādā* (shouted/called)" implies the existence of some distance between the "people of paradise" and the "people of the fire":

وَنَادَىٰٓ أَصْحَٰبُ ٱلْجَنَّةِ أَصْحَٰبَ ٱلنَّارِ أَن قَدْ وَجَدْنَا مَا وَعَدَنَا رَبُّنَا حَقًّا فَهَلْ وَجَدتُّم مَّا وَعَدَ رَبُّكُمْ حَقًّا قَالُوا۟ نَعَمْ فَأَذَّنَ مُؤَذِّنٌۢ بَيْنَهُمْ أَن لَّعْنَةُ ٱللَّهِ عَلَى ٱلظَّٰلِمِينَ ﴿٤٤﴾. (سورة الأعرافِ).

And the people of paradise shall call the people of the fire [saying]: "We have found what our Lord promised us to be true; have you too found what your Lord promised to be true?" They [the people of the fire] will say: "Yes." Then *adhdhana mu'adhihun* (a proclaimer will proclaim) in between them that the curse of Allah is upon the wrongdoers (7.44).

Similarly, the imperative verb أَذِّنْ "*adhdhin* (do proclaim)" in the following verse refers to an announcement that reaches far distances:

وَأَذِّن فِى ٱلنَّاسِ بِٱلْحَجِّ يَأْتُوكَ رِجَالًا وَعَلَىٰ كُلِّ ضَامِرٍ يَأْتِينَ مِن كُلِّ فَجٍّ عَمِيقٍ ﴿٢٧﴾. (سورة الحَج).

And *adhdhin* (proclaim) [O Muhammad!] among people about the Pilgrimage; they will come to you on foot and on every lean camel, coming from every remote path (22.27).

The clause "*adhdhana mu'adhdhinun*" in verse 12.70 suggests that Joseph's brothers had already moved some distance on their way back home when someone shouted to them accusing them of theft.

81. It is possible that all pronouns in verses 72-76 refer to Joseph, where the use of the plural form reflects the prestige of his position. Another possibility is that all of the dialogue in verses 70-75 occurred between Joseph's servants and his brothers. In this case, the speaker of the clause "I am responsible for delivering that" would be the proclaimer or one of his companions who had some authority

or was talking on behalf of Joseph. I think that both of these possible interpretations are unlikely.

According to the interpretation that I find more likely, Joseph was not present at the beginning of the dialogue between his servants and brothers in verse 12.70. It is logical to think that Joseph himself did not go with his servants to bring back his brothers for the investigation of the theft. That task did not require the presence of someone of his status. I also rule out the possibility that the scene in verse 12.76, which explicitly mentions Joseph, represents the first appearance for Joseph in the dialogue that involved his servants and brothers, particularly as his search of the luggage of his brothers means that he was aware of that dialogue. We need to specify the point in the conversation between Joseph's servants and his brothers at which he became present.

It is logical to suggest that Joseph's servants brought his brothers to him, so we simply need to determine the starting point of the conversation at Joseph's place. One possibility is that the change in the pronoun of the speaker from the plural to the singular form in verse 12.72 indicates the transition of the conversation to where Joseph was present. So, the speech in the first half of the verse, "they said: 'We have lost the drinking cup of the king'," was between Joseph's brothers and servants, whereas the second half of the verse, "and he who shall bring it shall have a camel load, and I am responsible for delivering that," happened at Joseph's place after his servants brought back his brothers to him. It is also possible, nevertheless, that the whole speech in this verse took place at Joseph's place. In both cases, the conversation about the theft, which is recounted in the following verses, would have occurred at Joseph's place and in his presence.

This interpretation means that that Joseph's brothers' conversation was with Joseph, who is referred to with the singular pronoun, and his men, who are referred to with the plural pronoun. In verse 12.72, for instance, the sentence "They said: 'We have lost'" refers to Joseph's entourage who were talking to his brothers, whereas the singular pronoun in the clause "I am responsible for delivering that" refers to Joseph.

82. The word وِعَآءِ "*wi'ā'*," which I have translated as "container," refers to the container of the luggage.

83. Aṭ-Ṭabaṭabā'ī thinks that it refers to the stealing charge that they leveled against Joseph and which he did not deny and expose to be a lie. Other exegetes, including al-Jalālayn, think it is the words of Joseph's brothers: "If he has stolen, a brother of his did indeed steal before." Another group of exegetes, including Ibn Kathīr who attributed this view to Ibn 'Abbās, have suggested that it is Allah's words: "You are in a worse situation, and Allah knows best [the truth of] what you describe." Al-Qurṭubī says that others have indicated that Joseph hid within himself the clause "You are in a worse situation," but voiced the sentence "and Allah knows best [the truth of] what you describe." The fact that the sentence "you are in a

worse situation, and Allah knows best [the truth of] what you describe" is preceded with "He said" indicates that Joseph did actually say "you are in a worse situation, and Allah knows best [the truth of] what you describe," so this is not what he kept secret.

84. For example, the following verse tells Prophet Muhammad how to deal with the disbelievers and refutes their claims:

ٱدْفَعْ بِٱلَّتِى هِىَ أَحْسَنُ ٱلسَّيِّئَةَ نَحْنُ أَعْلَمُ بِمَا يَصِفُونَ ﴿٩٦﴾. (سورة المؤمنون).

[O Muhammad!] Repel [evil] with the best [response]; We know best [the truth of] what they describe (23.96).

85. The verb "*khalaṣū*" means "took to an isolated place, away from people." This verb shares the same root with خالص "*khāliṣ*" which means "pure, unmixed with other material." It is used, for example, to describe pure gold.

The word نَجِيًّا "*najiyyān*" occurs also in verse 19.52 where Allah says about prophet Moses وَقَرَّبْنَـٰهُ نَجِيًّا "*wa qarrabnāhu najiyyān*," which means "and We drew him near [to Us], *najiyyān* (talking to him in private)." *Najiyyān* means "talking privately and from a close distance."

Therefore, I have translated خَلَصُوا۟ نَجِيًّا "*khalaṣū najiyyān*" into "they conferred privately."

86. The act of "bearing witness" must be based on "knowledge," as in the words of Joseph's brothers: "and we did not bear witness except to what we have known." On the contrary, the term غيب "*ghayb*" refers to the "unknown," "unseen" ...etc.

87. Allah described Jacob with the adjective كَظِيمٌ "*kaẓīm*," whose verb كظم "*kaẓama*" means "hid," "concealed," "restricted," or "restrained" within one's self. The active participle of "*kaẓama*" is كاظم "*kāẓim*"; it is used in the following verse: وَٱلْكَـٰظِمِينَ ٱلْغَيْظَ "*wal kāẓimīna al-ghayẓa* (and those who restrain [their] anger)" (from 3.134). "*Kaẓīm*" is an over-emphasized form of the active participle "*kāẓim*." It is worth noting that the passive participle of "*kaẓama*" is مكظوم "*makẓūm*," which means "restrained," "concealed" ...etc. Allah used this word to describe prophet Jonah who was "confined inside" the whale when he cried to Allah:

وَلَا تَكُن كَصَاحِبِ ٱلْحُوتِ إِذْ نَادَىٰ وَهُوَ مَكْظُومٌ ﴿١٢﴾. (سورة القلم).

And do not [O Muhammad!] be like the companion of the whale who cried while he was *makẓūm* (confined) [inside it] (from 68.48).

88. The verb "*taḥassasū*" literally means to reach to something via the "senses," which are called حواس "*ḥawās*" in Arabic, hence my translation of that verb as "trace."

Some exegetes think that the verb "*taḥassasū*" has the same meaning of تَجَسَّسُوا "*tajassasū* (spy)." There is, in fact, a significant difference. "Spying" is to try to secretly uncover information about something or someone. Allah has forbidden the believers from spying on each other, because it amounts to stealing information that the spy has no right to know, and to intruding on others' privacy. He prohibited spying in the same verse that proscribed backbiting and misguided suspicions:

يَـٰٓأَيُّهَا ٱلَّذِينَ ءَامَنُوا۟ ٱجْتَنِبُوا۟ كَثِيرًا مِّنَ ٱلظَّنِّ إِنَّ بَعْضَ ٱلظَّنِّ إِثْمٌ وَلَا تَجَسَّسُوا۟ وَلَا يَغْتَب بَّعْضُكُم بَعْضًا أَيُحِبُّ أَحَدُكُمْ أَن يَأْكُلَ لَحْمَ أَخِيهِ مَيْتًا فَكَرِهْتُمُوهُ وَٱتَّقُوا۟ ٱللَّهَ إِنَّ ٱللَّهَ تَوَّابٌ رَّحِيمٌ ﴿١٢﴾. (سورة الحُجرات).

O you who believe! Avoid most of suspicion, for surely some suspicion is a sin. And do no spy on or backbite each other. Would any of you like to eat the flesh of his dead brother? You abhor that. And be dutiful toward Allah. Surely, Allah is Relenting, Merciful (49.12).

89. Exegetes have disagreed on the exact meaning of مُزْجَـٰة "*muzjātin*," but there is consensus that it means "poor."

90. It is notable that Joseph's prayer for his brothers does not explicitly contain the word عسى "*'asā* (may)," hence put in brackets in the translation. This may be one way of stressing the prayer.

91. Some exegetes have mentioned a different way of reading this verse. They consider "today" as the first word in the clause "today [may] Allah forgive you," not the last word in "you shall not be rebuked today." This is a very unlikely reading because the clause "today [may] Allah forgive you" would then mean that Joseph specified "that particular day" as a date for Allah's forgiveness for his brothers. Although some have claimed that this interpretation means that Joseph knew through revelation that Allah forgave his brothers on "that day," the fact that the verb يَغْفِرُ "*yaghfiru* (forgive)" is in present tense undermines this view.

In fact, Prophet Muhammad's saying that I cited earlier leaves no doubt that "today" should be read as the last word in the clause "you shall not be rebuked today."

92. Verses 21.59-60 talk about Abraham's destruction of the idols of his people, which led to their attempt to burn Abraham alive. He is described in verse 21.60 as فتى "*fatā*," i.e. "young man":

قَالُوا۟ مَن فَعَلَ هَـٰذَا بِـَٔالِهَتِنَآ إِنَّهُۥ لَمِنَ ٱلظَّـٰلِمِينَ ﴿٥٩﴾ قَالُوا۟ سَمِعْنَا فَتًى يَذْكُرُهُمْ يُقَالُ لَهُۥٓ إِبْرَٰهِيمُ ﴿٦٠﴾. (سورة الأنبيَاءِ).

They [the disbelievers] said: "Who has done this to our gods? Surely he is one of the wrongdoers" (21.59). They [some of them] said: "We have heard a *fatā* (young man) with the name of Abraham mention them [negatively]" (21.60).

93. There is a subtle difference between Jacob's sons' speech to their father and their acknowledgement to Joseph: "By Allah! Allah has indeed preferred you over us, and we have been sinners" (from 12.91). They used إِن "*in*" and the particle لَ "*lām*" at the beginning of the word لَخَـٰطِـِٔينَ "*lakhāṭi'īn*" in their speech to their brother in the clause that I have translated as "we have been sinners," whereas they used إِنَّا "*innā*" in the similar clause that I have translated as "we have certainly been sinners." Both clauses represent a clear acknowledgement of erring, but the over-stressed "*innā*" carries additional emphasis and certainty that they sinned, which I have reflected in my translation by the use of the word "certainly." This change in the use of words has a subtle reference to the continuation of the positive change that Joseph's brothers were going through as they moved from one state to another by Allah's favor. The speech of Joseph's brothers to their father, which took place after they witnessed the miracle of restoring his sight by the blessed shirt of Joseph, shows that they became absolutely certain that what they did to their father and brother was wrong.

94. see the interpretation of the next verse.

95. This is another verse which makes clear that the meaning of the Beautiful Name لَطِيفٌ "*Laṭīf*" is "subtle" and "undetectable by the senses":

لَّا تُدْرِكُهُ ٱلْأَبْصَـٰرُ وَهُوَ يُدْرِكُ ٱلْأَبْصَـٰرَ وَهُوَ ٱللَّطِيفُ ٱلْخَبِيرُ ﴿١٠٣﴾. (سورة الأنعام).

Eyes cannot reach Him, and He can reach every eye, and He is the *Laṭīf* (Subtle), the Aware (6.103).

96. Note that apart from verse 12.93, the word مُلْك "*mulk* (kingship)" is preceded by مِنَ "*min* (a share of)" in another verse:

أَمْ لَهُمْ نَصِيبٌ مِّنَ ٱلْمُلْكِ فَإِذًا لَّا يُؤْتُونَ ٱلنَّاسَ نَقِيرًا ﴿٥٣﴾ أَمْ يَحْسُدُونَ ٱلنَّاسَ عَلَىٰ مَآ ءَاتَىٰهُمُ ٱللَّهُ مِن فَضْلِهِۦ فَقَدْ ءَاتَيْنَآ ءَالَ إِبْرَٰهِيمَ ٱلْكِتَـٰبَ وَٱلْحِكْمَةَ وَءَاتَيْنَـٰهُم مُّلْكًا عَظِيمًا ﴿٥٤﴾. (سورة النِّسَاءِ).

Or have they [the Children of Israel] a share of *mulk* (property), in which case they would not give a farthing to people? (4.53). Or do they envy people for the favor that Allah has given them? We have given the family of Abraham the Book, Wisdom, and great kingship (4.54).

The word "*mulk*" in verse 4.53, which I have translated as "property," is preceded by نَصِيبٌ مِّنَ "*naṣībun min* (a share of)" to underline the limitedness of that property. This is mentioned in the context of emphasizing the niggardliness of the Children of Israel who would not share with other people some of what Allah gave them. Verse 4.54 talks about another bad attribute of those people: their envy for people for what Allah had given them. In this verse, Allah said "great kingship" instead of "a share of kingship" to stress the greatness of His favor to the family of Abraham. This confirms my view that preceding "property" in the first verse with "a share of" stresses the limitedness of that property. These two verses compare the niggardliness of the Children of Israel, despite their limited property, with the generosity of Allah, who owns everything. They imply that if kingship and properties were in the hand of the Children of Israel, they would not give anything to people.

97. Additionally, the term "*mulk*," as I have mentioned in my comment on verse 4.53, can also mean "property" in general, not necessarily "kingship." In this case, it may be suggested that Joseph owned a lot, but was not a king.

98. I need to address a misinterpretation that some might think confirm that Joseph did become a king. The men that Joseph sent after his brothers attributed the drinking cup to the king: "They said: 'We have lost the drinking cup of the king; and he who shall bring it shall have a camel load, and I am responsible for delivering that'" (12.72). Allah, however, did not say "the drinking cup of the king" in His speech about what Joseph did with the drinking cup: "So when he furnished them with their provisions, he put the drinking cup in his brother's luggage. Then a proclaimer proclaimed: 'O camel caravanners! You are certainly thieves" (12.70). Then, Joseph referred to the king's drinking cup with "our property" in "He said: 'Allah forbid that we should seize other than the person with whom we found our property, otherwise we would certainly be unjust'" (12.79). This, actually, does not mean that Joseph was the king.

Joseph was speaking and acting on behalf of the king, so it is logical for him to use the phrase "our property." Let us also remember what we said above about Joseph's reception of his brothers in the king's place.

The indisputable proof that these verses do not mean that Joseph was the king is that in the same encounter in which Joseph referred to the king's drinking cup with "our property," his brothers were calling him "the 'Azīz," not "the king": "They said: 'O 'Azīz! He has a father who is a very old man, therefore retain one of us instead of him; surely we see you to be one of the good-doers' (12.78). He said: 'Allah forbid that we should seize other than the person with whom we found our property, otherwise we would certainly be unjust'" (12.79). We have already seen that the "'Azīz" and the "king" could not have been one and the same person.

99. The "jinn" are different creatures from human beings. The latter are created of "clay"; jinn are created of "fire." The jinn were created before humans.

100. These are examples:

وَإِذْ صَرَفْنَآ إِلَيْكَ نَفَرًا مِّنَ ٱلْجِنِّ يَسْتَمِعُونَ ٱلْقُرْءَانَ فَلَمَّا حَضَرُوهُ قَالُوٓا۟ أَنصِتُوا۟ فَلَمَّا قُضِىَ وَلَّوْا۟ إِلَىٰ
قَوْمِهِم مُّنذِرِينَ ﴿٢٩﴾ قَالُوا۟ يَٰقَوْمَنَآ إِنَّا سَمِعْنَا كِتَٰبًا أُنزِلَ مِنۢ بَعْدِ مُوسَىٰ مُصَدِّقًا لِّمَا بَيْنَ يَدَيْهِ يَهْدِىٓ إِلَى
ٱلْحَقِّ وَإِلَىٰ طَرِيقٍ مُّسْتَقِيمٍ ﴿٣٠﴾ يَٰقَوْمَنَآ أَجِيبُوا۟ دَاعِىَ ٱللَّهِ وَءَامِنُوا۟ بِهِۦ يَغْفِرْ لَكُم مِّن ذُنُوبِكُمْ وَيُجِرْكُم مِّنْ
عَذَابٍ أَلِيمٍ ﴿٣١﴾ وَمَن لَّا يُجِبْ دَاعِىَ ٱللَّهِ فَلَيْسَ بِمُعْجِزٍ فِى ٱلْأَرْضِ وَلَيْسَ لَهُۥ مِن دُونِهِۦٓ أَوْلِيَآءُ أُو۟لَٰٓئِكَ فِى
ضَلَٰلٍ مُّبِينٍ ﴿٣٢﴾. (سورة الأحقاف).

And when We turned toward you [O Muhammad!] a group of jinn to listen to the Qur'an. So, when they were in its presence, they said [to each other]: "Listen." So, when it was finished, they returned to their people, warning them (46.29). They said: "O our people! We have heard a Book that has been sent down after Moses, confirming that which was before it, guides to the truth and to a straight path (46.30). O our people! Respond to the caller of Allah and believe in Him, so that He forgives you of your sins and protects you from a painful punishment" (46.31). And whoever does not accept the caller of Allah, he shall not frustrate [Allah's will] on the earth, and he shall not have guardians besides Him; those are in manifest error (46.32).

قُلْ أُوحِيَ إِلَيَّ أَنَّهُ ٱسْتَمَعَ نَفَرٌ مِّنَ ٱلْجِنِّ فَقَالُوٓا۟ إِنَّا سَمِعْنَا قُرْءَانًا عَجَبًا ﴿١﴾ يَهْدِىٓ إِلَى ٱلرُّشْدِ فَـَٔامَنَّا بِهِۦ وَلَن نُّشْرِكَ بِرَبِّنَآ أَحَدًا ﴿٢﴾ وَأَنَّهُۥ تَعَـٰلَىٰ جَدُّ رَبِّنَا مَا ٱتَّخَذَ صَـٰحِبَةً وَلَا وَلَدًا ﴿٣﴾ وَأَنَّهُۥ كَانَ يَقُولُ سَفِيهُنَا عَلَى ٱللَّهِ شَطَطًا ﴿٤﴾ وَأَنَّا ظَنَنَّآ أَن لَّن تَقُولَ ٱلْإِنسُ وَٱلْجِنُّ عَلَى ٱللَّهِ كَذِبًا ﴿٥﴾ وَأَنَّهُۥ كَانَ رِجَالٌ مِّنَ ٱلْإِنسِ يَعُوذُونَ بِرِجَالٍ مِّنَ ٱلْجِنِّ فَزَادُوهُمْ رَهَقًا ﴿٦﴾ وَأَنَّهُمْ ظَنُّوا۟ كَمَا ظَنَنتُمْ أَن لَّن يَبْعَثَ ٱللَّهُ أَحَدًا ﴿٧﴾.

(سورة الجِـنّ).

Say [O Muhammad!]: "It has been revealed to me that a group of jinn have heard, so they said: 'Surely, we have heard a wonderful Qur'an (72.1). That guides to righteousness, so we have believed in it, and we will not ascribe partners to our Lord (72.2). And that, exalted be the majesty of our Lord, He has taken neither a consort nor a son (72.3). And that the foolish amongst us used to forge extravagant lies against Allah (72.4). And that we thought that humans and jinn would not utter a lie against Allah (72.5). And that human men used to seek refuge with jinn men, so they increased them in tiredness (72.6). And that they thought, as you think, that Allah would not resurrect anyone'" (72.7).

101. Note that both verses 12.80 and 12.110 use the verb إستيئس "*istay'asa*," not يئس "*ya'isa*." The later is used in other verses in the Qur'an. Both verbs mean "despair."

102. BCE stands for "Before the Common Era."

103. These documents are named after the Swedish consul in Egypt Signor Anastasi who sold them to the British Museum in 1839.

104. This book uses the King James Version of the Bible.

105. For instance, one Egyptian song glorifying the new city describes it as being "full of food and provisions" (p. 470). In a letter to his superior, one Egyptian scribe described Pi-Ramesse as follows:

The Residence is pleasant in life; its field is full of everything good; it is (full) of supplies and food every day, its *ponds* with fish, and its lakes with birds. Its meadows are verdant with grass; its banks bear dates; its melons are abundant on the sands.... Its granaries are (so) full of barley and emmer (that) they come near to the sky. Onions and leeks are *for food*, and lettuce of the *garden*, pomegranates, apples, and olives, figs of the orchard, sweet wine of *Ka*-of-Egypt, surpassing honey, red *wedj*-fish of the canal of the Residence City, *which* live on lotus-flowers, *bedin*-fish of the *Hari*-waters,.... (*p.* 471).

These quotations are taken from *Ancient Near Eastern Texts Relating to the Old Testament*, edited by J. B. Pritchard (Princeton: Princeton University Press, 1950).

106. For more details about the topic of this section, I recommend consulting our book *History Testifies to the Infallibility of the Qur'an: Early History of the Children of Israel* (Malaysia: A. S. Noordeen, 1999), pp. 21-23.

107. *History Testifies to the Infallibility of the Qur'an: Early History of the Children of Israel* (Malaysia: A. S. Noordeen, 1999).

108. There is a longer discussion of this subject in our book *History Testifies to the Infallibility of the Qur'an: Early History of the Children of Israel* (Malaysia: A. S. Noordeen, 1999).

109. In fact, the Bible starts with an account of the creation of the universe. The details and timelines suggested by this account are thoroughly rejected by modern science.

110. We have studied critically the origin of this concept and its significance in our book *History Testifies to the Infallibility of the Qur'an: Early History of the Children of Israel* (Malaysia: A. S. Noordeen, 1999), pp. 69-78.

111. The existing books of the Old Testament which the Jews call Torah holds very little resemblance to the Torah that Allah revealed to Moses.

General Index

Index of Qur'anic Verses